ARITHMETIC AND ALGEBRA

Ramanujan Mathematical Society

Little Mathematical Treasures

Editorial Policy

In times past, mathematics was studied and researched by a select few—an elite class who valued the subject for its intellectual elegance and perhaps also for its philosophic connotations. But today it is studied and practised by an extremely large number of individuals, for mathematics has acquired a pivotal role in the sustenance of a technologically advanced society.

Broadly speaking, there are two distinct groups of students to whom expository material in mathematics may be addressed:

(a) students who have a deep interest in mathematics and wish to pursue a career involving research and teaching of mathematics;
(b) students who are good at mathematics but wish to pursue a career in some other discipline.

Clearly such students require suitable material (in addition to contact with inspiring teachers and practising mathematicians) to nurture their talent in the subject.

To this list we may add professionals in industry and government and teachers in mathematics and other disciplines who require a good understanding of certain areas of mathematics for their professional work.

The proposed series is addressed to mathematically mature readers and to bright students in their last two years of school education. It is envisaged that the books will contain expository material not generally included in standard school or college texts. New developments in mathematics will be presented attractively using mathematical tools familiar at the high school and undergraduate levels. There will be problem sets scattered through the texts which will serve to draw the reader into a closer hands-on study of the subject. Readers will be invited to grapple with the subject, and so experience the creative joy of discovery and contact with beauty.

A thing of beauty is a joy forever.... So it is with mathematics. The discoveries of Archimedes, Apollonius and Diophantus have been sources of joy from very ancient times. It is our hope that these books will serve our readers in a similar manner.

Proposals for publication of a book in the series is invited with a draft of the proposed book. The decision of the Editorial Board will be final.

Ramanujan Mathematical Society

LITTLE MATHEMATICAL TREASURES

ARITHMETIC AND ALGEBRA

Numbers and the beginnings of Algebra

SHAILESH A SHIRALI
Rishi Valley School
Andhra Pradesh

Universities Press

ARITHMETIC & ALGEBRA: NUMBERS AND THE BEGINNINGS OF ALGEBRA

UNIVERSITIES PRESS (INDIA) PRIVATE LIMITED

Registered Office
3-6-747/1/A and 3-6-754/1. Himayatnagar, Hyderabad 500 029 (Telangana), India
info@universitiespress.com; www.universitiespress.com

Distributed by
Orient Blackswan Private Limited

Registered Office
3-6-752, Himayatnagar, Hyderabad 500 029 (Telangana), India

Other Offices
Bengaluru, Chennai, Guwahati, Hyderabad, Kolkata,
Mumbai, New Delhi, Noida, Patna

First published 2012
Reprinted 2021, 2024

Cover and book design

ISBN 978 81 7371 767 3

Set in Life BT 11/13.6 *by*
Orient BlackSwan

501994

Printed in India by
Avantika Printers Private Limited, New Delhi 110 020

Published by
Universities Press (India) Private Limited
3-6-747/1/A & 3-6-754/1, Himayatnagar,
Hyderabad 500 029, Telangana, India.

This book is dedicated to all students who love mathematics,

And also to those who do not . . . ;

May they join the tribe!

Contents

Dedication	*v*
Preface	*xi*
1. The World of Numbers	**1**
1.1 The unending supply of numbers	1
1.2 Roman numerals	4
1.3 Hindu–Arabic numerals	6
1.4 Positive and negative	9
1.5 Addition and subtraction	13
1.6 Multiplication and division	19
1.7 Number patterns	36
1.8 Palindromic entertainment	40
1.9 Miscellaneous problems I	42
1.10 Miscellaneous problems II	44
1.11 Miscellaneous problems III	46
2. Beginnings of Algebra	**48**
2.1 Framing sentences	48
2.2 Expressing patterns	50
2.3 Laws of algebra	52
2.4 Using algebra to explain patterns	53
2.5 Using algebra to discover properties	55
2.6 Factorisation	56
2.7 Equations	60
2.8 Closing quotes	69
3. Families of Integers	**70**
3.1 Odd and even	71
3.2 Multiples of 3	73
3.3 Multiples of 5	76
3.4 Prime and composite	77
3.5 GCD and LCM	83
3.6 Euclid's algorithm	87
3.7 Perfect numbers	90

3.8 Squares and cubes 97
3.9 Triangular numbers 109
3.10 Powers of 2 116
3.11 Miscellaneous problems 119

4. Fractions, Decimals and Percentages **122**

4.1 Fractions as numbers 123
4.2 Equivalent fractions 126
4.3 Arithmetic with fractions 127
4.4 Decimal fractions 135
4.5 Percentages 137
4.6 Fractions on the number line 142
4.7 Rational numbers 143
4.8 Miscellaneous exercises 148

5. Fractions: Special Topics **150**

5.1 Recurring decimals 150
5.2 Powers of integers---on a clothes line! 159
5.3 Cyclic numbers 160
5.4 Decimal expansion of $1/p$ 162
5.5 Irrational numbers 164
5.6 Unit fractions 166
5.7 Mischievous fractions 167
5.8 Farey sequences 169
5.9 Miscellaneous exercises 170

6. Ratio and Proportion **175**

6.1 Ratios for unit conversion 175
6.2 Rate 176
6.3 Dimensionless ratios 177
6.4 Proportion 180
6.5 Results concerning proportion 182
6.6 Continued proportion 184
6.7 Historical note 187
6.8 Approximations to pi 188
6.9 The tangram puzzle 190

7. Indices and Exponents **193**

7.1 Introduction 193
7.2 The laws of indices 195

7.3 Big numbers	196
7.4 The four twos	198
7.5 Visualising big numbers	200
7.6 Negative exponents	202
7.7 Fractional exponents	204
7.8 Growth patterns	210
7.9 Exponential notation in science	212
7.10 Three diversions	216
8. Polynomials	**222**
8.1 Notion of a polynomial	222
8.2 Degree of the zero polynomial	224
8.3 Alternate definition	224
8.4 Multiplication	226
8.5 Division	227
8.6 GCD	230
8.7 Roots of a polynomial	231
8.8 The remainder theorem	235
8.9 Symmetric polynomials	236
9. Expansions in Algebra	**240**
9.1 Homogeneous expressions	241
9.2 Expansions using shortcuts	241
9.3 Binomial expansions I	242
9.4 Using the Pascal triangle	248
9.5 Binomial expansions II	249
9.6 Squares of multinomials	250
9.7 Sum and product formulas	254
9.8 Difference of two squares	255
9.9 Visual representations	255
9.10 Miscellaneous expansions	258
9.11 A claim of Ramanujan's	259
10. Factorisation of Polynomials	**265**
10.1 Difference of two squares	266
10.2 Application to integer factorisation	268
10.3 Factorisation by breaking up an expression	269
10.4 Factorisation of quadratic trinomials	271
10.5 A more complex example	275

10.6 Using the factor theorem 276
10.7 A square investigation 283

11. Linear Equations **288**

11.1 Introduction to equations 288
11.2 Genesis of equations 290
11.3 Solution sets 292
11.4 Solving an equation 294
11.5 Linear equations in two unknowns 301
11.6 Application I: Clock problems 310
11.7 Application II: Pythagorean triples 311
11.8 Application III: Squares in AP 313
11.9 Application IV: Unit fractions 316

12. Problem Corner **322**

12.1 Appetisers 322
12.2 For the junior mathlete 326

13. Investigations **333**

13.1 Mischievous cancellations 333
13.2 Mischievous square roots 333
13.3 Prime numbers 334
13.4 Digital sums 334
13.5 Digital reversals 335
13.6 Squares and 2006 . . . 336
13.7 Squares and cubes 336
13.8 Still more squares 337
13.9 And yet more squares . . . 337
13.10 Accommodating numbers 338

Answers to Exercises **339**

Index **345**

Preface

I discovered that Nature was constructed in a wonderful way, and our task is to find out its mathematical structure.
— Albert Einstein, quoted in EINSTEIN: HIS LIFE AND UNIVERSE

I have written this book for students of mathematics in classes 7–10, to help them journey into a world of pattern, power and beauty, a world with great value for human society. Journeying into such a world can bring beauty into human lives, and be the source of a lifelong creative pursuit.

But for this, you—the student—must read and work through the book with care and patience. It will not always be easy; after all, reading a book on mathematics is not like reading your favourite storybook. It requires you to understand definitions and work through carefully presented arguments that justify and persuade you to accept certain statements. This may mean hard work on your part, but it is worth the trouble, for mathematics is not a subject where we simply make claims; we also explain them, link them with other claims, and prove or disprove them.

Reading this book also requires you to tackle problems which are not just 'drill exercises' where all you need to do is apply a formula; you will need to play the part of a mathematical detective on the trail of a mystery when working through such problems. You may get stuck every once in a while. But you must not fear this—it is all part of a great journey.

I have tried to use an algebraic approach all through the book, whether in explaining facts about arithmetic (for example, number patterns) or in presenting proofs in geometry, which will appear in the two books on geometry, planned as part of the series. This is intentional; it is because the algebraic way of thinking has immense power. In the book on geometry, I have used the modern approach based on transformations and functions, which too has a base of algebra underneath it. This is one of the great discoveries of recent times, and it has brought new life to a subject more than two millennia old.

The logo for the series is M^{POWER}. It is our earnest and committed belief that mathematics is a great agent for empowerment. May this journey empower you, may it be enchanting, and may it be a source of inspiration and creative joy.

Acknowledgement

The guiding force behind this work is Professor Phoolan Prasad (Department of Mathematics, Indian Institute of Science, Bangalore). He has been very keen that such a book be written for the benefit of school-children in this country. For this, I thank him most sincerely. It has been a pleasure knowing him and working with him all these years.

I also thank Professor V G Tikekar (formerly with the Department of Mathematics, Indian Institute of Science, Bangalore) for looking through the initial efforts with a critical but friendly eye, and suggesting numerous changes and improvements.

I also thank Ms Javanthi Singaram, Universities Press, who examined the book with an extremely observant and critical eye and helped correct many typographical and stylistic errors.

Shailesh A Shirali

Chapter 1

The World of Numbers

1.1 The unending supply of numbers

How many whole numbers are there? Take any large number, and add 1 to it; we get a larger number. By adding 1 to 1000 we get 1001; by adding 1 to 100000 we get 100001; by adding 1 to 100000000 we get 100000001. We can do this to any number, and we do not ever have to stop. This means that there is an endless supply of numbers--they just go on and on and on!

Using multiplication, it is even easier to produce very large numbers. For example, if we do the multiplication $3 \times 3 \times 3 \times \cdots \times 3$ with one hundred 3s, we get the following huge 48-digit number (which mathematicians write as 3^{100}):

$$515377520732011331036461129765621272702107522001.$$

If we put in another hundred 3s into the multiplication, we get a number (written as 3^{200}) with 96 digits; it is much too large to write in one line. And the number 3^{300} has 144 digits. Why stop there? The number 3^{1000} has 478 digits.

Continuing this way, we can in a simple manner produce very large numbers indeed, and they may be so large that we would find it impossible to form any physical picture of these numbers, in terms of imagining that many objects piled up in a heap. (I can imagine a heap of 10 books, or a heap of 100 coins, or a heap of 10000 grains of rice; but I cannot imagine 1000000000 objects piled up together.) There is clearly no limit to the size of the numbers we can produce by doing simple multiplication.

Exercises

1. Compute the number $2 \times 2 \times 2 \times \cdots \times 2$ with 10 twos in the product. (The number is written in short form as 2^{10}.)

2. Compute the number 3^{10}.

3. If I add 2^{10} and 3^{10}, will the answer be more than 2^{11} or less? Think out the answer without doing any calculations, and then check by actual calculation whether you got the right answer.

4. If I stack 1000 one-rupee coins in a vertical column, how high will the column be, roughly?

5. If I lay out 100000 matchsticks in a straight line, joined tip to tip, roughly how long will the line be?

6. I go for a long walk and count my steps; I find at the end that I have walked 5000 steps. Roughly what distance have I walked?

We can make do with just ten digits!

One of the wonderful things about the **WHOLE NUMBERS**,

$$0,\ 1,\ 2,\ 3,\ 4,\ 5,\ 6,\ 7,\ 8,\ 9,\ 10,\ 11,\ 12,\ \ldots$$

is that their supply is endless. But there is another equally wonderful thing about them: though there are an endless number of them, to write them down we need just *ten* symbols—namely, the digits 0, 1, 2, 3, 4, 5, 6, 7, 8 and 9—and nothing more. We were able to write the 48-digit number 3^{100} (above) using just these ten digits. *And that is so for any number, however large*: we do not need any other digits to represent the numbers. That is the great strength of the system of numeration discovered by the Indians more than two thousand years ago (and maybe the Chinese too). It is called the **BASE TEN** system or the **DECIMAL** system.

The system uses the successive *powers* of 10, i.e., the numbers

$$1, \quad 10, \quad 100, \quad 1000, \quad 10000, \quad 100000, \quad \ldots.$$

So, when we write the numbers 231, 708, and 2307, we mean the following:

$$\begin{aligned} 231 &= 2\times 100 + 3\times 10 + 1, \\ 708 &= 7\times 100 + 0\times 10 + 8\times 1, \\ 2307 &= 2\times 1000 + 3\times 100 + 0\times 10 + 7. \end{aligned}$$

What if we had just one digit?

You may say that we could represent numbers even if we had just one single digit, namely 1. You are right, of course. In this system, we would represent one by 1, two by 11 ('two ones'), three by 111 ('three ones'), four by 1111 ('four ones'), five by 11111 ('five ones'), and so on. Obviously we can represent any number this way, no matter how large. But what a terribly wasteful system it would be! We would have to represent ten by

$$1111111111,$$

twenty by

$$11111111111111111111,$$

and thirty by

$$111111111111111111111111111111.$$

As you can see, doing arithmetic in such a world is simply too tedious. (Try to multiply seven and eight in this system, and you will see the difficulty for yourself.) Far back in history, people must have counted their sheep and cows in just this way, but as other systems came along, this system got forgotten, which is perhaps just as well. (But note that it has not been discarded entirely; when we use a tally system to count votes in an election, or to count the runs scored by a batsman in a cricket match, it is this number system that we are really using.)

Could we do with just two digits, or just three?

The answer is "Yes." It is indeed possible to do all of arithmetic using just two digits, namely 0 and 1, and this way of representing numbers is known as the **BINARY NUMBER SYSTEM**. The world of computers—on which we depend so much these days—uses the binary system. (Of course, computers use binary numbers only for their *internal* operation; if you sit at a terminal and type out something, or if you use the Internet, you are not likely to see any binary numbers on the screen.)

There is also a **TERNARY NUMBER SYSTEM**, in which there are just three digits, namely 0, 1 and 2. But this is not the place to explain how either of these systems works. We shall do so in a later chapter.

EXERCISES

1. What number comes just before one million? Write it in decimal notation.

2. Using the digits $4, 5, 7, 8, 0, 0$ no more than once each, what is the largest number that can be made?

3. Between which two powers of 10 does the number 2341 occur? What about the numbers 45132 or 716789?

4. Fill in the boxes with powers of 10 so that the statement reads correctly:

$$24318 = 24 \times \square + 3 \times \square + 18 = 243 \times \square + 18.$$

1.2 The Roman system of numeration

Way back, during the times of the Romans (Julius Caesar and Mark Antony and others; perhaps Asterix too?), numbers were written quite differently. The numbers from 1 to 10 were written as follows:

1	2	3	4	5	6	7	8	9	10
I	**II**	**III**	**IV**	**V**	**VI**	**VII**	**VIII**	**IX**	**X**

You will observe the following:

- **I** has been used for 1, and **V** for 5;
- when **I** is placed to the *left* of **V**, it has the effect of *subtracting* 1 from 5 (giving 4, or **IV**), but when it is placed to the *right* of **V**, it has the effect of *adding* 1 to 5 (giving 6, or **VI**);
- **X** is used for 10; placing a **I** before the **X** has the effect of subtracting 1 from 10 (giving 9, or **IX**); placing it after the **X** has the effect of adding 1 to 10 (giving 11, or **XI**).

But note the really important thing: *there is no symbol for* 0. This great and very useful invention came a bit later, from ancient India. Apparently it was discovered a long time back, but the rules for working with this symbol were clearly stated only in the fifth century AD, by the great Indian mathematician Āryabhaṭa.

Here is how we write the numbers from 11 to 20 in the Roman system:

11	12	13	14	15	16	17	18	19	20
XI	**XII**	**XIII**	**XIV**	**XV**	**XVI**	**XVII**	**XVIII**	**XIX**	**XX**

Here are the numbers from 21 to 25:

21	22	23	24	25
XXI	**XXII**	**XXIII**	**XXIV**	**XXV**

and from 26 to 30:

26	27	28	29	30
XXVI	**XXVII**	**XXVIII**	**XXIX**	**XXX**

As you will see, things are getting a bit awkward already, and we have only reached 30; we still have a long way to go! The numbers from 31 to 39 are written in much the same way, with **XXXI** for 31, **XXXV** for 35 and **XXXIX** for 39; but 40 is written as **XL**, because the symbol for 50 is **L**, and 40 is 10 less than 50. It is not hard to see why the Romans had to invent a separate symbol for 50, for if they did not then they would start getting large strings of symbols, with 50 itself having to be written as **XXXXX**. But unfortunately they had to do much the same thing once they got close to a hundred. They chose '**C**' for a hundred (from the Latin word 'century' for 100); now 90 gets written as **XC**, 110 as **CX**, and so on.

Now the thing about this approach is that more and more symbols have to be invented. We cannot stop at a hundred! So the Romans had **D** for 500 and **M** for 1000 ('**M**' comes from the word 'millennia,' meaning 'thousand'). Here is how the Romans wrote some large numbers:

Number	Expanded form	Roman form
786	$500+200+50+30+6$	**DCCLXXXVI**
982	$900+80+2$	**CMLXXXII**
1234	$1000+100+100+30+4$	**MCCXXXIV**
2003	$1000+1000+3$	**MMIII**
3421	$3000+400+20+1$	**MMMCDXXI**

You will see that there is a definite logic to the system. By stacking together more and more **M**s, one can write down very large numbers. But to do this, the price we have to pay is heavy—the strings of letters get harder and harder to handle. Indeed, soon they start to get unmanageable! But the real drawback of this system is that it makes arithmetic look very hard. Even simple addition becomes a most daunting task. Thus, $3421+786$ takes the following form in the Roman system:

$$\texttt{MMMCDXXI} + \texttt{DCCLXXXVI}.$$

And multiplication would be next to impossible! So how did the Romans manage to do any arithmetic? Surely they needed to do computations, if only to account for payment of salaries, number of slaves captured, and so on? Apparently, they did not use their system of numeration to do arithmetic. Instead they used an **ABACUS**—not the modern kind, which has beads strung on wires, but one where pebbles are placed in grooves upon a board. (In Latin these pebbles are called *calculi* and that is where the familiar word 'calculate' comes from.) To do their calculations they probably used the abacus along with some tables that had already been prepared.

Is the Roman system still in use?

It is interesting to note that though the Roman system of numeration is no longer used in mathematics, it is still used for other purposes; e.g., in clock faces, for numbering chapters within a book, and in general to make things look a bit more fancy. And we still use these Roman words in everyday language: 'century' for 100 (think of Don Bradman's 29 centuries in Test cricket, Steve Waugh's 32, and Sunil Gavaskar's 34; how many will Sachin Tendulkar get?); in referring to our century as the '21st century;' in using the word 'millennium' for 1000, and so on.

1.3 The Hindu–Arabic system of numeration

The decimal place value system which we use with such ease today first evolved in ancient India, sometime between 200 BC and 500 AD (there are no clear records to indicate the exact date), but it was Āryabhaṭa who first clearly stated the rules for working with 0, in his great book, ĀRYABHATĪYĀ. To honour this achievement, the first satellite launched by India was named after Āryabhaṭa. (However Āryabhaṭa did not get it completely right; his rule for division by 0 was wrong, and it was only some centuries later that the correction was made.)

Somewhere around the seventh or eighth century AD, Arab traders and other Arab visitors to India started to carry knowledge of the system back to their home. In the ninth century AD, an official translation of the influential book written by the Indian mathematician Brahmagupta in the seventh century AD, BRAHMA SPHUTA SIDDHĀNTA (which translates roughly as 'Revised System of Brahma'), was commissioned by one of the early caliphs, and soon after that there appeared an extremely important work by the Arab mathematician Al-Khowarizmi (AD 790–850), HISAB-AL-JABR WA-AL-MUQABALA (this translates roughly as 'Calculation for Integration and Equations'), which he wrote after a long visit to India. The word 'algebra' comes from the title of this work, and Al-Khowarizmi is remembered in the word 'algorithm' (used so often today by computer scientists and mathematicians).

In this work, Al-Khowarizmi developed the system of algebra and included a detailed account of the Indian place value system. The system took root in the Arab world fairly quickly, and by and by, as a result of Arab trade with Italy and other centres in the Mediterranean region, it entered Europe too. In the thirteenth century, the mathematician Leonardo of Pisa (central Italy), better known as Fibonacci ('son of Bonacci') took it upon himself to educate the rest of Europe in its use, and did so in great style in his book LIBER ABACI ('Book of the Abacus'). It was as a result of such efforts that this system of numeration finally took root in Europe. Full acceptance came a bit slowly, though; nearly three centuries later, in fact. But by the time the Scientific Revolution came to Europe, in the late fifteenth century, the decimal place value system was fully in use.

The strength of the place value system

The great strength of the place value system is that it allows us to write numbers in a compact form, occupying very little space, and to do multiplication and division with ease, even when large numbers are involved. Once a civilization comes in contact with such a system, it finds it impossible to go back to the old system. (It is no different for us; once we get used to running water, or electricity, or cars, or telephones and the Internet, it seems impossible to think of life without these things.)

One needs to do just one single calculation in arithmetic to see why the place value system is so vastly superior to any other numeration system; simply try the following multiplication.

$$\begin{array}{r} 1\ 2\ 3\ 4 \\ \times \quad 3\ 4\ 2\ 1 \\ \hline \\ \hline \end{array}$$

It is quite easy to do. But now try to do the same using Roman numerals.

```
      M C C X X X I V
×     M M M C D X X I
─────────────────────

─────────────────────
```

Not quite that easy to do! Even the addition problem:

```
      M C C X X X I V
+     M M M C D X X I
─────────────────────

─────────────────────
```

presents a challenge. Thinking about doing such a multiplication would be enough to cause a headache!

We close this section with a quote from a very famous mathematician of the eighteenth century.

> *The ingenious method of expressing every possible number using a set of ten symbols (each symbol having a place value and an absolute value) emerged in India. The idea seems so simple nowadays that its significance and profound importance are no longer appreciated. Its simplicity lies in the way it [helped] calculation and placed arithmetic foremost amongst useful inventions. The importance of this invention is more readily appreciated when one considers that it was beyond the two greatest men of antiquity, Archimedes and Apollonius.*
>
> Simon Laplace (1749–1827)

EXERCISES

1. Express the following numbers, given in usual Hindu–Arabic notation, in Roman notation.

   41, 73, 103, 586, 1123, 5081

2. Express the numbers, given in Roman notation, using ordinary Hindu-Arabic notation.

   XVIII, **XCVII**, **MCXIXIV**, **LCXXXIV**,

3. Find the sum **XVIII** + **XCVII** + **MCX**.

4. What is the product of **XVIII** and **XCVII**?

1.4 Positive and negative

The numbers we experience in our daily life are numbers like $1,2,3,4,5,\ldots$. I may have *one* house, *two* parents, *three* rooms in my house, *four* pets, *five* fingers on my hand, a set of *six* tea-cups, *seven* classes in a day, *eight* friends, *nine* days before my examinations, and so on. These numbers are all *positive* numbers, and our everyday experience with numbers may suggest that only these kinds of numbers exist. Let us arrange these numbers in a line.

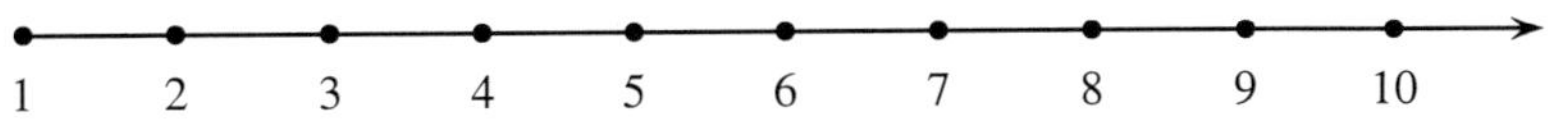

Figure 1.1

This line is known as the **NATURAL NUMBER LINE**. The arrow at its end is a way of reminding us that the natural numbers go on forever. Now observe that:

- A movement one unit to the right corresponds to **ADDITION** by 1. It takes you from any given number to what is called the **SUCCESSOR** of that number (e.g., it takes you from 4 to 5; so 5 is the successor of 4).

- A movement one unit to the left corresponds to **SUBTRACTION** by 1. It takes you from any given number to what is called the **PREDECESSOR** of that number (e.g., it takes you from 5 to 4; so 4 is the predecessor of 5).

Using algebraic symbols: If n stands for any number, then we write $n+1$ for its successor, and $n-1$ for its predecessor.

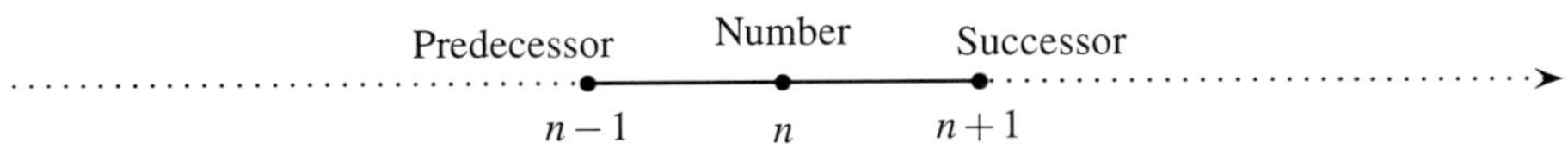

Figure 1.2

Numbers to the left of a number are **LESS**, than that number, and those to the right are **GREATER** than the number. We use the symbols ‘$<$’ and ‘$>$’ to denote ‘less than’ and ‘greater than’, respectively; so we have $4 < 5$, $5 > 3$, and so on.

There are two other symbols that are very much like ‘$<$’ and ‘$>$’; they are ‘$\leq$’ and ‘$\geq$’. Writing ‘$\leq$’ is very much like writing ‘$<$’ but now you allow for the possibility that the numbers on the two sides of the symbol are equal. For example, we can write $5 \leq 5$, and $5 \leq 6$; both these are correct statements. Similarly, we can write $7 \geq 7$, and $7 \geq 5$. But we *cannot* write $4 \leq 3$ or $7 \geq 10$ (we would need to put a slanted line across the symbol to indicate that the relation is wrong: $4 \not\leq 3$, $7 \not\geq 10$, and so on). The symbol '$\leq$' is read as 'less than or equal to', and '$\geq$' as 'greater than or equal to.'

What happens if I try to move one unit to the left of 1? This may look impossible to do; it may seem that we have reached the 'edge of the world,' and if we try moving further to the left then we may fall off. (In the early days, sailors who believed that the world was flat had the great fear that if they reached the edge of the world they would fall off!) The great discovery that human beings made many, many centuries ago in India, is that it is very convenient if we extend the number line to the left—not just by one unit, but *indefinitely*. If we do this we get the picture shown below. (The arrow marks at the left and right tell you that the picture can be extended both ways, indefinitely.)

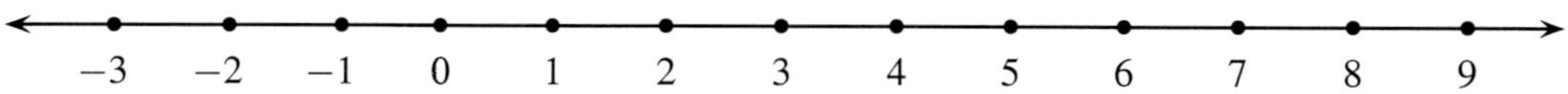

Figure 1.3

The number one unit to the left of 1 (i.e., the predecessor of 1) is called **ZERO**, and it is written as 0. If we proceed still further to the left, then we get what are called the **NEGATIVE NUMBERS**. The number one unit to the left of 0 is written as -1; we call it 'negative 1.' If we move one more unit to the left we reach -2 (we call it 'negative 2') then we reach -3 ('negative 3'), and so on. The numbers we get this way are called **NEGATIVE INTEGERS**.

Note that -1 is just a short form for $0-1$. We get the very same result from the operations $2-3$ ('from 2 move 3 steps to the left') and $10-11$ ('from 10 move 11 steps to the left').

Similarly, -2 is a short form for $0-2$, and we get the same result from the operations $3-5$ and $24-26$.

Do negative numbers really exist?

Of course they do—they exist just in the same way that positive numbers exist! It is true that they are not **COUNTING** numbers; we would never be able to point to a heap having a negative number of objects. But negative numbers do show up in daily life in a variety of ways. Some examples are given below.

- *There can be temperatures below zero!* If you have ever lived in a very cold place, you can watch how the minimum temperature steadily drops as winter approaches. One day it may reach 0°C, and in the days to come it may even drop below this level, i.e., below zero. Or if you happen to be fond of trekking in the high Himalayas, you may experience the temperature steadily coming down as you climb up towards the top of a mountain.

- *There are places below sea-level!* I can climb up a high mountain, but I can also go down into a mine, or into a swimming pool, or in a bathyscape into the underwater world. During the Second World War, U-boats and submarines moved around in the oceans, below the surface of the water, and fought great battles. If I can say that I went down to a depth of 5 m, then surely I can say with as much accuracy that I climbed up to a height of −5 m? (It may sound a bit odd, but that's only because we are not used to that kind of language; there is nothing wrong as such with the sentence.)
- *I could go into debt!* If I owe you ₹ 100, then as far as my balance is concerned, what I have is ₹ −100. If I withdraw all the money in my savings bank account and then take an 'overdraft' (i.e., I borrow still more money), what I have in my account with the bank is a *negative* amount. Banks do not permit us to carry negative balances for too long!

What these examples show is that there are many daily-life situations where it makes sense to talk of negative numbers. We may not find them as 'real' as the positive numbers, but they are certainly very useful and convenient.

Just as there is no boundary to the number line as we move to the right (i.e., there is no largest number), there is no boundary in the other direction either; we can produce negative numbers as far away from 0 as we may want, because there is no limit to how many steps we can take to the left.

From now on these numbers, (positive, negative and zero) will be called the **INTEGERS**. (Note that 0 has no sign.) If we imagine all the integers to be put in one single bag, then that bag is referred to, for short, as **Z**. (The letter 'Z' was first used by the Germans, because the word for integers in the German language is 'Zahlen.') Some people prefer to write the name as $\mathbb{Z}$, but we shall stick to **Z**. (Teachers may prefer $\mathbb{Z}$, because it is easier to write on a blackboard!)

Absolute value

The **SIGN** of an integer tells us on which side of 0 it is, i.e., whether it is negative (left side) or positive (right side). If we forcibly remove the sign from the number, then what is left behind is called its **ABSOLUTE VALUE**. We use a double-bar notation, | |, to denote absolute value.

Thus we have:

$$|-3| = 3 = |3|, \qquad |-5| = 5 = |5|, \qquad |-6| = 6 = |6|, \qquad |-9| = 9 = |9|,$$

and so on.

What are all the integers whose absolute value is no more than 3? This is the same as asking for all those integers n for which $-3 \le n \le 3$. They are, of course, -3, -2, -1, 0, 1, 2, 3; observe that there are seven of them. And the integers that are no more than 6 in absolute value are -6, -5, -4, -3, -2, -1, 0, 1, 2, 3, 4, 5, 6; there are thirteen such integers.

Gaps between integers

The **GAP** or **DISTANCE** between two integers is the absolute value of their difference. For example, the gap between 11 and 20 is $|11-20|$ (or $|20-11|$, it does not matter which way you write it, because the two are the same), i.e., the gap is 9. Obviously, the gap can never be a negative number; it is at least 0.

How many integers are there within a distance of 7 from 53? The integers within a distance of 7 from 53 are:

$$46,\ 47,\ 48,\ 49,\ 50,\ 51,\ 52,\ 53,\ 54,\ 55,\ 56,\ 57,\ 58,\ 59,\ 60,$$

so there are 15 such integers. They are the integers n such that $46 \le n \le 60$.

EXERCISES

1. List all the integers whose absolute value is no more than 4.
2. List all the integers whose absolute value is no more than 10.
3. How many integers are there whose absolute value is no more than 50? Can you give the answer without having to list all these integers?
4. How many integers are there whose absolute value is no more than 100? No more than 500? (Give the answers without preparing the actual lists.)
5. List the integers whose difference from 11 is no more than 5.
6. List the integers whose difference from 7 is no more than 19.

7. How many integers are there whose difference from 21 is no more than 31?

8. I think of a number and tell you that the gap between it and 50 is 13. What could the number be?

9. I think of a number and tell you that the gap between it and 75 is 22. I now compute the gap between 50 and that number. What could my answer be?

10. I think of some number n, calculate the gap between it and 50, then calculate the gap between the number calculated and 20. I get 9 as the answer. What could my number n have been?

1.5 Addition and subtraction with integers

Now that we know what integers are, we need to know how to do arithmetic with them; i.e., how to do addition, subtraction, multiplication and division. You are already familiar with these operations when done on the whole numbers. Now we extend the operations to the integers.

The commutativity of addition

One of the first observations we make about addition of integers is that it does not matter in which order we do it. For example, $3+4$ is the same as $4+3$, and $6+9$ is the same as $9+6$. This property is called **COMMUTATIVITY OF ADDITION**. It is true because of the very nature of addition itself.

Thus, $3+4$ can be thought of as follows: *From the point* 0 *on the number line, move* 3 *units to the right, and then move* 4 *units to the right*, while $4+3$ has the following meaning: *From the point* 0 *on the number line, move* 4 *units to the right, and then move* 3 *units to the right*. Both actions bring you to the same point, corresponding to the number 7. That is, both actions result in the following: *Move* 7 *units to the right*. So the effect of adding 3 and then 4 is the same as that of adding 4 and then 3. The same feature is seen with any two numbers, not just 3 and 4. Mathematicians describe this feature by stating that *addition commutes*, or *addition is commutative*.

In symbols, we write $a+b=b+a$, where a and b are any two integers whatever.

This may seem to be too obvious to need pointing out! But note that there *are* situations in which the order in which we do things matters. For example, wearing your socks and then wearing your shoes is not quite the same as wearing your shoes and then wearing your socks! Here the two operations (wearing your socks, and wearing your shoes) do *not* commute. Cooking provides interesting examples where operations commute and others where operations do not commute.

Even in mathematics we find situations where the order can matter; for example, $6-4$ is not the same as $4-6$. We describe this by stating that *subtraction is not commutative in general*. In symbols, we write: $a-b \neq b-a$ in general. Here, the symbol '$\neq$' means 'is not equal to'; for example, we have $2 \neq 3$, and $7 \neq 10$.

Remarks

- You may wonder why we have had to add the words 'in general.' The reason is that for some choices of a and b, it might just happen that $a-b=b-a$; but 'in general' it does not happen. Can you see for which choices it will happen that $a-b=b-a$?

- Note that if $6-4$ is regarded as an *addition* of integers, that is, as

  $$6+(-4),$$

  then commutativity gets restored, for $6+(-4)$ is the same as $(-4)+6$. The first one means:

  > *From the point* 0, *move* 6 *units to the right, and then from there, move* 4 *units to the left,*

  while the second one means:

  > *From the point* 0, *move* 4 *units to the left, and then from there, move* 6 *units to the right.*

  Both actions bring you to the same point, corresponding to the number 2.

Subtraction as the reverse of addition

We have seen how, on the number line, addition by 1 results in a *movement to the right by* 1 *unit*, whereas subtraction by 1 results in a *movement to the left by* 1 *unit*. This tells us that subtraction by any number *reverses* the effect of addition by that number.

Now, subtraction by 1 is the same as addition by -1; subtraction by 2 is the same as addition by -2, and so on. Therefore, the 'antidote' to 'addition by 1' is 'addition by -1'; the antidote to 'addition by 2' is 'addition by -2'; and so on.

Instead of 'antidote' mathematicians prefer to say **ADDITIVE INVERSE**; 'additive' because we are talking about addition, and 'inverse' because we are trying to undo the effect of addition. So they write: -1 *is the additive inverse of* 1; -2 *is the additive inverse of* 2; and so on.

Here are two everyday situations where we see the additive inverse in action.

- If we borrow ₹ 100 from a friend and then return the money to him or her the next day, the net effect is nil—i.e., no sum of money is owed by either one of us to the other. The net amount owed may be expressed as $100+(-100)$, and this equals 0.

- Imagine that we throw a ball straight up into the air; it reaches its highest point, then falls back into our hands. If its highest point is at a height of 5 m from the point where it was thrown, then on its forward journey it gets displaced by 5 m; on its return journey it gets displaced by -5 m, because 'down' is in the opposite direction to 'up'. Hence, the net displacement is $5+(-5)=0$ m.

Antidotes in real life!

It often happens in daily life that we want to undo the effect of an action. Here are some examples.

- After eating spicy food, we may need to take an antacid tablet to undo its effects!

- While writing text on a computer, we may in haste delete a sentence, and then realise that we should not have done so. Luckily, the error can easily be corrected, because computers have an 'undo' option.

- The inverse operation to tying a knot (say on your shoelaces) is that of untying the knot.

The inverse of the inverse

What is the additive inverse of -1? To reverse the effect of addition by -1 (which is the same as subtraction by 1), we must add 1, for to reverse the effect of moving 1 unit to the left we must move 1 unit to the right. *So the additive inverse of* -1 *is* 1. We write:

$$-(-1)=1.$$

This is an important property. We similarly get:

$$-(-2) = 2, \quad -(-3) = 3, \quad -(-4) = 4,$$

and so on; in symbols, we have: $-(-a) = a$, for any integer a. *The inverse of the inverse is the original number.*

The identity property

By the nature of 0 we have the following:

$$1+0=1, \quad 2+0=2, \quad 3+0=3, \quad 4+0=4, \quad \ldots.$$

So if we think of ADDING 0 as an 'action' then it is an action that 'does nothing'; the number on which we 'do' the action remains the same after the operation. An action or operation of this kind in mathematics is called an **IDENTITY OPERATION.** Zero is known as the **ADDITIVE IDENTITY**, or the **IDENTITY ELEMENT FOR ADDITION.**

We can think of other actions of this kind. If we ask a person to turn around completely (i.e., through 360°), standing at some fixed point, then at the end he will be facing the same direction as before; the action has in effect done nothing.

The bar notation

Sometimes we use a 'bar' notation for negative numbers: we write $\bar{1}$ for -1, $\bar{2}$ for -2, and so on. We can write numbers in a different way using this notation, by mixing the bar notation with the usual one. For example, $2\bar{3}$ means $20+(-3)$, so $2\bar{3}$ is the same as 17. (Note that the bar in $2\bar{3}$ covers only the 3, and not the 2.) Similarly, $1\bar{2}$ is the same as 8; $3\bar{4}2$ is the same as 262; and $10\bar{4}$ is the same as 96.

The rules for addition/subtraction using the bar notation are as follows:

$$1+\bar{1}=0, \quad 2+\bar{1}=1, \quad 1+\bar{2}=\bar{1}, \quad 5+\bar{2}=3, \quad 3-\bar{1}=4,$$

and so on.

To convert a number from the mixed notation to the usual one, we may use the base ten structure; thus, $3\bar{4}2 = (3\times 100)+(\bar{4}\times 10)+2 = 300-40+2 = 262$. Or we may work from the units end at the right and proceed to the left. Each time we meet a 'bar' number we mentally remove the bar and then replace this number by its complement from 10; then we take away 1 from the digit to its left. We thus proceed leftwards, doing the same thing to each 'bar' number. Thus, to write $3\overline{4}2$ in the usual way, we start at the units end, put down 2 unchanged, then in place of $\overline{4}$ we write the complement of 4 from 10, i.e., 6, and take away 1 from the digit to its left; therefore, we replace 3 by 2. We get the answer 262. (If the number itself is negative, this answer may not be very useful; e.g., try it for $\overline{3}\,\overline{4}2 = -338$.)

Complementary addition

Using the bar notation, we can do subtraction a bit differently, by treating it as an *addition*. Let us look at some examples.

- To do $347 - 139$, we write the subtraction as an addition, of 347 and $\overline{1}\,\overline{3}\,\overline{9}$:

$$\begin{array}{rccc} & 3 & 4 & 7 \\ + & \overline{1} & \overline{3} & \overline{9} \\ \hline & 2 & 1 & \overline{2} \\ \hline \end{array}$$

  So the answer is $21\overline{2} = 208$.

- Similarly, to do $356 - 219$, we write:

$$\begin{array}{rccc} & 3 & 5 & 6 \\ + & \overline{2} & \overline{1} & \overline{9} \\ \hline & 1 & 4 & \overline{3} \\ \hline \end{array}$$

  So the answer is $14\overline{3} = 137$.

- Here is an example using larger numbers. In the addition problem below, we must find the number represented by $****$.

$$\begin{array}{rcccc} & 2 & 4 & 3 & 1 \\ + & 1 & 5 & 7 & 9 \\ + & * & * & * & * \\ \hline & 7 & 3 & 2 & 5 \\ \hline \end{array}$$

  To find the unknown number, we perform an addition:

$$\begin{array}{rcccc} & 7 & 3 & 2 & 5 \\ + & \overline{2} & \overline{4} & \overline{3} & \overline{1} \\ + & \overline{1} & \overline{5} & \overline{7} & \overline{9} \\ \hline & 4 & \overline{6} & \overline{8} & \overline{5} \\ \hline \end{array}$$

The answer is $4\,\overline{6}\,\overline{8}\,\overline{5}$. This can be converted step by step into the usual form:

$$\begin{array}{rcccc} & 4 & \overline{6} & \overline{8} & \overline{5} \\ \rightarrow & 4 & \overline{6} & \overline{9} & 5 \\ \rightarrow & 4 & \overline{7} & 1 & 5 \\ \rightarrow & 3 & 3 & 1 & 5 \end{array}$$

The required answer is 3315. Check: We have: $2431+1579+3315=7325$.

The bar notation is non-standard and is not used too often, but it is useful to know it. You will meet it later when you study a topic called **LOGARITHMS**.

The cancellation law; associativity of addition

Suppose a and b are two integers, and we are told that $a+c=b+c$ for some third integer c, then we can conclude right away that $a=b$. This feature of addition is called the **CANCELLATION LAW FOR ADDITION**. It allows us to 'cancel' the c on the two sides of the equality.

Another feature which we mention briefly here, because it will allow us to make certain connections a little later, is that of **ASSOCIATIVITY**: if a,b,c are any three integers, then

$$a+(b+c)=(a+b)+c.$$

There is no such result for subtraction: $a-(b-c)$ is not in general the same as $(a-b)-c$. We say that *addition has the property of associativity; subtraction does not.*

EXERCISES

1. We said above that 'in general' $a-b$ is not the same as $b-a$. For what numbers a,b does it happen that the two are the same (i.e., $a-b=b-a$)?

2. An 'easier' way of doing the subtraction $912-699$ is to add 1 to both numbers and then do $913-700$, instead. Why does this give us the correct answer? Which law of arithmetic are we using here?

3. Write the following numbers, which are given in mixed notation, in usual notation:

$$2\,\overline{3}\,4, \quad 4\,\overline{1}\,2, \quad 1\,\overline{2}\,3\,\overline{4}.$$

4. Explain why $21\bar{2} = 208$.

5. What number must be added to 271 to give 812? Find the answer using complementary addition.

6. What number must be added to 3482 to give 9216?

7. Find the number represented by $****$ in the following addition problem:

$$\begin{array}{rcccc} & 3 & 1 & 7 & 2 \\ + & 2 & 3 & 0 & 4 \\ + & * & * & * & * \\ \hline & 9 & 2 & 4 & 1 \\ \hline \end{array}$$

8. In what situations will it happen that $a-(b-c)$ is the same as $(a-b)-c$?

1.6 Multiplication and division with integers

You are already familiar with how multiplication is done, using multiplication tables (which are best committed to memory—all the way till the '12 times' table) and the 'long multiplication' method. You also know how to perform divisions using the 'long division' method. Here, we will draw your attention to certain important features of multiplication and division, and their relation to addition and subtraction.

There are two different symbols commonly used for multiplication: '$\times$' and '$\cdot$'. Each one has its advantages. Whichever symbol we use, when we read it aloud we say "times". For example, we may write

$$3 \times 7 = 21, \quad \text{or} \quad 3 \cdot 7 = 21,$$

and we say this aloud as: "3 times 7 is 21". Sometimes, when using letter symbols in algebra, the sign for multiplication is dropped altogether; we write ab to denote $a \times b$ or $a \cdot b$.

Multiplication by positive integers is essentially repeated addition. When we write '2×3' or '2 times 3', what we mean is '$3+3$'. Similarly, '5×7' means '$7+7+7+7+7$' (with five 7s).

We can represent multiplication by positive integers using diagrams. If we let 3 be represented as a row of three unit squares, □□□, then the product 2×3 can be represented as a double row of three unit squares: 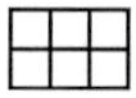. As the figure has 6 unit squares, this may be regarded as a way to show that $2 \times 3 = 6$, using a diagram.

Remark

In India it has become quite common to use the word 'into' while talking about multiplication. We shall avoid this as it can cause some confusion with division. So, we shall say "7 times 9 equals 63", and *not* "7 into 9 equals 63".

Commutativity

While discussing addition we said that if a, b are any two integers, then $a+b=b+a$. A similar statement may be made for multiplication; namely, we have the relation $a \times b = b \times a$.

We shall only give illustrations of why this is true. To check that $2 \times 3 = 3 \times 2$, we only need to verify whether $3+3$ is the same as $2+2+2$. The two are indeed the same. (Note: 'verify' means the same as 'check'.) Or, if we use diagrams, we need to verify that the following two grids have the same number of unit squares:

2×3 3×2

Figure 1.4

Both grids have 6 squares, and the check is over.
To check that $5 \times 7 = 7 \times 5$, we draw grids with more squares:

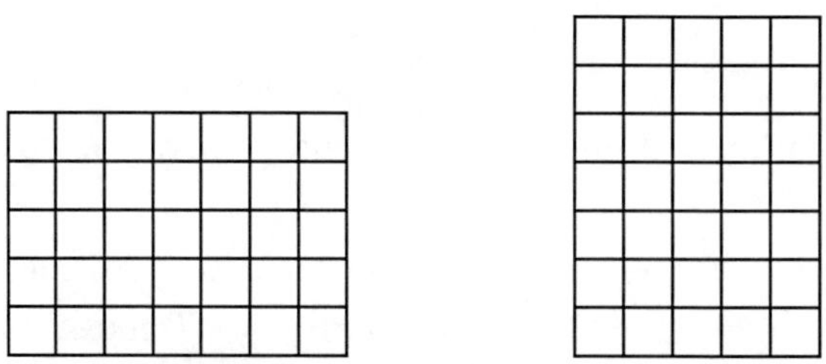

5×7 7×5

Figure 1.5

It will be noticed that each grid when turned through a quarter of a full turn (that is, through 90°) looks like the other one. So they are in some ways the 'same' grid, and they have the same number of unit squares.

The multiplicative identity

Just as there is an identity element for addition, namely 0, there is also an identity element for multiplication; it is the number 1. For we have:

$$1\times 0=0,\quad 1\times 1=1,\quad 1\times 2=2,\quad 1\times 3=3,\quad 1\times 4=4,$$

and so on; in general, $1\times a=a$ for any integer a. Because of this, 1 is called the **MULTIPLICATIVE IDENTITY.**

The element 0 is special when it comes to multiplication; no other integer behaves like it. For we have:

$$0\times 0=0,\quad 0\times 1=0,\quad 0\times 2=0,\quad 0\times 3=0,\quad 0\times 4=0,$$

and so on; $0\times a=0$, and $a\times 0=0$ for any integer a. Zero has a way of dragging everything down to its level!

The cancellation law

For multiplication too, we have a cancellation law. Thus, if $a\times b=a\times c$, and $a\neq 0$, then we can say that $b=c$; we can 'cancel' the a that is present on both sides. *But it is crucial that we have $a\neq 0$ when we state this.* The reason for insisting on this should be clear; it is because $a\times 0=0$ for every integer a.

Distributivity of multiplication over addition

We now come to an extremely important rule which connects addition and multiplication. Without it, we would not be able to do much arithmetic! The rule states simply that if a,b,c are any three integers, then

$$a\times(b+c) \;=\; a\times b \;+\; a\times c.$$

We see that the multiplication symbol ($\times$) has 'distributed' itself over the addition symbol ($+$).

For example, we have $2 \times (3+4) = 2 \times 3 + 2 \times 4$. To check this, note that on the left we have $2 \times 7 = 14$, and on the right we have $6+8$ which is also 14.

Using grids, there is a simple way of seeing that the two sides are equal. The quantity $2 \times (3+4)$ or 2×7 is represented as usual by a 2×7 grid. The quantities 2×3 and 2×4 are represented by two grids, joined but kept apart by a line ℓ as shown in Figure 1.6. If we blank out this line, then the two grids are the same, and so the numbers they represent are the same.

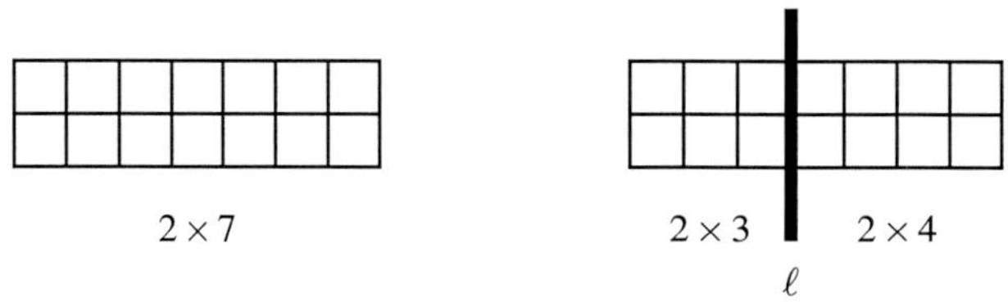

Figure 1.6

As stated earlier, the law of distributivity is *crucial* to arithmetic, and it is taken to apply *as a rule*—that is, it is true for any three numbers a, b, c, no matter what their signs are. *It is this rule that will persuade us that* $a \times 0 = 0$ *for any a.* Let us see why.

PROOF THAT $\mathbf{a \times 0 = 0}$: In the rule $a \times (b+c) = a \times b + a \times c$, let c be equal to 0; then we get

$$a \times (b+0) = a \times b + a \times 0.$$

Now $b+0$ is just b, so the statement becomes

$$a \times b = a \times b + a \times 0.$$

Seeing the quantity $a \times b$ on both sides, we use the law of cancellation to conclude that

$$a \times 0 = 0.$$

This will work no matter what value is given to a. In the same way we get $0 \times a = 0$.

So if we accept the law of distributivity, then we are also 'duty bound' to accept that $a \times 0 = 0$. This illustrates the importance of the law.

Below, when we work out the laws of multiplication for negative numbers, we shall see the rule in action yet again.

Rules for multiplication of negative numbers

You may have noticed that the grids used above were for showing the multiplication of *positive* numbers: 2×3, 5×7, and so on. But what shall we do for something like $2\times(-3)$? We certainly cannot draw a grid with -3 squares on its side! So what is $2\times(-3)$ equal to?

Well, we will not try to draw a grid in this case. Instead, we shall use the law of distributivity. We have already accepted that

$$a\times(b+c) \;=\; a\times b \;+\; a\times c.$$

In this statement let $a=2$, $b=3$, and $c=-3$. The statement then becomes

$$2\times\Big[3+(-3)\Big] \;=\; 2\times 3 \;+\; 2\times(-3).$$

On the left side we get, first: $3+(-3)=0$, and then: $2\times 0=0$. So the quantity on the left side is 0. Therefore the quantity on the right side must be 0. But this means that the two quantities

$$2\times 3, \qquad 2\times(-3)$$

are additive inverses of each other. Since $2\times 3=6$, we get $2\times(-3)=-6$.

We can show, arguing similarly, that for any two numbers a,b, the numbers

$$a\times(-b), \qquad -(a\times b)$$

are additive inverses of each other; in other words, $a\times(-b)=-(a\times b)$.

Negative times negative

What about a product like $(-2)\times(-3)$? The numbers $(-2)\times(-3)$ and $(-2)\times 3$ are additive inverses of each other. Also, $(-2)\times 3$ and 2×3 are additive inverses of each other. But the inverse of the inverse is just the original number! This means that

$$(-2)\times(-3), \qquad 2\times 3$$

are the *same* number. So we have: $(-2)\times(-3)=2\times 3=6$.

In the same way we show that for any two numbers a,b,

$$\boxed{(-a)\times(-b)=a\times b\ .} \tag{1.1}$$

Here is another way that mathematicians prove the above statement. The proof uses in a clever way the properties of associativity of addition and distributivity of multiplication over addition. It looks at the following expression:

$$\Big[a \times b\Big] + \Big[a \times (-b)\Big] + \Big[(-a) \times (-b)\Big].$$

The expression has two addition signs, and because addition is associative, we may do either one first. If we start with the first one, we get

$$\begin{aligned} & \Big[a \times b + a \times (-b)\Big] + (-a) \times (-b) \\ = \; & a \times \Big[b + (-b)\Big] + (-a) \times (-b) \\ = \; & a \times 0 + (-a) \times (-b) \\ = \; & (-a) \times (-b). \end{aligned}$$

However if we do the second addition first, we get

$$\begin{aligned} & a \times b + \Big[a \times (-b) + (-a) \times (-b)\Big] \\ = \; & a \times b + \Big[a + (-a)\Big] \times (-b) \\ = \; & a \times b + 0 \times (-b) \\ = \; & a \times b. \end{aligned}$$

So we see that the expression we began with is at the same time equal to $a \times b$ and to $(-a) \times (-b)$. This means, of course, that $a \times b = (-a) \times (-b)$.

The facts noted above may be written in words as follows:

$$\begin{array}{lcrcl} \text{Positive} & \times & \text{Positive} & = & \text{Positive}, \\ \text{Positive} & \times & \text{Negative} & = & \text{Negative}, \\ \text{Negative} & \times & \text{Positive} & = & \text{Negative}, \\ \text{Negative} & \times & \text{Negative} & = & \text{Positive}. \end{array}$$

It may be simpler to show these relations in a box:

×	Positive	Negative
Positive	Positive	Negative
Negative	Negative	Positive

You must always remember the above multiplication facts.

Parity

The **EVEN NUMBERS** are the numbers

$$2, \quad 4, \quad 6, \quad 8, \quad 10, \quad 12, \quad 14, \quad \ldots,$$

and the **ODD NUMBERS** are the numbers

$$1, \quad 3, \quad 5, \quad 7, \quad 9, \quad 11, \quad 13, \quad \ldots.$$

Here is one way of seeing what is 'odd' about the odd numbers. If we have an odd number of marbles, and we arrange them in pairs, then in the end one marble will be left out. This one is the 'odd man out;' it has no 'mate.' For example, if we have 7 marbles, the picture will look like this:

[● ●   ● ●   ● ●   ●]

Notice the marble left with no mate—the 'lonely marble.'

The oddness or evenness of a number is called its **PARITY**. The numbers 2, 4, 6, 8, 10, 12, ... all share the same parity, and the numbers 1, 3, 5, 7, 9, 11, ... likewise share the same parity.

What makes parity nice to study, and useful too, are the following simple rules which you may have noticed on your own:

- *If we add two even numbers or two odd numbers, we get an even number. That is,* ***the sum of two numbers with the same parity is an even number.***
- *If we add an odd number and an even number, we get an odd number. That is,* ***the sum of two numbers with opposite parity is an odd number.***

For example, if we add the two even numbers 6 and 10, we get 16, which is even; if we add the two odd numbers 5 and 13, we get 18, which is even; and if we add the numbers 5 and 12 (an odd number and an even number), we get 17, which is odd.

If we keep in mind the picture shown above, we will be able to understand why this happens. For example, if we have to do the addition $5+7$, we get the following picture:

[● ●   ● ●   ●] + [● ●   ● ●   ● ●   ●]

The two lonely marbles can be teamed up together, and we get the following picture:

[● ●   ● ●   ● ●   ● ●   ● ●   ● ●]

We see that the sum is an even number, because no marble is left unpaired.

For multiplication too there is such a rule:

- *If we multiply two odd numbers we get an odd number.*
- *If we multiply an even number with any number, we get an even number.*

For example, the multiplication 5×9 yields 45, an odd number, whereas $6 \times 7 = 42$ and $4 \times 8 = 32$ both yield even numbers.

The parity rules may be shown in a table as below.

+	Even	Odd
Even	Even	Odd
Odd	Odd	Even

×	Even	Odd
Even	Even	Even
Odd	Even	Odd

Parity check

Parity sometimes comes of use in checking a calculation. The idea is simple: *Parity cannot be lost*. For example, if someone were to tell you that

$$21 + 32 + 57 + 165 + 312 \;=\; 586,$$

you would quickly be able to tell that the answer is *wrong*; for, on the left side we have

$$\text{Odd} + \text{Even} + \text{Odd} + \text{Odd} + \text{Even},$$

which must be Odd as there are three Odds and two Evens. As the answer given (586) is Even, it must be wrong.

Similarly, we can immediately say that the statement $23 \times 12 = 275$ is wrong, because 23×12 must certainly be Even.

Parity checks are made use of by computers when they read data from some source, to see if any error has happened in recording or storing the data. You should find out how they do this—look it up on the Web.

Remark

The manner in which parity stays intact may remind you of of the conservation laws of physics: *Conservation of energy* and *Conservation of momentum*. Here we seem to have a conservation law in mathematics. The resemblance has more to it than one may suspect!

Digital roots

Let any positive integer be given. We find the sum of its digits. If the answer is greater than 10, then we find the sum of the digits of the answer; then we find the sum of the digits of *that* answer. We continue doing this till we get an answer which is a single-digit number. This answer is called the **DIGITAL ROOT** of the integer we started out with.

For example, take the integer 123456; its sum of digits is $1+2+3+4+5+6$ which gives 21. As the answer is more than 10, we find the sum of *its* digits; we get $2+1=3$. As the answer is a single-digit number, we stop the computation here. So the digital root of 123456 is 3.

Similarly, the digital root of 456 is 6 (the calculations are: $4+5+6=15$, $1+5=6$), and the digital root of 8765 is 8 (the calculations: $8+7+6+5=26$, $2+6=8$).

For convenience, if n is a given integer, we shall call its digital root $\text{DR}(n)$. So $\text{DR}(123456)=3$, $\text{DR}(456)=6$, and $\text{DR}(8765)=8$.

Patterns in digital roots

We find some nice patterns in the digital roots of multiples of certain numbers. For example, take the *multiples of* 3:

$$3, \quad 6, \quad 9, \quad 12, \quad 15, \quad 18, \quad 21, \quad 24, \quad 27, \quad 30, \quad \ldots.$$

Their digital roots are, respectively:

$$3, \quad 6, \quad 9, \quad 3, \quad 6, \quad 9, \quad 3, \quad 6, \quad 9, \quad 3, \quad \ldots.$$

We get the numbers 3, 6, 9, 3, 6, 9, 3, 6, 9, 3, ...: a sequence of numbers that repeats after every three steps, made up of the single digit multiples of 3.

Digital roots of the multiples of 9

Let us do the same with the multiples of 9:

$$9, \quad 18, \quad 27, \quad 36, \quad 45, \quad 54, \quad 63, \quad 72, \quad 81, \quad \ldots.$$

The digital roots are:

$$9, \quad 9, \quad 9, \quad 9, \quad 9, \quad 9, \quad 9, \quad 9, \quad 9, \quad \ldots.$$

The digital roots are all the same.

Digital roots of the multiples of 11

For the multiples of 11 there is once again a pattern, but it takes a bit longer to see. The multiples of 11 are:

$$11, \quad 22, \quad 33, \quad 44, \quad 55, \quad 66, \quad 77, \quad 88, \quad 99, \quad \ldots.$$

The digital roots are:

$$2,\ 4,\ 6,\ 8,\ 1,\ 3,\ 5,\ 7,\ 9,\ 2,\ 4,\ 6,\ 8,\ 1,\ 3,\ 5,\ 7,\ 9, \ldots.$$

After this we get the same numbers again: 2, 4, 6, 8, 1, 3, 5, 7, 9, and so on. So there is a pattern here too, but it is harder to spot: *the numbers repeat after every nine steps, and every digit except* 0 *appears in the chain.*

Digital roots of the multiples of 2

What comes as a surprise is that the multiples of 2 give us the same pattern as the multiples of 11: the same digits, and in the same order! For, the multiples of 2 are:

$$2, \quad 4, \quad 6, \quad 8, \quad 10, \quad 12, \quad 14, \quad 16, \quad 18, \quad \ldots.$$

Their digital roots are:

$$2, \quad 4, \quad 6, \quad 8, \quad 1, \quad 3, \quad 5, \quad 7, \quad 9, \quad \ldots.$$

After this we get the same numbers again, just as before: 2, 4, 6, 8, 1, 3, and so on.

Other cases of duplication of pattern

If you do some computations on your own, you will find that the multiples of 3 and 12 yield the same chain (namely, 3, 6, 9, 3, 6, 9, ...).

Similarly, the multiples of 4 and 13 yield the same chain (namely, 4, 8, 3, 7, 2, 6, 1, 5, 9, and then the numbers repeat in the same order).

A surprising connection between digital roots and 9

What makes digital roots extremely useful is the following fact, which may come as a big surprise in the beginning: *If we add 9 to a positive integer, then the digital root remains the same.* This can be summarised by writing: *If n is a positive integer, then* $\mathrm{DR}(n) = \mathrm{DR}(n+9)$. Look at these examples:

- $\mathrm{DR}(31) = 4$, and $\mathrm{DR}(40) = 4$;
- $\mathrm{DR}(123) = 6$, and $\mathrm{DR}(132) = 6$;
- $\mathrm{DR}(126) = 9$, and $\mathrm{DR}(135) = 9$;
- $\mathrm{DR}(91) = 1$, and $\mathrm{DR}(100) = 1$;
- $\mathrm{DR}(31568) = 5$, and $\mathrm{DR}(31577) = 5$.

This means that if we 'cast out nines' from a number (i.e., we subtract multiples of 9 from the number, as many times as we wish), then so long as we do not let the numbers go below 0, the digital root always remains the same. So, for example, the following numbers have the same digital root:

$$3476, \quad 3467, \quad 3458, \quad 3449, \quad 3440, \quad 3431, \quad 3422, \quad 3413, \quad \dots.$$

EXERCISES

1. Find the digital roots of 345621 and 8796341.
2. Write down the first 15 multiples of 5, and then write down their digital roots. What pattern do you see?
3. Write down the first 15 multiples of 14, and then write down their digital roots. What pattern do you see?
4. Compare the chain of digital roots that we got from the multiples of 2 with the chain that we got from the multiples of 4. What do you find?
5. I think of a positive integer and tell you that it is 1 more than a multiple of 9. What could be its digital root?
6. I think of a positive integer and tell you that it is 5 more than a multiple of 9. What could be its digital root?

7. Which positive integers have (a) a digital root of 5 (b) a digital root of 9 (c) a digital root of 3 (d) a digital root of 7.

8. Is there any positive integer with more than one digit whose sum-of-digits is equal to itself?

9. If the digital root of a number is equal to itself, what could the number be?

10. If the digital roots of the integers n and $2n$ are the same, what can be said about n?

11. If the digital roots of the integers n and $3n$ are the same, what can be said about n?

The digital root stays intact!

Take any addition 'sum', say $a+b=c$. What relation exists between the digital roots of a,b,c? What if it is a multiplication rather than an addition? What if it is an equality featuring both multiplication and addition? We study some examples.

- Take any addition $37+213=250$.

  The digital roots are $\mathrm{DR}(37)=1$, $\mathrm{DR}(213)=6$ and $\mathrm{DR}(250)=7$.

  Replacing each number in the equality $37+213=250$ by its digital root, we get $1+6$ on the left side, and 7 on the right side. Since $1+6=7$, *equality continues to hold true*.

- Take the addition $431+716=1147$.

  The digital roots are: $\mathrm{DR}(431)=8$, $\mathrm{DR}(716)=5$, and $\mathrm{DR}(1147)=4$.

  Replacing each number in the equality $431+716=1147$ by its digital root, on the left side we get $8+5$, and on the right side we get 4. Since $8+5$ gives 13, and the digital root of 13 is 4, *equality continues to hold true*.

- Take the multiplication $71\times 23=1633$.

  The digital roots are: $\mathrm{DR}(71)=8$, $\mathrm{DR}(23)=5$, and $\mathrm{DR}(1633)=4$.

  If we replace each number in the equality $71\times 23=1633$ by its digital root, we get 8×5 on the left side, and 4 on the right side. Since $8\times 5=40$, and the digital root of 40 is 4, *equality continues to hold true*.

- Take the statement $(41 \times 35) + 123 = 1558$.

  The digital roots this time are: $\mathrm{DR}(41) = 5$, $\mathrm{DR}(35) = 8$, $\mathrm{DR}(123) = 6$, and $\mathrm{DR}(1558) = 1$.

  If we replace each number in the given statement by its digital root, we get $(5 \times 8) + 6$ on the left side, and 1 on the right side. If we work out $(5 \times 8) + 6$ we get $40 + 6 = 46$, and the digital root of 46 is 1. So we get the same digital root (namely, 1) on both sides; *equality continues to hold true.*

It appears, then, that in any relation between integers involving addition and multiplication, *if we replace every number by its digital root, and do the arithmetic with* these *numbers instead of the original numbers, then equality is maintained: the digital roots of the two sides are equal.*

The 'casting out nines' rule

Using the observation made above, we now describe a method by which addition and multiplication may be checked.

Say that we have done some calculations with some numbers, and we now wish to check the calculation. We replace all the given numbers by their digital roots, and then repeat the calculation. If the answers on the two sides have *different* digital roots, then we have definitely gone wrong in our calculation. For example, suppose that someone tells us that

$$123 \times 456 = 56188.$$

The digital roots are:

$$\mathrm{DR}(123) = 6, \quad \mathrm{DR}(456) = 6, \quad \mathrm{DR}(56188) = 1.$$

Now $6 \times 6 = 36$, and the digital root of 36 is 9. So we get 9 as the digital root on the left side, and 1 as the digital root on the right side. *The two digital roots are different!* Therefore, the calculation is wrong. (You should check that the correct answer is $123 \times 456 = 56088$. The given answer is wrong in one digit.)

Similarly, if someone tells us that

$$3124 \times 51349 = 160414376,$$

we can check his arithmetic by calculating the digital roots:

$$\mathrm{DR}(3124) = 1, \quad \mathrm{DR}(51349) = 4, \quad \mathrm{DR}(160414376) = 5.$$

On the left side we have 1×4 which is 4, and on the right side we have 5. As the two are not equal, we know for sure that there has been a mistake in the calculation. (The correct answer is 160414276.)

You should be able to work out for yourself why the rule of casting out nines works.

Remark

If the digital roots on the two sides of the calculation are equal, then nothing definite can be said. The calculation *might* be correct or not, but we cannot say for sure. So the rule of casting out nines works in one direction only. *It reveals errors, but does not verify correctness.* The same is true of the parity check mentioned earlier in the chapter.

EXERCISES

1. Take the addition $451 + 718 = 1169$. Replace each number by its digital root, and check that the digital roots on both sides are the same.

2. Do the same for the multiplication $451 \times 718 = 323818$.

3. A friend tells you that $6512 + 4067 = 10479$. Check the statement using the rule of casting out nines.

4. Do the same for the statement that $651 \times 407 = 274957$.

5. It was stated above that "if the digital roots on the two sides are equal, then nothing definite can be said. The calculation *might* be correct or not, but we cannot say for sure." Give an example of a wrong addition statement where the digital roots on the two sides are the same.

6. Give an example of a wrong multiplication statement where the digital roots on the two sides are the same.

7. Explain why the digital roots of n and $n+9$ are the same for any positive integer n.

Division

Division is, of course, the inverse operation or 'antidote' to multiplication; so the 'antidote' to multiplication by 2 is division by 2, and so on.

In any division, say $56 \div 7 = 8$, which we also write as

$$\frac{56}{7} = 8,$$

the number being divided (56 in this case) is the **DIVIDEND**, the number by which we are dividing (7 in this case) is the **DIVISOR**, and the answer obtained (8 in this case) is the **QUOTIENT**. So we have:

$$\frac{\text{Dividend}}{\text{Divisor}} = \text{Quotient}.$$

Write N for the number being divided, i.e., the dividend, D for the divisor, and Q for the quotient; then $N \div D = Q$, i.e.,

$$\frac{N}{D} = Q.$$

This may also be written as: $N = D \times Q$. For example, the relation $56 \div 7 = 8$ may also be written as $56 = 7 \times 8$.

Sometimes the remainder does not work out exactly, and a **REMAINDER** is left; e.g., in the division $30 \div 7$. Here we get a quotient of 4, and a remainder of 2 is left. Writing R for the remainder, we get an important relation:

$$\boxed{N \;=\; D \times Q \;+\; R}.$$

For example, in the division $30 \div 7$, $N = 30$, $D = 7$, $Q = 4$, and $R = 2$; and we have

$$30 = (4 \times 7) + 2.$$

In the relation $N = (D \times Q) + R$, there are *four* quantities. If any three of them are known, then the fourth one can be found.

For example, if we are told that when 138 is divided by a certain divisor, the quotient is 19, and the remainder is 5, then we have $N = 138$, $Q = 19$, and $R = 5$. Since the remainder is 5, we subtract 5 from the dividend N, and get $138 - 5 = 133$. This number when divided by the divisor gives 19 exactly, so the divisor D is $133 \div 19$ which works out to 7. This is the required answer.

EXERCISES

1. In dividing 167 by some number, we get a quotient of 11 and a remainder of 2. What is the divisor?

2. In dividing a certain number by 31 we get a quotient of 133 and a remainder of 4. What is the number?

3. I think of a certain number. I multiply it by 2, add 1 to the answer, then multiply this answer by 3 and add 1, and then I multiply *this* answer by 4 and add 1. In the end I get 185. What number had I thought of at the start?

"Thou shalt not divide by 0"

An oddity about division is that there is one particular number which we must never permit as a divisor—the number 0. *Division by* 0 *is an illegal operation in mathematics.*

It is not for nothing that we say this. If division by 0 were allowed, it would wreck all of arithmetic! Suppose we needed the value of $9 \div 0$. Not knowing what it is, we call it 'a'; we have now:

$$\frac{9}{0} = a.$$

This would mean that $9 = 0 \times a$. But $0 \times a = 0$ (any number when multiplied by 0 yields 0). So we get $9 = 0$, an unhappy state of affairs! Such a difficulty happens no matter which number we try to divide by zero.

To avoid this confusion, mathematicians have decided on a simple rule: ***Thou shalt not divide by zero***. It is regarded as one of the absolute never-to-be-violated 'commandments' of mathematics. ***Division by zero is much like a computer virus; if permitted, it would destroy the whole edifice of arithmetic.***

Here is another way of seeing why division by zero is an impossible operation. Suppose we had to compute $20 \div 1$. We say to ourselves, "the multiples of 1 are $1, 2, 3, 4, 5, \ldots$; we reach 20 on the twentieth step, with no remainder left; hence the quotient is 20, with no remainder."

What if we had to compute $20 \div 3$? We say to ourselves, "the multiples of 3 are $3, 6, 9, 12, \ldots$; no multiple of 3 equals 20 exactly, but $6 \times 3 = 18$, and $20 - 18 = 2$; hence the quotient is 6, and the remainder is 2."

What if we had to compute $20 \div 8$? The multiples of 8 are $8, 16, 24, \ldots$; no multiple of 8 equals 20 exactly, but $2 \times 8 = 16$, and $20 - 16 = 4$; hence the quotient is 2, and the remainder is 4.

What if we had to compute $20 \div 0$? The multiples of 0 are $0, 0, 0, 0, \ldots$. No matter how many multiples we take, we do not move away from 0 at all, and we make no progress whatever with the division; the remainder is always the same, and we get stuck in an endless loop! Hence, division by 0 is an impossible task.

This includes the division $0 \div 0$. On seeing that $1 \div 1 = 1$, $2 \div 2 = 1$, $3 \div 3 = 1$, and so on, we may be tempted to write

$$\frac{0}{0} = 1.$$

But even this leads us into difficulties! To see why, suppose we accept that $\frac{0}{0} = 1$. Add 1 to both sides; then we get

$$\frac{0}{0} + 1 = 2, \quad \therefore \frac{0 + (1 \times 0)}{0} = 2, \quad \therefore \frac{0+0}{0} = 2,$$

i.e., $\dfrac{0}{0} = 2$. This leads to the equality $1 = 2$. And no one would want that to happen!

Remark

In connection with the division $0 \div 0$ we mention an interesting incident in the life of the Indian mathematician Srinivasa Ramanujan, when he was but a young boy. His arithmetic teacher had said that if three bananas were given to three boys, each boy would get a banana, and he had generalised this idea. This prompted Ramanujan to ask: "Sir, if no banana is distributed to no student, will everyone still get a banana?"

Short-cut for multiplication by 5

There are some numbers with which multiplication is easier to perform than with other numbers. For example, suppose that we have to multiply some number by 5. Since 5 is half of 10, we can achieve the result by multiplying by 10 and then dividing by 2. Since multiplication by 10 is achieved simply by placing an extra 0 at the units end, we get the following rule for multiplication by 5: *Place a* 0 *at the units end of the given number, and then divide the result by* 2. You will find that with some practice this can be done mentally.

For example, to find 31×5, we do $310 \div 2$, i.e., we find half of 310; the answer is 155.

To find 433×5, we do $4330 \div 2$; the answer is 2165.

Short-cut for multiplication by 25

We can state a similar rule for multiplication by 25; now we use the fact that 25 is a quarter of 100, i.e., $100 \div 4$. So multiplication by 25 is achieved by placing two 0s at the units-end of the number, and then dividing the result by 4.

EXERCISES

1. State a similar rule for multiplication by 125.
2. State a similar rule for multiplication by 625.
3. Study the following multiplications of some two-digit numbers by 11:

   $$14 \times 11 = 154, \qquad 17 \times 11 = 187,$$

   $$23 \times 11 = 253, \qquad 34 \times 11 = 374.$$

   Using these examples, what rule can you state for multiplication of two-digit numbers by 11?

   What happens in the case of the multiplications 19×11, 28×11, 37×11, and so on? How would you modify your rule to fit these multiplications?
4. Now study multiplication of some three-digit numbers by 11:

   $$135 \times 11 = 1485, \qquad 231 \times 11 = 2541,$$

   $$452 \times 11 = 4972, \qquad 625 \times 11 = 6875.$$

   What rule can you state for multiplication of three-digit numbers by 11?

   In what situations will you need to modify the rule?
5. Find a simple rule for multiplication of two-digit numbers by 101.

1.7 Number patterns

In this section we describe some nice patterns found in the integers.

Colour patterns

We first arrange the positive integers in a 10-column array, one column for each units digit. The first column has all the numbers whose units digit is 1; the second column has all the numbers whose units digit is 2; and so on. The tenth and last column has all the numbers whose units digit is 0. We get the array shown in Figure 1.7 (we have only shown the numbers from 1 till 100).

1	2	3	4	5	6	7	8	9	10
11	12	13	14	15	16	17	18	19	20
21	22	23	24	25	26	27	28	29	30
31	32	33	34	35	36	37	38	39	40
41	42	43	44	45	46	47	48	49	50
51	52	53	54	55	56	57	58	59	60
61	62	63	64	65	66	67	68	69	70
71	72	73	74	75	76	77	78	79	80
81	82	83	84	85	86	87	88	89	90
91	92	93	94	95	96	97	98	99	100

Figure 1.7 The integers from 1 till 100 arranged in a square grid

Next, we select some number (call it D) and *shade all the squares containing the multiples of that number*; all other squares are left unshaded. Depending on which number D we select, nice patterns emerge. For example, if we choose $D = 2$ we get the picture shown in Figure 1.8 (we have shown only the squares themselves, leaving out the numbers that they contain, to avoid a clutter):

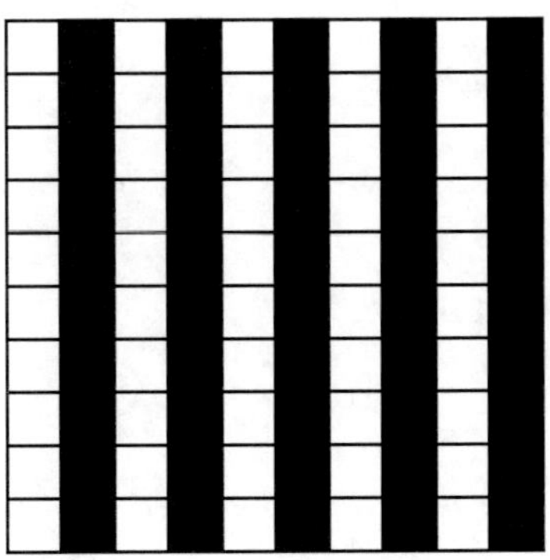

Figure 1.8 Multiples of 2

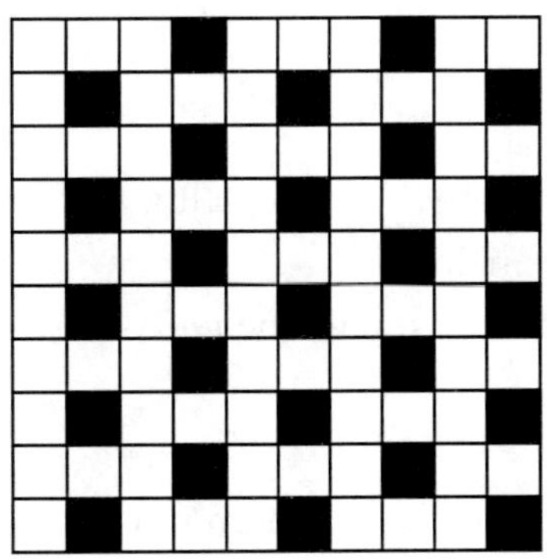

Figure 1.9 Multiples of 4

If we choose $D = 4$ we get the pattern shown in Figure 1.9.

And if we choose $D = 3$ we get the pattern shown in Figure 1.10.

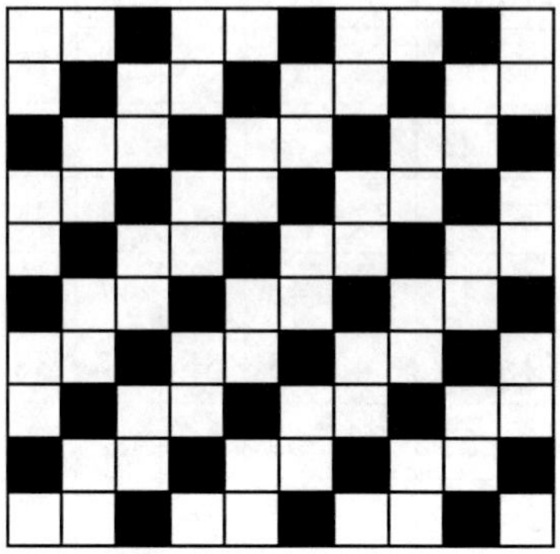

Figure 1.10 Multiples of 3

Squares

If we multiply a number with itself, we get what is called the **SQUARE** of that number. For example, if we do 6×6, we get 36. We write this as: $6^2 = 36$; the little '2' at the top tells us the number of 6s in the multiplication. Similarly, we get:

$$4^2 = 16, \quad 5^2 = 25, \quad 9^2 = 81, \quad 11^2 = 121,$$

and so on, these being short forms for $4 \times 4 = 16$, $5 \times 5 = 25$, and so on.

Let us make a list of the squares, starting with $0^2 = 0$; we get

$$0, \quad 1, \quad 4, \quad 9, \quad 16, \quad 25, \quad 36, \quad 49, \quad 64, \quad 81, \quad \dots,$$

with the dots (...) indicating that there are more to come, only we have not bothered to write them down.

Now we list only the *units digits* of these numbers. What do we find?

$$0, \quad 1, \quad 4, \quad 9, \quad 6, \quad 5, \quad 6, \quad 9, \quad 4, \quad 1, \quad 0, \quad 1, \quad 4, \quad 9, \quad 6, \quad 5, \quad \dots.$$

We spot a definite pattern now: *Between each zero and the next one, the digits repeat in exactly the same order. Moreover, the digits read the same left-to-right and right-to-left.* The portion between any 0 and the next one is:

$$1, \quad 4, \quad 9, \quad 6, \quad 5, \quad 6, \quad 9, \quad 4, \quad 1.$$

Note that this string of digits is a **PALINDROME**—it reads the same both ways.

Cubes

If we multiply a number with itself *twice*, we get what is called the **CUBE** of that number. For example, if we do this to 6 we get $6 \times 6 \times 6 = 216$. We write this as: $6^3 = 216$; the little '3' at the top tells us the number of 6s in the multiplication. We get, similarly, $4^3 = 64$, $5^3 = 125$, $9^3 = 729$, etc. Here is a list of the cubes, starting with $0^3 = 0$:

$$0, \quad 1, \quad 8, \quad 27, \quad 64, \quad 125, \quad 216, \quad 343, \quad \ldots.$$

If we list only the units digits of the cubes, here is what we get:

$$0, \quad 1, \quad 8, \quad 7, \quad 4, \quad 5, \quad 6, \quad 3, \quad 2, \quad 9, \quad ,\ldots.$$

Observe that *all ten digits appear in this list*. Following the '9', the same ten digits appear again, and in the same order. We see some interesting pairings in this list; e.g., if the units digit of a number is 8, then the units digit of the cube is 2, and if the units digit of a number is 2, then the units digit of the cube is 8. Also, if the units digit of a number is 7, then the units digit of the cube is 3, and if the units digit of a number is 3, then the units digit of the cube is 7.

We shall study the families of squares and cubes in greater detail in the next chapter.

Powers of 2

We now do a similar exercise with the numbers

$$2, \quad 2\times 2, \quad 2\times 2\times 2, \quad 2\times 2\times 2\times 2, \quad 2\times 2\times 2\times 2\times 2, \quad \ldots.$$

These numbers are called the **POWERS** of 2, and they are written more conveniently as

$$2^1, \quad 2^2, \quad 2^3, \quad 2^4, \quad 2^5, \quad \ldots.$$

The little '5' at the top in 2^5 tells us that there are *five* 2s in the multiplication.

Here are the powers of 2 till 2^{12}:

$$\begin{array}{llll} 2^1 = 2, & 2^2 = 4, & 2^3 = 8, & 2^4 = 16, \\ 2^5 = 32, & 2^6 = 64, & 2^7 = 128, & 2^8 = 256, \\ 2^9 = 512, & 2^{10} = 1024, & 2^{11} = 2048, & 2^{12} = 4096, \end{array}$$

and so on.

Just as we did for the squares and the cubes, we list only the units digits of these numbers; we get

$$2, \quad 4, \quad 8, \quad 6, \quad 2, \quad 4, \quad 8, \quad 6, \quad 2, \quad 4, \quad \ldots.$$

The pattern straight away jumps out at us: the digits 2, 4, 8, 6 repeat again and again in that order!

We shall study the family of powers of 2 in greater detail in the next chapter.

EXERCISES

1. Do the colouring exercise using (a) $D = 5$, (b) $D = 6$, (c) $D = 7$.

   Make a note describing the kinds of patterns you see.

2. Do the colouring exercise using (a) $D = 9$, (b) $D = 11$.

   What relationship do you see between the patterns in these two cases?

3. List the units digits of the powers of 3, i.e., of the numbers $3^1 = 3$, $3^2 = 3 \times 3$, $3^3 = 3 \times 3 \times 3$, and so on. What pattern do you find?

4. List the units digits of the powers of 7, i.e., of the numbers $7^1 = 7$, $7^2 = 7 \times 7$, $7^3 = 7 \times 7 \times 7$, and so on. What pattern do you find?

5. Now we shift from the units digit to the *tens digit*.

   List the tens digits of the powers of 2. You will have to leave out the very first power from your list (i.e., $2^1 = 2$). Go as far down the list as you can. What pattern do you find? (You may have to calculate lots of numbers till you spot a pattern.)

6. Do the same for the tens digits of the powers of 3. (This time you need not leave out any powers from your list.)

1.8 Palindromic entertainment

We conclude this chapter with some entertainment—featuring curiosities from the world of **PALINDROMIC NUMBERS**. These are numbers that read the same both ways (left-to-right and right-to-left), e.g., 12321 or 9210129. We shall exhibit some *palindromic squares* and some *palindromic cubes*.

It is tempting to guess that if a number is palindromic and has enough 0s distributed in a regular way within its digits, then its square too will be palindromic. There are a good many instances which will support this guess, for example,

$$\begin{aligned} 11^2 &= 121, \\ 101^2 &= 10201, \\ 1001^2 &= 1002001, \\ 10201^2 &= 104060401, \\ 1001001^2 &= 1002003002001, \end{aligned}$$

and so on. But this will not always work; for example, $10301^2 = 106110601$ is not palindromic (though it comes close). In the other direction, there are non-palindromic numbers whose squares are palindromes:

$$\begin{aligned} 26^2 &= 676 \\ 264^2 &= 69696 \\ 307^2 &= 94249 \\ 836^2 &= 698896 \end{aligned}$$

You may enjoy looking for more such instances.

As of now, the largest known non-palindromic number whose square is a palindrome is 831775153121251039203514; its square,

$$691849905349880612384525525483216088943509948196,$$

is a 48-digit number.

The situation for cubes is *very* different; we find that most palindromic cubes arise from palindromic numbers. For example,

$$\begin{aligned} 101^3 &= 1030301, \\ 111^3 &= 1367631, \\ 10101^3 &= 1030607060301, \\ 11011^3 &= 1334996994331, \\ 110011^3 &= 1331399339931331, \\ 1001001^3 &= 1003006007006003001. \end{aligned}$$

Incredibly, to date *just one* case has been found of a non-palindromic number whose cube is palindromic! This is the number 2201:

$$2201^3 = 10662526601.$$

Apart from this and the instance $7^3 = 343$, *in every other case the number being cubed is made up solely of* 1*s and* 0*s*.

For fourth powers, computer searches have produced only the following instances, which are not very interesting:

$$\begin{aligned} 11^4 &= 14641, \\ 101^4 &= 104060401, \\ 1001^4 &= 1004006004001, \\ 10001^4 &= 10004000600040001, \end{aligned}$$

and so on. *No instance has been found where the fourth root is not of the form* $100\cdots01$.

For powers > 4, *computer searches have found nothing at all*—except for the trivial case of 1, which is of no interest! Mathematicians have conjectured that there do not exist any non-trivial palindromic n^{th} powers when $n > 4$.

EXERCISES

1. Verify that 2285^2 and 2636^2 are palindromes.

2. By examining a list of squares, find the smallest palindromic square which is not the square of a palindromic base.

3. See if you can explain 'why' 11^2, 11^3 and 11^4 are palindromic, but 11^5 is not.

4. See if you can explain why the following are palindromic:

$$11^2, \quad 111^2, \quad 1111^2, \quad 11111^2, \quad \ldots, \quad \underbrace{111111111}_{\text{nine ones}}{}^2,$$

whereas the following are *not*:

$$\underbrace{1111111111}_{\text{ten ones}}{}^2, \qquad \underbrace{11111111111}_{\text{eleven ones}}{}^2, \qquad \underbrace{111111111111}_{\text{twelve ones}}{}^2.$$

1.9 Miscellaneous problems I

1. Suppose we assume that $\dfrac{0}{0} = 5$. What difficulties would we get into?

2. The sum of the integers from 1 to 100 is known to be 5050. (Let us assume that someone did the calculations for us!) Use this information to find the sum of the integers from 101 to 200.

3. The sum of the integers from 1 to 1000 is known to be 500500. Use this information to find the sum of the integers from 1001 to 2000.

4. The sum of the numbers from 1 to 300 is known to be 45150. Use this information to find the sum of the *odd* numbers from 1 to 300 (include the number 1 in the sum).

5. A certain number is added to its square, and the answer is 756. What is the number?

6. A certain number is added to its square, and the answer is 2256. What is the number?

7. A certain number is subtracted from its square, and the answer is 4422. What is the number?

8. A certain number is added to its cube, and the answer is 6878. What is the number?

9. A certain number is added to its cube, and the answer is 9282. What is the number?

10. If we arrange all the numbers that are not multiples of 3 in a line, like this:

$$1, 2, 4, 5, 7, 8, 10, 11, 13, 14, 16, 17, 19, 20, \ldots,$$

what would be the 100th and 1000th numbers in this sequence?

11. If we arrange all the numbers that are *not* multiples of 5 in a line, like this:

$$1, 2, 3, 4, 6, 7, 8, 9, 11, 12, 13, 14, 16, 17, 18, 19, \ldots,$$

what would be the 100th and 1000th numbers in this sequence?

12. If we arranged all the numbers that are not squares (we may call them the *non-square numbers*) in a line like this:

$$2, 3, 5, 6, 7, 8, 10, 11, 12, 13, 14, 15, 17, 18, 19, 20, 21, \ldots,$$

what would be the 100th and 1000th numbers in this sequence?

13. If we arrange all the numbers that are either multiples of 2 or multiples of 3, but not both, in a line like this:

$$2, 3, 4, 8, 9, 10, 14, 15, 16, 20, 21, 22, 26, 27, 28, \ldots,$$

what would be the 100th and 1000th numbers in this sequence?

14. If we arrange all the numbers that are either multiples of 2 or multiples of 5, but not both, in a line like this:

$$2,\ 4,\ 5,\ 6,\ 8,\ 12,\ 14,\ 15,\ 16,\ 18,\ 22,\ 24,\ 25,\ 26,\ 28,\ 32,\ 34,\ 35,\ \dots,$$

what would be the 100th and 1000th numbers in this sequence?

15. If we arrange all the numbers that are either multiples of 3 or multiples of 5, but not both, in a line like this:

$$3,\ 5,\ 6,\ 9,\ 10,\ 12,\ 18,\ 20,\ 21,\ 24,\ 25,\ 27,\ 33,\ 35,\ 36,\ 39,\ 40,\ \dots,$$

what would be the 100th and 1000th numbers in this sequence?

16. From the numbers $1,2,3,\dots,1000$, I discard all those that are divisible by 2 or by 5 or by both 2 and 5. How many numbers are left?

17. Find a positive integer n such that $\frac{1}{3}n$ is a square and $\frac{1}{2}n$ is a cube. How many such integers are there below 10000?

1.10 Miscellaneous problems II

In each of the problems 1–7, you will see a statement together with a question: True-or-false? What you need to do is this: for each statement, investigate whether it is **always true** or **sometimes true/sometimes false**.

If you think the statement is false, then give an example showing that it is false. In other words, **disprove** the statement!

If you think the statement is true, then give an argument showing why it is true. In other words, **prove** the statement! (Your argument should show that the statement is *always* true.)

Either way, have fun!

1. True or false: *The sum of any two consecutive numbers is odd.*

2. True or false: *The sum of any three consecutive numbers is divisible by* 3.

3. True or false: *The sum of any four consecutive numbers is divisible by* 4.

4. True or false: *The sum of any five consecutive numbers is divisible by* 5.

5. True or false: *The sum of any two consecutive odd numbers is divisible by* 4.

6. True or false: *The product of any two consecutive numbers is even.*

7. True or false: *The product of any three consecutive numbers is divisible by* 6.

8. There is precisely one four-digit number that has the following property: *If its digits are reversed, then the number so obtained is* 4 *times the original number.* Find the number.

9. There is precisely one four-digit number that has the following property: *If its digits are reversed, then the number so obtained is* 9 *times the original number.* Find the number.

10. There is precisely one four-digit number that has the following property: *If its digits are reversed, then the number so obtained is* $2/3$ *of the original number.* What is the number?

11. There is precisely one five-digit number that has the following property: *If its digits are reversed, then the number so obtained is* 4 *times the original number.* What is the number?

12. I think of any three-digit number, and make a six-digit number by writing the same three digits *twice* (e.g., if I think of 156, then I get the number 156156). I find that this six-digit number is always divisible by 13. Why?

13. In the above problem, if I divide the six-digit number successively by 7, 11, and 13, I find that the divisions all work out perfectly, with no remainders left. Moreover, in the end I get back the number I had at the start! For example, if I think of 156, then I get the number 156156, and now:

$$\frac{156156}{7} = 22308, \qquad \frac{22308}{11} = 2028, \qquad \frac{2028}{13} = 156.$$

Why does this happen?

14. I think of any two-digit number, and then make a six-digit number by writing the same two digits *three times* in a row (e.g., if I think of 15, then I get the number 151515). I find that the six-digit number I get is always divisible by 37. Why?

15. I think of a two-digit number, and then make an eight-digit number by writing the same two digits *four times* in a row (e.g., if I think of 19, then I get the number 19191919). I find that the eight-digit number I get is always divisible by 137. Why?

16. I think of a two-digit number, and then make a ten-digit number by writing the same two digits *five times* in a row (e.g., if I think of 23, then I get the number 2323232323). I find that the ten-digit number I get is always divisible by 41. Why?

1.11 Miscellaneous problems III

1. In this problem, we express the **CUBES** as sums of consecutive odd numbers.

   Examine the following list:

$$\begin{aligned}
1^3 &= 1 = 1\\
2^3 &= 8 = 3+5\\
3^3 &= 27 = 7+9+11\\
4^3 &= 64 = 13+15+17+19, \ \ldots
\end{aligned}$$

   Observe that 3^3 has been written as a sum of *three* consecutive odd numbers, 4^3 has been written as a sum of *four* consecutive odd numbers and so on.

   Do the same for 5^3, 6^3, 7^3 and 8^3. Then state a general rule based on your observations.

   Is there a way of explaining 'why' this rule works?

2. Once again we study a connection between cubes and lists of consecutive numbers.

   Examine the following list:

$$\begin{aligned}
1 &= 0^3+1^3\\
2+3+4 &= 1^3+2^3\\
5+6+7+8+9 &= 2^3+3^3\\
10+11+12+13+14+15+16 &= 3^3+4^3
\end{aligned}$$

   State a general rule based on your study of this list. Is there a way of explaining 'why' this rule works?

3. Now we study a connection between squares and lists of consecutive numbers.

Examine the following list:

$$\begin{aligned} 1^2 &= 1 \\ 1^2 - 2^2 &= -(1+2) \\ 1^2 - 2^2 + 3^2 &= 1+2+3 \\ 1^2 - 2^2 + 3^2 + 4^2 &= -(1+2+3+4) \end{aligned}$$

State a general rule based on your study of this list. Is there a way of explaining 'why' this rule works?

4. Take any three digits, and arrange them in any order you please. For example, you may choose the digits 2, 3 and 5, and arrange them as $(3,5,2)$. Now we form two-digit numbers using this arrangement, by joining adjacent pairs of digits, keeping the order in mind. So from $(3,5,2)$ we get the two-digit numbers 35, 52, 23. We get the last number by coming 'around the circle' and joining 2 and 3.

   Next, we *reverse the order* of the digits and do the same with this arrangement. We get the arrangement $(2,5,3)$, and the two-digit numbers are 25, 53 and 32.

   Compare the values of $35^2+52^2+23^2$ and $25^2+53^2+32^2$. What do you find?

   Repeat the experiment with some other three digits. What do you find?

   Now for the hard part: *explain* what you have found.

5. In the above problem what happens if we use *two-digit numbers* instead of digits? For example, we may select the numbers 71, 13 and 24 and arrange them in that order, getting $(71,13,24)$. The reverse order is $(24,13,71)$, so we must compare

$$7113^2+1324^2+2471^2 \qquad \text{and} \qquad 2413^2+1371^2+7124^2.$$

   What do we find now?

Chapter 2

Beginnings of Algebra

Algebra can be thought of as *lazy man's arithmetic*; it is a way of doing arithmetic in a clever way, by using symbols that can be replaced by actual numbers (just as in a code) any time we wish. It may also be thought of as *generalised arithmetic*.

We shall see shortly that this simple step places great power in our hands, particularly when we combine it with another important practice of mathematicians—*making repeated use of known patterns*.

As someone said wisely, "Algebra is kind—she gives you more than you ask for ...". You will soon see the truth of this.

2.1 Framing sentences

We have already used a bit of algebra in Chapter 1, but without saying so in so many words. We cover a bit of the same ground here, and show how statements in algebra (Alg) are framed when we are given some condition or property. We start by looking at some examples.

Alg-1. By how much does a quantity x exceed a quantity y?

Answer: $x-y$.

Alg-2. The product of two numbers is 100, and z is one of the numbers. What is the other number?

Answer: The other number is $\dfrac{100}{z}$.

Alg-3. I walk at a uniform speed of s km per hour, and I walk for t hours. How much distance do I cover?

Answer: I travel st km.

Alg-4. N sweets are equally divided among m children. How many sweets does each child get?

Answer: Each child gets $\frac{N}{m}$ sweets.

Alg-5. If the middle number of a triple of consecutive integers is y, what are the other two numbers?

Answer: The other two numbers are $y-1$ and $y+1$.

Alg-6. If n is an odd number, what are the next two odd numbers?

Answer: $n+2$ and $n+4$.

Alg-7. The product of two numbers x and y is six times their sum. Express this fact using algebra.

Answer: $xy = 6(x+y)$.

Alg-8. The largest of four consecutive integers is k, and the sum of the squares of these integers is 1374. Express this fact using algebra.

Answer: $(k-3)^2 + (k-2)^2 + (k-1)^2 + k^2 = 1374$.

Alg-9. I divide a by b and get a quotient q, and a remainder r. Express this fact using algebra.

Answer: $a = bq + r$.

Alg-10. A boy is x years old. Five years back his brother's age was twice his age. What is the brother's age now, in terms of x?

Answer: As the boy's present age is x years, five years back it would have been $x-5$ years, and so the brother's age five years back would have been twice this, that is, $2(x-5)$ years. So the present age of the brother is $2(x-5)+5$ years.

These examples show how we substitute numbers with letters and thereby get statements in the language of algebra.

2.2 Expressing patterns in the language of algebra

We now study some examples showing how observed arithmetic patterns are translated into the language of algebra.

EXAMPLE 1. Consider triples of consecutive integers such as $(3,4,5)$ or $(7,8,9)$; we notice that *in any such triple, twice the middle number equals the sum of the two outer numbers* (e.g., $2\times 4 = 3+5$, $2\times 8 = 7+9$, and so on). (It is not difficult to see why this will always be true.)

We shall write this observation in symbols by using x to denote the first number in the triple; then the next number is $x+1$, and the one after that is $x+2$. The observation now translates into the following:

$$2(x+1) \;=\; x \;+\; (x+2) \tag{2.1}$$

Here, $2(x+1)$ means 2 times $(x+1)$.

Observe how the compact statement (2.1) contains all the individual examples listed earlier ($2\times 4 = 3+5$, $2\times 8 = 7+9$, $\ldots$) and many, many more. So it contains a lot of information!

Note the steps involved: we noticed a certain pattern, and then stated it in a general form that includes the examples studied, as *specific instances*. The keyword here is 'general'. *Generalisation is crucial to mathematics.*

Remarks

- A small change in the allotment of symbols will allow us to get a neater formulation: we let x denote the *middle* number in the triple (rather than the first one); then the two other numbers are $x-1$ and $x+1$. The translated statement now becomes: $2x \;=\; (x-1)+(x+1)$.

- Note that our having expressed a property in the language of algebra does not make it true! Till we have demonstrated it in a convincing manner, using the accepted rules of algebra, it will remain a speculation, and nothing more.

- In this particular instance, it is easy to see why the stated relation must be true: we simply note that the middle number exceeds the least number by 1, and the largest number exceeds the middle number by the same amount (1).

EXAMPLE 2. On studying lists of four consecutive integers we notice that *the sum of the outer two numbers is equal to the sum of the middle two numbers*. For example, for the list 4, 5, 6, 7, we have: $4+7=11=5+6$.

To translate this observation into algebra, we write x for the least integer; then the list is x, $x+1$, $x+2$, $x+3$, and the observation translates into the following statement:

$$x+(x+3) \;=\; (x+1)+(x+2). \tag{2.2}$$

EXAMPLE 3. Triples of consecutive integers yield another nice pattern when we compare the *product of the two outer numbers* with the *square of the middle number*. For example, for the triple $(3,4,5)$ we get:

$$3\times 5=15, \qquad 4^2=16, \qquad 16-15=1.$$

For the triple $(7,8,9)$ we get:

$$7\times 9=63, \qquad 8^2=64, \qquad 64-63=1.$$

We see the same behaviour for other triples, and speculate that *the difference is always* 1. In other words,

$$\boxed{(\text{middle number})^2 \;-\; \text{product of two outer numbers} \;=\; 1.}$$

This is written in everyday language, and uses many words. To put it in symbols, we say: let x denote the middle number in any three consecutive integers; then the other two numbers are $x-1$ and $x+1$, and we write:

$$\boxed{x^2-(x-1)\cdot(x+1) \;=\; 1.} \tag{2.3}$$

Of course, $(x-1)\cdot(x+1)$ means '$(x-1)$ times $(x+1)$'.

EXAMPLE 4. When we study lists of *four* consecutive integers such as $(3,4,5,6)$ or $(7,8,9,10)$, we notice a pattern similar to the one noted above, when we compare the *product of the two outer numbers* with the *product of the two middle numbers*. For example, for $(3,4,5,6)$ we get:

$$3\times 6=18, \qquad 4\times 5=20, \qquad 20-18=2.$$

For $(7,8,9,10)$ we get:

$$7\times 10=70, \qquad 8\times 9=72, \qquad 72-70=2.$$

We now speculate that *the difference is always* 2, i.e.,

$$\boxed{\text{product of middle two numbers} \; - \; \text{product of outer two numbers} \; = \; 2.}$$

In symbols: let x be any number; then the next three consecutive numbers are $x+1$, $x+2$ and $x+3$, and we write:

$$\boxed{(x+1)\cdot(x+2) \; - \; x\cdot(x+3) \; = \; 2.} \tag{2.4}$$

EXAMPLE 5. Consider the number $63^2 = 63 \times 63$. Instead of computing it directly, we express it as follows: $63^2 = (60+3)^2$, and now:

$$\begin{aligned}
(60+3)^2 &= (60+3)\times(60+3) \\
&= (60+3)\times 60 \; + \; (60+3)\times 3 \\
&= 60^2 \; + \; (3\times 60) \; + \; (60\times 3) \; + \; 3^2 \\
&= 60^2 \; + \; (2\times 60\times 3) \; + \; 3^2 \\
&= 3600 \; + \; 360 \; + \; 9 \; = \; 3969.
\end{aligned}$$

In the same way we can write

$$\begin{aligned}
73^2 &= 70^2 \; + \; (2\times 70\times 3) \; + \; 3^2 \; = \; 4900+420+9 \; = \; 5329, \\
81^2 &= 80^2 \; + \; (2\times 80\times 3) \; + \; 1^2 \; = \; 6400+480+1 \; = \; 6881,
\end{aligned}$$

and so on. Observing the pattern, and generalising, we are ready to make the leap to an algebraic statement. We write:

$$\boxed{(a+b)^2 \; = \; a^2+2a\cdot b+b^2 \quad \text{for any two positive numbers } a \text{ and } b.} \tag{2.5}$$

2.3 Laws of algebraic operations

In arithmetic we learn how to *add* two given numbers, to *multiply, subtract* and *divids* them. Now, having brought in letters to represent numbers, we must learn how to do the same with them. But this presents no mystery, for we simply treat them as 'numbers in disguise', which means that they must behave exactly as numbers do. So we require that for these letters or symbols:

- *Commutativity of addition and multiplication continues to be true.* This only means that $a+b=b+a$ and $a\cdot b=b\cdot a$ for any two symbols a and b. Note that '$a\cdot b$' means '$a\times b$'. Sometimes we leave out the 'times' symbol and write ab for $a\times b$ or $a\cdot b$.

- *Distributivity of multiplication over addition and subtraction continues to be true.* This means that for any three symbols a, b and c, we have

$$a\cdot(b+c) = a\cdot b+a\cdot c, \qquad a\cdot(b-c) = a\cdot b-a\cdot c,$$
$$(b+c)\cdot a = b\cdot a+c\cdot a, \qquad (b-c)\cdot a = b\cdot a-c\cdot a.$$

- 0 *continues to act as the additive identity, and* 1 *as the multiplicative identity.* This means that for any symbol a, we have $a+0=a$, and $a\times 1=a$. (Here we do use the 'times' symbol, as it is awkward to write $a1$.)

  Note that as both addition and multiplication are commutative, we also have the relations $0+a=a$ and $1\times a=a$ for any symbol a.

It is important to realise the significance of the phrase 'any symbol' in these statements. It tells us that *if we use some other symbols, then the statements continue to be true*; so we also have: $x+y=y+x$, $x\cdot(y+z)=x\cdot y+x\cdot z$, and so on.

The laws stated above allow us to write the following.

- $x+x=2x$, because if we add a number to itself, the result is the same as when we multiply it by 2; and $2x$ means just that—the result of multiplying x by 2. (We could also write it as $2\cdot x$ or as $2\times x$, but these may cause some confusion.)

- $x+x+x=3x$, $\quad 2x+3x+7x=12x$, $\quad 9x-4x=5x$, $\quad$ and so on.

- $2(x+1)=2x+2$, which we get by applying the distributivity law, as in $2\times(3+4)=(2\times 3)+(2\times 4)$.

2.4 Using algebra to explain patterns

In this section we show how algebra can explain the number patterns noted above.

- We first consider (2.1): "twice the middle number in a triple of consecutive integers equals the sum of the first and last numbers". If the three numbers are x, $x+1$ and $x+2$, then twice the middle number is:

$$2(x+1) = 2x+2,$$

  and the sum of the first and last numbers is:

$$x+(x+2) = (x+x)+2 = 2x+2.$$

Both yield the same answer. This explains the observed pattern. Note how we used the properties of distributivity and associativity.

If we use instead the 'neater' formulation mentioned above, we get the result even more quickly: $(x-1)+(x+1)=2x$.

- We may similarly explain (2.2): "in any list of four consecutive integers, the sum of the outer two numbers equals the sum of the middle two numbers".

  Let the four numbers be x, $x+1$, $x+2$ and $x+3$. Then the sum of the outer two numbers equals $x+(x+3)=2x+3$, while the sum of the middle two numbers equals $(x+1)+(x+2)=2x+3$. As both yield the same sum $(2x+3)$, the observation is explained.

- The above two examples may have seemed too simple, so we try something more challenging. Let us see if we can use algebra to demonstrate the truth of (2.3). If we do so convincingly, it will be a sort of 'test case' for algebra.

  Let us consider the product $(x-1)\cdot(x+1)$. Using distributivity we get:

$$\begin{aligned}(x-1)\cdot(x+1) &= (x-1)\cdot x+(x-1)\cdot 1\\ &= x^2-x+x-1\\ &= x^2-1.\end{aligned}$$

  The difference between x^2-1 and x^2 is clearly 1, so we have demonstrated that equality (2.3) is true. Since x can be replaced by any number whatever, *we know for certain that the observed property will hold true for any three consecutive numbers whatever.*

- Now let us check if we can use algebra to demonstrate that (2.4) is true.

  Let us consider the product $(x+1)\cdot(x+3)$. Using distributivity we get:

$$\begin{aligned}(x+1)\cdot(x+2) &= (x+1)\cdot x+(x+1)\cdot 2\\ &= x^2+x+2x+2\\ &= x^2+3x+2,\\ x\cdot(x+3) &= x^2+3x.\end{aligned}$$

  Therefore,

$$(x+1)\cdot(x+2)-x\cdot(x+3) = (x^2+3x+2) - (x^2+3x) = 2.$$

  So equality (2.4) is true. *We can now be certain that the observed property is true for every collection of four consecutive integers.*

2.5 Using algebra to discover properties

The efforts made above can be turned in a different direction to *find* such properties. In doing so, we see the great power of algebra.

EXAMPLE 6. Let x denote any number. If x is even then the even number that precedes x is $x-2$, and the even number that follows x is $x+2$. Observe that if we were to replace 'even' by 'odd' everywhere in the above sentence, it remains valid.

Now consider the three numbers $x-2$, x, $x+2$. They represent either *three consecutive even numbers* or *three consecutive odd numbers*. If we compute the product of the outer two of the three numbers we get $(x-2)(x+2)$, which simplifies to x^2-4; for

$$(x-2)\cdot(x+2) \;=\; (x-2)\cdot x+(x-2)\cdot 2 \;=\; x^2-2x+2x-4 \;=\; x^2-4.$$

If we compute the square of the middle number we get x^2. Comparing these two results we see that the second one exceeds the first one by 4, *and this is so for any x whatever*. So we have found something here!

For any three consecutive even numbers, or any three consecutive odd numbers, the square of the middle number exceeds the product of the outer two numbers by 4.

For example, take the consecutive even numbers 10, 12, 14; we get $12^2=144$ and $10\times 14=140$. As predicted, the two answers differ by 4.

EXAMPLE 7. Let x denote any number, and consider the five consecutive numbers x, $x+1$, $x+2$, $x+3$ and $x+4$. If we discard the middle one, and search for relations which might hold between the remaining four, we find soon enough that

$$\boxed{(x+1)\cdot(x+3) \;-\; x\cdot(x+4) \;=\; 3.} \tag{2.6}$$

To check this, note that $(x+1)\cdot(x+3)=x^2+4x+3$, and $x\cdot(x+4)=x^2+4x$.

How can equality (2.6) be interpreted? The obvious way is:

In any set of five consecutive integers, let the central one be discarded. Then in the remaining numbers, the product of the middle two exceeds the product of the outer two by 3.

For example, consider the consecutive integers 11, 12, 13, 14, 15. Ignoring the central number, we are left with 11, 12, 14, 15. The product of the middle two is now $12 \times 14 = 168$, and the product of the outer two is $11 \times 15 = 165$. As predicted, the former number exceeds the latter by 3.

EXAMPLE 8. Consider any four consecutive positive integers, say x, $x+1$, $x+2$, $x+3$. Let us explore what happens if we add their squares. We get

$$\begin{aligned} & x^2+(x+1)^2+(x+2)^2+(x+3)^2 \\ = \; & x^2+\left(x^2+2x+1\right)+\left(x^2+4x+4\right)+\left(x^2+6x+9\right) \\ = \; & 4x^2+12x+14. \end{aligned}$$

Observing the form of the answer, we note that it is made up of three parts:

- $4x^2$, which is a multiple of 4 no matter what the value of x;
- $12x$, which too is a multiple of 4 no matter what the value of x; and
- 14, which leaves a remainder of 2 when divided by 4.

This tells that the quantity $x^2+(x+1)^2+(x+2)^2+(x+3)^2$ leaves a remainder of 2 when divided by 4, no matter what the value of x. So we arrive at the following:

The sum of the squares of four consecutive integers leaves a remainder of 2 *when divided by* 4.

Consider the integers 10, 11, 12, 13; the sum of their squares is $10^2+11^2+12^2+13^2$, which equals 534. You can verify that this leaves a remainder of 2 when divided by 4.

2.6 Factorisation

Earlier we had found using direct multiplication that

$$\left.\begin{aligned} x^2-1 &= (x-1)\cdot(x+1), \\ x^2-4 &= (x-2)\cdot(x+2). \end{aligned}\right\} \tag{2.7}$$

In exactly the same way as we got these, we can show that

$$\boxed{x^2-y^2 = (x-y)\cdot(x+y).} \tag{2.8}$$

For, $(x-y)\cdot(x+y) = (x-y)\cdot x + (x-y)\cdot y = x^2 - x\cdot y + x\cdot y - y^2 = x^2 - y^2$.

In this equality if we substitute $y = 1$ or $y = 2$ then we get back the relations shown above. And if we substitute other values for y, say $3, 4, \ldots$, then we get more such relations.

Equality (2.8) is called the **DIFFERENCE OF TWO SQUARES** formula. It is very frequently used in mathematics, in all sorts of connections.

Equalities (2.7) and (2.8) can be regarded as giving **FACTORISATIONS** of the expressions x^2-1, x^2-4 and x^2-y^2, respectively. And this reveals an important and pretty connection between the factorisation of *numbers* and equality (2.8).

We substitute positive integers for x and y, with $x > y$. If x and y are not consecutive integers, then $x-y$ is strictly greater than 1. Obviously, so is $x+y$, and this means that $(x-y)\cdot(x+y)$ is a product of two integers both strictly greater than 1. Therefore, x^2-y^2 is a composite number! So:

The difference between the squares of two non-consecutive integers is a composite number.

Examples:

- $5^2 - 2^2 = 21$ is divisible by $5-2=3$ and also by $5+2=7$;
- $15^2 - 4^2 = 209$ is divisible by $15-4=11$ and also by $15+4=19$;
- $21^2 - 8^2 = 377$ is divisible by $21-8=13$ and also by $21+8=29$;
- $41^2 - 12^2 = 1537$ is divisible by $41-12=29$ and also by $41+12=53$.

More factorisations

Other such results can be obtained. We had begun the above discussion by looking at the factorisation of x^2-1. Now we look at the factorisations of similar expressions, like x^3-1, x^4-1, etc. We factorise them by using an ingenious trick—that of adding and subtracting the same quantity to different parts of the expression. The idea is that *if a quantity A can be written as $B+C$ in such a way that both B and C are divisible by a common quantity k, then k must be a divisor of A as well.*

For the expression x^3-1 we may write x^3-1 as $x^3-x^2+x^2-1$. (We add and subtract x^2. Think of x^3-x^2 as B, and x^2-1 as C.) Now $x^3-x^2 = x^2\cdot(x-1)$, so B evidently has the factor $x-1$. And x^2-1 also has the factor $x-1$; this is from the equality (2.7) above. *Therefore, $x-1$ is a divisor of x^3-1.* Indeed, we have:

$$x^3-1 \;=\; x^3-x^2+x^2-1 \;=\; x^2\cdot(x-1)+(x+1)\cdot(x-1) \;=\; (x-1)\cdot\left(x^2+x+1\right);$$

so the factorisation of x^3-1 is

$$\boxed{x^3-1 = (x-1)\cdot\left(x^2+x+1\right).} \tag{2.9}$$

In the same way, we get the factorisation of x^4-1; the same trick works: we add and subtract x^3 and *use the just-found factorisation of* x^3-1:

$$\begin{aligned} x^4-1 &= x^4-x^3+x^3-1 \\ &= x^3\cdot(x-1)+\left(x^2+x+1\right)\cdot(x-1) \\ &= (x-1)\cdot\left(x^3+x^2+x+1\right); \end{aligned}$$

so the factorisation of x^4-1 is

$$\boxed{x^4-1 = (x-1)\cdot\left(x^3+x^2+x+1\right)} \tag{2.10}$$

For the factorisation of x^5-1, the same idea works yet again, and now we use the factorisation of x^4-1; we get

$$\boxed{x^5-1 = (x-1)\cdot\left(x^4+x^3+x^2+x+1\right).} \tag{2.11}$$

And so we proceed, each time using the result previously found; we ascend as though on a ladder. By now we see a general pattern beginning to emerge from the dust and smoke of the battle. We must be quick to grab hold of this pattern! After all, that is an essential part of algebra. So we write, for any positive integer n:

$$\boxed{x^n-1 = (x-1)\cdot\left(x^{n-1}+x^{n-2}+\cdots+x^2+x+1\right).} \tag{2.12}$$

The three dots in the middle $(\cdots)$ tell us that there are more such terms in the middle, and they follow the pattern. For example:

$$x^6-1 = (x-1)\cdot\left(x^5+x^4+x^3+x^2+x+1\right).$$

From equality (2.12) we deduce that if x is an integer greater than 2 (this makes $x-1$ greater than 1), then x^n-1 is a composite number (for the other factor also exceeds 1). So, we may now assert with confidence that the following numbers are composite, and we can say this without even bothering to compute them in full:

- $4^{10}-1$ is composite; it is divisible by $4-1=3$;
- $6^{12}-1$ is composite; it is divisible by $6-1=5$;

- $12^{18} - 1$ is composite; it is divisible by $12 - 1 = 11$;
- $20^{30} - 1$ is composite; it is divisible by $20 - 1 = 19$;
- $642^{77} - 1$ is composite; it is divisible by $642 - 1 = 641$;

and so on.

In the last example, no one would want to actually compute the number $642^{77} - 1$; it is a number with 217 digits!

What happens if x = 2?

Recall that we had said above that x must be greater than 2. What if $x = 2$? Then we must revise our assertions. Equality (2.12) tells us that

$$2^n - 1 \;=\; 2^{n-1} + 2^{n-2} + \cdots + 2^2 + 2 + 1. \tag{2.13}$$

This does not yield any factorisation—*but it gives us something else, just as interesting and as valuable!* For $n = 3$, it tells us that the sum $2^2 + 2 + 1 = 2^3 - 1$ (which may be checked: $2^2 + 2 + 1 = 4 + 2 + 1 = 7$, and $2^3 - 1 = 8 - 1 = 7$); for $n = 4$ it tells us that the sum $2^3 + 2^2 + 2 + 1 = 2^4 - 1$ (check: $2^3 + 2^2 + 2 + 1 = 8 + 4 + 2 + 1 = 15$, and $2^4 - 1 = 16 - 1 = 15$), and so on. So:

> *For any positive integer n, the sum of the quantities* $1, 2, 2^2, 2^3, 2^4, \ldots, 2^{n-1}$ *is equal to* $2^n - 1$. *In other words, the sum of a consecutive stretch of powers of* 2, *starting with* $1, 2, 4, \ldots$ *and going up to some power, is* 1 *less than the next power of* 2.

This has come as a gift, unexpectedly! We now see the truth of the saying, "Algebra is kind—she gives you more than you ask for ...".

Mersenne primes

We had stated above that equality (2.13) does not yield a factorisation of $2^n - 1$. Unlike the numbers $3^n - 1$, $4^n - 1$, $5^n - 1$, ..., which are *never* prime for $n > 1$, it *is* possible for $2^n - 1$ to be prime. Such primes are called **MERSENNE PRIMES**. They are named after Father Marin Mersenne (1588–1648) of France who was the first to study them. A few such primes are listed.

n	2	3	5	7	13	17	19
$2^n - 1$	3	7	31	127	8191	131071	524287

The table may give the impression that $2^n - 1$ is prime for any prime value of n. But this is not so; when $n = 11$ we get $2^{11} - 1 = 2047 = 23 \times 89$, and when $n = 23$ we get $2^{23} - 1 = 8388607 = 47 \times 178481$. However, it *is* true that if $2^n - 1$ is a prime number, then so is n.

Mersenne primes are a source of great interest to number theorists.

Assigning different values to x

Equality (2.12) yields more results. Substitute $x = 3$ in the equality; then we get

$$2 \times \left(3^{n-1} + 3^{n-2} + \cdots + 3^2 + 3 + 1\right) = 3^n - 1. \tag{2.14}$$

To illustrate this, let $n = 6$; then on the left we get

$$\begin{aligned} 2 \times \left(3^5 + 3^4 + 3^3 + 3^2 + 3 + 1\right) &= 2 \times (243 + 81 + 27 + 9 + 3 + 1) \\ &= 2 \times 364 = 728, \end{aligned}$$

and on the right we get $3^6 - 1 = 729 - 1 = 728$.

If we substitute $x = 4$ in equality (2.12), we get another interesting relation:

$$3 \times \left(4^{n-1} + 4^{n-2} + \cdots + 4^2 + 4 + 1\right) = 4^n - 1. \tag{2.15}$$

We can get any number of such nice results, by assigning different values to x.

2.7 Equations

One of the important uses of algebra is in finding unknown quantities that have been described by some given condition(s). For example, if we ask:

> *What is that integer with the property that when it is multiplied by* 3, *and* 7 *is added to the result, we get* 34?

Of course, this question is easy enough that it can be solved by trial-and-error, or by guessing, or by reversing the steps given. But we shall solve it *using algebra*. Let x denote the number to be found. If it is multiplied by 3, and 7 is then added to the result, we get $3x + 7$, and we are told that this is equal to 34. Hence:

$$3x + 7 = 34, \qquad \therefore\ 3x = 34 - 7 = 27, \qquad \therefore\ x = 27 \div 3 = 9.$$

So the number we seek is 9. Now we can check that it fits the stated condition: $3 \times 9 = 27$, and $27 + 7 = 34$.

Equations come in different shapes and sizes. They have a set of **UNKNOWNS** (in the above example there was just one unknown, which we called x) which satisfy some conditions expressed in the form of equalities (or, at times, inequalities). The unknowns are traditionally denoted by x, y, z, w, ... (letters at the tail end of the alphabet). Finding their values is called **SOLVING THE EQUATION**. We shall shortly learn a number of methods for doing this, including the *function approach*, the *use of graphs*, etc. (In general, we do not admit 'trial-and-error' as a method of solution of equations, at least not in the obvious sense.)

Some equations give rise to just one solution, i.e., just one possible set of values for the unknown; we say that the solution is **UNIQUE** in such cases. In other cases, the equation may admit **MULTIPLE SOLUTIONS**.

For example, consider the equation $(x-1)\cdot(x-3) = 8$. One solution, which is easy to spot, is $x = 5$ (check: $4 \times 2 = 8$). But, less obviously, there is the solution $x = -1$. You may check that it works: $(-2) \times (-4) = 8$. So the equation $(x-1)(x-3) = 8$ has at least two different solutions, $x = 5$ and $x = -1$. (Later you will learn that there can be no more solutions.)

Or we may have an equation which features *two* unknowns, e.g., $x + y = 5$. There are *infinitely many* pairs (x, y) of integers satisfying the equation; e.g., $x = 5, y = 0$; or $x = 4$, $y = 1$; or $x = 3$, $y = 2$; $x = -1$, $y = 6$; ....

Sometimes we meet equations which are satisfied by *all* of the numbers that are available; for example, the equation $x^2 - 1 = (x-1)\cdot(x+1)$. We have seen earlier that this relation is always true. Such equations are called **IDENTITIES** in algebra. We have already seen several identities in the previous section: (2.8), which gives the factors of $x^2 - y^2$; (2.9), which gives the factors of $x^3 - 1$; etc.

Sometimes we meet equations that have *no solutions* at all. This happens when the conditions that describe the unknown(s) somehow contradict one another. For example, if the given equation is $x = x + 1$ then it is obvious that we will not be able to find any number x that satisfies the equation, because the equation has a contradiction within itself. If the equation is $x^2 + 1 = 0$, then again we are unable to find any integer x satisfying this condition. Equations can come in varying degrees of difficulty; some are easy to solve, others are computationally very difficult to solve, even if one has access to a powerful computer. We now look at some examples of different types of equations. Later we will be devoting a full chapter to this topic.

EXAMPLE 9. *Find six consecutive integers whose sum is* 333.

Let x denote the least of the integers; then the six integers are $x, x+1, x+2, x+3, x+4, x+5$, and their sum is

$$x+(x+1)+(x+2)+(x+3)+(x+4)+(x+5) = 6x+15.$$

Hence we have:

$$\begin{aligned} 6x+15 &= 333, \\ 6x &= 333-15 = 318, \\ \therefore\ x &= 318 \div 6 = 53, \end{aligned}$$

and we see that the required integers are $53, 54, 55, 56, 57, 58$. (Please check that their sum is 333.)

EXAMPLE 10. *Find a pair of consecutive integers such that four times the larger one exceeds three times the smaller one by* 100.

Let x denote the smaller integer; then the larger integer is $x+1$, and the stated condition yields:

$$\begin{aligned} 4(x+1)-3x &= 100, \\ 4x+4-3x &= 100, \\ x+4 &= 100, \\ \therefore\ x &= 96. \end{aligned}$$

Hence, the two integers are 96 and 97.

(Check: $4 \times 97 = 388$, $3 \times 96 = 288$, and $388 - 288 = 100$.)

EXAMPLE 11. *Find three consecutive positive integers such that the sum of the squares of the smallest one and the largest one exceeds the square of the middle one by* 326.

We use x to denote the integer in the *middle*; then the other two integers are $x-1$ and $x+1$. Their squares are $(x-1)^2$ and $(x+1)^2$, so the stated condition translates into the following equation:

$$(x-1)^2+(x+1)^2-x^2 = 326.$$

Since $(x-1)^2 = x^2-2x+1$ and $(x+1)^2 = x^2+2x+1$, we get, on substitution:

$$x^2-2x+1+x^2+2x+1-x^2 = 326.$$

The expression on the left simplifies to x^2+2, so we have: $x^2+2=326$, hence $x^2=324$. Looking up a table of squares, we find

$$17^2 = 289, \quad 18^2 = 324, \quad 19^2 = 361.$$

Since $18^2=324$, we get $x=18$. [We also have $(-18)^2=324$, i.e., $x=-18$; but as the problem said 'positive integer' we do not consider this possibility.]

So the three consecutive integers which had to be found are 17, 18, 19.

(Check: $17^2+19^2-18^2=289+361-324=326$).

EXAMPLE 12. *Find five consecutive positive integers such that the sum of their squares is* 2215.

As earlier, we use the symbol x to denote the middle integer. Then the five integers are:

$$x-2, \quad x-1, \quad x, \quad x+1, \quad x+2,$$

and the sum of their squares is

$$\begin{aligned} & (x-2)^2+(x-1)^2+x^2+(x+1)^2+(x+2)^2 \\ = \; & \left(x^2-4x+4\right)+\left(x^2-2x+1\right)+x^2+\left(x^2+2x+1\right)+\left(x^2+4x+4\right) \\ = \; & 5x^2+10. \end{aligned}$$

Using the given information, we get:

$$\begin{aligned} 5x^2+10 &= 2215, \\ 5x^2 &= 2205, \\ \therefore\ x^2 &= \frac{2205}{5} = 441. \end{aligned}$$

Once again, we use a table of squares to get $x=21$. (We disregard the possibility that $x=-21$, as we want x to be positive.)

So the five numbers are 19, 20, 21, 22, 23. (Check: $19^2+20^2+21^2+22^2+23^2=2215$.)

EXAMPLE 13. *Find two consecutive integers given that the difference between their squares is* 29.

It is natural to let the integers be x and $x+1$. Note that in this problem we have not specified that the integers must be positive. We are told that the difference between x^2 and

$(x+1)^2$ equals 29. Depending on which of the two squares is the larger one, the above statement could translate into two possible equations:

$$(x+1)^2 - x^2 = 29, \quad \textbf{or} \quad x^2 - (x+1)^2 = 29.$$

We must examine both these possibilities. We shall use identity (2.5), which yields: $(x+1)^2 = x^2 + 2x + 1$, and therefore $(x+1)^2 - x^2 = 2x + 1$. Substituting this into the above, we get:

- If $(x+1)^2 - x^2 = 29$, then

$$\begin{aligned} 2x+1 &= 29, \\ 2x &= 29-1 = 28, \\ \therefore x &= \frac{28}{2} = 14. \end{aligned}$$

- If $x^2 - (x+1)^2 = 29$, then

$$\begin{aligned} -2x-1 &= 29, \\ -2x &= 29+1 = 30, \\ \therefore x &= -\frac{30}{2} = -15. \end{aligned}$$

So either of the two pairs $14, 15$ *or* $-15, -14$ *fits the stated requirement.*

(Check: $15^2 - 14^2 = 225 - 196 = 29$, and $(-15)^2 - (-14)^2 = 225 - 196 = 29$.)

Déscartes on algebra

Being able to correctly translate conditions given in *words* into statements using *symbols* is a skill that the student will have to learn, for it is a vital part of algebra.

Here is a remarkable and expressive quote from René Déscartes, in the book LA GEOMETRIE, in which he performed a 'marriage' of algebra and geometry and laid out the foundations and methods of a brand new chapter in mathematics—**COORDINATE GEOMETRY** (also called **ANALYTIC GEOMETRY**).

> *If, then, we wish to solve any problem, we first suppose the solution already effected, and give names to all the lines that seem needful for its construction—to those that are unknown as well as to those that are known. Then, making no distinction between*

known and unknown lines, we must unravel the difficulty in any way that shows most naturally the relations between these lines, until we find it possible to express a single quantity in two ways. This will constitute an equation since the terms of one of these two expressions are together equal to the terms of the other.

So Déscartes is telling us to: (a) 'assume' that the problem is solved; (b) give names to all the quantities, making no distinction between the knowns and unknowns; (c) express the relations between the knowns and unknowns using the language of algebra; and (d) find a single quantity that can be expressed in two different ways. By this means we get an equation, which we then solve.

EXERCISES

1. Verify the factorisation: $a^2 - b^2 = (a-b)(a+b)$.
2. Verify the factorisation: $a^3 - b^3 = (a-b) \cdot (a^2 + ab + b^2)$.
3. Verify the factorisation: $a^4 - b^4 = (a-b) \cdot (a^3 + a^2b + ab^2 + b^3)$.
4. Verify the factorisation: $a^5 - b^5 = (a-b) \cdot (a^4 + a^3b + a^2b^2 + ab^3 + b^4)$.
5. Guess the factorisation of $a^n - b^n$ where n represents any positive integer.
6. Verify the factorisation: $a^3 + b^3 = (a+b) \cdot (a^2 - ab + b^2)$.
7. Verify the factorisation: $a^5 + b^5 = (a+b) \cdot (a^4 - a^3b + a^2b^2 - ab^3 + b^4)$.
8. Guess the factorisation of $a^n + b^n$ where n represents any *odd* positive integer.
9. Factorise the following expressions:

   (a) $x^2 + 4x + 3$;
   (b) $x^2 + 10x + 9$;
   (c) $x^2 - 12x + 35$;
   (d) $x^3 - 8$;
   (e) $x^3 + 27$;
   (f) $x^4 - 16$.

10. Show that $2^{31} + 3^{31}$ is not a prime number.
11. Show that $4^{66} + 7^{66}$ is not a prime number.
12. Using algebra, factorise the number 899.

13. Using algebra, factorise the number 973.

14. Find (a) a two-digit number and (b) a three-digit number which is a divisor of the number $5^{33} - 2^{33}$.

15. Find a three-digit number which is a divisor of the number $8^{33} - 5^{33}$.

16. Find a three-digit number which is a divisor of the number $7^{33} - 4^{33}$.

17. Show that 11 and 37 are divisors of the number $7^{33} + 4^{33}$.

18. Show that 13 and 49 are divisors of the number $8^{15} + 5^{15}$.

19. Show that $2^{11} + 2^{12} + 2^{13} + 2^{14} + 2^{15} + 2^{16} + 2^{17} + 2^{18} + 2^{19} = 2^{20} - 2^{11}$.

20. ✪ Find the factors of $a^4 + a^2b^2 + b^4$.

21. ✪ Find the factors of $x^4 + 4$. (The problem is quite challenging at this stage, but is well worth an attempt.)

22. ✪ Let n represent a positive integer. Find all possible values of n, given that $n^2 - 4$ is a prime number.

23. ✪ Let n represent a positive integer. Find all possible values of n, given that $n^3 - 8$ is a prime number.

24. Write 195 as the sum of two parts in such a way that two times one part equals three times the other part.

25. In a two-digit number the tens digit exceeds the units digit by 3. The sum of the number and the number obtained by reversing the digits is 121. Express the given information in terms of a suitable equation, and hence find the number.

26. The square of a given number exceeds the number by 42. Express the given information as a suitable equation.

27. A number is such that when the square of half the number is subtracted from 7 times the number, the result is 3 times the number. Express this information in terms of a suitable equation, and hence find the number.

28. In a stretch of four consecutive integers, it is found that the product of the second and fourth integers exceeds the product of the first and third integers by 45. Express this statement using algebra, and hence find the four integers.

29. In a stretch of six consecutive integers, it is found that the product of the second, fourth and sixth integers exceeds the product of the first, third and fifth integers by 543. Express this statement using algebra, and hence find the six integers.

30. Four consecutive integers are required such that the product of the second and third integers exceeds the product of the first and fourth integers by 4. Do you think any such integers exist?

31. Using algebra show that in any three consecutive numbers, the sum of the squares of the smallest and largest numbers exceeds twice the square of the middle one by 2.

32. Using algebra show that in any four consecutive numbers, the sum of the squares of the smallest and largest numbers exceeds the sum of the squares of the other two numbers by 4.

33. In any five consecutive integers, let A be the sum of the squares of the first, third and fifth integers, and let B be the the sum of the squares of the second and fourth integers. Show using algebra that $2A - 3B = 10$.

    For example, if the integers are 12, 13, 14, 15, 16, then $A = 12^2 + 14^2 + 16^2 = 596$, and $B = 13^2 + 15^2 = 394$. Check that $2 \times 596 - 3 \times 394 = 10$.

34. In any six consecutive integers, let A be the sum of the squares of the first, second, fifth and sixth integers, and let B be the the sum of the squares of the third and fourth integers. Show using algebra that $A - 2B = 16$.

    For example, if the integers are 12, 13, 14, 15, 16, 17, then $A = 12^2 + 13^2 + 16^2 + 17^2 = 858$, and $B = 14^2 + 15^2 = 421$. Check that $858 - 2 \times 421 = 16$.

35. (a) Using algebra show that the sum of the squares of any *five* consecutive integers is a multiple of 5.

    (b) Using algebra show that the sum of the squares of any *seven* consecutive integers is a multiple of 7.

36. Using algebra show that the sum of the squares of any nine consecutive integers, when divided by 9, leaves a remainder of 6.

37. Is it true that the sum of the squares of any eleven consecutive integers is a multiple of 11?

38. From the list of non-negative integers (1, 2, 3, 4, 5, 6, 7, ...) we form a new one by computing *products of consecutive pairs of numbers from the list*; we get:

$$2, \ 6, \ 12, \ 20, \ 30, \ 42, \ \ldots.$$

Now we *add consecutive pairs of numbers from the new list* and then *divide by* 2; we get:

$$4, \ 9, \ 16, \ 25, \ 36, \ \ldots.$$

These are just the perfect squares! How do you explain this finding using algebra?

Note that we miss the very first perfect square (namely, 1). How should we modify the above description so that we get 1 too?

39. Now we work with the list of *odd numbers*.

From the list of odd positive integers (1, 3, 5, 7, 9, 11, ...) we form a new one by computing the *products of consecutive pairs of numbers from the list*; we get:

$$3, \ 15, \ 35, \ 63, \ 99, \ \ldots.$$

Now we *add consecutive pairs of numbers from the new list* and then *divide by* 2; we get:

$$9, \ 25, \ 49, \ 81, \ \ldots.$$

These are the odd perfect squares! How do you explain this finding using algebra?

Note that we once again miss the very first odd perfect square (namely, 1). How should we modify the above description so that we get 1 too?

40. ✪✪ Examining the products of *four* consecutive integers, we find to our surprise that *the product of any four consecutive integers is* 1 *less than a perfect square*. Thus we have:

$$\begin{aligned} 1\times2\times3\times4 &= 24 = 5^2-1,\\ 2\times3\times4\times5 &= 120 = 11^2-1,\\ 3\times4\times5\times6 &= 360 = 19^2-1,\\ 4\times5\times6\times7 &= 840 = 29^2-1, \end{aligned}$$

and so on. How would you use algebra to account for this property? (The problem is quite challenging at this stage, but is well worth an attempt.)

2.8 Closing quotes

We close the chapter with some nice comments about algebra. Caution: Some of the statements are rather tongue-in-cheek!

- *Algebra is generous; she often gives more than is asked of her.*—Jean Le Rond d'Alembert (1717–83), French mathematician
- *Algebraic symbols are used when you do not know what you are talking about.*
- *When you learn to read, you start with a, b, c. But when you learn algebra, you start with x, y, z.*
- *As long as algebra is taught in school, there will be prayer in school.*—Cokie Roberts

Chapter 3

Families of Integers

God created the integers, all else is the work of man.

Leopold Kronecker (1823–1891)

If we look closely at the family of integers, we find a large number of sub-families—families within families. In this chapter, we examine some of these families and note some of their properties.

Notation and symbols

Throughout, we shall use the following symbols: $\mathbf{N}$ is the set of natural or counting numbers, and $\mathbf{Z}$ is the set of integers, so:

$$\begin{aligned} \mathbf{N} &= \{1,\ 2,\ 3,\ 4,\ 5,\ 6,\ 7,\ 8,\ 9,\ 10,\ 11,\ 12,\ 13,\ 14,\ \ldots\}, \\ \mathbf{Z} &= \{\ldots,\ -5,\ -4,\ -3,\ -2,\ -1,\ 0,\ 1,\ 2,\ 3,\ 4,\ 5,\ \ldots\}. \end{aligned}$$

Sometimes it turns out to be convenient to use symbols like $2\mathbf{N}$, $2\mathbf{Z}$, $2\mathbf{N}+1$, $2\mathbf{Z}+1$, etc, which are defined below:

- If we double every number in $\mathbf{N}$, then we get the set $2\mathbf{N}$; this is the set of *even positive integers* (or *even numbers*):

$$2\mathbf{N} = \{2,\ 4,\ 6,\ 8,\ 10,\ 12,\ 14,\ 16,\ 18,\ 20,\ \ldots\};$$

- If we double every integer in $\mathbf{Z}$, then we get the set $2\mathbf{Z}$ of even integers:

$$2\mathbf{Z} = \{\ldots,\ -8,\ -6,\ -4,\ -2,\ 0,\ 2,\ 4,\ 6,\ 8,\ \ldots\};$$

- If we multiply each number in $\mathbf{N}$ by 3, then we get the set $3\mathbf{N}$:

$$3\mathbf{N} = \{3,\ 6,\ 9,\ 12,\ 15,\ 18,\ 21,\ 24,\ 27,\ 30,\ \ldots\};$$

- If we multiply each integer in $\mathbf{Z}$ by 3, then we get the set $3\mathbf{Z}$:

$$3\mathbf{Z} = \{\ldots,\ -12,\ -9,\ -6,\ -3,\ 0,\ 3,\ 6,\ 9,\ 12,\ \ldots\};$$

- If we multiply every number in $\mathbf{N}$ by 10, then we get the set $10\mathbf{N}$:

$$10\mathbf{N} = \{10,\ 20,\ 30,\ 40,\ 50,\ 60,\ 70,\ 80,\ 90,\ 100,\ \ldots\};$$

- If we multiply every integer in $\mathbf{Z}$ by 10, then we get the set $10\mathbf{Z}$:

$$10\mathbf{Z} = \{\ldots,\ -40,\ -30,\ -20,\ -10,\ 0,\ 10,\ 20,\ 30,\ 40,\ \ldots\};$$

and so on. More such symbols will soon be introduced and used.

Remark

We shall often use the following terms to mean the same thing: ‘number’, ‘natural number’, ‘positive integer’. Generally this should not be a source for confusion.

3.1 Odd integers and even integers

The simplest two sub-families of $\mathbf{Z}$ that we shall examine are the families of odd integers and even integers. By definition, an even integer is one that leaves no remainder when divided by 2, whereas an odd integer leaves a remainder of 1 when divided by 2. So the even integers are

$$\ldots,\ -10,\ -8,\ -6,\ -4,\ -2,\ 0,\ 2,\ 4,\ 6,\ 8,\ 10,\ \ldots.$$

and the odd integers are

$$\ldots,\ -11,\ -9,\ -7,\ -5,\ -3,\ -1,\ 1,\ 3,\ 5,\ 7,\ 9,\ 11,\ \ldots.$$

Both families clearly have an unending supply of integers. We shall refer to them as ‘**Even**’ and ‘**Odd**’ respectively. However, we could also call them $2\mathbf{Z}$ and $2\mathbf{Z}+1$.

Remark

The reason for calling the second family $2\mathbf{Z}+1$ should be clear: if we double all the integers in $\mathbf{Z}$ and then add 1 to all the resulting integers, we get the family **Odd**. If we *subtract* 1 from all the integers in $2\mathbf{Z}$, we get exactly the same family; so we could equally well call it $2\mathbf{Z}-1$ instead of $2\mathbf{Z}+1$. Note that $2\mathbf{Z}+2$ is the same as $2\mathbf{Z}$, for by adding 2 to all the integers in $2\mathbf{Z}$, we get exactly the same set of integers.

If we restrict our attention to only the positive numbers (that is, to $\mathbf{N}$), then we get the sets:

$$\begin{aligned} 2\mathbf{N} &= \{2,\ 4,\ 6,\ 8,\ 10,\ \ldots\}, \\ 2\mathbf{N}+1 &= \{3,\ 5,\ 7,\ 9,\ 11,\ \ldots\}, \\ 2\mathbf{N}+2 &= \{4,\ 6,\ 8,\ 10,\ 12,\ \ldots\}, \\ 2\mathbf{N}-1 &= \{1,\ 3,\ 5,\ 7,\ 9,\ \ldots\}, \end{aligned}$$

Observe that $2\mathbf{N}$ is *not* the same as $2\mathbf{N}+2$, and $2\mathbf{N}-1$ is *not* the same as $2\mathbf{N}+1$. We see that $\mathbf{N}$ and $\mathbf{Z}$ behave differently in this respect.

Parity

If two given integers are both in **Even** or both in **Odd**, we say that *they have the same parity*, and if they are in different families, we say that *they have opposite parity*. So 12 and 26 have the same parity; 15 and 32 have opposite parity; and 13 and −7 have the same parity.

As noted in Chapter 1, if we take any two integers in *even* and add them, then the sum is always in *even*. For instance, we have:

$$4+8=12, \quad 10+10=20, \quad 18+(-2)=16, \quad 14+(-18)=-4, \quad \ldots.$$

We shall write this fact for short as '**Even** + **Even** = **Even**.' Another way of writing it is:

$$2\mathbf{Z}+2\mathbf{Z}=2\mathbf{Z}.$$

If we work, instead, with odd integers, we find a similar pattern to that for $2\mathbf{Z}$:

$$1+3=4, \quad 5+11=16, \quad 7+(-17)=-10, \quad 19+(-3)=16, \quad \ldots.$$

So we also have: '**Odd** + **Odd** = **Even**'; otherwise written as:

$$(2\mathbf{Z}+1)+(2\mathbf{Z}+1)=2\mathbf{Z}.$$

Both facts may be easily explained if we use the 'dots' model described in Chapter 1 (in the section 'Parity').

EXERCISES

1. Explain why **Even** + **Odd** = **Odd**. Use the dots model.

2. Complete the following:

$$\begin{aligned} \textsf{Even} \times \textsf{Even} &= ? \\ \textsf{Even} \times \textsf{Odd} &= ? \\ \textsf{Odd} \times \textsf{Even} &= ? \\ \textsf{Odd} \times \textsf{Odd} &= ? \end{aligned}$$

3. Explain why **Even** × **Odd** = **Even** and **Odd** × **Odd** = **Odd**.

4. "If the sum of two integers is **Even**, then the two integers have the same parity." Explain this statement.

5. "If the sum of two integers is **Odd**, then the two integers have opposite parity." Explain this statement.

6. Suppose that an integer X has a divisor Y. If X and Y are both **Odd**, what can you say about the quotient $X \div Y$?

7. Suppose that an integer X has a divisor Y. What can you say about the quotient $X \div Y$ if X is even, but Y is **Odd**? What can you say about the quotient $X \div Y$ if X and Y are both **Even**?

3.2 Multiples of 3, non-multiples of 3

In the above section we placed each integer into one or the other of two categories, depending on its divisibility by 2. Instead of using a divisor of 2 we could use other divisors, for example, 3.

When a positive integer is divided by 3, there are three possible things that might happen: there may be no remainder (we shall call this 'a remainder of 0'), or a remainder of 1, or a remainder of 2. The families of positive integers that yield these possibilities are listed below:

$$\begin{aligned} \text{Remainder} = 0: &\quad \{3,\ 6,\ 9,\ 12,\ 15,\ 18,\ 21,\ \ldots\}, \\ \text{Remainder} = 1: &\quad \{1,\ 4,\ 7,\ 10,\ 13,\ 16,\ 19,\ \ldots\}, \\ \text{Remainder} = 2: &\quad \{2,\ 5,\ 8,\ 11,\ 14,\ 17,\ 20,\ \ldots\}. \end{aligned}$$

We shall call the first set $3\mathbf{N}$. A natural choice of name for the second set is $3\mathbf{N}+1$ (just like $2\mathbf{N}+1$, above), and for the third set $3\mathbf{N}+2$. We shall extend all three sets in a natural manner to include the negative integers too:

$$\begin{aligned} 3\mathbf{Z} &= \{\ldots, -12, -9, -6, -3, 0, 3, 6, 9, \ldots\}, \\ 3\mathbf{Z}+1 &= \{\ldots, -11, -8, -5, -2, 1, 4, 7, 10, \ldots\}, \\ 3\mathbf{Z}+2 &= \{\ldots, -10, -7, -4, -1, 2, 5, 8, 11, \ldots\}. \end{aligned}$$

Just like we did for the families $2\mathbf{Z}$ and $2\mathbf{Z}+1$, let us now see how these three families behave under addition and multiplication. First, we add pairs of integers in $3\mathbf{Z}$:

$$3+9=12, \quad 6+15=21, \quad 12+(-15)=-3, \quad (-15)+(-12)=-27, \quad \ldots.$$

We see right away that the sum of two integers in $3\mathbf{Z}$ belongs to the same family. So we get:

$$3\mathbf{Z}+3\mathbf{Z}=3\mathbf{Z}.$$

But this is surely not very surprising: if we add two multiples of 3, we will surely get a multiple of 3. We similarly find that

$$\begin{aligned} 3\mathbf{Z}+(3\mathbf{Z}+1) &= 3\mathbf{Z}+1, \qquad & (3\mathbf{Z}+1)+(3\mathbf{Z}+1) &= 3\mathbf{Z}+2, \\ 3\mathbf{Z}+(3\mathbf{Z}+2) &= 3\mathbf{Z}+2, \qquad & (3\mathbf{Z}+1)+(3\mathbf{Z}+2) &= 3\mathbf{Z}, \end{aligned}$$

and so on. To see what the statement $(3\mathbf{Z}+1)+(3\mathbf{Z}+2)=3\mathbf{Z}$ means, we study these examples:

$$1+5=6, \quad 7+14=21, \quad 10+(-13)=-3, \quad (-2)+17=15.$$

In each case the answer is a multiple of 3, i.e., it is in $3\mathbf{Z}$. The meanings of the other statements can be understood similarly.

For multiplication too we can make such statements. If we multiply any two integers in $3\mathbf{Z}$, the answer will always be in the same set; for example, we have

$$3\times 6=18, \quad 6\times 9=54, \quad 9\times 12=108.$$

So we write: $3\mathbf{Z}\times 3\mathbf{Z}=3\mathbf{Z}$.

EXERCISES

1. Give examples to illustrate the following addition facts:

$$3\mathbf{Z}+(3\mathbf{Z}+1)=3\mathbf{Z}+1,$$
$$(3\mathbf{Z}+1)+(3\mathbf{Z}+1)=3\mathbf{Z}+2,$$
$$(3\mathbf{Z}+1)+(3\mathbf{Z}+2)=3\mathbf{Z}.$$

2. Give examples to illustrate the following multiplication facts:

$$3\mathbf{Z}\times(3\mathbf{Z}+1)=3\mathbf{Z},$$
$$(3\mathbf{Z}+1)\times(3\mathbf{Z}+1)=3\mathbf{Z}+1,$$
$$(3\mathbf{Z}+1)\times(3\mathbf{Z}+2)=3\mathbf{Z}+2.$$

Using different symbols

A nice pattern emerges if we hide the symbol $3\mathbf{Z}$ which comes repeatedly in all these statements and, instead, write **1** for $3\mathbf{Z}+1$, **2** for $3\mathbf{Z}+2$, and **0** for $3\mathbf{Z}$ (think of $3\mathbf{Z}$ as $3\mathbf{Z}+0$ to see the consistency in the notation), respectively.

Here is how the addition and multiplication tables now look:

+	0	1	2
0	0	1	2
1	1	2	0
2	2	0	1

×	0	1	2
0	0	0	0
1	0	1	2
2	0	2	1

Observe how **0** behaves very much like the ordinary 0, for addition as well as multiplication (in other words, it behaves just like the usual additive identity: **0** plus any number equals that number; **0** times any number equals **0**), and **1** behaves much like the ordinary 1 for multiplication (it behaves like the multiplicative identity: **1** times any number equals that number). Also, in the first table, observe the 'wrap around' effect.

This 'world' is called the MOD 3 or the 'modulo 3' world; it has just three numbers (**0**, **1** and **2**). We shall meet such worlds later in the book.

3.3 Multiples of 5, non-multiples of 5

We can construct and explore the **MOD** 5 or the modulo 5 world just as we did for the mod 3 world. Here we put the integers into *five* different categories, according to the remainders they leave on division by 5. So we give the name $5\mathbf{Z}$, or **0**, to the set of integers that are divisible by 5:

$$\{\ldots, -20, -15, -10, -5, 0, 5, 10, 15, 20, \ldots\},$$

the name $5\mathbf{Z}+1$, or **1**, to the set of integers that leave a remainder of 1 when divided by 5:

$$\{\ldots, -19, -14, -9, -4, 1, 6, 11, 16, 21, \ldots\};$$

the name $5\mathbf{Z}+2$, or **2**, to the set of integers that leave a remainder of 2 when divided by 5:

$$\{\ldots, -18, -13, -8, -3, 2, 7, 12, 17, 22, \ldots\},$$

and so on. In the end we get five sets, which we call, respectively:

$$5\mathbf{Z}, \quad 5\mathbf{Z}+1, \quad 5\mathbf{Z}+2, \quad 5\mathbf{Z}+3, \quad 5\mathbf{Z}+4.$$

But it is most convenient to hide the '$5\mathbf{Z}$' and call them simply **0**, **1**, **2**, **3**, **4**.

Having defined them, we now construct the addition and multiplication tables for these entities. Here is what we get:

+	0	1	2	3	4
0	0	1	2	3	4
1	1	2	3	4	0
2	2	3	4	0	1
3	3	4	0	1	2
4	4	0	1	2	3

×	0	1	2	3	4
0	0	0	0	0	0
1	0	1	2	3	4
2	0	2	4	1	3
3	0	3	1	4	2
4	0	4	3	2	1

The table tells us, for example, that in the mod 5 world, $\mathbf{1}+\mathbf{3}=\mathbf{4}$, $\mathbf{2}\times\mathbf{4}=\mathbf{3}$, $\mathbf{1}\times\mathbf{2}\times\mathbf{3}\times\mathbf{4}=\mathbf{4}$, and so on.

Observe, yet again, how **0** behaves like the ordinary 0, for both addition and multiplication, and how **1** behaves like the ordinary 1 for multiplication. And once again we see the wrap around effect in the addition table.

Modular arithmetic

There is a definite risk here that we could get confused between the **2** of the mod 3 world and the **2** of the mod 5 world! Generally, however, we shall not deal with them at the same time. If it ever does happen that way, then to avoid confusion we may write mod 2, or mod 3, or mod 5, or whatever, like this: 2 mod 3 (short for $3\mathbf{Z}+2$), 1 mod 5 (short for $5\mathbf{Z}+1$),and so on.

By choosing different divisors we get different worlds, and we can construct as many of them as we wish. Arithmetic done in these worlds is called **MODULAR ARITHMETIC**. For more on this topic, please consult the author's book FIRST STEPS IN NUMBER THEORY, or visit the following web page:

`http://www.math.rutgers.edu/~erowland/modulararithmetic.html`

EXERCISES

1. In the mod 7 world, what do $\mathbf{4}+\mathbf{5}$ and $\mathbf{4}\times\mathbf{5}$ equal?
2. In the mod 6 world, calculate: $\mathbf{2}+\mathbf{3}$ and $\mathbf{2}\times\mathbf{3}$.
3. Observe from the above exercise that the product of **2** and **3** in the mod 6 world is **0**. In the mod 5 world, can you find two numbers, neither of them equal to **0**, whose product is **0**?
4. In the mod 7 world, can you find two numbers, neither of them equal to **0**, whose product is **0**?
5. In the mod 8 world, can you find two numbers, neither of them equal to **0**, whose product is **0**?
6. In the mod 10 world, can you find two numbers, neither of them equal to **0**, whose product is **0**?
7. Consider the mod 12 world. In what way does the arithmetic of ordinary clocks correspond to this world? (Hint: What could $\mathbf{9}+\mathbf{4}$ mean when talking about time? How about: '9 a.m. plus 4 hours equals 1 p.m.'?)

3.4 Prime numbers, composite numbers

In this section we describe briefly two important families in **N** which have played a vital role in the growth of number theory: the families of prime numbers and composite numbers.

Some positive integers can be written as products of *strictly smaller* positive integers. For example, we have:

$$\begin{aligned} 8 &= 2 \times 4, \\ 12 &= 3 \times 4, \\ 15 &= 3 \times 5, \\ 56 &= 7 \times 8, \end{aligned}$$

and so on. Such integers are called **COMPOSITE NUMBERS**.

But for some positive integers there is simply no way that we can express them as products of smaller integers. For example, 5 is such a number: the only way of writing 5 as a product of two positive integers is 1×5, and here we have *not* been able to use only numbers smaller than 5. The same thing can be said for the numbers 2, 3, 7, 11, and 13. Such numbers are called **PRIME NUMBERS**. So a positive integer $p > 1$ is a prime number if its only divisors are 1 and p. The next two prime numbers after 13 are 17 and 19.

What about the integer 1 itself? Though 1 obviously cannot be factorised into positive integers smaller than itself, mathematicians prefer to give it a special status, and to not call it either prime or composite; rather, it is called a **UNIT**. We shall briefly discuss the reason behind this at the end of this section.

So we get three sub-families of **N**, as shown below:

$$\begin{aligned} \textsf{Units} &= \{1\}, \\ \textsf{Primes} &= \{2,\ 3,\ 5,\ 7,\ 11,\ 13,\ 17,\ 19,\ 23,\ \ldots\}, \\ \textsf{Composites} &= \{4,\ 6,\ 8,\ 9,\ 10,\ 12,\ 14,\ 15,\ 16,\ \ldots\}. \end{aligned}$$

Neither of the families, **Primes** and **Composites**, has a 'last' integer; no matter how far we travel on the number line, we meet integers that are in **Primes**, and integers that are in **Composites**.

It is of course not surprising that the family **Composites** has indefinitely large integers in it; for, we can with ease produce very large integers belonging to this family. For example, the integer 2^{100} (the product $2 \times 2 \times 2 \times \cdots \times 2$, with a hundred 2s) is composite, since we can write it as a product of integers all smaller than itself (namely, all 2s); so we have here a really large composite integer:

$$2^{100} = 1267650600228229401496703205376.$$

Here is an even larger composite integer:

$$3^{100} = 515377520732011331036461129765621272702107522001.$$

A still larger composite integer is obtained by multiplying all the integers from 1 till 50, i.e., the product $1 \times 2 \times 3 \times 4 \times \cdots \times 49 \times 50$ (the three dots indicate that there are more numbers between 4 and 49, only, we have not listed them):

$$30414093201713378043612608166064768844377641568960512000000000000.$$

Clearly, the following composite number is larger still:

$$1 \times 2 \times 3 \times 4 \times 5 \times \cdots \times 98 \times 99 \times 100.$$

But it is too large to print here; it has a hundred and fifty-eight digits!

So we can go on in this way and generate, with ease, composite numbers that exceed any given limit.

Surprisingly, in the family **Primes** too there are prime numbers larger than any given limit. A big difference between this family and **Composites**, however, is that finding large composite numbers is very easy to do, whereas finding large prime numbers is a very difficult task.

Some large prime numbers

Here are some five-digit prime numbers:

$$20011, \quad 40009, \quad 55001, \quad 77003, \quad 86711.$$

Here are some ten-digit prime numbers:

$$2000000137, \quad 3000000511, \quad 6000000901.$$

Here are two 20-digit prime numbers:

$$30000000000000000109, \qquad 70000000010000000033.$$

And here is one with 60 digits:

$$500000000000000000000000000000000000000000000000000000000131.$$

But we cannot easily recognise these as prime numbers. *This is a basic difficulty about prime numbers.*

Remark

The large number of zero digits in the above numbers make them difficult to read. Here is another way in which we can write such numbers:

- 20_6137 for 2000000137 (the subscript '6' indicates six zeros);
- 30_6511 for 3000000511;
- $30_{16}109$ for 30000000000000000109 (it has 16 zeros);

The 60-digit prime number $500\ldots00131$ displayed above would be written as $50_{56}131$.

Fundamental theorem of arithmetic

An extremely important feature about the family of prime numbers is this: *Every positive integer can be written in essentially just one way as a product of prime numbers.* By 'essentially just one way' we mean that we do not distinguish between $6 = 2 \times 3$ and $6 = 3 \times 2$, in which the same factors occur, but in some different order. For example, we have:

$$\begin{aligned} 12345 &= 3 \times 5 \times 823, \\ 23456 &= 2 \times 2 \times 2 \times 2 \times 2 \times 733, \\ 34567 &= 13 \times 2659, \\ 45678 &= 2 \times 3 \times 23 \times 331, \\ 56789 &= 109 \times 521, \\ 123456789 &= 3 \times 3 \times 3607 \times 3803. \end{aligned}$$

In each case, there is no essentially different way of writing the given number as a product of prime numbers; and this is so for every positive integer. This statement is called the **FUNDAMENTAL THEOREM OF ARITHMETIC**.

Unsolved problems

What is most remarkable about the prime numbers is that though we know a lot about them, there are also lots and lots of questions for which the answers are not known!

Here is an example of such a question. Pairs of primes that differ by 2 are called *twin primes*, e.g.,

$$\{3, 5\}, \quad \{11, 13\}, \quad \{29, 31\}, \quad \{59, 61\}, \quad \{71, 73\}.$$

How many such pairs are there? Is there a largest possible pair of twin primes, or can indefinitely large pairs of such primes be found? No one knows the answer to these questions! All that we know today is that there *seems* to be no limit to how many twin primes there are. For example, here is a pair of large twin primes:

$$\{18409199, \quad 18409201\}.$$

And here is a larger pair:

$$\{1000000000002371, \quad 1000000000002373\}.$$

Many more such questions can be listed.

A list of the primes below 100

Given below are all the primes till 100; there are exactly 25 of them. Try to memorise the list. It may come in useful some day!

$$\begin{array}{rrrrr} 2, & 3, & 5, & 7, & 11, \\ 13, & 17, & 19, & 23, & 29, \\ 31, & 37, & 41, & 43, & 47, \\ 53, & 59, & 61, & 67, & 71, \\ 73, & 79, & 83, & 89, & 97. \end{array}$$

Notice that 2 is the only prime that is an even number. For this reason, it is said to be the oddest prime!

Why is 1 not listed as a prime number?

Suppose we *did* designate 1 to be prime. What consequences would this have? The following would all be prime factorisations of 10:

$$10 = 1 \times 2 \times 5 = 1^2 \times 2 \times 5 = 1^3 \times 2 \times 5 = 1^4 \times 2 \times 5 = \cdots.$$

We would get an infinite number of such representations, simply by including more and more 1s, and these representations would *not* all be 'essentially the same'.

Hence, *an immediate consequence of designating* 1 *as a prime number is that the Fundamental Theorem of Arithmetic would no longer be valid—at least, not in its stated form.* To 'rescue' the theorem, we would have to restate it with an additional clause which may read something like this: "except for the prime 1, which may occur to any power".

Most mathematicians reject such awkward statements, because they spoil the symmetry and inherent pattern within mathematics. Ultimately, the loss of pattern and symmetry means a loss of power, because it is from its pattern that mathematics derives its great power. So it is simpler to *not* call 1 a prime number.

EXERCISES

1. Verify that there are exactly 25 prime numbers below 100 (that is, the table given above is full and complete).

2. Find the prime numbers in the following list:

$$187, \quad 199, \quad 209, \quad 257, \quad 277$$

3. Find the first pair of twin primes that exceed 100.

4. Find the first pair of twin primes that exceed 200.

5. Find the prime factorisations of the following four numbers:

$$861, \qquad 957, \qquad 1001, \qquad 1295$$

6. Find the prime factorisations of the following four numbers:

$$1309, \qquad 1547, \qquad 1729, \qquad 3731$$

   The third number listed, 1729, is called *Ramanujan's number*, because of an incident that happened when Ramanujan was in hospital, being treated for tuberculosis; the incident is described by his friend Prof. GH Hardy. Apparently, Hardy had remarked to Ramanujan, when he visited him in hospital, that the number of the taxi in which he arrived was 1729, and that the number did not seem too interesting. Ramanujan replied immediately that that was not the case, and that in fact 1729 has an extremely special property: it is the *smallest positive number that can be written as the sum of two perfect cubes in two different ways*. The fact that 1729 can be written as such a sum, and in two different ways, can be seen from the following:

$$9^3 + 10^3 = 729 + 1000 = 1729,$$
$$1^3 + 12^3 = 1 + 1728 = 1729.$$

Hardy remarked later that to Ramanujan, every integer was a sort of personal friend.

7. Find the least positive integer which when multiplied by 30 gives a perfect square.

8. Find the least positive integer which when multiplied by 90 gives a perfect square.

9. Find the smallest positive integer which when multiplied by 12345 gives a perfect square.

10. Find the least positive integer which when multiplied by 30 gives a perfect cube.

3.5 GCD (or HCF) and LCM

Consider the two numbers 16 and 28. The divisors of 16 are $1, 2, 4, 8, 16$; and the divisors of 28 are $1, 2, 4, 7, 14, 28$. Let us list all their *common divisors*—i.e., the numbers common to both these lists; they are:

$$1, \quad 2, \quad 4.$$

These are all the divisors shared by the two numbers. Observe that 4 is the largest among them. This number is called the **GREATEST COMMON DIVISOR** or the **HIGHEST COMMON FACTOR** of 16 and 28. In this book we will call it the 'greatest common divisor', shortening it to GCD; so we write: $\text{GCD}(16, 28) = 4$. In the same way, we get: $\text{GCD}(28, 42) = 14$, $\text{GCD}(50, 75) = 25$ and $\text{GCD}(12, 25) = 1$.

We can find the GCD of more than two numbers; for example, we have:

$$\text{GCD}(12, 14, 16) = 2, \qquad \text{GCD}(15, 35, 75) = 5.$$

In the first example, 2 is the largest divisor common to $12, 14, 16$.

If two integers have no common factors other than 1, then their GCD is 1; we say that the two numbers are **COPRIME**, or **RELATIVELY PRIME**. For example, the numbers 12 and 25 are coprime, as are 21 and 32.

We may similarly define the **LEAST COMMON MULTIPLE** or the LCM of two numbers, also called the **LOWEST COMMON MULTIPLE**. For example, consider the two numbers 16 and 20; the multiples of 16 are:

$$16,\ 32,\ 48,\ 64,\ \mathbf{80},\ 96,\ 112,\ \ldots.$$

and the multiples of 20 are:

$$20,\ 40,\ 60,\ \mathbf{80},\ 100,\ 120,\ 140,\ \ldots.$$

The least number common to both lists (displayed in bold) is 80; we call it the least common multiple of 16 and 20, and we write: $\text{LCM}(16,20) = 80$. As earlier, we can talk of the LCM of more than two numbers; e.g., we have:

$$\text{LCM}(2,3,4) = 12, \qquad \text{LCM}(3,4,5,6) = 60.$$

Computing the GCD

If we know the prime factorisations of the numbers involved, then computing their GCD is easy. For example, take the numbers 16 and 28. We have:

$$16 = 2^4, \qquad 28 = 2^2 \times 7.$$

Any common factor of 16 and 28 would have to be made up only of 2s, because the prime factor 7 is a divisor of 28 but not of 16, and there are no other prime factors available. So the greatest common factor of 16 and 28 is $2^2 = 4$.

Or take the numbers 60 and 126; since

$$60 = 2^2 \times 3 \times 5, \qquad 126 = 2 \times 3^2 \times 7,$$

any common factor of 60 and 126 would have to be made up only of 2s and 3s, as 5 divides only 60, and 7 divides only 126. The GCD is clearly equal to $2 \times 3 = 6$.

Here is one way of carrying out this procedure. We make an array listing the primes contained in the two numbers, and the *number of times* they occur in their prime factorisations. For example, let the given numbers be 60 and 126. In the top row, we list all the primes (2, 3, 5, 7, ...) that divide the two numbers, and in the next two rows we list, for each of the numbers (60 and 126), *the number of times these primes occur in their respective prime factorisations*. (The symbol '#2' means 'number of 2s'. Similarly, '#3' means 'number of 3s', and so on.) Thus, since $60 = 2^2 \times 3^1 \times 5^1 \times 7^0$, we have two 2s, one 3, one 5 and no 7s; so we write the numbers 2, 1, 1, 0 in the row marked '60'.

Number	#2	#3	#5	#7
60	2	1	1	0
126	1	2	0	1
GCD	1	1	0	0

Similarly, since $126 = 2^1 \times 3^2 \times 5^0 \times 7^1$, in the row marked '126' we write the numbers 1, 2, 0, 1.

To fill the last row (labelled 'GCD'), for each cell we select the *least number* lying above it in the rows corresponding to the given two numbers. The first entry is 1, because 1 is the least among 2 and 1; the second entry is 1, because 1 is the least number among 1 and 2; following this, we have two 0s. (If the two entries had been equal, then both of them would have qualified for being 'least'.) These entries give the powers to which the primes occur in the required GCD. Therefore, $\text{GCD}(60, 126) = 2^1 \times 3^1 = 6$.

The procedure works just as well if we have to compute the GCD of three or more numbers. For example, if the numbers are $240 = 2^4 \times 3 \times 5$, $440 = 2^3 \times 5 \times 11$, and $5600 = 2^5 \times 5^2 \times 7$, then the primes that collectively divide these numbers are $2, 3, 5, 7, 11$, and we get the following array:

Number	#2	#3	#5	#7	#11
240	4	1	1	0	0
440	3	0	1	0	1
5600	5	0	2	1	0
GCD	3	0	1	0	0

Therefore, $\text{GCD}(240, 440, 5600) = 2^3 \times 5^1 = 8 \times 5 = 40$.

Computing the LCM

The nice thing about the method described above is that the very same array also gives us the LCM. Now, instead of selecting the least number, we select the *largest* number. As earlier, if the two entries are equal, then both of them would qualify for being 'largest'.

Thus, for the numbers 60 and 126 we get the following array:

Number	#2	#3	#5	#7
60	2	1	1	0
126	1	2	0	1
LCM	2	2	1	1

Therefore, $\text{LCM}(60,126) = 2^2 \times 3^2 \times 5^1 \times 7^1 = 4 \times 9 \times 5 \times 7 = 1260$.

The same procedure works if there are three or more numbers whose LCM we require. For example, for the numbers 240, 440, 5600 we get the following array:

Number	#2	#3	#5	#7	#11
240	4	1	1	0	0
440	3	0	1	0	1
5600	5	0	2	1	0
LCM	5	1	2	1	1

Therefore,

$$\text{LCM}(240,440,5600) = 2^5 \times 3^1 \times 5^2 \times 7^1 \times 11^1 = 32 \times 3 \times 25 \times 7 \times 11 = 184800.$$

A relation between the GCD and the LCM

If we are dealing with just two numbers, then there is a simple and neat relation between the GCD and LCM: if a and b are given numbers, then

$$\boxed{\text{GCD}(a,b) \times \text{LCM}(a,b) = a \times b.} \tag{3.1}$$

Problems 4 and 5 in the Exercises on p.89 ask you to find an explanation for this identity. Here, we only illustrate it with two examples.

- Consider the numbers 16 and 20; their GCD is 4, and their LCM is 80. Observe that $4 \times 80 = 16 \times 20$.
- Consider the numbers 60 and 126; their GCD is 6, and their LCM is 1260. Observe that $6 \times 1260 = 60 \times 126$.

If we are dealing with three or more numbers, we can find similar relations, but they are more complicated.

3.6 Euclid's algorithm for the GCD

The method described in Section 3.5 for computing GCDs demands that we know the prime factors of each number involved. But this can act as a disadvantage; what if we do not know all the prime factors? Then we have to first go through a lengthy exercise to get all the prime factors.

We now describe another method called the *Euclidean algorithm*; it was first stated by Euclid in THE ELEMENTS, as Proposition VII.3 (this means that it occurs in Book VII). It works directly with the given numbers; the prime factors of the numbers are not required. Moreover, it yields the desired result with great speed, even if the numbers involved are large. It is also called **EUCLID'S DIVISION ALGORITHM**.

The principles on which it works are very simple indeed. First, note that b is a divisor of a, then $\text{GCD}(a,b) = b$. Also, note that $\text{GCD}(a,b) = \text{GCD}(b,a)$. Finally, suppose that d is a divisor of two given numbers a and b. *Then, d divides $a+b$ as well as $a-b$.* More generally, d is a divisor of every one of the following numbers:

$$a+b, \quad a-b, \quad a+2b, \quad a-2b, \quad 2a+b, \quad 2a-b, \quad \ldots.$$

That is, *a common divisor of the numbers a and b is also a divisor of any number formed through the addition or subtraction of multiples of a and b.*

This idea can be extended in the reverse direction to yield the following: *A common divisor of a and $a-b$ is also a common divisor of a and b.* In particular, we can say that the following pairs of numbers all have exactly the same GCD:

$$(a,b), \quad (a,a-b), \quad (a,a+b), \quad (a-b,b), \quad (a+b,b), \quad \ldots.$$

For example:

- $\text{GCD}(16,28) = 4 = \text{GCD}(16,12)$;
- $\text{GCD}(44,77) = 11 = \text{GCD}(44,33)$;
- $\text{GCD}(20,28) = 4 = \text{GCD}(20,8)$.

We summarise below the key properties of GCD:

1. $\text{GCD}(a,b) = \text{GCD}(a,a-b) = \text{GCD}(a,a-2b) = \text{GCD}(a,a-3b) = \cdots$.
2. If b is a divisor of a, then $\text{GCD}(a,b) = b$; in particular, $\text{GCD}(a,a) = a$.
3. $\text{GCD}(a,b) = \text{GCD}(b,a)$.

Using these properties it is possible to compute the GCD of any two given numbers.

EXAMPLE 1. Let us see how these principles are used to find, for example, the GCD of 60 and 126:

$$\begin{aligned}\text{GCD}(60,126) &= \text{GCD}(60,66) && \text{because } 66 = 126-60;\\ &= \text{GCD}(60,6) && \text{because } 6 = 66-60;\\ &= 6 && \text{because 6 is a divisor of 60.}\end{aligned}$$

So the required GCD is 6.

Here are two more examples. We now give the working directly, without any explanation in brackets.

- To compute $\text{GCD}(240,440)$:

$$\text{GCD}(240,440) = \text{GCD}(240,200) = \text{GCD}(40,200) = 40.$$

- To compute $\text{GCD}(16,28)$:

$$\text{GCD}(16,28) = \text{GCD}(16,12) = \text{GCD}(4,12) = 4.$$

The method is indeed very fast in its operation! And we can make it still faster by doing several of the subtractions at a single time.

EXAMPLE 2. To find $\text{GCD}(54,675)$ we first divide 675 by 54, and find that it goes 12 times (because $54 \times 12 = 648$), with remainder 27; hence:

$$\text{GCD}(54,675) = \text{GCD}(54,675-648) = \text{GCD}(54,27) = 27.$$

In the first step we have in effect subtracted 54 from 675 'twelve times' all at once.

Finding the GCD of three numbers

To find the GCD of three numbers, we apply the Euclidean method *twice*, using the following idea:

$$\text{If } \text{GCD}(a,b) = d, \text{ then } \text{GCD}(a,b,c) = \text{GCD}(d,c).$$

For example, suppose that we want the GCD of 540, 6750 and 16065. We first compute the GCD of 540 and 6750. Since the division $6750 \div 540$ leaves a remainder of 270, we have:

$$\text{GCD}(540,6750) = \text{GCD}(540,270) = 270,$$

so we must now compute $\text{GCD}(16065,270)$.

Since $16065 \div 270$ leaves a remainder of 135, we get,

$$\text{GCD}(270, 16065) = \text{GCD}(270, 135) = 135.$$

So the required GCD is 135.

We can obviously extend this to the computation of the GCD of more than three numbers.

EXERCISES

1. Find the GCD of 504 and 540 using the prime factorisation method.

2. Find the GCD of 504 and 540 using the Euclidean algorithm.

3. Suppose b is a divisor of a. Explain why $\text{GCD}(a,b) = b$.

4. Suppose a and b are coprime. Explain why $\text{LCM}(a,b) = ab$.

5. Explain why $\text{GCD}(a,b) \times \text{LCM}(a,b)$ is equal to $a \times b$. (Use the reasoning from the previous problem.)

6. What can you say about the GCD of two consecutive positive integers?

7. Suppose $\text{GCD}(a,b) = d$. What will be the GCD of a^2 and b^2?

8. Suppose a and b are coprime integers. Are $a+b$ and $a-b$ necessarily coprime? What could the largest possible value of $\text{GCD}(a+b, a-b)$?

9. Let a be any positive integer. Find all possible values of $\text{GCD}(a, a+2)$.

10. Let a be any positive integer. Find all possible values of $\text{GCD}(a, a+3)$.

11. Let a be any positive integer. Find all possible values of $\text{GCD}(a, a+4)$.

12. Let a be any positive integer. What can be said about $\text{GCD}(a, 2a+1)$?

13. Let d be the GCD of two positive integers a and b. What can be said about the GCD of $a \div d$ and $b \div d$?

14. Let a be any positive integer. What can be said about $\text{GCD}(a, a^2+1)$?

15. Find all possible pairs of positive integers with $\text{GCD} = 10$ and $\text{LCM} = 120$.

16. Find all possible pairs of positive integers with GCD $= 6$ and LCM $= 210$.

17. Find all possible pairs of positive integers with GCD $= 6$ and LCM $= 240$.

18. Suppose the GCD of two numbers is d, and their LCM is d^2. What could be the two numbers?

19. The following statement has been claimed in a well-known text book.

    Let the GCD *of any three integers a, b, c be X, and let their* LCM *be Y; then X^2Y is equal to abc.*

    The statement is false! Show that the statement does not always hold, by finding three numbers a, b and c for which the relation fails. (In other words, find a 'counter-example' to the claim made by the book.)

20. In the previous problem, we asked you to *disprove* some statement. Now we ask you to verify and then prove the correct version of this statement, which reads as follows: *Let a, b and c be any three positive integers; then*

$$\left(\frac{\mathrm{LCM}(a,b,c)}{\mathrm{GCD}(a,b,c)}\right)^2 = \frac{\mathrm{LCM}(a,b)}{\mathrm{GCD}(a,b)} \cdot \frac{\mathrm{LCM}(b,c)}{\mathrm{GCD}(b,c)} \cdot \frac{\mathrm{LCM}(c,a)}{\mathrm{GCD}(c,a)}.$$

    Another way of writing this is:

$$\frac{\mathrm{LCM}(a,b,c)}{\mathrm{GCD}(a,b,c)} = \frac{abc}{\mathrm{GCD}(a,b)\cdot\mathrm{GCD}(b,c)\cdot\mathrm{GCD}(c,a)}.$$

    What might be the corresponding relation for four numbers?

3.7 Perfect numbers

The number 6 has the curious feature that *the sum of all its proper divisors equals itself.* For, its proper divisors are $1, 2, 3$, and their sum is 6. This property gives rise to the notion of *perfectness* in numbers.

We say that a positive integer is **PERFECT** if the sum of all its proper divisors exactly equals itself. So 6 is perfect, and it happens to be the smallest such number. After 6 the next such number is 28. To see why, we list its proper divisors; they are:

$$1,\ 2,\ 4,\ 7,\ 14,$$

and the sum of the divisors is $1+2+4+7+14 = 28$.

Most numbers are not perfect. Checking a number for the property may seem tedious, but if we know the prime factors of the number, it is easy. Take the number 154. Its prime factorisation is:

$$154 = 2 \times 7 \times 11.$$

Consequently, its factors must be made up of these primes and no others, and are the following numbers:

$$1,\ 2,\ 7,\ 11,\ 2\times 7,\ 2\times 11,\ 7\times 11,\ 2\times 7\times 11.$$

That is, its factors are the following:

$$1,\ 2,\ 7,\ 11,\ 14,\ 22,\ 77,\ 154.$$

Of these, the last one is not a proper factor. So the sum of the proper factors is,

$$1+2+7+11+14+22+77 = 288,$$

which exceeds 154; so 154 is *not* perfect. This method can be applied to any integer, provided we know its prime factors.

It takes a while before we find the next perfect number after 28; a trial-and-error search would certainly test one's patience! Eventually we find that 496 and 8128 are perfect. We ask you to check these claims in the exercise below. After 8128, the next few perfect numbers are the following:

$$\begin{aligned}
(2^{13}-1)\,2^{12} &= 33550336\\
(2^{17}-1)\,2^{16} &= 8589869056\\
(2^{19}-1)\,2^{18} &= 137438691328\\
(2^{31}-1)\,2^{30} &= 2305843008139952128
\end{aligned}$$

As you can see, perfect numbers are quite scarce. Finding them by trial-and-error would be a very slow process indeed; imagine how long it would take to get to 137438691328. But luckily, there is a better method. It was described by Euclid in his book THE ELEMENTS, in Proposition IX.36 (i.e, it occurs in Book IX):

> *Add together, starting from* 1 *and without skipping any number, as many of the numbers*
>
> $$1,\quad 2,\quad 4,\quad 8,\quad 16,\quad 32,\quad 64,\quad \ldots,$$
>
> *as are needed for the sum to be prime, and then multiply the answer with the very last number added. The product is a perfect number.*

Let us see how this works.

(a) The sum $1+2=3$ is a prime number. Multiplying it with the last number added (namely, 2), we get the perfect number 6.

(b) The sum $1+2+4=7$ is a prime number. Multiplying it with the last number added (namely, 4), we get the perfect number 28.

(c) The sum $1+2+4+8+16=31$ is a prime number. Multiplying it with the last number added (namely, 16), we get the perfect number 496.

(d) The sum $1+2+4+8+16+32+64=127$ is prime. Multiplying it with the last number added (namely, 64), we get the perfect number 8128.

Euclid's method may be expressed more compactly thus: *Let n be a positive integer such that the number $P=2^n-1$ is prime. Then the number $\frac{1}{2}P(P+1)$ is perfect.*

For example, let $n=5$; then $P=2^5-1=31$, which is prime, and we get the perfect number $\frac{1}{2}(31\times 32)=486$.

Even perfect numbers, odd perfect numbers

Euclid's prescription will naturally always give an *even* number, becausc in the end we multiply by an even number (in fact, by a power of 2). This observation gives rise to two questions.

- *Do there exist any even perfect numbers other than those given by Euclid's method?* The answer is: *No*, and this was first shown in the eighteenth century by the great Swiss mathematician Leonhard Euler (1707–1783).

- *Do there exist any odd perfect numbers?* You may be astonished to learn that no one knows the answer to this question! It is yet another of those things about prime numbers to which no answer is currently known.

You may wonder, *Why were the Greeks so interested in perfect numbers?* In fact, they were interested in many more aspects about whole numbers. The reason behind this has a bit to do with how the Greeks thought about life, about friendship, about God, and so on. Look up an encyclopedia to see why the Greeks considered whole numbers to be so important.

The game of Aliquot

An older name for 'proper divisor' is **ALIQUOT PART**. Thus, a prime number has just one aliquot part, the number 1, and 1 itself has no aliquot part.

In the game of Aliquot, some number is chosen to start the game, and two players take turns subtracting an aliquot part of the number left by their opponent. The last player who is able to do such a subtraction is the winner. So, the object of the game is to reach the number 1, as this will leave one's opponent without a move. For example, if the initial number is 36, and the two players are A and B, then a possible game history would be:

$$36 \xrightarrow{A} 30 \xrightarrow{B} 27 \xrightarrow{A} 18 \xrightarrow{B} 16 \xrightarrow{A} 8 \xrightarrow{B} 4 \xrightarrow{A} 2 \xrightarrow{B} 1,$$

and B would be the winner, as A is unable to make a move. Could A have played differently and forced a victory?

It is interesting to examine the strategies that the players can adopt, and in what way they depend on the choice of the initial number.

Euclid of Alexandria

Euclid lived around 300 BC in Alexandria, in Greece, and was certainly the best known mathematician of the Greek era. He founded a great school of mathematics at Alexandria during the reign of Ptolemy I, who was one of the trusted generals of Alexander the Great. THE ELEMENTS are still in use 2000 years after they were written!

Figure 3.1 Euclid of Alexandria, and his famous school of geometry—a portrayal by Raphael (*Source*: `http://en.wikipedia.org/wiki/Euclid`)

Euclid is said to have told Ptolemy I, when the emperor asked whether there was any short way of mastering the subject, "There is no royal road to geometry." He is also reported to have offered "threepence" to a student who wanted to know what he would get by learning geometry.

No one knows what Euclid looked like—but that has not stopped artists from depicting him! Figure 3.1 shows a picture of a statue of Euclid in Oxford University, together with a portrayal of Euclid's school made by the great Renaissance painter Raphael.

Amicable numbers

Closely related to the topic of perfect numbers is another such topic, once again of Greek origin. Consider the numbers 220 and 284. Their prime factorisations are the following:

$$220 = 2 \times 2 \times 5 \times 11, \qquad 284 = 2 \times 2 \times 71.$$

From these we get the lists of proper factors of the two numbers:

Number	*List of proper factors*
220	1, 2, 4, 5, 10, 11, 20, 22, 44, 55, 110
284	1, 2, 4, 71, 142

It follows that the sum of the proper factors of 220 is

$$1+2+4+5+10+11+20+22+44+55+110 = 284,$$

and the sum of the proper factors of 284 is

$$1+2+4+71+142 = 220.$$

How curious! For each number, the sum of the proper factors has yielded the other number! Such pairs of numbers are known as *amicable numbers*, so named by the Greeks (well, in Greek, not in English!).[1] They had a high regard for such number pairs; they probably felt that friends should behave towards one another as amicable numbers do!

Remark

Another way of defining amicable numbers is the following. *Two numbers m and n form an amicable pair if the sum-of-all-divisors of each one is $m+n$*, where 'sum-of-all-divisors'

[1] The word 'amicable' means 'friendly' or 'peacable'. Think of words like 'amiable'.

includes the number itself as one of the divisors. For example, the two numbers 220 and 284 have the same sum-of-all-divisors, namely, 504, which equals $220+284$.

This definition may seem less natural, but it has the advantage of suggesting how to define 'amicable triples'.

Searching for amicable pairs

Finding such pairs of numbers is far from easy. The following whimsical story has been narrated to illustrate the difficulty.

Amicable pairs and amicable triples

After $\{220,284\}$ the next few amicable number pairs are

$$\{1184,1210\}, \quad \{2620,2924\}, \quad \{5020,5564\},$$
$$\{6232,6368\}, \quad \{10744,10856\}, \quad \{12285,14595\},$$
$$\{17296,18416\}, \quad \{63020,76084\}.$$

Once upon a time there lived a king who considered himself a great mathematician. Unfortunately, he went around jailing all the local mathematicians, because he was jealous of them. One day he offered one of his mathematician-prisoners a chance of escape, through the following challenge: "Either you remain in prison for the rest of your life or you give me a problem to solve and I will let you go free—but only till I find the answer; as soon as I discover the solution, I will order your execution." The prisoner knew a bit about numbers and happily accepted the deal; he posed the following problem to the king:

> The sum of all the proper divisors of 220 is $1+2+4+5+10+11+20+22+44+55+110=284$, and the sum of all the proper divisors of 284 is $1+2+4+71+142=220$. Find me another pair of such numbers!

The king never did solve the problem, and the prisoner was able to live a full and happy life, pursuing further properties of amicable pairs of numbers.

Many of these pairs were found by Arab mathematicians. In 1866, a 16-year old Italian boy, Nicolò Paganini, found the first pair listed above, $\{1184,1210\}$; strangely, it had been missed by the Arab mathematicians, and by mathematicians such as Fermat and Euler. Today, more than a million pairs of amicable numbers are known.

One can invent more such families. An **AMICABLE TRIPLE** is defined to be a triple (a,b,c) of positive integers, such that for each one, the sum-of-all-divisors is $a+b+c$.

This means that the sum of the proper divisors of a is $b+c$, the sum of the proper divisors of b is $c+a$, and the sum of the proper divisors of c is $a+b$. An example of such a triple is:

$$\{123228768,\ 103340640,\ 124015008\}.$$

For each of these three numbers, the sum-of-all-divisors is 350584416, which equals the sum of the three numbers. (Computations dealing with such large numbers are best left to the computer!)

EXERCISES

1. Verify that 496 is a perfect number.
2. Verify that 8192 is a perfect number.
3. Find the sum of the proper factors of the number $2 \times 2 \times 5 \times 5$.
4. Find the sum of the proper factors of the number $2 \times 3 \times 5 \times 7$.
5. If the sum of the proper divisors of a number is *less* than the number, we say that the number is **DEFICIENT**, and if the sum of the proper divisors exceeds the number we say that the number is **ABUNDANT**. Verify that 5 is a deficient number, and that 12 is an abundant number.
6. "Every prime number is deficient." Why?
7. "If we double any prime number greater than 3, the answer is deficient." Why?
8. "If we double an abundant number, the answer is abundant." Why?
9. "A multiple of an abundant number is itself abundant." Why?
10. Let p represent a prime number exceeding 6. Show that $6p$ is an abundant number.
11. Show how one can list as many abundant numbers as one may wish.
12. Verify that $\{1184, 1210\}$ are a pair of amicable numbers.
13. Verify that $\{2620, 2924\}$ are a pair of amicable numbers.
14. Verify that $\{5020, 5564\}$ are a pair of amicable numbers.
15. Verify that $\{1980,\ 2016,\ 2556\}$ form an amicable triple.

3.8 Squares and cubes

In this section we shall take a brief look at the set of perfect squares, which we shall call **Squares**, or $\mathscr{S}$ for short:

$$\text{Squares} = \{1,\ 4,\ 9,\ 16,\ 25,\ 36,\ 49,\ 64,\ 81,\ 100,\ 121,\ 144,\ 169,\ 196,\ \ldots\},$$

and at the set of perfect cubes, which we shall call **Cubes**, or $\mathscr{C}$ for short:

$$\text{Cubes} = \{1,\ 8,\ 27,\ 64,\ 125,\ 216,\ 343,\ 512,\ 729,\ 1000,\ 1331,\ 1728,\ \ldots\}.$$

The set of fourth powers, **FourthPowers**, is:

$$\text{FourthPowers} = \{1,\ 16,\ 81,\ 256,\ 625,\ 1296,\ 2401, 4096,\ 6561,\ 10000,\ \ldots\},$$

but we shall not study this sequence for now.

Table 3.1, Table 3.2 and Table 3.3 (below) give lists of squares, cubes and fourth powers till some point (99^2, 49^3, 19^4, respectively; we have stopped here as the numbers get too big to display properly in a table). We feel that these tables are worth remembering.

In the tables, **T** and **U** stand, respectively, for 'tens digit' and 'units digit'. So, to find 47^2, we go to Table 3.1 and look for the entry in row **4** and column **7**; we see that $47^2 = 2209$. Similarly, we get $23^3 = 12167$ (from Table 3.2), and $13^4 = 28561$ (from Table 3.3).

Table 3.1 A list of perfect squares, from 0^2 till 99^2

T \ U	**0**	**1**	**2**	**3**	**4**	**5**	**6**	**7**	**8**	**9**
0	0	1	4	9	16	25	36	49	64	81
1	100	121	144	169	196	225	256	289	324	361
2	400	441	484	529	576	625	676	729	784	841
3	900	961	1024	1089	1156	1225	1296	1369	1444	1521
4	1600	1681	1764	1849	1936	2025	2116	2209	2304	2401
5	2500	2601	2704	2809	2916	3025	3136	3249	3364	3481
6	3600	3721	3844	3969	4096	4225	4356	4489	4624	4761
7	4900	5041	5184	5329	5476	5625	5776	5929	6084	6241
8	6400	6561	6724	6889	7056	7225	7396	7569	7744	7921
9	8100	8281	8464	8649	8836	9025	9216	9409	9604	9801

Table 3.2 A list of perfect cubes, from 0^3 till 49^3

T \ U	0	1	2	3	4	5	6	7	8	9
0	0	1	8	27	64	125	216	343	512	729
1	1000	1331	1728	2197	2744	3375	4096	4913	5832	6859
2	8000	9261	10648	12167	13824	15625	17576	19683	21952	24389
3	27000	29791	32768	35937	39304	42875	46656	50653	54872	59319
4	64000	68921	74088	79507	85184	91125	97336	103823	110592	117649

Table 3.3 A list of perfect fourth powers, from 0^4 till 19^4

T \ U	0	1	2	3	4	5	6	7	8	9
0	0	1	16	81	256	625	1296	2401	4096	6561
1	10000	14641	20736	28561	38416	50625	65536	83521	104976	130321

Patterns in the sequence of perfect squares

A study of the **Squares** table reveals a lot of patterns. For example, look at the column marked **1**, giving the squares of numbers with units digit 1. Naturally, the squares too have 1 for their units digit; but of more interest are the tens digits in that column. We find the following sequence of tens digits:

$$0,\ 2,\ 4,\ 6,\ 8,\ 0,\ 2,\ 4,\ 6,\ 8,\ 0,\ 2,\ \ldots.$$

The pattern is unmistakable: the digits $0, 2, 4, 6, 8$ occur again and again, and in that order.

The tens digits of the entries in the column marked **2** show a similar pattern:

$$0,\ 4,\ 8,\ 2,\ 6,\ 0,\ 4,\ 8,\ 2,\ 6,\ 0,\ 4,\ \ldots.$$

The connection between this sequence and the previous one is immediately visible to the eye—the second sequence is exactly *twice* the first sequence (but with the 'carries' thrown away). Similarly, the tens digits in the entries of the column marked **4** have a repetitive pattern:

$$1,\ 9,\ 7,\ 5,\ 3,\ 1,\ 9,\ 7,\ 5,\ 3,\ 1,\ 9,\ \ldots.$$

Observe that the repeating portion has five digits in each case.

Explaining the pattern when the last digit is 1

It is fun to try explaining these patterns. Let us study what happens when we square a number whose last digit is 1. Call the 'rest' of the number $\ldots cba$, where $a, b, c, \ldots$ are digits; then, in digit form, the number has the appearance $\ldots cba1$. Now let us do a long multiplication of the number with itself:

$$\begin{array}{rrrrrr} & & \ldots & c & b & a & 1 \\ \times & & \ldots & c & b & a & 1 \\ \hline & & \ldots & c & b & a & 1 \\ & \ldots & ac & ab & a^2 & a & \\ \hline & & \ldots & \ldots & \ldots & 2a & 1 \\ \hline \end{array}$$

Observe that in the last row, we get $a + a = 2a$ in the tens place. There may be some 'carry' from $2a$ into the hundreds place, but the important part is the 2; it shows that we have to *double* the digit a to get the digit in the tens place of the answer. This explains the sequence $0, 2, 4, 6, 8, 0, \ldots$; these digits are obtained by doubling $0, 1, 2, 3, 4, 5, \ldots$ and retaining only the units digits.

Explaining the pattern when the last digit is 4

Similarly, to understand the sequence $1, 9, 7, 5, 3, 1, \ldots$ in the tens digits of the squares of numbers with units digit 4, we study the long multiplication

$$\begin{array}{rrrrrrr} & & \ldots & c & b & a & 4 \\ \times & & \ldots & c & b & a & 4 \\ \hline & & \ldots & 4c & 4b & 4a & 16 \\ & \ldots & ac & ab & a^2 & 4a & \\ \hline & & \ldots & \ldots & \ldots & 8a & 16 \\ \hline \end{array}$$

In the bottom row we have written 16 in the units place, and $8a$ in the tens place; this comes from $4a + 4a = 8a$. Of course, the 1 in 16 does not remain in the units column; it gets 'carried' to the tens place, so we actually get the following picture:

$$\begin{array}{cccccc} & \dots & c & b & a & 4 \\ \times & \dots & c & b & a & 4 \\ \hline & \dots & \dots & \dots & 8a+1 & 6 \\ \hline \end{array}$$

If we let a take the values $0,1,2,3,4,5,\dots$ in turn, then $8a+1$ takes these values in turn: $1,9,17,25,33,41,\dots$. Hence, the units digit of $8a+1$ takes the following values: $1,9,7,5,3,1,\dots$. Now the reason for the pattern is revealed.

Explaining the pattern when the last digit is 5

There are patterns in the hundreds place too, and they can be similarly explained. One such pattern is obtained by studying column **5**; i.e., the squares of numbers with 5 as the units digit. From the table we construct the following array:

15^2	25^2	35^2	45^2	55^2	65^2	75^2	85^2	95^2	105^2	...
225	625	1225	2025	3025	4225	5625	7225	9025	11025	...

All these squares have 25 as their last two digits (this may not come as a surprise). If we delete these two digits, then what remains is the sequence

$$2, \quad 6, \quad 12, \quad 20, \quad 30, \quad 42, \quad 56, \quad 72, \quad 90, \quad 110, \quad \dots.$$

The pattern is instantly revealed when we write these numbers as

$$1 \times 2, \ 2 \times 3, \ 3 \times 4, \ 4 \times 5, \ 5 \times 6, \ 6 \times 7, \ 7 \times 8, \ 8 \times 9, \ 9 \times 10, \ 10 \times 11, \ \dots.$$

We therefore arrive at the following rule.

> *To find the square of a number with units digit 5, let n represent the 'rest' of the number. Compute the quantity $n \times (n+1)$, then place the digits 2 and 5 after the product, in that order; i.e., append a '25' to the product $n(n+1)$. This yields the desired answer.*

For example, to find 145^2 we compute 14×15; we get 210. The desired answer is, therefore, 21025; that is, $145^2 = 21025$. Similarly, from $23 \times 24 = 592$ we get $235^2 = 59225$.

To understand the reason behind the observed pattern, we once again set up the long multiplication array:

$$\begin{array}{cccc} & & n & 5 \\ \times & & n & 5 \\ \hline & & 5n & 25 \\ & n^2 & 5n & \\ \hline & n^2 & 10n & 25 \\ \hline \end{array}$$

The number in the units column (namely, 25) cannot stay in that form; we must carry the 2 into the tens column. After doing so, we get this array:

$$\begin{array}{cccc} & & n & 5 \\ \times & & n & 5 \\ \hline & & 5n & 25 \\ & n^2 & 5n & \\ \hline & n^2 & 10n+2 & 5 \\ \hline \end{array}$$

More carries need to be done: from the entry $10n+2$ in the tens column, we must carry n to the hundreds column. Now we get the following picture:

$$\begin{array}{cccc} & & n & 5 \\ \times & & n & 5 \\ \hline & n^2+n & 2 & 5 \\ \hline \end{array}$$

Observe that the hundreds place has the expression n^2+n, which equals $n \times (n+1)$. So we have found the desired explanation.

Another observation that is plainly visible in the units digits is that only some digits can occur in the units place, namely

$$0, \quad 1, \quad 4, \quad 5, \quad 6, \quad 9.$$

No other digit can occur as the units digit of a square. We can never have a square whose last digit is 2, 3, 7 or 8. On the other hand, no such thing happens for cubes; any digit can occur as the last digit.

Gaps between consecutive perfect squares

Yet another pattern that we observe is about the *gaps* between consecutive perfect squares. We see that

$$1^2-0^2=1, \quad 2^2-1^2=3, \quad 3^2-2^2=5, \quad 4^2-3^2=7, \quad 5^2-4^2=9, \quad \ldots.$$

So the sequence of gaps is

$$1,\ 3,\ 5,\ 7,\ 9,\ 11,\ 13,\ 15,\ 17,\ \ldots.$$

In other words, the sequence of gaps is identical to the sequence of odd numbers. This observation gives rise to a very striking and pleasing property:

$$\begin{aligned} 1 &= 1^2, \\ 1+3 &= 2^2, \\ 1+3+5 &= 3^2, \\ 1+3+5+7 &= 4^2, \\ 1+3+5+7+9 &= 5^2, \\ 1+3+5+7+9+11 &= 6^2, \end{aligned}$$

and so on. We can therefore get the sequence of squares using only addition!

What we have just found can be described compactly as follows: *The partial sums of the sequence of odd positive integers are just the squares.* (Here the term 'partial sum' refers to finding the sum of a consecutive block of numbers starting from the first one and going to some point.) Shown below is a 'proof-without-words' for this relation. Try to explain why it works!

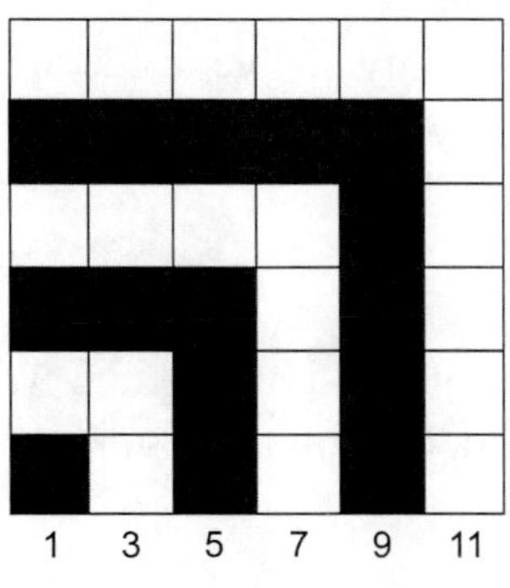

Finding the cubes using partial sums

There is a similar way to get the sequence of cubes, but it is more complicated and harder to explain. Noting that we get the sequence of odd numbers by 'throwing out' every second number (i.e., throwing out all the even numbers), we start with the sequence of positive integers,

$$1,\ 2,\ 3,\ 4,\ 5,\ 6,\ 7,\ 8,\ 9,\ 10,\ 11,\ 12,\ \ldots,$$

and throw out from this sequence *every third number*; we get the sequence

$$1,\ 2,\ 4,\ 5,\ 7,\ 8,\ 10,\ 11,\ 13,\ 14,\ \ldots.$$

We now compute the partial sums of this sequence, i.e., the sums $1,\ 1+2,\ 1+2+4,$ $1+2+4+5,$ and so on; we get the sequence

$$1,\ 3,\ 7,\ 12,\ 19,\ 27,\ 37,\ 48,\ 61,\ 75,\ \ldots.$$

From this sequence we throw out every *second term*; we are left with the sequence

$$1,\ 7,\ 19,\ 37,\ 61,\ \ldots.$$

Finally we compute the partial sums of *this* sequence of numbers; we get

$$1,\ 8,\ 27,\ 64,\ 125,\ \ldots,$$

and this is just the sequence of cubes!

Multiplication using a table of perfect squares

It turns out that multiplication can be done using a table of squares. For simplicity, we shall assume that the two numbers we wish to multiply are both odd or both even, and that we have available a long list of squares. We shall make repeated use of the following *identity* which comes from algebra:

$$\boxed{(a+b)^2-(a-b)^2=4ab,} \tag{3.2}$$

which may be written after division by 4 as

$$\left(\frac{a+b}{2}\right)^2-\left(\frac{a-b}{2}\right)^2=ab.$$

So, to find $a \times b$, we first compute $\frac{1}{2}(a+b)$ and $\frac{1}{2}(a-b)$, respectively, look up their squares, and then do a subtraction.

For example, to compute 37×59, we compute $\frac{1}{2}(59+37) = 48$ and $\frac{1}{2}(59-37) = 11$; then we get, using a table of squares,

$$48^2 - 11^2 = 2304 - 121 = 2183.$$

So, the answer is 2183.

Similarly, to compute 19×91, we have: $\frac{1}{2}(91+19) = 55$, $\frac{1}{2}(91-19) = 36$, and $55^2 - 36^2 = 3025 - 1296 = 1729$. Hence, $19 \times 91 = 1729$.

Factorisation using a table of perfect squares

Surprisingly, even **PRIME FACTORISATION** (the 'opposite' of multiplication) may be achieved using a table of perfect squares; the idea is due to Pierre Fermat. Once again, we make use of the identity

$$a^2 - b^2 = (a+b) \times (a-b).$$

Here is how we use the identity. Suppose we wish to find the prime factors of 187. We add the squares to it in turn, starting from 1^2, and *continue till we get a perfect square*, thus:

$$\begin{aligned} 187+1^2 &= 187+1 = 188 && \text{(not a square)},\\ 187+2^2 &= 187+4 = 191 && \text{(not a square)},\\ 187+3^2 &= 187+9 = 196 = 14^2 && \text{(square number)}. \end{aligned}$$

On the third step we have obtained a perfect square; so we have $187 + 3^2 = 14^2$, and therefore,

$$187 = 14^2 - 3^2 = (14+3) \times (14-3) = 17 \times 11.$$

Similarly, to find the factors of 989, we work as shown below:

$$\begin{aligned} 989+1^2 &= 989+1 = 990 && \text{(not a square)},\\ 989+2^2 &= 989+4 = 993 && \text{(not a square)},\\ 989+3^2 &= 989+9 = 998 && \text{(not a square)}, \end{aligned}$$

$$\begin{aligned}
989+4^2 &= 989+16 &&= 1005 && \text{(not a square)},\\
989+5^2 &= 989+25 &&= 1014 && \text{(not a square)},\\
989+6^2 &= 989+36 &&= 1025 && \text{(not a square)},\\
989+7^2 &= 989+49 &&= 1038 && \text{(not a square)},\\
989+8^2 &= 989+64 &&= 1053 && \text{(not a square)},\\
989+9^2 &= 989+81 &&= 1070 && \text{(not a square)},\\
989+10^2 &= 989+100 &&= 1089 = 33^2 && \text{(a square number)}.
\end{aligned}$$

Finally, we have obtained a perfect square: $989+10^2 = 33^2$, and so,

$$989 = 33^2 - 10^2 = (33+10)\times(33-10) = 43\times 23.$$

EXERCISES

1. The sequence of last digits of the squares of the integers 0, 1, 2, 3, …, 8, 9, 10, i.e.,

   $$0,\ 1,\ 4,\ 9,\ 6,\ 5,\ 6,\ 9,\ 4,\ 1,\ 0$$

   is **PALINDROMIC**; that is, it reads the same both ways. Explain this feature.

   (Words that read the same left-to-right and right-to-left are called *palindromes*; e.g., words like MADAM and DAD. It is an interesting challenge to find the longest palindrome. Here are two palindromic sentence: "A Santa at NASA" and "Madam I'm Adam". Find other such crazy sentences!)

2. Consider the sequence of tens digits in the squares of numbers whose last digit is 9:

   $$8,\ 6,\ 4,\ 2,\ 0,\ 8,\ 6,\ 4,\ 2,\ 0,\ \ldots$$

   Explain the pattern you see in this sequence.

3. You may have noticed that *the last two digits of a perfect square are never both odd*; if the units digit is odd, then the tens digit is even, and if the tens digit is odd, then the units digit is even. Why is this so? How would you explain it?

4. If the units digit and tens digit of a perfect square are the same, say a, what could be the value of a?

5. Find the smallest perfect square whose last two digits are equal and not 0.

6. Use the table of squares to do the following multiplications:

$$17 \times 53, \quad 29 \times 91, \quad 42 \times 66.$$

7. In describing how a table of perfect squares may be used to multiply two given numbers a and b, why did we want the numbers to have the same parity? What modification is needed if we do not want to impose this condition?

8. Find the factors of 689 and 1003 using the method described above.

9. Find the factors of 893 and 1363.

10. Find the factors of 3953.

11. For what kinds of numbers will the factorisation method described above take a very long time to provide the answer? (For such numbers, this is an inefficient method for factorisation, and we have to look for alternatives.)

12. Explain, using the identity

$$a^2 - b^2 = (a+b) \times (a-b),$$

why the sequence of gaps between consecutive perfect squares is identical to the sequence of odd numbers.

13. How many four-digit perfect squares are there?

14. How many five-digit perfect cubes are there?

15. Observe from the table of perfect cubes that

the last digit of 0^3 is 0,
the last digit of 1^3 is 1,
the last digit of 4^3 is 4,
the last digit of 5^3 is 5,
the last digit of 6^3 is 6,
the last digit of 9^3 is 9.

We also observe that

the last digit of 2^3 is 8, while the last digit of 8^3 is 2,

the last digit of 3^3 is 7, while the last digit of 7^3 is 3.

How do you explain these features?

16. Construct for yourself a table of *fifth powers* of the numbers 1, 2, 3, 4, ..., and verify the following statement:

    The units digit of the fifth power of any number is the same as the units digit of that number.

17. How would you explain the pleasing pattern seen below?

$$\begin{aligned}
1^2 &= 1,\\
11^2 &= 121,\\
111^2 &= 12321,\\
1111^2 &= 1234321,\\
11111^2 &= 123454321,\\
111111^2 &= 12345654321,\\
1111111^2 &= 1234567654321,\\
11111111^2 &= 123456787654321,\\
111111111^2 &= 12345678987654321.
\end{aligned}$$

18. How would you explain the pleasing pattern seen below?

$$\begin{aligned}
6^2+8^2 &= 1\times 100,\\
66^2+88^2 &= 121\times 100,\\
666^2+888^2 &= 12321\times 100,\\
6666^2+8888^2 &= 1234321\times 100,\\
66666^2+88888^2 &= 123454321\times 100,\\
666666^2+888888^2 &= 12345654321\times 100,\\
6666666^2+8888888^2 &= 1234567654321\times 100,
\end{aligned}$$

and so on.

19. There are several instances where the sum of two perfect squares is itself a perfect square; for example,

$$3^2+4^2=9+16=25=5^2.$$

From this relation we get a triple of numbers $(3,4,5)$ called a **PYTHAGOREAN TRIPLE**, so-named after the great and mystical mathematician Pythagoras of Samos (He lived in the sixth century BC, at about the same time as Socrates.) Another such triple is $(5,12,13)$. Please verify that it satisfies the stated property.

Find three more such triples, avoiding those where the numbers in the triple share a common factor. [In the Pythagorean triple $(6,8,10)$ the numbers share the factor 2.]

20. Mathematicians have found (much to their surprise!) that no such instances of the above kind can be found for cubes; it is simply not possible to find integers a,b,c, none of them zero, such that $a^3+b^3=c^3$. But it is extremely hard to explain why this should be so.

Find instances where the sum of *three* positive cubes is equal to another cube. Also find instances where the sum of two positive cubes is equal to the sum of two other positive cubes.

21. The great French mathematician Joseph-Louis Lagrange showed in the eighteenth century that *every positive integer can be written as a sum of no more than four perfect squares*. For example, the number 210 can be written as $196+9+4+1$, i.e., as $14^2+3^2+2^2+1^2$.

Express the numbers 454, 746 and 1398 as sums of no more than four perfect squares.

22. Here is an arithmetical curiosity:

$$1^3+5^3+3^3=1+125+27=153.$$

So the number 153 has the feature that it is equal to the sum of the cubes of its digits.

Find other numbers with this property. (There are exactly three other three-digit numbers that have this property.)

23. Rather surprisingly, if we change 'cubes' to 'squares' in the above problem, we find that the only numbers having the property are 0 and 1. In other words, if we want to find numbers that are equal to the sum of the squares of their digits, then the only such numbers are 0 and 1; there are no 'non-trivial' examples.

However, we can look for 'close misses' where the sum of the squares differs by 1 from the original number. An example of such a number is 35, because $3^2+5^2=34$, which differs from 35 by 1. Find other two-digit close misses, where the difference between the number and the sum of the squares of its digits is 1.

24. Make a list of cubes of numbers whose units digit is 5 and study the list. You will get the following:

125,	3375,	15625,	42875,	91125,
166375,	274625,	421875,	614125,	857375,
1157625,	1520875,	1953125,	2460375,	3048625,
3723875,	4492125,	5359375,	6331625,	7414875.

What pattern do you see in their last two digits?

25. If you delete the units and tens digits of the numbers shown above, then you will get the following:

1,	33,	156,	428,	911,
1663,	2746,	4218,	6141,	8573,
11576,	15208,	19531,	24603,	30486,
37238,	44921,	53593,	63316,	74148.

Can a pattern be found in these numbers?

3.9 Triangular numbers

The perfect squares studied above are a type of **FIGURATE NUMBER**; they come from a sequence of geometric figures, as seen in Figure 3.2.

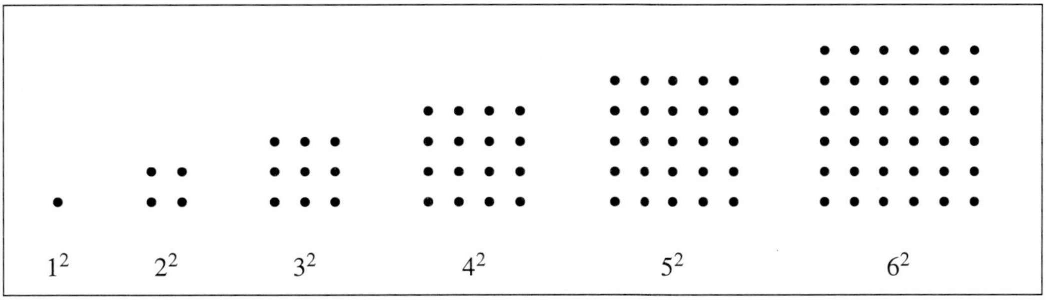

Figure 3.2

We now study another kind of figurate number, the **TRIANGULAR NUMBERS**, which are formed from triangular rather than square arrays. The first few figures of the sequence are shown in Figure 3.3. You should be able to extend the sequence on your own.

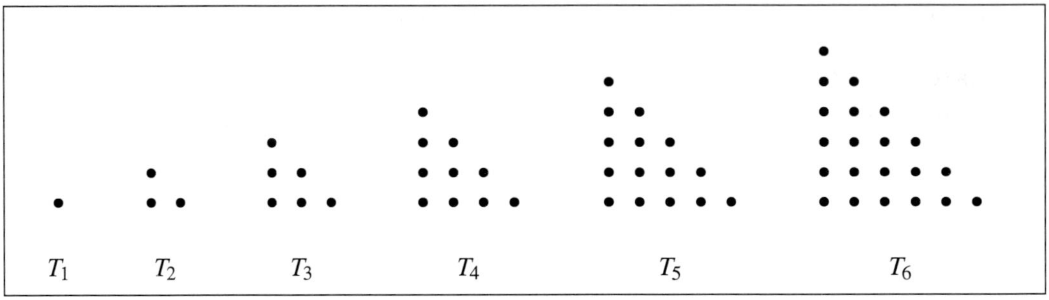

Figure 3.3

The number of dots in the nth figure is called the nth triangular number and is denoted by T_n. Therefore,

$$T_1 = 1, \qquad T_2 = 3, \qquad T_3 = 6, \qquad T_4 = 10, \qquad T_5 = 15, \qquad T_6 = 21.$$

For the sake of convenience, we agree to say that $T_0 = 0$. We can readily see how this sequence is to be extended. The next few numbers are $T_7 = 28$, $T_9 = 36$ and $T_{10} = 45$. Note that

$$\begin{aligned} T_1 &- 1, \\ T_2 &= 1+2, \\ T_3 &= 1+2+3, \\ T_4 &= 1+2+3+4, \\ T_5 &= 1+2+3+4+5, \end{aligned}$$

and, in general, T_n is the sum of the integers $1, 2, 3, \ldots, n-1, n$ for each positive integer n. Table 3.4 displays the triangular numbers till T_{99}.

The sequence of triangular numbers, which we shall call **TriangleNum**, or $\mathscr{T}$ for short, has many unexpected properties, just like **Squares**.

Note, firstly, that

$$\begin{aligned} 2T_1 &= 1 \times 2, \\ 2T_2 &= 2 \times 3, \\ 2T_3 &= 3 \times 4, \end{aligned}$$

Table 3.4 A list of triangular numbers, from T_0 till T_{99}

T \ U	0	1	2	3	4	5	6	7	8	9
0	0	1	3	6	10	15	21	28	36	45
1	55	66	78	91	105	120	136	153	171	190
2	210	231	253	276	300	325	351	378	406	435
3	465	496	528	561	595	630	666	703	741	780
4	820	861	903	946	990	1035	1081	1128	1176	1225
5	1275	1326	1378	1431	1485	1540	1596	1653	1711	1770
6	1830	1891	1953	2016	2080	2145	2211	2278	2346	2415
7	2485	2556	2628	2701	2775	2850	2926	3003	3081	3160
8	3240	3321	3403	3486	3570	3655	3741	3828	3916	4005
9	4095	4186	4278	4371	4465	4560	4656	4753	4851	4950

$$\begin{aligned} 2T_4 &= 4\times 5, \\ 2T_5 &= 5\times 6. \end{aligned}$$

The general pattern seems to be that

$$2T_n = n\times(n+1), \qquad \therefore\ T_n = \frac{n(n+1)}{2}.$$

Let us show why this relationship is true. One of the nicest ways was found by the great mathematician Carl Friedrich Gauss when he was just a boy. We illustrate the idea using T_5. Write the defining relation for T_5 in two ways, as shown below:

$$\begin{aligned} T_5 &= 1+2+3+4+5, \\ T_5 &= 5+4+3+2+1. \end{aligned}$$

Observe that we have simply reversed the order of the summands (i.e., the numbers being summed) in the second line. Naturally, this does not change the answer. Now we add the two lines, *vertically*; we get

$$2T_5 = (1+5)+(2+4)+(3+3)+(4+2)+(5+1).$$

The nice thing that happens is that inside each bracket we get *exactly* the same sum! (Each sum is 6.) Since there are 5 such bracketed terms, we get

$$2T_5 = \underbrace{6+6+6+6+6}_{5 \text{ times}} = 5 \times 6,$$

and therefore,

$$T_5 = \frac{5 \times 6}{2}.$$

In exactly the same way we see that for any positive integer n,

$$\boxed{T_n = \frac{n(n+1)}{2}.} \tag{3.3}$$

You should write the justification of this relation in full.

Other features of the triangular numbers

- ***Parity***. Write O for 'odd' and E for 'even'. Starting with $T_0 = 0$, which is even and therefore of type E, we get the following sequence:

  $$E,\ O,\ O,\ E,\ E,\ O,\ O,\ E,\ E,\ O,\ O,\ E,\ E,\ O,\ O,\ E,\ E,\ O,\ O,\ E,\ \ldots.$$

  We see that the string $\overline{E,O,O,E}$ repeats again and again, for ever.

- ***Divisibility by 3***. Write D for 'divisible by 3' and N for 'not divisible by 3'. Starting with $T_0 = 0$, which is divisible by 3 and is therefore of type D, we get the following sequence:

  $$D,\ N,\ D,\ D,\ N,\ D,\ D,\ N,\ D,\ D,\ N,\ D,\ D,\ N,\ D,\ D,\ N,\ D,\ D,\ N,\ \ldots.$$

  We see that the string $\overline{D,N,D}$ repeats again and again. The remainders in the divisions are

  $$0,\ 1,\ 0,\ 0,\ 1,\ 0,\ 0,\ 1,\ 0,\ 0,\ 1,\ 0,\ 0,\ 1,\ 0,\ \ldots.$$

  We see an endless repetition of the string $\overline{0,1,0}$. Strangely, we do not see a 2 anywhere in the sequence! *This means that no triangular number is of the form* $3k+2$.

- ***Divisibility by 5***. Starting with $T_0 = 0$, we divide each triangular number by 5 and record only the remainder left; we get the following numbers:

  $$0,\ 1,\ 3,\ 1,\ 0,\ 0,\ 1,\ 3,\ 1,\ 0,\ 0,\ 1,\ 3,\ 1,\ 0,\ 0,\ 1,\ 3,\ 1,\ 0,\ 0,\ \ldots.$$

We see an endless repetition of the string $\overline{0,1,3,1,0}$. And we see no 2 or 4 anywhere in the sequence.

- ***Sums of pairs of consecutive triangular numbers.*** Observe that

$$\begin{aligned} T_0+T_1 &= 1 = 1^2, \\ T_1+T_2 &= 4 = 2^2, \\ T_2+T_3 &= 9 = 3^2, \\ T_3+T_4 &= 16 = 4^2, \\ T_4+T_5 &= 25 = 5^2. \end{aligned}$$

In general, we have: $T_{n-1}+T_n = n^2$ for every positive integer n.

- If we multiply the triangular numbers by 8 and add 1 to the result, we get the squares of the odd numbers:

$$\begin{aligned} 8T_0+1 &= 1 = 1^2, \\ 8T_1+1 &= 9 = 3^2, \\ 8T_2+1 &= 25 = 5^2, \\ 8T_3+1 &= 49 = 7^2, \\ 8T_4+1 &= 81 = 9^2. \end{aligned}$$

In general, we have: $8T_n+1 = (2n+1)^2$.

- ***Sums of reciprocals.*** If we compute the partial sums of the *reciprocals* of the triangular numbers, a nice pattern emerges:

$$\begin{aligned} \frac{1}{T_1} &= \frac{1}{1}, \\ \frac{1}{T_1}+\frac{1}{T_2} &= \frac{4}{3}, \\ \frac{1}{T_1}+\frac{1}{T_2}+\frac{1}{T_3} &= \frac{3}{2}, \\ \frac{1}{T_1}+\frac{1}{T_2}+\frac{1}{T_3}+\frac{1}{T_4} &= \frac{8}{5}, \\ \frac{1}{T_1}+\frac{1}{T_2}+\frac{1}{T_3}+\frac{1}{T_4}+\frac{1}{T_5} &= \frac{5}{3}, \end{aligned}$$

$$\frac{1}{T_1}+\frac{1}{T_2}+\frac{1}{T_3}+\frac{1}{T_4}+\frac{1}{T_5}+\frac{1}{T_6} = \frac{12}{7},$$
$$\frac{1}{T_1}+\frac{1}{T_2}+\frac{1}{T_3}+\frac{1}{T_4}+\frac{1}{T_5}+\frac{1}{T_6}+\frac{1}{T_7} = \frac{7}{4},$$

and so on. If we write the fractions in unsimplified form as follows,

$$\frac{2}{2},\quad \frac{4}{3},\quad \frac{6}{4},\quad \frac{8}{5},\quad \frac{10}{6},\quad \frac{12}{7},\quad \frac{14}{8},\quad \ldots,$$

then the pattern becomes instantly visible.

EXERCISES

1. Find a simple formula for the nth term in the sequence of fractions obtained above,

$$\frac{2}{2},\quad \frac{4}{3},\quad \frac{6}{4},\quad \frac{8}{5},\quad \frac{10}{6},\quad \frac{12}{7},\quad \frac{14}{8},\quad \ldots.$$

2. Show that $\dfrac{1}{2T_n} = \dfrac{1}{n} - \dfrac{1}{n+1}$.

3. Explain why the triangular numbers have the parity pattern $\overline{E,O,O,E}$.

4. Explain why the triangular numbers yield the pattern $\overline{D,N,D}$ with regard to divisibility by 3.

5. Explain why the triangular numbers yield the pattern $\overline{0,1,3,1,0}$ when they are divided by 5 and only the remainders are retained.

6. Explore the divisibility of the triangular numbers by 4. You will find (perhaps to your surprise) that the pattern is a good deal more complicated than the ones you get from divisibility by 2, 3 or 5. See if you can find an explanation.

7. Explore the divisibility of the triangular numbers by 6. Once again, you will find a somewhat complicated pattern. See if you can find an explanation.

8. Study the sequence of units digits of the triangular numbers, and verify that they form a repeating pattern. Find the length of the repeating portion.

9. Find a pictorial proof for the relation $2T_n = n \times (n+1)$. (Hint: Think of the right side as representing the area of a rectangle.)

10. Explain why $T_{n-1} + T_n = n^2$ for all n. Find a pictorial proof.

11. Explain why $8T_n + 1 = (2n+1)^2$. Look for a pictorial proof.

12. The number 1 is both a triangular number and a perfect square. Find other numbers of this kind. List as many as you can, and identify some patterns in your collection.

13. The numbers 3 and 6 are both triangular numbers, and the larger one is *twice* the smaller one. Find other instances of pairs of triangular numbers with this property. Identify some patterns in your collection.

14. The numbers 1 and 3 are both triangular numbers, and the larger one is *three times* the smaller one. Find other instances of pairs of triangular numbers that have this property. Identify some patterns in your collection.

15. The numbers 3 and 15 are both triangular numbers, and the larger one is *five times* the smaller one. Find other instances of pairs of triangular numbers that have this property. Identify some patterns in your collection.

16. It is not possible to find pairs of triangular numbers in which one number is *four times* the other one. Try to explain why this is so.

    In fact, the following is true, though you may find it hard at this point to see why:

    > *Given any non-square integer k greater than* 1, *it is possible to find pairs of triangular numbers such that the larger one is k times the smaller one. But if* $k > 1$ *is a perfect square, then this is not possible.*

17. If we compute the *squares* of the triangular numbers 0, 1, 3, 6, 10, 15, 21, 28, 36, 45, 55, ..., we get the numbers

    $$0,\ 1,\ 9,\ 36,\ 100,\ 225,\ 441,\ 784,\ 1296,\ 2025,\ 3025,\ \ldots.$$

    If we compute the differences between the successive terms in this sequence, we get these numbers:

    $$1,\ 8,\ 27,\ 64,\ 125,\ 216,\ 343,\ 512,\ 729,\ 1000,\ \ldots.$$

    We have obtained the cubes! Does this come as a surprise? Should it?

    Explain the pattern we have found.

18. As a teenager, Gauss discovered (and *proved*) that *every positive integer can be written as a sum of no more than three triangular numbers.* (He recorded this discovery in his secret diary by writing "Eureka! Num $= \triangle + \triangle + \triangle$".)

    For example, we have $150 = 120 + 15 + 15 = T_{15} + T_5 + T_5$.

    Express the numbers 50, 100 and 500 as sums of no more than three triangular numbers.

3.10 Powers of 2

The last family that we shall study in this chapter is the family of powers of 2, which we shall call Power2:

$$\text{Power2} = \{2,\ 4,\ 8,\ 16,\ 32,\ 64,\ 128,\ 256,\ 512,\ 1024,\ 2048,\ 4096,\ \ldots\}.$$

Occasionally, we shall find it convenient to start the sequence with 1 rather than with 2.

We catalogue a few properties of this sequence below.

- ***Units digit.*** Examining the sequence of units digits of the powers of 2, we spot a pattern almost immediately:

  $$2,\quad 4,\quad 8,\quad 6,\quad 2,\quad 4,\quad 8,\quad 6,\quad \ldots.$$

  We see that the units digits show a repetition every four steps, with the string $2,4,8,6$ repeating indefinitely.

- ***Last two digits.*** If we consider not just the units digit but the tens and units digits, considered as a two-digit block, i.e., as a two-digit number (which could be regarded as the remainder left when the number is divided by 100), then this sequence too has a repetitive pattern; but it is harder to spot, as the repeating portion is much longer. Here is the sequence of last two digits of the powers of 2:

  $$\begin{gathered} 02,\ 04,\ 08,\ 16,\ 32,\ 64,\ 28,\ 56,\ 12,\ 24, \\ 48,\ 96,\ 92,\ 84,\ 68,\ 36,\ 72,\ 44,\ 88,\ 76, \\ 52,\ 04,\ 08,\ 16,\ 32,\ 64,\ 28,\ 56,\ 12,\ 24, \\ 48,\ 96,\ 92,\ 84,\ 68,\ 36,\ 72,\ 44,\ 88,\ 76,\ \ldots. \end{gathered}$$

  Observe that '02' does not occur again in the sequence.

With the very first entry omitted, the sequence repeats itself after every 20 terms, the repeating portion being the string

$$04,\ 08,\ 16,\ 32,\ 64,\ 28,\ 56,\ 12,\ 24,\ 48,$$
$$96,\ 92,\ 84,\ 68,\ 36,\ 72,\ 44,\ 88,\ 76,\ 52.$$

After '52' we get 04 once again, then 08, 16, 32, and so on.

- ***Partial sums***. We compute the partial sums of the powers of 2, i.e., the sums

  $$1, \quad 1+2, \quad 1+2+4, \quad 1+2+4+8, \quad 1+2+4+8+16, \quad \dots;$$

  note that this time we have chosen to start the sequence with a 1. Here are the sums we get:

  $$1, \quad 3, \quad 7, \quad 15, \quad 31, \quad 63, \quad 127, \quad \dots.$$

  The pattern here is striking—*each partial sum is* 1 *less than the next power of* 2. We seem to have found, therefore, that:

  The sum of the numbers $1, 2^1, 2^2, 2^3, \dots, 2^{n-1}, 2^n$ *is equal to* $2^{n+1}-1$.

- *Expressing the positive integers as sums of powers of* 2. If we have a system of weight measures where the weights in kilograms are precisely the powers of 2, i.e., 1 kg, 2 kg, 4 kg, 8 kg, 16 kg, 32 kg, ..., then we find that *every integral weight can be measured on a pan balance using just these weights, no weight having to be used more than once*. For example, we have $3=2+1,\ 5=4+1,\ 6=4+2,\ 7=4+2+1,\ 11=8+2+1,$ and so on.

  We may express this property as follows: *Each positive integer can be written as a sum of distinct powers of* 2. Here the word 'distinct' tells us that no power of 2 is used more than once.

Explanations

We shall show how to explain first and third statements above.

- Consider the units digits of the first four powers of 2; they are the numbers 2, 4, 8, 6, in that order.

Each power of 2 is obtained by multiplying the *previous power* by 2. Since the units digit of 2^4 is 6, to get the units digit of 2^5, we simply multiply 6 by 2, retaining only the units digit of the answer; we get 2. (Check: $2^5 = 32$, whose units digit is 2.) Continuing: since $2 \times 2 = 4$, the units digit of 2^6 will be 4; since $4 \times 2 = 8$, the units digit of 2^7 will be 8; and since $8 \times 2 = 16$, whose units digit is 6, the units digit of 2^8 will be 6.

The cycle is now complete, because we have once again got 6 as the units digit; the units digits of $2^5, 2^6, 2^7, 2^8$ are the same, respectively, as the units digits of $2^1, 2^2, 2^3, 2^4$. Repeating these steps, we find that the units digits of $2^9, 2^{10}, 2^{11}, 2^{12}$ are the same, respectively, as the units digits of $2^5, 2^6, 2^7, 2^8$. Hence, 2, 4, 8 and 6 will repeat again and again as the units digits, and in that order.

Much the same reasoning works if we consider the block of last two digits, but we shall not take up the matter here.

- Now we consider the partial sums.

  Let X represent the sum of the numbers

$$1, \quad 2^1, \quad 2^2, \quad 2^3, \quad \ldots, \quad 2^{n-1}, \quad 2^n.$$

Doubling each of the numbers in this list, we see that $2X$ is the sum of the numbers

$$2^1, \quad 2^2, \quad 2^3, \quad 2^4, \quad \ldots, \quad 2^n, \quad 2^{n+1}.$$

These two lists have many numbers in common; indeed, the numbers

$$2^1, \quad 2^2, \quad 2^3, \quad 2^4, \quad \ldots, \quad 2^n$$

occur in both lists. However, 1 occurs only in the list for X, whereas 2^{n+1} occurs only in the list for $2X$; so if we delete 1 from the first list and 2^{n+1} from the second one, we will get two identical lists. It follows that

$$X - 1 = 2X - 2^{n+1}.$$

This tells us that

$$X = 2^{n+1} - 1,$$

and this is precisely what we wanted to show.

EXERCISES

1. Express the numbers 50, 101, 1003 and 2005 as sums of distinct powers of 2.

2. Examine the sequence of units digits of the powers of 3, i.e., the sequence

$$3, \quad 9, \quad 27, \quad 81, \quad 243, \quad 729, \quad 2187, \quad 6561, \quad 19683, \quad 59049, \quad \ldots,$$

   and show that the units digits repeat in a four-step cycle, the repeating portion being 3, 9, 7, 1.

3. Compute the partial sums of the powers of 3, starting with 1 rather than 3. The first few partial sums are:

$$\begin{aligned} 1 &= 1, \\ 1+3 &= 4, \\ 1+3+9 &= 13, \\ 1+3+9+27 &= 40, \\ 1+3+9+27+81 &= 121. \end{aligned}$$

   Try to find a pattern in the answers. That is, try to find a formula for the sum of the numbers $1, 3^1, 3^2, 3^3, \ldots, 3^{n-1}$ and 3^n. Next, *prove* the formula!

4. Explore whether the sequence of last two digits of the powers of 3 show a repetitive behaviour.

5. We stated above (but did not justify) that each positive integer can be written as a sum of distinct powers of 2.

   Can every positive integer be written as a sum of distinct powers of 3? Or are there some integers that cannot be written this way? Explore the question as thoroughly as you can.

3.11 Miscellaneous problems

1. Among the numbers from 1 till 300, how many are not divisible by either 2 or by 3?

2. Among the numbers from 1 till 600, how many are not divisible by either 3 or by 5?

3. Which positive integer is one-ninth of its own square?

4. Which positive integer is one-ninth of its own cube?

5. Which is the smallest positive integer that is a perfect square and at the same time a perfect cube?

6. Which is the smallest positive integer that is twice a perfect square, and at the same time three times a perfect cube?

7. Which is the smallest positive integer that is three times a perfect square, and at the same time twice a perfect cube?

8. Which integer below 100 has the largest number of divisors?

9. Which integer between 100 and 200 has the largest number of divisors?

10. How many divisors does the number $2^{10} = 1024$ have?

11. How many divisors does the number 3^{100} have?

12. How many divisors does the number 4^{100} have?

13. How many divisors does the number 6^{100} have?

14. List the divisors of the number $2^4 \times 3^4$.

15. Based on your answer to the preceding question, state the number of divisors of the number $2^{10} \times 3^{10}$.

16. How many divisors does the number $3^{15} \times 5^{15}$ have?

17. Let n be any odd, positive integer. Show that $2n$ has twice the number of divisors that n has.

18. Let n be any positive integer which is *not* divisible by 3. Compare the number of divisors, respectively, of $3n$ and n. What relationship do you find between them?

19. Give two examples of numbers which have exactly six divisors.

20. Give two examples of numbers which have exactly 12 divisors.

21. Give two examples of numbers which have exactly 15 divisors.

22. What can you say about the family of numbers which have precisely two divisors? (Here we include the number itself as a divisor; e.g., the number 10 has the divisors 1, 2, 5 and 10.)

23. What can you say about the family of numbers which have precisely three divisors?

24. What can you say about the family of numbers which have precisely four divisors? Show that this family is made up of two smaller families.

25. What can you say about the family of numbers which have precisely five divisors?

Chapter 4

Fractions, Decimals and Percentages

What do we get if we divide 4 by 2? We all know that we will get 2, but it is fun to illustrate this using *pictures* or *dot diagrams*. Using dots, we see that $\boxed{\bullet\ \bullet\ \bullet\ \bullet}$ may be written as $\boxed{\bullet\ \bullet}\ \boxed{\bullet\ \bullet}$, or as two copies of $\boxed{\bullet\ \bullet}$, and so

$$\boxed{\bullet\ \bullet\ \bullet\ \bullet} \div 2 = \boxed{\bullet\ \bullet}.$$

Similarly, we know that if we divide 6 by 2, we get 3; the dot diagram for this is:

$$\boxed{\bullet\ \bullet\ \bullet\ \bullet\ \bullet\ \bullet} \div 2 = \boxed{\bullet\ \bullet\ \bullet}.$$

If we divide 6 by 3, we get 2;

$$\boxed{\bullet\ \bullet\ \bullet\ \bullet\ \bullet\ \bullet} \div 3 = \boxed{\bullet\ \bullet}.$$

Long back, mathematicians evolved a neat way of writing such relations:

$$\frac{4}{2} = 2, \qquad \frac{6}{2} = 3, \qquad \frac{6}{3} = 2.$$

These may respectively be read aloud as follows:

- "4 divided by 2 gives 2";
- "6 divided by 2 gives 3";
- "6 divided by 3 gives 2".

We can write many such relations:

$$\frac{21}{3} = 7, \qquad \frac{33}{3} = 11, \qquad \frac{52}{4} = 13, \qquad \frac{65}{5} = 13.$$

Another way of writing $\frac{21}{3}$ is $21/3$, but we prefer the first way. (We give a reason for this on page 124.)

4.1 Fractions as numbers

When we write something like $\frac{21}{3}$, we call it a **FRACTION**. There are two ways of thinking about a fraction.

(I) We may think of it as an *instruction* or a *command*: ***Divide* 21 *by* 3.**

(Of course, as we are polite people, we will first say *Please*.)

(II) Or we may think of $\frac{21}{3}$ as a *number*, obtained from the division $21 \div 3$. So $\frac{21}{3}$ is *simply another way of writing* 7; because, if we divide 21 by 3, then that is what we get.

In this book, it is meaning (II) that we shall give throughout to fractions. So *we shall think of a fraction as a number written in the form of a division.*[1]

This is a crucial step—regarding fractions as numbers, and thereby placing them alongside other numbers that we already know. We consider this step to be so important that we shall write the statement in a box:

> *Fractions are numbers, and we can do arithmetic with them.*

Fractions are generally written in the form $\frac{a}{b}$ where a and b are integers, with $b \neq 0$. This restriction should never be forgotten, because division by zero is not allowed. The 'bar' between the two numbers is called the **FRACTION BAR**. (Later, we shall relax the restriction that a and b should be integers.)

The number above the fraction bar is called the **NUMERATOR** of the fraction, and the number below the bar is called the **DENOMINATOR**. For $\frac{21}{3}$, the numerator is 21 and the denominator is 3. We pronounce it as '21 upon 3' or '21 by 3'.

---

[1]The possibility of looking at a statement in two ways arises in many other contexts. For example, consider the expression $3+5$. We may think of it as an instruction or a command, "Add 3 to 5". Or we may think of $3+5$ as the *number* obtained from the addition $3+5$.

Now we can say why we prefer to write $\frac{21}{3}$ and not $21/3$; when we write $21/3$, it is not clear what lies above the fraction bar. Is the number $2\frac{1}{3}$ (i.e., 2 and $1/3$), or is it $\frac{21}{3}$? A similar confusion can arise if we write $2/3+1$. Does this mean $\frac{2}{3+1}$ or $\frac{2}{3}+1$? Our notation must be clear, with no room for wrong interpretation.

The fraction $\frac{21}{3}$ is only one of the many different ways of writing the number 7. Here are some other ways:

$$\frac{7}{1}, \quad \frac{14}{2}, \quad \frac{28}{4}, \quad \frac{35}{5}, \quad \frac{42}{6}, \quad \frac{49}{7}, \quad \ldots.$$

These fractions, being different ways of writing the same number (namely, 7) are said to be **EQUIVALENT** to one another; they are called **EQUIVALENT FRACTIONS**. The fractions shown above are pronounced as "7 upon 1", "14 upon 2", "28 upon 4", "35 upon 5", and so on.

We now examine a few fractions more closely.

- *The fraction* $\frac{m}{1}$. The integer m and the fraction $\frac{m}{1}$ are regarded as identical, since $m \div 1 = m$.

  We similarly have: $\frac{2m}{2} = m$, $\frac{3m}{3} = m$ and so on.

- *The fraction* $\frac{7}{3}$. Since 3 does not divide (or 'go') exactly into 7, this fraction is not equal to any integer. But 3 does go 2 times into 7, with remainder 1 (since $2 \times 3 = 6$, and $7-6=1$); so we may write any of the following, which all mean the same thing:

$$\frac{7}{3} = 2 \text{ and } \frac{1}{3}; \qquad \frac{7}{3} = 2+\frac{1}{3}; \qquad \frac{7}{3} = 2\frac{1}{3}.$$

- *The fraction* $\frac{1}{2}$. If we were given the command *Divide* 1 *by* 2, we would not know how to proceed because 2 does not go into 1 even once. So what do we do with this fraction?

  The answer is that we do not need to 'do' anything; *we keep the fraction as it is*. Just as 2 and 3 and 4 are numbers with definite properties, so too $\frac{1}{2}$ is a number with definite properties.

  Now 2 is the number with the property that if we double it, we get 4; and 3 is the number with the property that if we double it, we get 6. Similarly, $\frac{1}{2}$ *is the number with the property that if we double it, we get* 1. So we have:

$$2 \times \frac{1}{2} = 1, \qquad \frac{1}{2}+\frac{1}{2} = 1.$$

- *The fraction* $\frac{2}{3}$. In the same way, $\frac{2}{3}$ is the number with the property that if we multiply it by 3, then we get 2:

$$3 \times \frac{2}{3} = 2, \qquad \frac{2}{3} + \frac{2}{3} + \frac{2}{3} = 2.$$

Proper fractions, improper fractions

- Fractions in which the numerator is less than the denominator, like $\frac{2}{3}$ or $\frac{3}{7}$, are called **PROPER FRACTIONS**.

- Fractions in which the numerator equals or exceeds the denominator, like $\frac{3}{3}$, $\frac{5}{5}$, $\frac{3}{2}$, or $\frac{9}{7}$, are called **IMPROPER FRACTIONS**.

Fractions and units

A useful way of thinking about fractions is in terms of a **UNIT**. Imagine a circular cake (or, if you prefer, a *roti* or a *dosa*) divided into two equal pieces. Regarding the whole cake as one unit, each piece now represents $\frac{1}{2}$ (of the unit). Since the two pieces together make the whole cake, we have: $\frac{1}{2} + \frac{1}{2} = 1$. See Figure 4.1 (I).

If, instead, the cake is divided into three equal pieces, then each piece represents $\frac{1}{3}$. If we take any two pieces, then together they represent $\frac{2}{3}$. Since the third piece represents $\frac{1}{3}$, we can say that $\frac{2}{3} + \frac{1}{3} = 1$. Figure 4.1 (II) illustrates these relations.

In Figure 4.1 (III), we imagine the cake divided into four pieces, of which one person takes three pieces, and another person takes the remaining piece. This illustrates the relation $\frac{3}{4} + \frac{1}{4} = 1$.

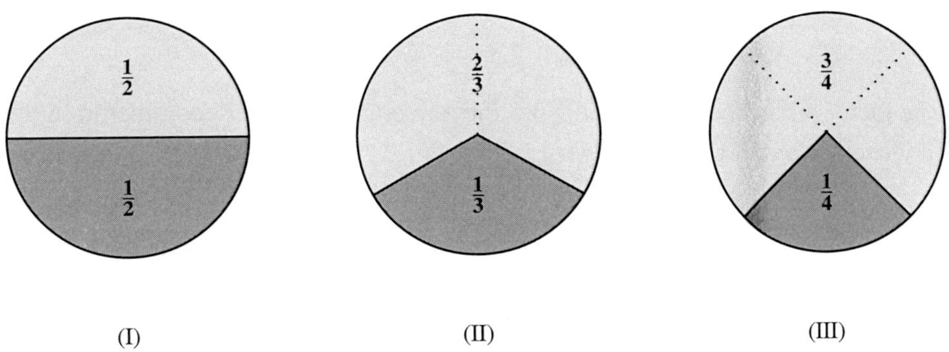

Figure 4.1

4.2 Equivalent fractions

As described above, fractions that represent the same number are called equivalent fractions; for example,

$$\frac{3}{8}, \quad \frac{6}{16}, \quad \frac{9}{24}, \quad \frac{12}{32}, \quad \ldots.$$

are equivalent fractions. To see why, we draw pictures as shown in Figure 4.2. Here we see three rectangles of the same size divided respectively into 8 equal strips, 16 equal strips, and 24 equal strips. In (a), 3 of the 8 strips have been shaded; in (b), 6 of the 16 strips have been shaded; and in (c), 9 of the 24 strips have been shaded. But if we disregard the strips, the actual *amount* that has been shaded is exactly the same in each case. This illustrates the equality $\frac{3}{8} = \frac{6}{16} = \frac{9}{24}$.

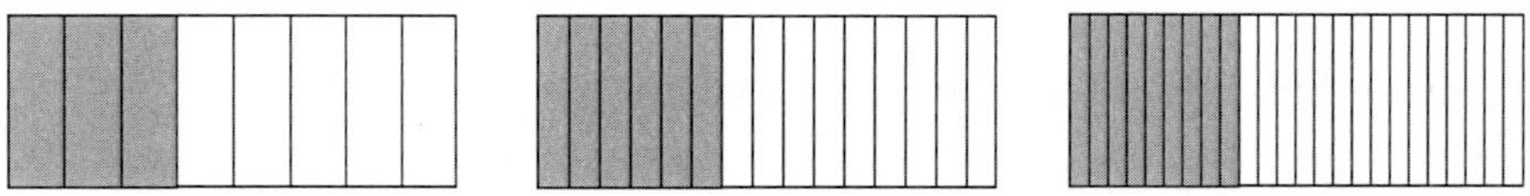

(a) 8 strips (b) 16 strips (c) 24 strips

Figure 4.2

On studying these fractions, we see that when the numerator and denominator share a factor, then the factor can be divided out; we call this **CANCELLATION**, and we say that we are **CANCELLING** the common factor, and the fraction we get after cancellation is equivalent to the original one. For example, we may write:

$$\frac{12}{32} = \frac{4 \times 3}{4 \times 8} = \frac{3}{8}.$$

Here the factor 4 has been cancelled from the numerator and the denominator. In general, we can write, for any non-zero integer c:

$$\frac{a \times c}{b \times c} = \frac{a}{b}.$$

We must have $c \neq 0$, because to get a from $a \times c$, we must divide by c, and division by 0 is not permitted.

If there is no common factor between the numerator and the denominator of a fraction, the fraction is said to be in its **LOWEST TERMS**. Mathematicians like to use another word for such fractions—they call them **IRREDUCIBLE** (they cannot be 'reduced' further). Here are some examples of irreducible fractions:

$$\frac{3}{8}, \quad \frac{4}{9}, \quad \frac{5}{6}, \quad \frac{12}{25}.$$

For a fraction that is not in lowest terms, the action of cancelling common factors between the numerator and denominator is called **REDUCING TO LOWEST TERMS**. For example:

$$\frac{10}{32} = \frac{5}{16}, \quad \frac{28}{63} = \frac{4}{9}, \quad \frac{38}{171} = \frac{2}{9}.$$

Here is a puzzle which you may enjoy tackling: *Using the ten digits* $0, 1, 2, \ldots, 9$ *just once each, form two positive integers a and b such that* $\frac{a}{b} = \frac{1}{2}$.

4.3 Arithmetic with fractions

Having decided that fractions are numbers, we must now learn how to add, subtract, multiply and divide them with one another. Naturally, the laws of arithmetic that hold true for integers must continue to remain valid, namely:

Commutativity of addition, commutativity of multiplication: $a + b = b + a$, and $a \times b = b \times a$;

Associativity of addition, associativity of multiplication: $(a+b)+c = a+(b+c)$, and $(a \times b) \times c = a \times (b \times c)$;

Distributivity of multiplication over addition: $a \times (b+c) = (a \times b) + (a \times c)$.

We want these rules to remain valid—*because if they lose their validity, then we would not be able to do arithmetic with fractions any more, and then fractions would not be of much use to us*. That is, we want to *extend* the laws of arithmetic from the domain of the integers to the domain of the fractions, in a smooth and harmonious manner. It is natural to want this; after all, the integers are part of the family of fractions, and it would be strange to have different sets of laws for them.

Note that fractions, like other numbers, can be **SIGNED**; so we can have fractions such as

$$-\frac{2}{3}, \quad -\frac{7}{5}, \quad -\frac{14}{19}, \quad -\frac{25}{11}, \quad -\frac{3}{19},$$

and so on. Note that $-\frac{2}{3}$ may be thought of as either $\frac{-2}{3}$ or $\frac{2}{-3}$; the two ways are equivalent, but the first one is preferred. The rules of arithmetic that we derive, below, must hold good for signed fractions as well.

Addition and subtraction

To add or subtract two given fractions, *we first replace each one by an equivalent one, in such a way that the two fractions to be added have the same denominator*. Let us see why we need to do this. Take an addition like $\frac{1}{2}+\frac{1}{3}$. In pictorial form, it looks like Figure 4.3.

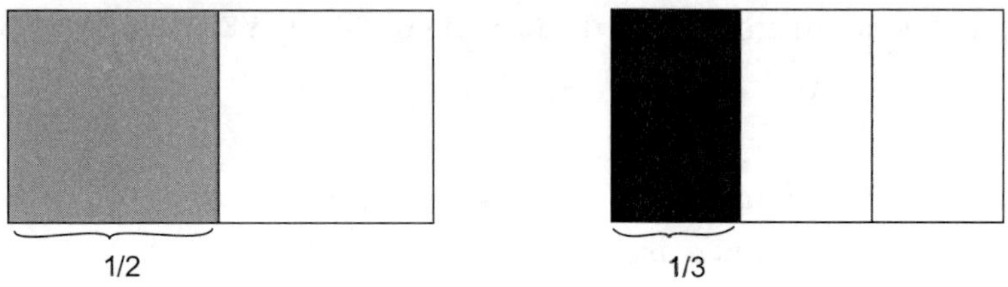

Figure 4.3

But the picture does not reveal the answer. So we make the grids in the pictures finer, in such a way that the two pictures can sensibly be placed 'one over the other', and then it is easy to see what the sum should be. Now look at Figure 4.4.

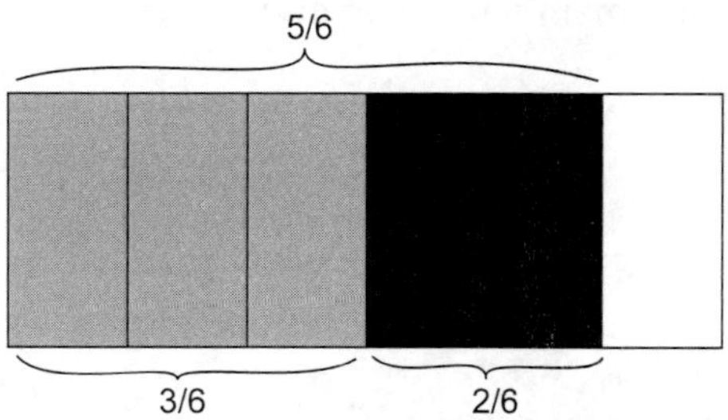

Figure 4.4

The grid drawn now shows that the sum is $\frac{5}{6}$. (In Figure 4.4 we have written $5/6$ rather than $\frac{5}{6}$. This is to avoid having to write the fraction in too small a font.)

What we have done is essentially this:

$$\begin{aligned} \frac{1}{2} &= \frac{3}{6}, \\ \frac{1}{3} &= \frac{2}{6}, \\ \therefore\ \frac{1}{2}+\frac{1}{3} &= \frac{3}{6}+\frac{2}{6} = \frac{5}{6}. \end{aligned}$$

This method tells us how to add or subtract two given fractions: *we replace both the fractions by equivalent ones, so that the resulting fractions have the same denominator;*

then we add or subtract the two numerators, as the case may be. The common denominator is clearly the LCM of the denominators of the given fractions.

EXAMPLE 1. *To add $\frac{3}{10}$ and $\frac{7}{15}$, we first find* LCM$(10,15) = 30$, *and now:*

$$\frac{3}{10}+\frac{7}{15} = \frac{9}{30}+\frac{14}{30} = \frac{23}{30}.$$

Similarly, to subtract $\frac{5}{12}$ from $\frac{11}{21}$, we first compute LCM$(12,21) = 84$, and now:

$$\frac{11}{21}-\frac{5}{12} = \frac{44}{84}-\frac{35}{84} = \frac{9}{84} = \frac{3}{28}.$$

Remark

It is not always essential that we compute the LCM—*any common multiple of the two denominators will do*; it does not have to be the *least* one. The most obvious common multiple of two numbers is their product; e.g., for 10 and 15 it would be $10 \times 15 = 150$. So to compute $\frac{3}{10}+\frac{7}{15}$ we do:

$$\frac{3}{10}+\frac{7}{15} = \frac{3\times 15}{150}+\frac{7\times 10}{150} = \frac{45}{150}+\frac{70}{150} = \frac{115}{150} = \frac{23}{30}.$$

The general rule is:

$$\boxed{\frac{a}{b}+\frac{c}{d} = \frac{ad+bc}{bd}.} \tag{4.1}$$

This rule or 'formula' is valid in all instances (i.e., for all a,b,c,d, with $b \neq 0$ and $d \neq 0$; they do not necessarily have to be integers). Such a formula is called an **IDENTITY** in algebra.

Multiplication and division

Fraction times whole number. For this, we must go back to the idea of a 'unit'. Take the multiplication $2 \times \frac{3}{7}$. Since $\frac{3}{7}$ represents 3 parts of a unit that has been divided into seven equal parts, $2 \times \frac{3}{7}$ (twice of $\frac{3}{7}$) represents 6 of those same parts (here 6 is 2×3); in other words,

$$2\times\frac{3}{7} = \frac{6}{7}.$$

Similarly,

$$3 \times \frac{5}{8} = \frac{15}{8},$$

because $\frac{5}{8}$ represents 5 parts of a unit that has been divided into eight equal parts, and $3 \times 5 = 15$.

The general rule is: if m is any whole number, then

$$\boxed{m \times \frac{a}{b} = \frac{ma}{b}.} \tag{4.2}$$

As earlier, this too is an identity.

Fraction divided by whole number. We do this in the same way—by thinking in terms of units. Thus,

$$\frac{6}{7} \div 2 = \frac{3}{7},$$

because $\frac{6}{7}$ represents 6 parts of a unit that has been divided into seven equal parts, and $6 \div 2 = 3$. Similarly, we have:

$$\frac{6}{7} \div 3 = \frac{2}{7}, \qquad \frac{6}{7} \div 6 = \frac{1}{7}.$$

In the case of a division like $\frac{6}{7} \div 5$, since 5 does not divide exactly into 6, we must first replace the fraction by a suitable equivalent fraction whose numerator is divisible by 5. A simple way to make this happen is to multiply both the numerator and the denominator of the given fraction by 5; we get:

$$\frac{6}{7} \div 5 = \frac{30}{35} \div 5 = \frac{6}{35}.$$

Similarly,

$$\frac{3}{11} \div 4 = \frac{12}{44} \div 4 = \frac{3}{44}.$$

The general rule is seen from these examples: if m is a whole number, then

$$\boxed{\frac{a}{b} \div m = \frac{a}{mb}.} \tag{4.3}$$

Fraction times fraction. To multiply two given fractions, say $\frac{2}{3} \times \frac{5}{6}$, we apply these rules in combination, by making it a two-step computation: first multiply $\frac{2}{3}$ by 5, and then divide the result by 6:

$$\frac{2}{3} \times 5 = \frac{10}{3}, \qquad \frac{10}{3} \div 6 = \frac{10}{18}.$$

So

$$\frac{2}{3} \times \frac{5}{6} = \frac{10}{18}.$$

Naturally, we reduce the answer to lowest terms and write it as $\frac{5}{9}$.

The general rule is: if $\frac{a}{b}$ and $\frac{c}{d}$ are any two fractions, then

$$\boxed{\frac{a}{b} \times \frac{c}{d} = \frac{ac}{bd}.} \tag{4.4}$$

This too is an identity.

Important remark. Observe that $\frac{a}{b} \div m$ and $\frac{a}{b} \times \frac{1}{m}$ yield the same answer, namely, $\frac{a}{mb}$. This tells us that:

***Division by** m **is the same as multiplication by** $\frac{1}{m}$.* (4.5)

Now the operation that is opposite to (i.e., reverses the effect of) 'division by m' is obviously 'multiplication by m', and the operation opposite to 'multiplication by $\frac{1}{m}$' is 'division by $\frac{1}{m}$'. We therefore deduce that:

***Multiplication by** m **is the same as division by** $\frac{1}{m}$.* (4.6)

The idea used here is, *if two operations yield the same result, then their opposites, or inverses, must yield the same result too.*

Fraction divided by fraction. The same idea works here—that of doing the computation in two steps. For example, consider $\frac{4}{11} \div \frac{3}{7}$. Since $\frac{3}{7}$ is $3 \times \frac{1}{7}$, division by $\frac{3}{7}$ is the same as division by 3 followed by division by $\frac{1}{7}$. So the first step is division by 3:

$$\frac{4}{11} \div 3 = \frac{4}{33}.$$

Next, we do $\frac{4}{33} \div \frac{1}{7}$. But, as we have already found, division by $\frac{1}{7}$ is the same as multiplication by 7. Therefore,

$$\frac{4}{33} \div \frac{1}{7} = \frac{4}{33} \times 7 = \frac{28}{33}.$$

So we get

$$\frac{4}{11} \div \frac{3}{7} = \frac{28}{33}.$$

The same answer would have been obtained from $\frac{4}{11} \times \frac{7}{3}$. The general rule is that division by $\frac{c}{d}$ is the same as multiplication by $\frac{d}{c}$, and so:

$$\boxed{\frac{a}{b} \div \frac{c}{d} = \frac{ad}{bc}.} \tag{4.7}$$

Idea of reciprocal of a fraction. If the product of two fractions is 1, then multiplication by either fraction is reversed (or 'undone') by multiplication by the other fraction. Such numbers are then said to be **RECIPROCALS** of each other. Clearly, the reciprocal of $\frac{a}{b}$ is $\frac{b}{a}$. This follows from associativity of multiplication. For example, consider the multiplication $\frac{2}{3} \times \frac{4}{7} \times \frac{7}{4}$:

$$\left(\frac{2}{3} \times \frac{4}{7}\right) \times \frac{7}{4} = \frac{8}{21} \times \frac{7}{4} = \frac{8 \times 7}{21 \times 4} = \frac{2}{3},$$

after cancelling the common factors. Associativity is seen after we bracket the multiplicands differently:

$$\frac{2}{3} \times \left(\frac{4}{7} \times \frac{7}{4}\right) = \frac{2}{3} \times 1 = \frac{2}{3}.$$

The 'of' operation. We often use the word 'of' in the following manner: "Please give me half of whatever you have". The 'of' here is understood to mean *multiplication*. So, if you have 30 marbles, and I ask you to give me half of what you have, what I am actually asking for is $\frac{1}{2} \times 30 = 15$ marbles. If I say, "Please give me one-third of what you have", what I am actually asking for is $\frac{1}{3} \times 30 = 10$ marbles. In arithmetic, the word 'of' indicates *multiplication*.

Why divide one fraction by another? In what kind of 'real life' situation would one want to divide one fraction by another? Here is an example:

> *In a canteen 'plate meal', $\frac{1}{4}$ of an apple is served on each plate. On how many plates can I serve the apple portion if I have just 3 apples?*

Since $3 \div \frac{1}{4} = 3 \times 4 = 12$, the answer is: 12 plates.

Here are two other 'stories' in which we would meet the division $3 \div \frac{1}{4}$.

1. *I am driving from city A to city B. I take 3 hours to do $\frac{1}{4}$ of the journey. How many hours does the full journey take?*
2. *If 3 halls are needed to hold $\frac{1}{4}$ of all the children in a school, how many halls would be needed to hold all the children?*

Comparing two fractions

If fractions represent numbers, then we ought to be able to place them in ORDER; that is, given any two fractions we ought to be able to say which represents the smaller number, and which represents the larger number.

For example, take the fractions $\frac{1}{3}$ and $\frac{1}{2}$. We would all agree, without thinking much about it, that $\frac{1}{2} > \frac{1}{3}$; but how do we show this? One way is to replace them with equivalent fractions having a common denominator, and then compare their numerators, which should maintain the same order. Since the LCM of 2 and 3 is 6, we write: $\frac{1}{2} = \frac{3}{6}$, and $\frac{1}{3} = \frac{2}{6}$. As $3 > 2$, we get $\frac{3}{6} > \frac{2}{6}$, and so $\frac{1}{2} > \frac{1}{3}$.

More generally, to compare $\frac{a}{b}$ and $\frac{c}{d}$, where both the denominators are positive, we replace both the fractions by equivalent fractions with common denominator bd. Since

$$\frac{a}{b} = \frac{ad}{bd}, \qquad \frac{c}{d} = \frac{bc}{bd},$$

we arrive at the following, known as the **CROSS-MULTIPLICATION RULE**:

> *If b and d are positive, then the fractions $\frac{a}{b}$ and $\frac{c}{d}$ bear the same order relation as the products ad and bc.*

EXERCISES

1. Compare the following pairs of fractions and state which one is bigger.

(a) $\frac{1}{3}$ and $\frac{2}{5}$;

(b) $\frac{2}{7}$ and $\frac{3}{8}$;

(c) $\frac{3}{11}$ and $\frac{5}{14}$;

(d) $\frac{4}{9}$ and $\frac{5}{11}$;

(e) $\frac{6}{13}$ and $\frac{9}{19}$;

(f) $\frac{11}{31}$ and $\frac{12}{35}$.

2. Find the least fraction which when added to $3\frac{2}{5} - 1\frac{1}{7} + 4\frac{4}{9}$ yields an integer.

3. Find the least fraction which when added to $4\frac{3}{7} - 2\frac{3}{8} + 5\frac{1}{3}$ yields an integer.

4. Simplify the sum $\frac{1}{2} + \frac{1}{6} + \frac{1}{12} + \frac{1}{20} + \frac{1}{30}$.

5. Invent two more 'stories' where we would meet the division $3 \div \frac{1}{4}$.

6. Find the smallest integer n such that the sum of the fractions $\frac{1}{1}, \frac{1}{2}, \frac{1}{3}, \frac{1}{4}, \ldots, \frac{1}{n}$ just exceeds $2\frac{1}{2}$.

7. In the problems below we use the following symbol: if n is a positive integer, then by $n!$ we mean the product of the integers $1, 2, 3, \ldots, n-1, n$. E.g., $3! = 6$, $4! = 1 \times 2 \times 3 \times 4 = 24$ and $5! = 120$.

(a) Simplify: $\dfrac{3!}{2!} \times \dfrac{5!}{6!}$.

(b) Simplify: $\dfrac{6!}{(3!)^2}$.

(c) Simplify: $\dfrac{4!}{3!} + \dfrac{4!}{4!}$.

(d) Simplify: $\dfrac{7!}{3!4!}$.

(e) Simplify: $\dfrac{3!}{5!} + \dfrac{4!}{6!}$.

(f) Verify that $\dfrac{9!}{4!5!} = \dfrac{8!}{4!4!} + \dfrac{8!}{3!5!}$.

(g) Verify that $\dfrac{10!}{3!7!} = \dfrac{9!}{3!6!} + \dfrac{9!}{2!7!}$.

(h) Verify that $\dfrac{8!}{3!5!} = \dfrac{7!}{3!4!} + \dfrac{7!}{2!5!}$.

8. ✪ Explain why the following are irreducible for any positive integer n:

$$\frac{n}{n+1}, \qquad \frac{n}{2n+1}, \qquad \frac{n}{3n+1}.$$

9. ✪ For which positive integers n is the fraction $\dfrac{n}{n+2}$ irreducible?

10. ✪ For which positive integers n is the fraction $\dfrac{n}{n+3}$ irreducible?

11. ✪ Using the ten digits $0,1,2,\ldots,8,9$ once each, form two positive integers a,b such that $\frac{a}{b}=\frac{1}{2}$.

12. ✪ Using the ten digits $0,1,2,\ldots,8,9$ once each, form two positive integers a,b such that $\frac{a}{b}=\frac{1}{3}$.

4.4 Decimal fractions

Fractions whose denominators are powers of 10 (for example, $\frac{3}{10}$, $\frac{21}{100}$, $\frac{397}{1000}$) are called **DECIMAL FRACTIONS**, and they are generally written in a more convenient manner as follows:

$$\frac{3}{10}=0.3, \qquad \frac{21}{100}=0.21, \qquad \frac{397}{1000}=0.397.$$

Now the fraction $\frac{397}{1000}$ can be written as

$$\frac{397}{1000}=\frac{300+90+7}{1000}=\frac{300}{1000}+\frac{90}{1000}+\frac{7}{1000}=\frac{3}{10}+\frac{9}{100}+\frac{7}{1000}.$$

We see that 0.397 is the same as $\frac{3}{10}+\frac{9}{100}+\frac{7}{1000}$. So the '3' in 0.397 has a value of $\frac{3}{10}$; this is its **PLACE VALUE**. Similarly, the '9' in 0.397 has a value of $\frac{9}{100}$, and the '7' in 0.397 has a value of $\frac{7}{1000}$; these are their respective place values. The 'dot' in 0.397 is called the **DECIMAL POINT**, and the digits after the decimal point are called the **DECIMAL DIGITS**. The number 0.397 is read out aloud as "zero point three nine seven".

From the above it should be clear that decimal notation works on a place value system, just like that for integers.

EXAMPLE 2. *Consider the number* 123.456*: it represents*

$$(1\times 100)+(2\times 10)+(3\times 1)+\left(4\times\frac{1}{10}\right)+\left(5\times\frac{1}{100}\right)+\left(6\times\frac{1}{1000}\right).$$

Here, 100 and 10 are powers of 10, while $\frac{1}{10}$, $\frac{1}{100}$ and $\frac{1}{1000}$ are *reciprocals of powers of* 10. Like the powers of 10 (namely, 10, 100, 1000, 10000, 100000, 1000000, ...), their supply is endless:

$$\frac{1}{10},\quad \frac{1}{100},\quad \frac{1}{1000},\quad \frac{1}{10000},\quad \frac{1}{100000},\quad \frac{1}{1000000},\quad \ldots.$$

They are the **NEGATIVE POWERS OF** 10. (Similarly, 1 is the **ZEROTH POWER OF** 10.) Later, we shall see that there are more compact ways of writing them. (They are written, respectively, as 10^{-1}, 10^{-2}, 10^{-3}, 10^{-4}, 10^{-5}, 10^{-6}, ... We shall say more about this, later.)

Note that if we include an extra zero at the end, *after* the decimal point, then it does not add any value to the number; for example, 3.2 is the same as 3.20, because $\frac{32}{10} = \frac{320}{100}$.

Addition of decimal fractions. Addition is done as for ordinary integers, e.g., to do $12.345 + 39.78$, we 'line up' the decimal points as shown below:

$$\begin{array}{rr} & 12.345 \\ + & 39.78 \\ \hline & 52.125 \\ \hline \end{array}$$

This may be understood in different ways, for example: 39.78 is the same as 39.780, so the addition corresponds to the addition of two fractions:

$$\frac{12345}{1000} + \frac{39780}{1000} = \frac{12345 + 39780}{1000} = \frac{52125}{1000},$$

and the decimal form of the last fraction is 52.125, as obtained earlier.

Multiplication of decimal fractions. Multiplication is handled as follows. Consider the product 12.34×3.2. Translated into fractions, this reads:

$$\frac{1234}{100} \times \frac{32}{10} = \frac{1234 \times 32}{100 \times 10} = \frac{39488}{1000},$$

hence the answer is 39.488. Using 'long multiplication', the working is done as follows:

$$\begin{array}{rr} & 12.34 \\ \times & 3.2 \\ \hline & 2468 \\ & 3702 \\ \hline & 39.488 \\ \hline \end{array}$$

Similarly, for the product 31.213×14.79, we write:

$$\begin{array}{rr} & 31.213 \\ \times & 14.79 \\ \hline & 461.64027 \\ \hline \end{array}$$

We see that the number of decimal digits in the product is always the *sum* of the numbers of decimal digits in the multiplicands.

In general, arithmetic with decimal fractions is done exactly as it is done for 'ordinary' integers, with the decimal point placed appropriately *after* all the additions, multiplications, etc., have been done.

4.5 Percentages

A **PERCENTAGE** is a fraction whose denominator is 100. The word 'percent' means *per cent*—with 100 as base; the original words are in Latin—*per centum*. When so written, the numerator is called the **RATE** per cent of the fraction.

EXAMPLE 3. *The fraction* $\frac{5}{100}$ *may also be written as '5 per cent' or '5 out of* 100'. *It is commonly written as* 5%. *Similarly, the fraction* $\frac{10}{100}$, *which is the same as* $\frac{1}{10}$, *is written as* 10%.

To express a given fraction as a percentage we must find an equivalent fraction with denominator 100. For example, for the fraction $\frac{2}{5}$, since 5 'goes' 20 times into 100, we have:

$$\frac{2}{5} = \frac{2 \times 20}{5 \times 20} = \frac{40}{100} = 40\%.$$

As the denominator of a percentage is always 100, it is easy to compare two percentages and see which one is greater; e.g., we have $7\% > 6\%$, and $19\% > 17\%$.

A very common use of percentages is in describing test scores. Thus, a score of 11 marks out of a maximum mark of 20 would be denoted by $\frac{11}{20}$ as a fraction, and by 55% as a percentage. A score of 19 marks out of 25 would be written as $\frac{19}{25}$ or 76%.

Percentages are made use of heavily in daily life, and particularly so in commercial applications. Some examples are given below.

PRICE DISCOUNT. A shopkeeper may advertise a '10% discount' to increase the sales of some item; this means that he is going to *reduce* his prices by $\frac{10}{100}$ or $\frac{1}{10}$. So if the unit price was ₹200 before the discount, it would be decreased by $\frac{1}{10} \times$ ₹200 = ₹20; the price would now be ₹180.

On the other hand, an economist may report on the price situation in the nation and say: "The cost of food has gone up by 7%". This means that, on the average, prices of food items have increased by 7%. So, if some food item used to cost ₹50, now its cost would be higher by $\frac{7}{100} \times$ ₹50 = ₹3.50; that is, the price would now be ₹53.50.

SALES TAX. Governments charge taxes on items sold in shops. The customer bears this cost, and the shopkeeper passes the sum to the Government. So sales tax is a sort of income to the Government, meant to be used for public benefit such as maintenance of roads. The tax is computed as a percentage; e.g., if the cost of an item is ₹ 200, and the sales tax is computed at the rate of 11%, then the price to the customer is

$$₹\,200 + ₹\left(\frac{11}{100} \times 200\right) = ₹\,(200+22) = ₹\,222.$$

PROFIT OR LOSS PERCENT. When an investment is made in a business venture, at the end of the year the profit or loss is computed by the accountant and reported to the investor. This is usually given as a percentage. Thus, a 'profit of 25%' means that an investor who invested a sum of ₹ 50,000 would get a profit of $\frac{25}{100} \times ₹\,50,000 = ₹\,12,500$.

COMMISSION PAID TO A BROKER. Sometimes we opt to make a financial transaction through an agent, in order to avoid inconveniences like standing in a queue. For example, we may purchase a train ticket through a travel agency. Or we may make an investment in the stock market through a broker; or we may buy or sell land through a real estate agent. All we do is to pay the agent our part of the money, and he or she then does the work for us. Of course, we have to bear some charge for this, and the charge is computed as a percentage. For example, the brokerage may be computed at, say, 3%. This means that the cost borne by us would be 3% greater than the cost incurred if we had done the work ourselves.

GROWTH RATE OF A POPULATION. In describing how the population of a country or region has changed over the course of a year, we use percentages. We may say, for example, "The population of Mumbai has increased by 3% over the last year"; or, "The number of people in the IT industry has been increasing at the rate of 11% for the last five years"and so on.

Here are some notable data.

- The population of Mumbai has increased at an average rate of nearly 3.2% per year over the last quarter of a century. This has meant a growth of population from 7.35 million in the year 1975 to 16.09 million in the year 2000.
- During the same time period (1975–2000), the population of New Delhi grew at an average rate of 4.1% per year, from 4.43 million to 12.44 million, and the population of Dhaka in Bangladesh grew at a rate of 7.0% per year.

- If a population grows by 10% each year, within just 80 years the population would get multiplied by a factor of over two thousand!

Solved examples

EXAMPLE 4. *Express the following as percentages:* $\frac{3}{16}$; $\frac{7}{20}$; $\frac{13}{40}$.

Dividing using long multiplication, we get:

$$\frac{3}{16} = 0.1875; \qquad \frac{7}{20} = 0.35; \qquad \frac{13}{40} = 0.325.$$

It follows that

$$\frac{3}{16} = 18.75\%; \qquad \frac{7}{20} = 35\%; \qquad \frac{13}{40} = 32.5\%.$$

EXAMPLE 5. *(a)* 20% *of which number is* 18*? (b)* 34% *of which number is* 170*?*

Write x for the desired number; then the equations to be solved are, for (a):

$$\frac{18}{x} = \frac{20}{100}, \qquad \therefore\ x = 18 \times \frac{100}{20} = 90, \qquad \therefore \text{ The desired number is 90;}$$

and for (b):

$$\frac{170}{x} = \frac{34}{100}, \qquad \therefore\ x = 170 \times \frac{100}{34} = 500, \qquad \therefore \text{ The desired number is 500.}$$

EXAMPLE 6. *The price of an item went up by* 10% *one week, and came down by* 10% *the next week. Did it come back to its original level?*

Since the actual price of the item is not given, we take it to be 100 units of money (the currency does not play a part; it could be in any currency). A 10% increase then takes the price to $100 + (10\% \times 100) = 110$ units.

The following week the price comes down by 10% of the *new* price; i.e., 10% of 110, and *not* 10% of 100. So the new price is

$$110 - (10\% \times 110) = 110 - 11 = 99.$$

So the price in the second week is 99 units. This means that it has *not* come back to its original level. Rather, the 'net' change is a *decrease*, by 1%.

EXAMPLE 7. *A customer is offered the following two alternatives for the purchase of a TV: (a) 20% discount on the after-sales-tax figure, with sales tax being levied at 5%; (b) 20% discount on the before-sales-tax figure, following which sales tax is levied at 5%). Which of these two is better for the customer?*

As earlier, since we are not told the actual price before sales tax and discounting, we take it to be 100 units. In alternative (a) we first levy the sales tax of 5% giving an after-tax price of $100+(5\%\times 100)=105$ units. Now we apply a discount of 20% on this figure:

$$105-(20\%\times 105) \;=\; 105-21 \;=\; 84.$$

This is the net price paid by the customer under alternative (a).

Under alternative (b), we first apply the 20% discount:

$$100-(20\%\times 100)=100-20=80$$

A sales tax of 5% is now levied on this figure:

$$80+(5\%\times 80) \;=\; 80+4 \;=\; 84.$$

This is the net price paid by the customer under alternative (b). We see that for the customer, the two alternatives are the same.

Remark

Should we have expected this answer? Or does it go against intuition? Many people would find it counter-intuitive, but in mathematical terms, it is simply an expression of the commutativity of multiplication: $ab=ba$. For, under alternative (a) the net price paid is 80% of 105% of the original price, and under alternative (b) the net price paid is 105% of 80% of the original price. Since $80\%\times 105\%=105\%\times 80\%$, the two options yield the same result.

EXAMPLE 8. *Express the following using algebra: "A is B% greater than C".*

To get A we must add $B\%$ of C to C:

$$A \;=\; C+(B\%\times C) \;=\; C+\left(\frac{B}{100}\times C\right) \;=\; C+\frac{BC}{100} \;=\; \frac{100C+BC}{100} \;=\; \frac{C(100+B)}{100}.$$

This is the desired relation.

EXAMPLE 9. *Does it make sense to talk of a percentage greater than* 100%?

Yes, of course. It may not be possible to get a test score exceeding 100%, but one *can* have a price increase of over 100%. For example, if the unit price of an item were to go up from ₹20 to ₹40, then the percentage increase would be

$$\frac{40-20}{20} \times 100\% = \frac{20}{20} \times 100\% = 100\%.$$

If the unit price were to go up from ₹20 to ₹50, then the percentage increase would be

$$\frac{50-20}{20} \times 100\% = \frac{30}{20} \times 100\% = 150\%.$$

A percentage increase of 200% would mean that the quantity has *tripled*, and a percentage increase of 300% would mean that the quantity has *quadrupled*.

Remark

On a lighter note we may add that there have been instances where a student writing an examination had so powerfully impressed the examiners that they awarded a mark greater than 100%! Such was the case with the great nuclear physicist Abdus Salam when he wrote his M.Sc. examination in pre-Independence Lahore (presently in Pakistan).

EXERCISES

1. If A is 50% of B, what percentage of A is B?

2. If A is 25% greater than B, what percentage of A is B?

3. If A is $x\%$ of B, what percentage of $5B$ is $2A$?

4. If the unit price of an item goes up by 10%, by what percentage must it come down to get back to its original level?

5. If the unit price of an item goes down by 20%, by what percentage must it go up to get back to its original level?

6. Which of these would be more attractive to a customer: two successive discounts of 10% on the sale price of an item, or a single discount of 20%?

7. Which of these would be more attractive to a customer: two successive discounts of 10% and 20%, respectively, on the sale price of an item, or a single discount of 30%?

8. The price of an item is reduced by 20% during one week. The following week the price is again brought down by 10%. By what percentage is the final price less than the original price?

9. *If A is B% of C, then C is D% more than A.* Given this statement, express D in terms of A, B and C.

10. If A is x% of B, and C is y% of D, what percentage of BD is AC?

4.6 Fractions on the number line

We have earlier seen how the integers may be placed on a number line. We now show how fractions may be defined and represented using the number line. The number line looks like this:

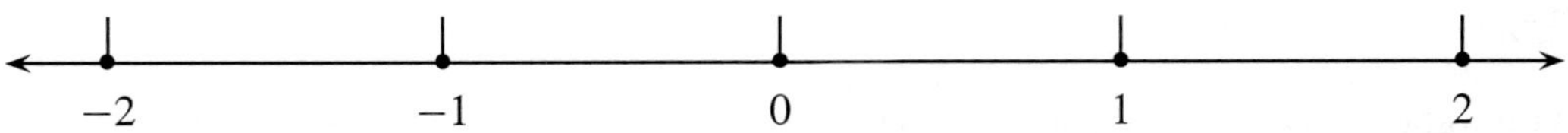

Figure 4.5

If we divide the portions between the successive tick marks into two equal parts and place ticks at the dividing points, then *the numbers represented by the points with tick marks are the fractions with denominator* 2:

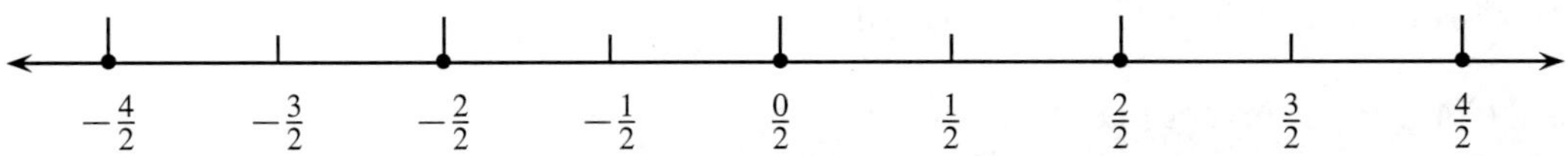

Figure 4.6

Comparing the two pictures, we see directly that 1 is the same as $\frac{2}{2}$, 2 is the same as $\frac{4}{2}$, and so on. Importantly, we see that 0 is the same as $\frac{0}{2}$.

If, instead, we divide the portions between successive marks into *three* equal parts and place ticks at the dividing points, then *the numbers represented by the points with tick marks are the fractions with denominator* 3:

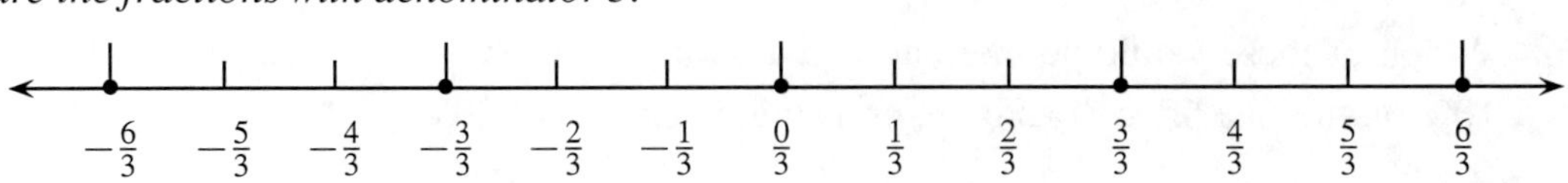

Figure 4.7

Comparing this with the original picture, we see directly that $1 = \frac{3}{3}$; $2 = \frac{6}{3}$; $0 = \frac{0}{3}$; and so on.

We can go on in this manner and define the fractions with denominator 4, with denominator 5, and so on.

4.7 Rational numbers

We know by now that fractions are numbers, and that we can do arithmetic with them—addition, subtraction, multiplication, and so on. Integers may be regarded as fractions in which the denominator divides exactly into the numerator; for example, the integer 3 may be written in any of the following equivalent forms:

$$\frac{3}{1}, \quad \frac{6}{2}, \quad \frac{9}{3}, \quad \frac{12}{4}, \quad \frac{15}{5}, \quad \ldots.$$

From now on, we shall think of integers as merely a special type of fraction. Thus, $\frac{a}{b}$ is an integer if b is a divisor of a.

The general name that mathematicians use for fractions is **RATIONAL NUMBER**. A rational number is defined to be one that can be written as one integer divided by another (which must naturally be non-zero). The family of such numbers includes all possible integers and all possible fractions.

If we put all the rational numbers into one basket, what do we get? There is no limit to how many fractions there are; their supply is endless. So the basket would have to be quite big! The collection of all the rational numbers is called the **SET OF RATIONAL NUMBERS**. Mathematicians like to use the symbol $\mathbf{Q}$ when they talk about this set. (Recall that the symbol for the collection of all integers is $\mathbf{Z}$, while the symbol for the collection of all positive integers is $\mathbf{N}$.)

We saw above how the fractions can be placed on the number line. The integers by themselves yield a picture like this:

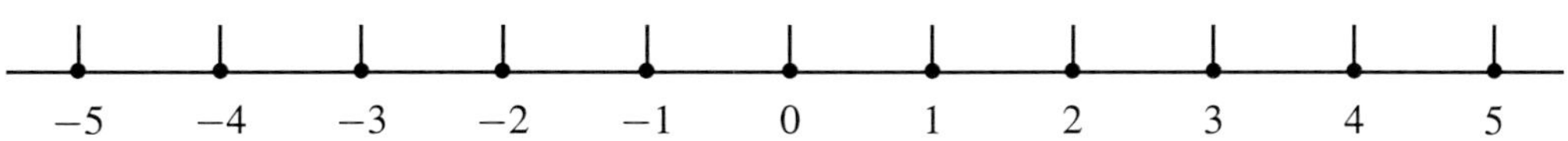

Figure 4.8

We naturally cannot show all the integers on the line, as there are too many of them; we would need a line that is endless in extent. We can, however, show *all the integers that lie between two given points on the line* (the above picture shows all the integers between

$-5\frac{1}{2}$ and $5\frac{1}{2}$.) But in the case of fractions, even if we limit our attention to a tiny portion of the line, *we still cannot show all the fractions belonging to that portion*. For example, let us look only at the portion of the line that extends from 0 to 1. Putting in all the fractions with denominators of 3 or less, we get the following picture:

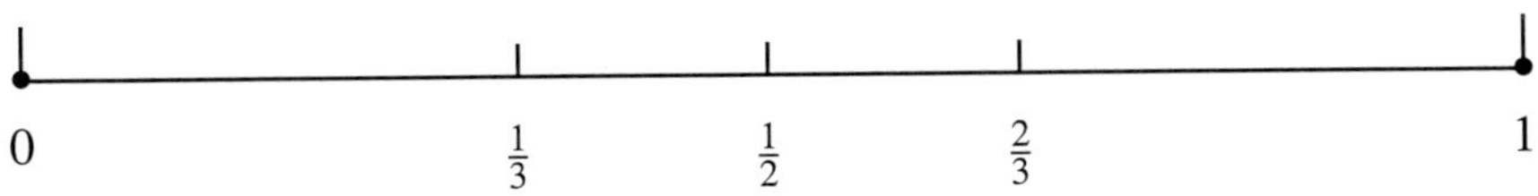

Figure 4.9

Now let us put in the fractions with denominator 4, namely, $\frac{1}{4}$ and $\frac{3}{4}$ (note that $\frac{2}{4}$ is already present, since $\frac{2}{4} = \frac{1}{2}$):

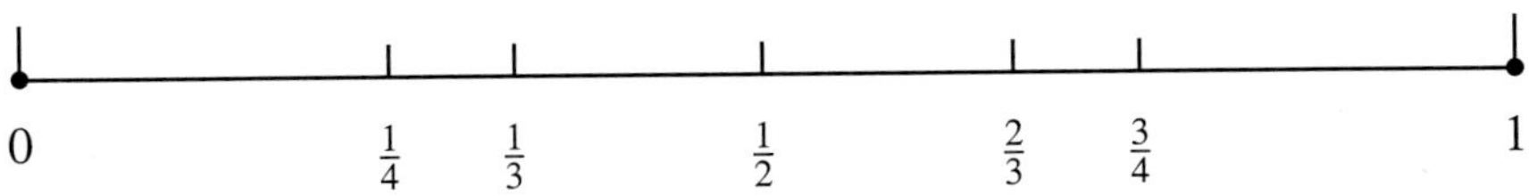

Figure 4.10

In this picture we do not see any of the fractions with denominator 5; so we put these in as well, and we get:

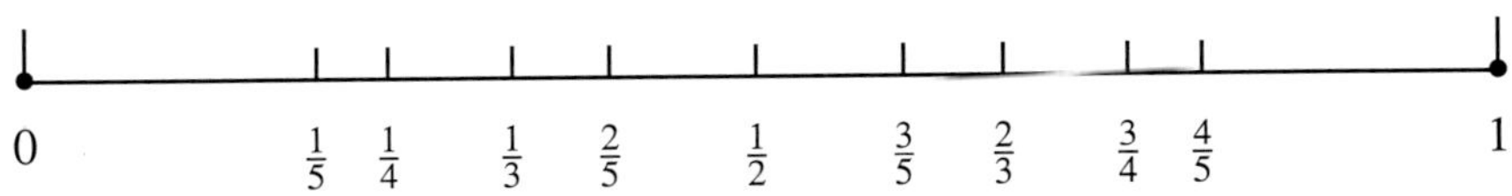

Figure 4.11

What about the fractions with denominator 6? Some of them are already marked ($\frac{2}{6} = \frac{1}{3}$; $\frac{3}{6} = \frac{1}{2}$; and $\frac{4}{6} = \frac{2}{3}$), but $\frac{1}{6}$ and $\frac{5}{6}$ are absent, so we put these in too:

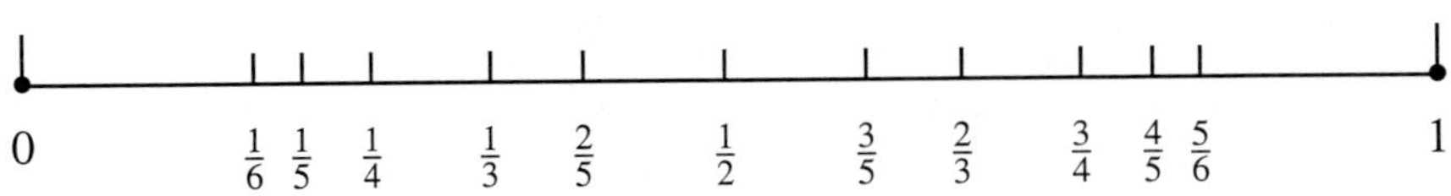

Figure 4.12

As you will easily see, this is an endless process. There are too many fractions to put in, and too little space to write them all down! We see here a vital difference between the collection of all the integers and the collection of all the fractions: both collections are limitless in number (the mathematician would say that both collections are **INFINITE** in size); but whereas the integers are neatly spaced out on the number line, with gaps of fixed length 1 between them, the fractions are 'tightly packed' on the same line, leaving no gaps of any length at all.

This means that in the set of rational numbers, we cannot speak of 'adjacency' or 'neighbourliness'. We can speak of two *integers* as being adjacent to each other (e.g., 2 and 3 are adjacent to each other—they are each other's neighbours), but we can never say this of two fractions. For example, $\frac{1}{3}$ and $\frac{1}{2}$ are not neighbours, because the fraction $\frac{2}{5}$ sits in-between them. And $\frac{1}{3}$ and $\frac{2}{5}$ are not neighbours either, because $\frac{3}{8}$ sits in-between them. And $\frac{1}{3}$ and $\frac{3}{8}$ are not neighbours either, because $\frac{4}{11}$ sits in-between them! We can go on like this for ever—because *between any two rational numbers, no matter how close, there lies at least one rational number.*

This simple observation leads to a wonderful conclusion. Given any two rational numbers x and y, we can always find another one lying between them; call it z. The same rule can be applied to x and z, and we get a rational number lying between x and z (and therefore also between x and y); call it w. Now the rule can be applied to x and w, and we get yet another rational number lying between x and w (and therefore also between x and y). This can be continued endlessly, so we arrive at the following very remarkable fact:

> *Between any two rational numbers—no matter how close—there are infinitely many rational numbers.*

Now you will see why we described the rational numbers as 'tightly packed' on the number line, leaving no gaps of any length! Mathematicians prefer to use the phrase 'densely packed': *The rational numbers are dense on the number line.*

Finding in-between rational numbers

A neat formula of finding a rational number which lies between two given rational numbers is the following:

> *If a, b, c, d are integers such that b and d are positive and $\frac{a}{b}$ and $\frac{c}{d}$ are unequal fractions, then the fraction $\frac{a+c}{b+d}$ lies in-between $\frac{a}{b}$ and $\frac{c}{d}$.*

EXAMPLE 10. Take the two fractions $\frac{2}{3}$ and $\frac{3}{4}$. Applying the rule, we get the fraction $\frac{2+3}{3+4}$ or $\frac{5}{7}$. It is not too hard to check that $\frac{5}{7}$ lies between $\frac{2}{3}$ and $\frac{3}{4}$. Indeed, the decimal forms of these fractions are:

$$\frac{2}{3} = 0.66666\ldots, \qquad \frac{5}{7} = 0.714285\ldots, \qquad \frac{3}{4} = 0.75, \qquad \therefore \frac{2}{3} < \frac{5}{7} < \frac{3}{4}.$$

We might prefer checking the order relations by computing the appropriate equivalent fractions. In this case, we have: $\text{LCM}(3,4,7) = 84$, and

$$\frac{2}{3} = \frac{56}{84}, \qquad \frac{5}{7} = \frac{60}{84}, \qquad \frac{3}{4} = \frac{63}{84}.$$

Since $56 < 60 < 63$, we get $\frac{2}{3} < \frac{5}{7} < \frac{3}{4}$.

EXAMPLE 11. We shall use the rule repeatedly to find different fractions between $x = \frac{1}{5}$ and $y = \frac{1}{4}$. From x and y, we get: $z = \frac{2}{9}$; then from x and z, we get $w = \frac{3}{14}$; then from x and w, we get $u = \frac{4}{19}$; then from x and u, we get $v = \frac{5}{24}$; etc. We may arrange these fractions in order as follows:

$$\frac{1}{5}, \quad \frac{5}{24}, \quad \frac{4}{19}, \quad \frac{3}{14}, \quad \frac{2}{9}, \quad \frac{1}{4}.$$

EXAMPLE 12. The rule can also be applied if negative integers are involved, but care is needed: we must write the fractions in the correct way, with *positive* denominators. For example, take the fractions $-\frac{2}{3}$ and $\frac{7}{5}$. Writing $-\frac{2}{3}$ as $\frac{-2}{3}$ and applying the rule, we get the fraction

$$\frac{-2+7}{3+5} = \frac{5}{8},$$

and it is easy to check that $\frac{5}{8}$ lies between $-\frac{2}{3}$ and $\frac{7}{5}$. But if we write $-\frac{2}{3}$ as $\frac{2}{-3}$ then when we apply the rule we get

$$\frac{2+7}{-3+5} = \frac{9}{2},$$

and this certainly does not lie between $-\frac{2}{3}$ and $\frac{7}{5}$.

EXAMPLE 13. The following statement derives from the one made above: *If a and b are unequal, positive integers, then the fraction $\frac{a+1}{b+1}$ lies in-between $\frac{a}{b}$ and* 1.

For example, $\frac{3}{5}$ lies between $\frac{2}{3}$ and 1, and $\frac{8}{5}$ lies between $\frac{7}{4}$ and 1.

The equal-fractions rule

In the above rule, we stated that $\frac{a}{b}$ and $\frac{c}{d}$ must be *unequal fractions*. What would happen if the fractions are equal? In this case the fraction $\frac{a+c}{b+d}$ gets 'squeezed' or 'sandwiched' between two equal numbers, which means that it must be equal to both of them! So we get another rule:

If a, b, c, d are integers such that b and d are positive and $\frac{a}{b} = \frac{c}{d}$, *then the fraction* $\frac{a+c}{b+d}$ *is equal to both of these fractions.*

This rule, called the **EQUAL-FRACTIONS RULE**, is useful in many situations. (It is found to be of use even in geometry!) It can be extended in many ways, e.g.:

1. If $\frac{a}{b}, \frac{c}{d}, \frac{e}{f}, \ldots$ are equal fractions, with $b, d, f, \cdots > 0$, then the fraction

$$\frac{a+c+e+\cdots}{b+d+f+\cdots}$$

is equal to all of them.

2. If a, b, c, d are integers such that b and d are positive and $\frac{a}{b} = \frac{c}{d}$, then

$$\frac{a}{b} = \frac{a+c}{b+d} = \frac{a+2c}{b+2d} = \frac{2a+c}{2b+d} = \frac{2a+3c}{2b+3d} = \cdots = \frac{c}{d},$$

$$\frac{a}{b} = \frac{a-c}{b-d} = \frac{a-2c}{b-2d} = \frac{2a-c}{2b-d} = \frac{2a-3c}{2b-3d} = \cdots = \frac{c}{d}.$$

In the second statement, it is assumed that none of the denominators is zero.

Remark

Some of these rules have a very long history, going back to the Greek era, though they were originally expressed in the language of ratio (we shall be studying this topic shortly). The following is known as the **RULE OF COMPONENDO**:

$$\text{If } \frac{a}{b} = \frac{c}{d}, \text{ then } \frac{a+b}{b} = \frac{c+d}{d},$$

and the following is the **RULE OF DIVIDENDO**:

$$\text{If } \frac{a}{b} = \frac{c}{d}, \text{ then } \frac{a-b}{b} = \frac{c-d}{d},$$

Combining the two, we get the **RULE OF COMPONENDO-DIVIDENDO**:

$$\text{If } \frac{a}{b} = \frac{c}{d}, \text{ then } \frac{a+b}{a-b} = \frac{c+d}{c-d}.$$

In all these statements, it is assumed that none of the denominators is zero.

4.8 Miscellaneous exercises

1. Among the gases in our atmosphere, by volume nitrogen accounts for 78%; oxygen accounts for 21%; carbon dioxide occurs to about 3 parts in 10,000. The remaining portion is mostly the 'noble gas' argon. What percentage of the atmosphere does argon occupy, by volume?

2. At a school party, $\frac{1}{3}$ of the people attending are students from school A and $\frac{1}{2}$ of the people are students from school B. The remaining people are all teachers from the two schools. If the number of teachers from A is 12, and the number of teachers from B is $1\frac{1}{2}$ times the number of teachers from A, find the total number of people at the party.

3. I go for a hike over a trail of length $17\frac{1}{2}$ km. I halt for rest every one-fifth of the journey. How much distance do I have left to cover when I take my third halt?

4. Referring to my hike in the previous problem, if I increase my speed by one quarter, by what percentage does the hiking time come down? (I walk at a uniform speed throughout the trail.)

5. I have two jugs in from of me, A and B. Jug A contains 200 ml of rum; jug B contains 200 ml of coffee. I take 20 ml of coffee from jug B and pour it into jug A. I now stir the mixture in jug A thoroughly, and pour back 20 ml of the mixture into jug B.

   (a) Of the 200 ml of mixture in jug B, what fraction is rum?

   (b) Of the 200 ml of mixture in jug A, what fraction is rum?

   (c) At the end of the exchanges, is there more rum in B or more coffee in A?

6. Four people (A, B, C and D) order a pot of tea. A drinks $\frac{1}{2}$ of the tea; after him, B drinks $\frac{1}{2}$ of what is left in the pot; then C drinks $\frac{1}{2}$ of what is left; and D finishes the rest. If D drinks 100 ml, how much tea was there in the pot at the start?

7. Four people (A, B, C and D) are sharing a jug of wine. A drinks $\frac{1}{2}$ of the wine; after him, B drinks $\frac{1}{3}$ of what is left in the jug; then C drinks $\frac{1}{4}$ of what is left; and D finishes the rest. If D drinks 2 cups of wine, how much wine was there in the jug at the start?

8. If the two sides of a rectangle are increased in length, respectively, by 20% and 30%, by what percentage does the area increase? (The area of a rectangle is obtained by taking the product of the two sides.)

9. If one side of a rectangle is increased in length by 20%, by what percentage must the other side be reduced in length so that the area of the rectangle stays unchanged?

10. (a) Given that $A = \frac{1}{3} + \frac{1}{4} + \frac{1}{5}$ and $B = \frac{1}{4} + \frac{1}{5} + \frac{1}{6}$, find by what percentage B is less than A.

    (b) Given that $A = \frac{1}{4} + \frac{1}{5} + \frac{1}{6}$ and $B = \frac{1}{8} + \frac{1}{9} + \frac{1}{10}$, find by what percentage A is more than B.

11. Let x denote the sum $\frac{1}{5} + \frac{1}{6} + \frac{1}{7} + \frac{1}{8}$. Without actually computing the value of x, show that x lies between $\frac{1}{2}$ and 1.

12. Let y denote the quantity $1 - \frac{1}{2} + \frac{1}{3} - \frac{1}{4} + \frac{1}{5} - \frac{1}{6} + \frac{1}{7} - \frac{1}{8} + \frac{1}{9} - \frac{1}{10}$. Without actually computing the value of y,

    (a) Show that y lies between $\frac{1}{2}$ and 1.

    (b) Show that y lies between $\frac{7}{12}$ and $\frac{5}{6}$.

Chapter 5

Fractions: Special Topics

In this chapter we continue our study of fractions, focusing on some of their unusual and special features.

5.1 Recurring decimals

For certain fractions, we find that their decimal forms 'end' at some point. For example, we have

$$\frac{1}{2} = 0.5, \qquad \frac{1}{4} = 0.25, \qquad \frac{3}{8} = 0.375, \qquad \frac{7}{40} = 0.175, \qquad \frac{11}{16} = 0.6875.$$

Such decimals are called **TERMINATING DECIMALS**; their decimal forms 'terminate'. The reason is easy to see: *the fractions can be written in equivalent forms in which the denominators are powers of* 10. For example, we have $\frac{1}{2} = \frac{5}{10} = 0.5$, and for the other fractions:

$$\frac{1}{4} = \frac{25}{100} = 0.25, \qquad \frac{3}{8} = \frac{375}{1000} = 0.375,$$

$$\frac{7}{40} = \frac{175}{1000} = 0.175, \qquad \frac{11}{16} = \frac{6875}{10000} = 0.6875.$$

But some fractions behave very differently. Let us see what happens when we try to get the decimal form of the fraction $\frac{1}{3}$. When we do the division, we find ourselves unable to 'end' the computation! The picture shows us why.

$$\begin{array}{r|l} & 0 \cdot 3\ \ 3\ \ 3\ \ 3\ \ 3\ \ 3\ \ 3\ \ \cdot\ \ \cdot \\ \hline 3 & 1 \cdot 0\ \ 0\ \ 0\ \ 0\ \ 0\ \ 0\ \ 0\ \ \cdot\ \ \cdot \end{array}$$

As you can check readily, each time the divisor goes 3 times into the dividend, and each time the remainder is 1. So the quotient-remainder pair are exactly the same each time, and we get an endless decimal:

$$\frac{1}{3} = 0.333333333333\ldots.$$

This is generally denoted by writing:

$$\frac{1}{3} = 0.\overline{3}.$$

The bar over the 3 is placed to indicate that it repeats endlessly. We call such a decimal fraction a **RECURRING DECIMAL**, or a **REPEATING DECIMAL**. The portion which repeats (a single '3' in this case) is called the **REPETEND**.

If we work out the decimal form of the fraction $\frac{1}{11}$ we get:

$$\begin{array}{r|l} & 0 \cdot 0\ \ 9\ \ 0\ \ 9\ \ 0\ \ 9\ \ 0\ \ \cdot\ \ \cdot \\ \hline 11 & 1 \cdot 0\ \ 0\ \ 0\ \ 0\ \ 0\ \ 0\ \ 0\ \ \cdot\ \ \cdot \end{array}$$

Here we observe that the quotients are alternately 0 and 9, and the pattern repeats every *two* divisions; so we write

$$\frac{1}{11} = 0.0909090909\ldots = 0.\overline{09}.$$

The bar is placed over the string '09' to show that it repeats endlessly. The repetend here is 09.

With some fractions, we find that there is an initial string of digits which appears just once and does not repeat after that; for example:

$$\frac{1}{6} = 0.166666666\ldots = 0.1\overline{6}.$$

Here we see an initial '1' which does not repeat. The portion which repeats is '6' (this is the repetend), so the bar covers only the 6, and not the 1.

This decimal is an example of a **MIXED RECURRING DECIMAL**. If there is no initial non-repeating portion, then it is a **PURE RECURRING DECIMAL**. Other examples of fractions that yield mixed recurring decimals are $\frac{5}{6}$ and $\frac{1}{12}$:

$$\frac{5}{6} = 0.566666\ldots = 0.5\overline{6}, \qquad \frac{1}{12} = 0.0833333\ldots = 0.08\overline{3}.$$

Which fractions yield terminating decimals?

We saw above that the decimal forms of the following fractions terminate:

$$\frac{1}{2}, \quad \frac{1}{4}, \quad \frac{3}{8}, \quad \frac{7}{40}, \quad \frac{11}{16},$$

whereas the decimal forms of the following fractions recur:

$$\frac{1}{3}, \quad \frac{1}{11}, \quad \frac{1}{6}, \quad \frac{5}{6}, \quad \frac{1}{12}.$$

Given any irreducible fraction (i.e., it has been reduced to its lowest terms), is there a simple way of knowing (without fully dividing out) whether its decimal form will be terminating, pure recurring, or mixed recurring? Indeed there is. Here is the rule which tells you which fractions will yield terminating decimals:

> *If the denominator of the fraction is a divisor of any power of* 10, *then the decimal form necessarily terminates.*

EXAMPLE 1. Consider the fraction $\frac{7}{8}$. The denominator is a divisor of 1000, because $8 \times 125 = 1000$. To find the decimal form, we multiply both the numerator and denominator by 125, getting:

$$\frac{7}{8} = \frac{125 \times 7}{125 \times 8} = \frac{875}{1000} = 0.875.$$

Or consider the fraction $\frac{19}{160}$. The denominator is a divisor of 100000, because $160 \times 625 = 100000$; so we have:

$$\frac{19}{160} = \frac{625 \times 19}{625 \times 160} = \frac{11875}{100000} = 0.11875.$$

The general idea is: if the fraction is $\frac{a}{b}$ and the denominator b is a divisor of a power of 10, say

$$c \times b = \text{some power of } 10,$$

then we have:

$$\frac{a}{b} = \frac{c \times a}{c \times b} = \frac{c \times a}{\text{that power of 10}},$$

and the decimal form becomes instantly 'visible'.

Let us push this line of thinking further. Since $10 = 2 \times 5$, the primes that divide any power of 10 are only 2 and 5. This tells us that if the denominator has to divide a power of 10, *it must not be divisible by any prime other than* 2 *and* 5; so it is either a power of 2, or a power of 5, or a product of a power of 2 and a power of 5.

EXAMPLE 2. Consider the fractions $\frac{15}{32}$, $\frac{61}{125}$ and $\frac{49}{160}$. Their denominators are not divisible by primes other than 2 and 5:

$$\begin{aligned} 32 &= 2 \times 2 \times 2 \times 2 \times 2 &= 2^5, \\ 125 &= 5 \times 5 \times 5 &= 5^3, \\ 160 &= 2 \times 2 \times 2 \times 2 \times 2 \times 5 &= 2^5 \times 5. \end{aligned}$$

As expected, we find that the decimal forms terminate:

$$\frac{15}{32} = 0.46875, \qquad \frac{61}{125} = 0.488, \qquad \frac{49}{160} = 0.30625.$$

In summary, we write the following:

> *Let $\frac{a}{b}$ be a fraction in lowest terms. Its decimal form terminates if the denominator b is of the form $(2 \times 2 \times \cdots \times 2) \times (5 \times 5 \times \cdots \times 5)$, that is, if b is a product of a power of* 2 *and a power of* 5*. This includes the possibility that b is a power of* 2 *alone, or a power of* 5 *alone.*

Which fractions yield recurring decimals?

Continuing the above line of thinking, we see that if the denominator of a fraction given in lowest terms is not a divisor of *any* power of 10, then the fraction just cannot be written in the form

$$\frac{\text{some integer}}{\text{some power of 10}}.$$

In this case, the decimal form is either pure recurring or mixed recurring.

But can it happen that a number does not divide *any* power of 10? Yes! Since the prime divisors of 10 are 2 and 5, this will happen precisely when the number has a prime divisor *other* than 2 and 5. For example, 6 will not be a divisor of any power of 10, as it has the prime divisor 3; nor will any of the following: 12, 15, 14, 21, etc. We deduce that:

The decimal form of a fraction $\frac{a}{b}$ given in lowest terms recurs if the denominator b has a prime divisor other than 2 and 5.

Why do we include the words “in lowest terms”? The reason may be illustrated by studying a specific example. Take the fraction $\frac{2}{5}$ which gives rise to a terminating decimal, 0.4. Next, consider the fraction $\frac{6}{15}$, which is equivalent to $\frac{2}{5}$. Its denominator is divisible by a prime number other than 2 and 5 (namely, by 3), yet it gives rise to a terminating decimal (namely, 0.4). So does this fact go against what was stated above? No, because $\frac{6}{15}$ is not in its lowest terms.

It remains only to check when we get a pure recurring decimal, and when we get a mixed recurring decimal. We take this up in the exercise set below.

EXERCISES

1. Work out the decimal forms of the following fractions:

$$\frac{2}{3}, \quad \frac{4}{9}, \quad \frac{7}{11}, \quad \frac{9}{11}.$$

2. Work out the decimal forms of the following fractions:

$$\frac{7}{12}, \quad \frac{8}{15}, \quad \frac{5}{22}, \quad \frac{12}{55}.$$

3. Work out the decimal forms of the following fractions:

$$\frac{1}{7}, \quad \frac{2}{7}, \quad \frac{3}{7}, \quad \frac{4}{7}, \quad \frac{5}{7}, \quad \frac{6}{7}.$$

4. Work out the decimal forms of the following fractions:

$$\frac{1}{13}, \quad \frac{2}{13}, \quad \frac{3}{13}, \quad \frac{4}{13}, \quad \frac{5}{13}, \quad \frac{6}{13}.$$

5. Find the fractions that yield the following decimal fractions:

$$0.1\overline{3}, \quad 0.1\overline{9}, \quad 0.2\overline{1}, \quad 0.3\overline{6}.$$

6. Find the fractions that yield the following decimal fractions:

$$0.\overline{13}, \quad 0.\overline{25}, \quad 0.\overline{19}, \quad 0.\overline{53}.$$

7. Which of the following will divide some power of 10?

$$8, \quad 9, \quad 15, \quad 20, \quad 25, \quad 30, \quad 40, \quad 48, \quad 64.$$

8. We found out above that the decimal form of $\frac{a}{b}$ (given in lowest terms) recurs if b is divisible by a prime number other than 2 and 5. Each of the following fractions gives rise to a recurring decimal fraction:

$$\frac{2}{3}, \quad \frac{5}{12}, \quad \frac{7}{15}, \quad \frac{5}{11}, \quad \frac{13}{22}, \quad \frac{20}{23}, \quad \frac{5}{27}, \quad \frac{19}{30}, \quad \frac{12}{19}, \quad \frac{13}{18}.$$

Separate out those which yield pure recurring decimals from those that yield mixed recurring decimals. Then study the list and see how, if you are given a fraction whose decimal form recurs, you will be able to predict whether it is of the pure recurring type or the mixed recurring type.

9. Study the decimal forms of $\frac{15}{32}$, $\frac{61}{125}$ and $\frac{49}{160}$:

$$\frac{15}{32} = 0.46875, \qquad \frac{61}{125} = 0.488, \qquad \frac{49}{160} = 0.30625.$$

Now study the prime factorisations of the denominators:

$$32 = 2 \times 2 \times 2 \times 2 \times 2, \quad 125 = 5 \times 5 \times 5, \quad 160 = (2 \times 2 \times 2 \times 2 \times 2) \times 5.$$

What relationship do you see between the *number of digits in the decimal forms* and the *prime factorisations*? You may need to study a few more examples before spotting the pattern. Try the following fractions: $\frac{73}{400}$, $\frac{89}{250}$ and $\frac{101}{625}$.

10. For which positive integers n will the decimal form of $\frac{1}{n}$ recur with a *one-digit repetend*? In other words, for which positive integers n does it happen that

$$\frac{1}{n} = 0.aaaaa\ldots$$

for some digit a?

11. For which positive integers n will the decimal form of $\frac{1}{n}$ recur with a *two-digit repetend*? In other words, for which positive integers n does it happen that

$$\frac{1}{n} = 0.ababababab\ldots$$

for some two unequal digits a and b? (Why do we state here that a and b must be unequal?)

12. For which positive integers n will it happen that the decimal form of $\frac{1}{n}$ recurs with a *three-digit repetend*? In other words, for which positive integers n does it happen that

$$\frac{1}{n} = 0.abcabcabcabcabc\ldots$$

for some three digits a, b and c, not all the same?

13. In the division shown below, each letter stands for some digit, and different letters represent different digits:

$$\frac{EVE}{DID} = 0.TALK\,TALK\,TALK\,TALK\ldots = 0.\overline{TALK}.$$

Find the 'code', i.e., which digit is represented by which letter.

14. In the division shown below, each letter stands for some digit, and different letters represent different digits:

$$\frac{NIR}{LON} = 0.FROWN\,FROWN\,FROWN\,FROWN\ldots = 0.\overline{FROWN}.$$

Find the 'code', i.e., which digit is represented by which letter.

15. Let a, b be digits, and let n be the number $a0b$ (i.e., with units digit b, tens digit 0, and hundreds digit a. Show that the decimal expansion of the fraction $\frac{n}{909}$ is

$$\frac{n}{909} = 0.aabb\,aabb\,aabb\,aabb\ldots = 0.\overline{aabb}.$$

Finding the fraction corresponding to a recurring decimal

If we are given a recurring decimal, how do we find the fraction that will produce it? Here is a simple way of proceeding.

EXAMPLE 3. We wish to find the fraction corresponding to the recurring decimal $0.23333333\ldots = 0.2\overline{3}$. Write x for this number:

$$x = 0.23333333\ldots.$$

Multiplying x by 10, and then by 100, we get the decimal forms of $10x$ and $100x$, as shown below:

$$100x = 23.3333333\ldots, \tag{5.1}$$

$$10x = 2.3333333\ldots. \tag{5.2}$$

Observe that *the portions after the decimal points of the numbers* $100x$ *and* $10x$ *are exactly the same*. So, if we subtract $10x$ from $100x$, the portion after the decimal point conveniently drops away, and we are left with

$$100x - 10x = 23 - 2 = 21.$$

It follows that $90x = 21$, and so

$$x = \frac{21}{90} = \frac{7}{30}.$$

So the required fraction is $\frac{7}{30}$.

Remark

You may possibly be troubled by the following thought: When we subtract $10x$ from $100x$, do the portions after the decimal point exactly cancel away? Is there not 'one extra' 3 in the decimal portion of $10x$ as compared with that of $100x$? The answer is, *No*. This is because the sequence of 3s in $0.233333\ldots$ is unending; *it has no 'last'* 3.

This may not entirely satisfy you; if so, you should be comforted by the fact that you are in good company, because many people are confounded by such questions! Another word for 'unending' is **INFINITE**, and the infinite holds many, many charming mysteries for those who study this topic. You will come to know about them when you study higher mathematics.

EXAMPLE 4. We wish to find the fraction that corresponds to the recurring decimal $0.21413413413413\ldots = 0.21\overline{413}$. Write x for this number:

$$x = 0.21413413413413\ldots.$$

Multiplying x by 100, and then by 100000, we get the decimal forms of $100x$ and $100000x$ respectively:

$$100000x = 21413.413413413413\ldots, \tag{5.3}$$

$$100x = 21.413413413413\ldots. \tag{5.4}$$

Observe—as earlier—that the portions after the decimal points of the two numbers are exactly the same. So if we subtract $100x$ from $100000x$, the portion after the decimal point drops away, and we are left with

$$99900x = 21413 - 21 = 21392.$$

It follows that

$$x = \frac{21392}{99900} = \frac{5348}{24975} \qquad \text{(after cancellation).}$$

Is 0.999 . . . equal to 1?

A question that frustrates many students is, *what is the fraction corresponding to the recurring decimal* $0.99999\ldots = 0.\overline{9}$. If we apply the method described above, and write $x = 0.99999\ldots$, then we get:

$$10x = 9.99999999\ldots, \tag{5.5}$$

$$x = 0.99999999\ldots. \tag{5.6}$$

Subtraction yields: $9x = 9$, and therefore, $x = 1$. Hence:

$$0.99999\ldots = 1.$$

Does this answer come as a surprise?

Another way to see the same thing is by considering what happens when the decimal form of $\frac{1}{3}$ is multiplied by 3. The answer ought to be 1, because $\frac{1}{3} \times 3 = 1$. Also, $\frac{1}{3} = 0.33333\cdots = 0.\overline{3}$, and therefore:

$$0.33333\cdots \times 3 = 0.99999\ldots = 0.\overline{9}$$

(note that there are no 'carries' in the multiplication). Comparing the two, we get $0.99999\cdots = 1$, as earlier.

Yet another way of seeing that $0.\overline{9}$ is the same as 1 is by examining the decimal form of the relation $\frac{1}{3} + \frac{2}{3} = 1$. The decimal equivalent of this relation is

$$0.33333\ldots + 0.66666\ldots = 0.99999\ldots.$$

Students often find it hard to accept that $0.99999\cdots = 1$, even though the logic of these explanations cannot be questioned! One way to make the answer look more 'reasonable' is to try subtracting $0.99999\ldots$ from 1. We find that we are unable to 'start' the subtraction anywhere at all, and the answer therefore is $0.00000\cdots = 0.\overline{0}$. Everyone would agree that this number is the same as 0, and this means that $0.99999\ldots$ is the same as 1.

5.2 Powers of integers—on a clothes line!

If we calculate the decimal form of $\frac{1}{99998}$, we find a most curious pattern:

$$\frac{1}{99998} = 0.00001\ 00002\ 00004\ 00008\ 00016\ 00032\ 00064\ 00128\ \ldots,$$

If we 'hide' the leading 0s in the blocks of this decimal expansion (which we have separated using blank spaces), we find the powers of 2 neatly arranged in sequence:

$$1, \quad 2, \quad 4, \quad 8, \quad 16, \quad 32, \quad 64, \quad 128, \quad \ldots.$$

It is as though 'the powers of 2 have been strung on a clothes line'.

Let us now calculate the decimal form of $\frac{1}{99997}$. Here is what we find:

$$\frac{1}{99997} = 0.00001\ 00003\ 00009\ 00027\ 00081\ 00243\ 00729\ 02187\ \ldots,$$

How curious! When we hide the 0s we see the powers of 3 strung on a line:

$$1, \quad 3, \quad 9, \quad 27, \quad 81, \quad 243, \quad 729, \quad 2187, \quad \ldots.$$

This behaviour seems to continue; in the decimal form of $\frac{1}{99996}$,

$$\frac{1}{99996} = 0.00001\ 00004\ 00016\ 00064\ 00256\ 01024\ 04096\ 16384\ \ldots,$$

we see the powers of 4 in sequence (1, 4, 16, 64, 256, ...). And in the decimal expansion of $\frac{1}{99995}$,

$$\frac{1}{99995} = 0.00001\ 00005\ 00025\ 00125\ 00625\ 03125\ 15625\ 78125\ \ldots,$$

we see the powers of 5 in sequence (namely, 1, 5, 25, 125, 625, ...). From these, we can readily guess the decimal forms of $\frac{1}{99994}$, $\frac{1}{99993}$, etc.

How do you explain this behaviour? Please explore the matter further! Does the property extend to fractions like $\frac{1}{99989}$, $\frac{1}{99988}$, $\frac{1}{99987}$, etc?

And what happens when the powers grow to more than five digits in size? What happens to the 'extra digits'? Where do they get placed?

You may be troubled by the fact that the decimal expansions of these fractions do not seem to either recur or terminate, though we know from our earlier findings that they *should* recur. What is happening here? Are we missing something?

5.3 Cyclic numbers

We do the following experiment: select any prime number $p > 5$, work out the decimal form of $\frac{1}{p}$, and find its repetend. (The decimal will certainly recur; do you see why?) We find, in a good many cases, that the repetend shows a curious property which may be described as **CYCLIC BEHAVIOUR**. For example, take the prime number 7. The decimal expansion of its reciprocal is:

$$\frac{1}{7} = 0.142857\ 142857\ 142857\ \ldots = 0.\overline{142857}.$$

The repetend here is 142857. The 'curious' property which this number has is that *its first six multiples are all cyclic forms of itself*:

$$142857 \times 1 = 142857, \qquad 142857 \times 2 = 285714,$$
$$142857 \times 3 = 428571, \qquad 142857 \times 4 = 571428,$$
$$142857 \times 5 = 714285, \qquad 142857 \times 6 = 857142,$$

and, finally, $142857 \times 7 = 999999$. The meaning of the word **CYCLIC** will become clear after we study the following figure:

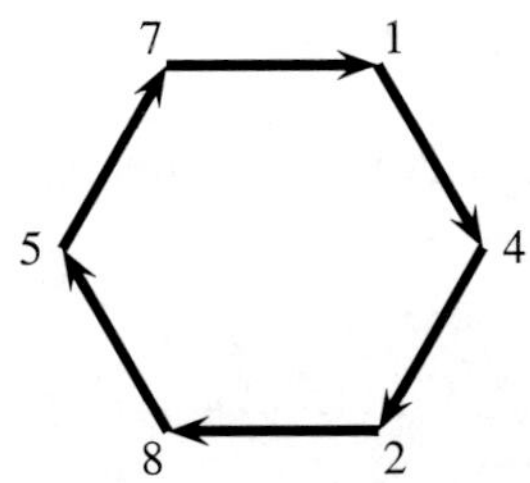

The 'cyclic order' of the digits is 1, 4, 2, 8, 5, 7, with the cycle 'wrapping around' to 1. When we multiply 142857 by 2, we get 285714; this has the same cyclic order of digits as 142857.

Likewise for the other multiples of 142857.

In view of this, we call 142857 a **CYCLIC NUMBER**. The cyclic property may be seen quite strikingly in the decimal expansions of the multiples of $\frac{1}{7}$:

$$\frac{1}{7} = 0.142857\ 142857\ 142857\ \ldots, \qquad \frac{2}{7} = 0.285714\ 285714\ 285714\ \ldots,$$
$$\frac{3}{7} = 0.428571\ 428571\ 428571\ \ldots, \qquad \frac{4}{7} = 0.571428\ 571428\ 571428\ \ldots,$$
$$\frac{5}{7} = 0.714285\ 714285\ 714285\ \ldots, \qquad \frac{6}{7} = 0.857142\ 857142\ 857142\ \ldots.$$

Similar behaviour is seen with the prime number 13. In the table below, we see the decimal expansions of the proper fractions with denominator 13:

$\frac{1}{13} = 0.076923\ 076923\ 076923\ \ldots,$	$\frac{2}{13} = 0.153846\ 153846\ 153846\ \ldots,$
$\frac{3}{13} = 0.230769\ 230769\ 230769\ \ldots,$	$\frac{4}{13} = 0.307692\ 307692\ 307692\ \ldots,$
$\frac{5}{13} = 0.384615\ 384615\ 384615\ \ldots,$	$\frac{6}{13} = 0.461538\ 461538\ 461538\ \ldots,$
$\frac{7}{13} = 0.538461\ 538461\ 538461\ \ldots,$	$\frac{8}{13} = 0.615384\ 615384\ 615384\ \ldots,$
$\frac{9}{13} = 0.692307\ 692307\ 692307\ \ldots,$	$\frac{10}{13} = 0.769230\ 769230\ 769230\ \ldots,$
$\frac{11}{13} = 0.846153\ 846153\ 846153\ \ldots,$	$\frac{12}{13} = 0.923076\ 923076\ 923076\ \ldots.$

Here we find *two* cyclic numbers; one is 076923, and it is associated with the fractions

$$\frac{1}{13},\quad \frac{3}{13},\quad \frac{4}{13},\quad \frac{9}{13},\quad \frac{10}{13},\quad \frac{12}{13}.$$

The other number is 153846, and it is associated with the following fractions:

$$\frac{2}{13},\quad \frac{5}{13},\quad \frac{6}{13},\quad \frac{7}{13},\quad \frac{8}{13},\quad \frac{11}{13}.$$

The grouping and cyclic behaviour are shown in the following figures:

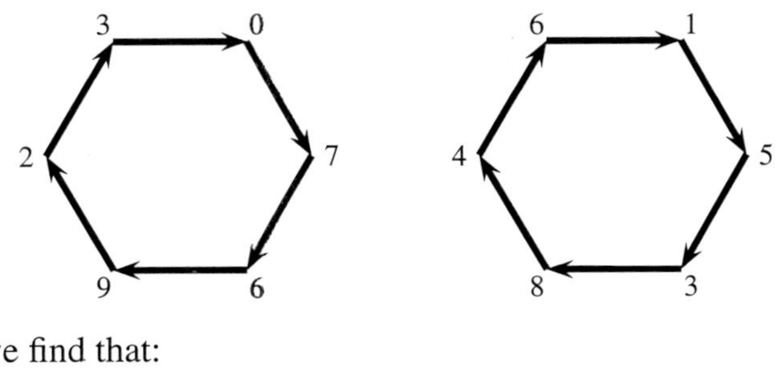

Probing further, we find that:

- when 076923 is multiplied by any of the numbers 1, 3, 4, 9, 10 or 12, the six multiples all have the same cyclic order as 076923.
- when 076923 is multiplied by any of the numbers 2, 5, 6, 7, 8 or 11, the six multiples all have the same cyclic order as 153846,

and, finally, $076923 \times 13 = 999999$.

Here is another property shared by the repetends of $\frac{1}{7}$ and $\frac{1}{13}$. If we list the repetends (142857 for $\frac{1}{7}$, 076923 and 153846 for $\frac{1}{13}$), 'slice' them into two numbers having the same number of digits, as shown below,

$$142 \mid 857, \qquad 076 \mid 923, \qquad 153 \mid 846,$$

and add the two numbers, we get the same answer in all the cases:

$$142 + 857 = 999, \qquad 076 + 923 = 999, \qquad 153 + 846 = 999.$$

There are obviously some very inviting mysteries lurking here!

5.4 Decimal expansion of 1/*p*

Above, we studied the decimal expansions of the reciprocals of the primes 7 and 13. If we study the repetends arising from other primes, we arrive at a striking conclusion. The results of our computations are shown in Table 5.1.

Examining the table, we see several common features:

- The number of digits in the repetend of $\frac{1}{p}$ is always *strictly less* than p. (There is a simple reason for this; see if you can find it.)

- For some primes p, the repetend has $p-1$ digits (this is the 'largest' it can get, if it is to be strictly less than p); this happens for $p = 7, 17, 19, 29, 47, 59, 61, \ldots$.

- For some primes p, the repetend has *half* the largest allowable number of digits, i.e., $\frac{p-1}{2}$ digits; this happens for $p = 13, 31, 43, 53, \ldots$.

- For all primes p, *the number of digits in the repetend is a divisor of* $p-1$.

  What has been noted in italics is an important and valuable discovery. It is related to a theorem about prime numbers first found and proved by the great seventeenth century French amateur mathematician Pierre de Fermat. It is called the **LITTLE FERMAT THEOREM**. You have probably heard of Fermat's name in connection with Fermat's Last Theorem.

  Here is a particular form of this theorem, relevant to our study of recurring decimals: *If* $p > 5$ *is a prime number, then* p *is a divisor of* $10^{p-1} - 1$. For example, 7 is a divisor of $10^6 - 1$, and 13 is a divisor of $10^{12} - 1$.

Table 5.1 Decimal expansions of the reciprocals of some primes

p	Decimal form of $\frac{1}{p}$	Number of digits in repetend
7	$0.\overline{142857}$	6
11	$0.\overline{09}$	2
13	$0.\overline{076923}$	6
17	$0.\overline{0588235294117647}$	16
19	$0.\overline{052631578947368421}$	18
23	$0.\overline{0434782608695652173913}$	22
29	$0.\overline{0344827586206896551724137931}$	28
31	$0.\overline{032258064516129}$	15
37	$0.\overline{027}$	3
41	$0.\overline{02439}$	5
43	$0.\overline{023255813953488372093}$	21
53	$0.\overline{0188679245283018867924528 3}$	26
79	$0.\overline{1265822784 81}$	13

For $p = 47$, we get a decimal with a 46-digit repetend (too big to put into the table):

$$\frac{1}{47} = 0.\overline{0212765957446808510638297872340425531914893617}.$$

Similarly, for $p = 59$, we get a decimal with a 58-digit repetend:

$$0.\overline{0169491525423728813559322033898305084745762711864406779661},$$

and for $p = 61$, we get a decimal with a 60-digit repetend:

$$0.\overline{016393442622950819672131147540983606557377049180327868852459}.$$

- In those cases where the repetend has an even number of digits, we find the same property as noted earlier for the fractions $\frac{1}{7}$ and $\frac{1}{13}$.

  That is, if we 'slice' the repetend into two numbers of equal length and add these two numbers, we get a number entirely made up of 9s. for example, for $p = 17$ the repetend is 0588235294117647, so we do:

$$05882352 + 94117647 = 99999999.$$

  Check that this works for $p = 19$, 23, 29, 47, 53, 59 and 61 too. (It does not apply for $p = 31$, $p = 37$, $p = 41$, as the repetends in these cases have an odd number of digits.)

5.5 Irrational numbers

We know now that any rational number gives rise either to a *terminating decimal* or to a *recurring decimal* (which could be pure or mixed). This gives rise to a natural question: *Are there numbers whose decimal forms neither terminate nor recur?* But this is easy to answer, for we can actually construct such numbers! Here is a simple example: the number

$$0.1\,01\,001\,0001\,00001\,000001\,0000001\,00000001\ldots,$$

made up of 0s and 1s, constructed in such a way that the number of 0s between the 1s steadily increases as we advance through the digits. This means that the digits neither terminate, nor do they recur.

It follows that *the above number cannot correspond to any rational number*; for if it did, then its decimal expansion would have to terminate or recur.

Such numbers are called **IRRATIONAL NUMBERS**. Any decimal whose digits neither terminate nor recur necessarily corresponds to an irrational number. This gives an easy recipé for generating more such numbers: all we need to ensure is that the decimal expansion neither terminates nor recurs. So the following numbers all belong to this family:

$$\begin{aligned} x &= 0.1212212221222212222212222221222\ldots, \\ y &= 0.101000100000100000001000000001\ldots, \\ z &= 0.1234567891011121314151617181920\ldots. \end{aligned}$$

For the number z, we have simply written the natural numbers in sequence (1, 2, 3, 4, ..., 10, 11, 12, ..., 19, 20, 21, ...) and strung them together to make a decimal number. Can you see why this decimal will not recur?

These numbers may seem rather 'artificial', for they do not appear in a natural manner; i.e., from some real problem. But there are more natural ways of coming across irrational numbers. One such number which is very famous is the square root of 2 (written as $\sqrt{2}$). It is that number which when multiplied by itself yields exactly 2. Let us try to see what this number is. A bit of experimentation with a calculator tells us that it must be *more* than 1.4, because $1.4 \times 1.4 = 1.96$, which falls short of 2; but it is *less* than 1.5, because $1.5 \times 1.5 = 2.25$, which exceeds 2. So we write:

$$1.4 < \sqrt{2} < 1.5.$$

Next, we find that $1.41 \times 1.41 = 1.9881 < 2$, but $1.42 \times 1.42 = 2.0164 > 2$; so:

$$1.41 < \sqrt{2} < 1.42.$$

Again, we find that $1.414 \times 1.414 = 1.999396 < 2$, but $1.415 \times 1.415 = 2.002225 > 2$; so

$$1.414 < \sqrt{2} < 1.415.$$

We can go on in this way and squeeze $\sqrt{2}$ into finer and finer intervals, and after some work we find that

$$1.414213562 < \sqrt{2} < 1.414213563.$$

The decimal expansion of $\sqrt{2}$ is found to be:

$$\sqrt{2} = 1.4142135623730950488016887242 0\ldots,$$

where the dots (...) tell us that more digits are to come—infinitely more of them!

You will notice that there is no sign of recurrence in the digits. Does this mean that $\sqrt{2}$ is irrational? Not really; our not seeing any sign of recurrence does not mean that it is not there!—it could just be that the repetend has an extremely large number of digits. (You could imagine a situation where the repetend is a number with a million digits. In this case we would see no sign of recurrence even if we were to list the first million digits of the decimal expansion!) So this *suggests* but does not *prove* what we are after.

What happens if we work directly with fractions instead? We are now looking for natural numbers a, b such that the fraction $\frac{a}{b}$ is in lowest terms, and its square equals 2.

The square of $\frac{a}{b}$ is $\frac{a}{b} \times \frac{a}{b} = \frac{a^2}{b^2}$, and for this to equal 2, the denominator must cancel exactly into the numerator. But as $\frac{a}{b}$ is in lowest terms, there are no prime factors in common between a and b. The prime factors of a^2 are exactly the same as those of a (only, they occur twice as many times), and the prime factors of b^2 are (similarly) the same as those of b. Therefore, there are no prime factors in common between a^2 and b^2. *So* $\frac{a^2}{b^2}$ *cannot be reduced to* 2. (In fact, it cannot be reduced at all; there are no factors to cancel.) Therefore, such a fraction does not exist! Hence we cannot find natural numbers a, b such that the square of $\frac{a}{b}$ equals 2. In other words, $\sqrt{2}$ is irrational.

Remarks

- Though it may not be visible in what we have written, we have used an important fact about prime factorisations of integers in the above proof of irrationality; namely, that there is essentially just one way to factorise a positive integer into prime numbers. This is the *fundamental theorem of arithmetic*. (We met this theorem earlier, in Chapter 3.)

- There are many other ways of proving that $\sqrt{2}$ is irrational. A nice article giving no less than *seven* of these proofs may be found at this link:
`http://www.ias.ac.in/resonance/December2007/p31-39.pdf`.

5.6 Unit fractions

Fractions such as $\frac{1}{2}, \frac{1}{3}, \frac{1}{4}, \frac{1}{5}, \frac{1}{6}, \ldots$, with numerator equal to 1, are called **UNIT FRACTIONS**. Mathematicians who study the history of mathematics have found that in ancient Egypt, some 3500 years back, fractions were generally written as *sums of unequal unit fractions*, though the fractions $\frac{2}{3}$ and $\frac{3}{4}$ too were allowed as summands (the reasons for this are not clear); hence, unit fractions are also called **EGYPTIAN FRACTIONS**. In the Egyptian system of arithmetic, it must have been convenient for some reason to express fractions in this manner. Here are some examples:

$$\frac{3}{4} = \frac{1}{2} + \frac{1}{4},$$

$$\frac{5}{6} = \frac{1}{2} + \frac{1}{3},$$

$$\frac{4}{11} = \frac{1}{3} + \frac{1}{33},$$

$$\frac{11}{17} = \frac{1}{2} + \frac{1}{7} + \frac{1}{238},$$

$$\frac{3}{7} = \frac{1}{3} + \frac{1}{11} + \frac{1}{231}.$$

It turns out that *any proper fraction* can be written in this way—as a sum of unequal unit fractions. You may be tempted to try proving this.

The Leibnitz triangle

The following construction produces an infinite triangular array of fractions called the **LEIBNITZ TRIANGLE**; it has a large number of interesting properties. At the top of the triangle (its apex) we place the fraction $\frac{1}{1}$. On the left border of the triangle we place, in turn, the fractions

$$\frac{1}{2}, \quad \frac{1}{3}, \quad \frac{1}{4}, \quad \frac{1}{5}, \quad \frac{1}{6}, \quad \ldots.$$

The rule used to find the remaining entries is the following: *each fraction is equal to the sum of the two fractions immediately below it* (i.e., the sum of the fraction immediately below it and to its *left*, and the fraction immediately below it and to its *right*). Hence, whenever three fractions x, y and z are placed in two consecutive rows as shown below, then $x = y + z$:

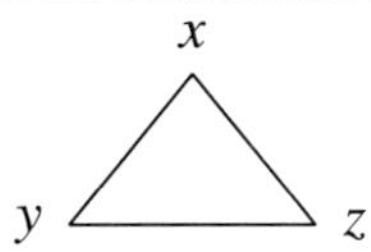

So the first three rows look like this:

$$\begin{array}{ccccc} & & \frac{1}{1} & & \\ & \frac{1}{2} & & \frac{1}{2} & \\ \frac{1}{3} & & \frac{1}{6} & & \frac{1}{3} \end{array}$$

Applying the rule repeatedly, we get the array shown in part in Figure 5.1. To our surprise, we find that all the fractions in the array are unit fractions. (Continue the array two or three rows further, and check for yourself.) There is nothing in the construction of the array that might suggest such a feature.

5.7 Mischievous fractions

The fraction $\frac{16}{64}$ displays the following somewhat mischievous property: if we write it in the normal manner,

$$\frac{16}{64},$$

$$
\begin{array}{ccccccccccccc}
 & & & & & & \frac{1}{1} & & & & & & \\
 & & & & & \frac{1}{2} & & \frac{1}{2} & & & & & \\
 & & & & \frac{1}{3} & & \frac{1}{6} & & \frac{1}{3} & & & & \\
 & & & \frac{1}{4} & & \frac{1}{12} & & \frac{1}{12} & & \frac{1}{4} & & & \\
 & & \frac{1}{5} & & \frac{1}{20} & & \frac{1}{30} & & \frac{1}{20} & & \frac{1}{5} & & \\
 & \frac{1}{6} & & \frac{1}{30} & & \frac{1}{60} & & \frac{1}{60} & & \frac{1}{30} & & \frac{1}{6} & \\
\cdots & & \cdots & & \cdots & & \cdots & & \cdots & & \cdots & & \cdots
\end{array}
$$

Figure 5.1 The first six rows of the Leibnitz triangle

and (illegally) 'cancel' the 6 which is common to the numerator and the denominator, we are left with $\frac{1}{4}$. Now we find, to our surprise, that

$$\frac{16}{64} = \frac{1}{4}.$$

The 'illegal cancellation' has resulted in a correct equality!

Are there other fractions with this property? We find that there is a whole family that can be generated from the above example. Indeed, the following fractions are all equal to $\frac{1}{4}$:

$$\frac{16}{64}, \quad \frac{166}{664}, \quad \frac{1666}{6664}, \quad \frac{16666}{66664}, \quad \frac{166666}{666664}, \quad \ldots.$$

In each case, an illegal cancellation of the common digits in the numerator and the denominator results in a correct equality at the end.

There are other such families. For example, the following fractions are all equal to $\frac{1}{5}$:

$$\frac{19}{95}, \quad \frac{199}{995}, \quad \frac{1999}{9995}, \quad \frac{19999}{99995}, \quad \frac{199999}{999995}, \quad \ldots.$$

See if you can find more such families!

5.8 Farey sequences

Earlier in the chapter we experimented with writing down, in ascending order, all fractions between 0 and 1 with denominators not exceeding 3; we got:

$$\frac{0}{1},\quad \frac{1}{3},\quad \frac{1}{2},\quad \frac{2}{3},\quad \frac{1}{1}.$$

Next we inserted all such fractions with denominator 4 that are not already present; we got:

$$\frac{0}{1},\quad \frac{1}{4},\quad \frac{1}{3},\quad \frac{1}{2},\quad \frac{2}{3},\quad \frac{3}{4},\quad \frac{1}{1}.$$

Such collections of fractions, when arranged in ascending order as shown, are called **FAREY SEQUENCES**. The first collection shown above, in which the denominators do not exceed 3, is called FAREY (3); the second one is called FAREY (4). Earlier we had computed FAREY (5) and FAREY (6) as well. We display them once again:

$$\text{FAREY}(3) = \left\{\frac{0}{1}, \frac{1}{3}, \frac{1}{2}, \frac{2}{3}, \frac{1}{1}\right\},$$

$$\text{FAREY}(4) = \left\{\frac{0}{1}, \frac{1}{4}, \frac{1}{3}, \frac{1}{2}, \frac{2}{3}, \frac{3}{4}, \frac{1}{1}\right\},$$

$$\text{FAREY}(5) = \left\{\frac{0}{1}, \frac{1}{5}, \frac{1}{4}, \frac{1}{3}, \frac{2}{5}, \frac{1}{2}, \frac{3}{5}, \frac{2}{3}, \frac{3}{4}, \frac{4}{5}, \frac{1}{1}\right\},$$

$$\text{FAREY}(6) = \left\{\frac{0}{1}, \frac{1}{6}, \frac{1}{5}, \frac{1}{4}, \frac{1}{3}, \frac{2}{5}, \frac{1}{2}, \frac{3}{5}, \frac{2}{3}, \frac{3}{4}, \frac{4}{5}, \frac{5}{6}, \frac{1}{1}\right\},$$

and so on. We can compute FAREY (1) and FAREY (2) too:

$$\text{FAREY}(1) = \left\{\frac{0}{1}, \frac{1}{1}\right\},$$

$$\text{FAREY}(2) = \left\{\frac{0}{1}, \frac{1}{2}, \frac{1}{1}\right\}.$$

And here is FAREY (7):

$$\left\{\frac{0}{1}, \frac{1}{7}, \frac{1}{6}, \frac{1}{5}, \frac{1}{4}, \frac{2}{7}, \frac{1}{3}, \frac{2}{5}, \frac{3}{7}, \frac{1}{2}, \frac{4}{7}, \frac{3}{5}, \frac{2}{3}, \frac{5}{7}, \frac{3}{4}, \frac{4}{5}, \frac{5}{6}, \frac{6}{7}, \frac{1}{1}\right\}.$$

Examining these collections, we discover something very striking:

In each Farey sequence, if $\frac{a}{b}$ and $\frac{c}{d}$ are any two adjacent fractions, then $ad - bc = -1$.

For example, in FAREY (5) we have the fractions $\frac{1}{2}$ and $\frac{3}{5}$ which are adjacent to each other; and we have: $1 \times 5 - 2 \times 3 = -1$. You may check that the property holds in each and every case.

Another striking property that these collections share is the following:

In each Farey sequence, if $\frac{a}{b}$, $\frac{c}{d}$, $\frac{e}{f}$ are any three consecutive fractions, then

$$\frac{c}{d} = \frac{a+e}{b+f}.$$

So to find the in-between fraction, we simply compute $\frac{a+e}{b+f}$ and then reduce it to lowest terms. For example, consider these three consecutive fractions in FAREY (6):

$$\frac{3}{5}, \quad \frac{2}{3}, \quad \frac{3}{4}.$$

Check that $\frac{3+3}{5+4} = \frac{2}{3}$.

5.9 Miscellaneous exercises

1. We showed above that $0.99999\ldots$ or $0.\overline{9}$ is the same as 1. Show in the same way that:

   - $0.299999\ldots$ or $0.2\overline{9}$ is the same as 0.3;
   - $0.5499999\ldots$ or $0.54\overline{9}$ is the same as 0.55;
   - $1.23499999\ldots$ or $1.234\overline{9}$ is the same as 1.235.

   The general rule will be clear from these examples.

2. Let n be any positive integer not divisible by 2 or 5; then we know that $\frac{1}{n}$ has a pure recurring decimal form. Verify that the following rule gives the repetend of this decimal:

   Divide the number $99999\ldots$, with an indefinite number of 9s, by n. Continue to insert 9s till the division works out exactly; that is, with no remainder. Then the quotient so obtained is the required repetend.

For example, in the case of $\frac{1}{7}$ we find that six 9s are required for the division to be exact; we get $999999 \div 7 = 142857$, so the repetend is 142857.

Verify that the rule gives the correct answer for the fractions $\frac{1}{13}$, $\frac{1}{17}$ and $\frac{1}{27}$.

Use the rule to find the repetends of the decimal forms of $\frac{1}{39}$ and $\frac{1}{41}$.

Another way of stating the above rule is: *Divide the number* 100000..., *with an indefinite number of* 0s, *by n. Continue to insert* 0s *till the remainder is* 1, *and then stop the division at that point. The quotient at that point is the required repetend.*

3. Is the following statement true?

   Given a positive integer n, the decimal form of $\frac{1}{n}$ is pure recurring if the units digit of n is 1, 3, 7 *or* 9. *If not, the decimal expansion is either terminating or mixed recurring.*

4. Earlier, we had found that

$$\frac{1}{99997} = 0.00001\ 00003\ 00009\ 00027\ 00081\ 00243\ 00729\ 02187\ \ldots.$$

   The decimal form does not give the appearance of recurring. Is this really so? Show that it is *not*.

5. Justify the claim made on page 164, that the decimal expansions of the numbers x, y, z shown below do not recur:

$$\begin{aligned} x &= 0.12122122212222122222122222221222\ldots, \\ y &= 0.1010001000000100000000100000000001\ldots, \\ z &= 0.1234567891011121314151617181920\ldots. \end{aligned}$$

6. On page 166 we presented a simple and neat argument, based on prime factorisation, to show that $\sqrt{2}$ is an irrational number. Show similarly that the numbers $\sqrt{3}$ and $\sqrt{5}$ are irrational.

7. We briefly studied the Leibnitz triangle above. There is another such triangular array of numbers which is much more famous, called the **PASCAL TRIANGLE**. Here is how it is constructed.

   The left and right borders of the triangle are entirely made up of 1s. To find the remaining entries we use the following rule: *each number is equal to the sum of the two numbers immediately above it*. So whenever three numbers x, y and z are placed in two consecutive rows as shown below, then $x = y + z$:

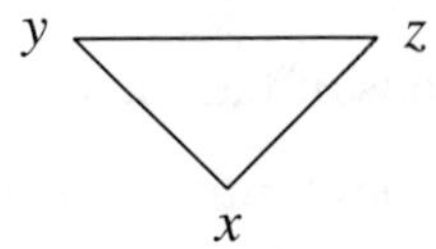

Applying the rule over and over again, we get the array shown in Figure 5.2.

1

1 1

1 2 1

1 3 3 1

1 4 6 4 1

1 5 10 10 5 1

… … … … … … …

Figure 5.2 The first six rows of the Pascal triangle

Explore connections between the Leibnitz triangle and the Pascal triangle. (Yes, there are many connections!)

8. *When is the sum of two unit fractions equal to another unit fraction?* Here are some obvious examples:

$$\frac{1}{4}+\frac{1}{4}=\frac{1}{2}, \qquad \frac{1}{6}+\frac{1}{6}=\frac{1}{3},$$

and so on. But these 'trivial' examples would not interest or impress anyone!

Much more interesting are the instances

$$\frac{1}{3}+\frac{1}{6}=\frac{1}{2}, \qquad \frac{1}{10}+\frac{1}{15}=\frac{1}{6}.$$

The summands in both these examples are unequal.

Find more instances of this kind, where the sum of two unequal unit fractions is equal to another unit fraction.

9. Observe that $6 = 2 \times 3$, and that $\frac{1}{2} - \frac{1}{3} = \frac{1}{6}$. This has enabled us to express $\frac{1}{6}$ as the difference between the reciprocals of two consecutive integers.

   Use this observation to similarly express the following unit fractions,

$$\frac{1}{12}, \quad \frac{1}{20}, \quad \frac{1}{30},$$

   as differences between the reciprocals of pairs of consecutive integers.

10. Based on your analysis of the previous problem, find a short way of computing the following sum without having to compute the LCM of the denominators:

$$\frac{1}{1\times 2} + \frac{1}{2\times 3} + \frac{1}{3\times 4} + \frac{1}{4\times 5} + \frac{1}{5\times 6} + \frac{1}{6\times 7} + \frac{1}{7\times 8} + \frac{1}{8\times 9} + \frac{1}{9\times 10}.$$

11. ✪ Find, similarly, a short way to compute the sum

$$\frac{1}{1\times 3} + \frac{1}{2\times 4} + \frac{1}{3\times 5} + \frac{1}{4\times 6} + \frac{1}{5\times 7} + \frac{1}{6\times 8} + \frac{1}{7\times 9} + \frac{1}{8\times 10} + \frac{1}{9\times 11}.$$

12. ***Pythagorean triples from even numbers.*** We studied *Pythagorean triples* in Chapter 3. These are triples of integers, say (a,b,c), such that $a^2 + b^2 = c^2$; for example, $(5,12,13)$. The triple is called *primitive* (or a PPT) if a, b, c are coprime.

    Here is a surprising recipé for generating such triples, using fractions. *Choose a pair of consecutive even numbers. Compute the sum of their reciprocals. Let the sum, written in lowest terms, be $\frac{a}{b}$. Then the triple $(a,b,b+1)$ is a* PPT.

    For example, from the pair of numbers $(4,6)$ we get:

$$\frac{1}{4} + \frac{1}{6} = \frac{10}{24} = \frac{5}{12} \quad \text{(in lowest terms)}.$$

    This yields the PPT $(5,12,13)$. Check: $5^2 + 12^2 = 25 + 144 = 169 = 13^2$.

    Similarly, from the pair of numbers $(6,8)$ we get:

$$\frac{1}{6} + \frac{1}{8} = \frac{14}{48} = \frac{7}{24} \quad \text{(in lowest terms)}.$$

    This yields the PPT $(7,24,25)$. Check: $7^2 + 24^2 = 49 + 576 = 625 = 25^2$.

    Verify that the pairs of numbers $(8,10)$ and $(10,12)$ also yield such triples.

13. In the above problem, explain why the computed triples have the Pythagorean property, and also why they are primitive.

14. ***Pythagorean triples from odd numbers.*** Instead of using even numbers, we may also use *odd* numbers. The recipé now becomes: *Choose a pair of consecutive odd numbers. Compute the sum of their reciprocals. Let the sum, written in lowest terms, be* $\frac{a}{b}$. *Then the triple* $(a, b, b+2)$ *is a* PPT.

    For example, from the pair of numbers $(3,5)$ we get: $\frac{1}{3}+\frac{1}{5}=\frac{8}{15}$. This yields the PPT $(8,15,17)$.

    Verify that the pairs $(5,7)$ and $(7,9)$ yield such triples, as claimed.

15. In the above problem, explain why the computed triples have the Pythagorean property, and also why they are primitive.

Chapter 6

Ratio and Proportion

The study of *ratio and proportion* naturally follows that of fractions, and we embark on this topic now. We shall see that these terms are widely used in daily life contexts.

Given two quantities A, B, by the words "**RATIO** of A to B" we mean the fraction $\frac{A}{B}$; that is, it is the division $A \div B$. It is generally written as $A : B$. It may be thought of as a way of comparing the two numbers A and B, by writing how many times B goes into A. Keeping in mind the definition of equivalent fractions, we see that the ratios

$$1:2, \qquad 2:4, \qquad 3:6, \qquad 4:8, \qquad \ldots$$

are all the same, as are the ratios

$$3:4, \qquad 6:8, \qquad 9:12, \qquad 12:16, \qquad \ldots.$$

In older times the two terms of the ratio were given names—the first term (denoted by A) was called the *antecedent*, and the second term (denoted by B) was called the *consequent*; but such fancy names are no longer in use.

6.1 Ratios for unit conversion

In the ratio $A : B$, if A and B arise as a result of measurements of some kind, then they will have *units* associated with them. If the measurements are of the 'same kind' (e.g., both may refer to lengths, or both may refer to weight), then the ratio $A : B$ gives the conversion from one unit to the other. Here are some examples.

- Suppose the lengths of objects are measured in *cm* as well as *inches*; then, writing A and B for the measurements in cm and inches, respectively, the ratio $A : B$ is the same for all objects, namely, 2.54 : 1. This is the ratio we must use when we convert from inches to cm. To convert from cm to inches, we use the ratio 1 : 2.54.

- Suppose the weights of objects are measured in kilogram (kg) as well as pounds (lb); then, writing A and B for the measurements in kg and lb, respectively, the ratio $A : B$ is the same for all objects, namely, 1 : 2.2. This is the ratio we must use when we convert from lb to kg. To convert from kg to lb, we use the ratio 2.2 : 1.

- Suppose the price of an item is given in a catalog in *dollars* ($) as well as *rupees* (₹); then, writing A and B for the prices in $ and ₹ respectively, the ratio $A : B$ is the same for all items (approximately 1 : 45). This is the ratio we must use when we convert from rupees to dollars. (Note, however, that this ratio changes over time. Sometimes the rupee gains on the dollar, which means that the ratio $A : B$ increases; and at other times—which happens rather more often—the dollar gains on the rupee, which means that the ratio $B : A$ increases. But there are some complications here—the ratio is a bit different when you *buy* dollars and when you *sell* dollars. For those interested in such currency-related matters, here is one of many references:
`http://en.wikipedia.org/wiki/Currency`

6.2 Rate

If A and B arise as a result of measurements of 'different kinds' (e.g., A may be the measurement of a distance, and B the measurement of a time interval), then the ratio $A : B$ has a unit attached to it, and is commonly known as a **RATE**. Here are some common examples of rates:

- *Speed* or *velocity* (obtained by the division of distance travelled by time taken for the journey); typical units are km/hr (kilometres per hour), m/s (metres per second); and mph (miles per hour),

- *Unit price* of a commodity (obtained by the division of price paid by quantity purchased, i.e., cost divided by quantity); typical units are ₹/kg, ₹/ton, ₹/litre and ₹/dozen.

- *Density* of a substance (obtained by the division of mass of an object made of the substance by the volume of the object); typical units are kg/m^3 (kilograms per cubic metre) and g/cm^3 (grams per cubic centimetre). In earlier times, highly student-unfriendly units such as lb/ft^3 (pounds per foot cubed) were in use; fortunately, no longer.

- *Annual rainfall* in some region (obtained by the division of the total rainfall measured over a period of several decades by the number of years); typical units are mm/year and cm/year (millimetres per year and centimetres per year).

Rates arise very often in scientific or technological contexts.

6.3 Dimensionless ratios

In the ratio $A : B$, if the terms A and B are pure numbers, with no units attached, or if they measure the same kind of thing and have the same unit, then the fraction $\frac{A}{B}$ is free of units; it is **DIMENSIONLESS**—that is, it is a pure number. Here are some examples.

- ***Specific gravity.*** For a solid or liquid, the ratio of the mass of any volume of the substance to the mass of the same volume of water is called the **SPECIFIC GRAVITY** or SG of that substance. By definition, the SG of water is 1. The specific gravities of some common solids and liquids are given in Table 6.1. Note the high values for platinum, gold, mercury, lead and silver, and the low values for cork and freshly fallen snow.

- ***Representative fraction of a map.*** A **MAP** is a schematic drawing of a region. It is *scaled down*, in the sense that distances in the actual region are uniformly scaled down so that the map has a convenient size; this makes it easy to use by unfolding it on, say, ones's desk or table. The scaling down must be *uniform*, so that the shape of an object in the map is the same as the shape in real life. A map also represents real life objects *schematically*: a river by a line in some colour, a railway line by a line with ticks, a town by a dot, a city by a heavier dot and so on.

  The scale used to draw the map is its **REPRESENTATIVE FRACTION** or **RF**; it compares the size of an object in the map with the size in real life. For example, in a map with RF equal to 1 : 100000, a distance of 1 cm on the map represents an actual distance of 100000 cm, i.e., 1 km. In a typical school atlas, the map of a country may have a RF of 1 : 10000000, so that a distance of 1 cm on the map represents an actual distance of 10000000 cm, i.e., 100 km. (Please look up your school atlas to see some typical RF values.)

Table 6.1 Approximate specific gravities of some well-known substances

Substance	SG
Alcohol	0.79
Cork	0.24
Gold (pure, 24 carat)	19.29
Granite	2.69
Ice	0.92
Iron (cast)	7.21
Ivory	1.84
Lead	11.35
Marble	2.56
Mercury	13.61
Mud (closely packed)	2.00
Mud (soft, loose)	1.73
Mud (wet)	1.60
Peanuts (shelled)	0.64
Peanuts (unshelled)	0.27
Platinum	21.51
Porcelain	2.40
Potatoes (white)	0.77
Pumice stone	0.64
Quartz	2.64
Salt	2.32
Sand (dry)	1.60
Sand (wet)	1.92
Sawdust	0.27
Silver	10.46
Snow (compacted)	0.48
Snow (freshly fallen)	0.16
Steel	7.85
Stone (crushed)	1.60
Sugar (brown)	0.72
Sugar (granulated)	0.85
Water (fresh)	1.00
Water (sea)	1.03

- ***Scale of an architectural drawing.*** In an architectural drawing, buildings are represented schematically (with walls represented by lines, doors by some symbol, windows by some other symbol, etc.).The scale factor for the drawing may be about 1 : 50.

- ***Scale of a photograph.*** In a passport-sized photograph, which is nothing but a scaled down picture of a person's face, the scale may be 1 : 5 or 1 : 10.

- ***Ratio of diagonal to side for a square.*** Squares of different sizes are shown in Figure 6.1 with the diagonal drawn in each one. The ratio of the *length of the diagonal* (d) to the *length of the side* (s) is the same for all the figures; namely, we have $d : s = \sqrt{2} : 1$.

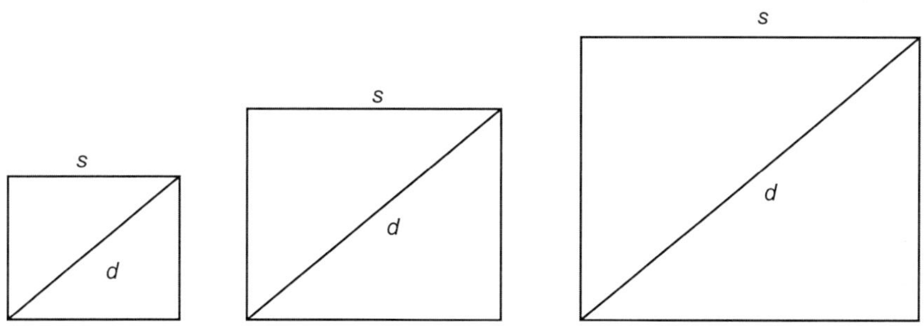

Figure 6.1

- ***Ratio of circumference to diameter for a circle.*** Circles of different sizes are shown in Figure 6.2 with the diameter drawn in each one. For each circle, the ratio of the *circumference* (C) to the *diameter* (D) is exactly the same; it is roughly $3.1416 : 1$.

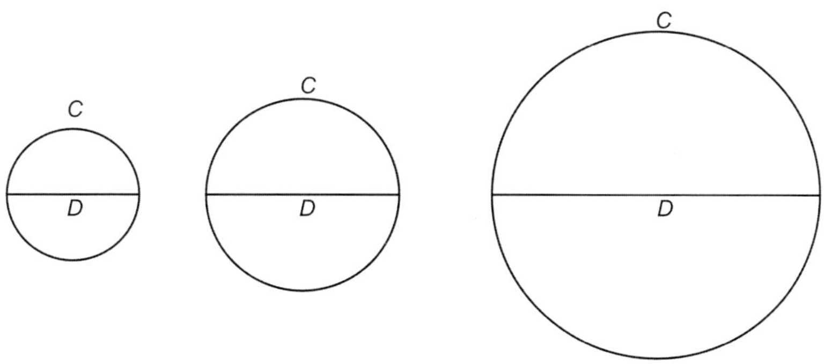

Figure 6.2

The number occurring in this ratio is a very famous one indeed, and it has been of great interest to mathematicians for the past 2000 years. It is denoted by the symbol π (pronounced 'pie'). It is found to be *irrational*, so we cannot give its value exactly as a fraction or as a decimal.

Here is π to fourteen decimal places:

$$\pi = 3.14159\,26535\,8979\ldots.$$

The dots $(\ldots)$ tell us that there are more decimal digits to follow.

A convenient fraction which is close to π is $\frac{22}{7}$. Its decimal expansion is $3.142857\ldots$, so it is accurate only to two decimal places. However it is used frequently, as its numerator and denominator are small and easy to use. Using it, we can say that the circumference of a wheel 70 cm in diameter is about 220 cm (i.e., 2.2 m).

Much more accurate, however, is the fraction $\frac{355}{113}$; it is accurate to six decimal places, for $\frac{355}{113} = 3.1415929\ldots.$

We shall say more about such approximations later in the chapter, when we study *incommensurable ratios*.

6.4 Proportion

When two ratios are equal, the statement that expresses their equality is called a **PROPORTION**. So if a, b, c and d are numbers such that the ratios $a:b$ and c and d are equal, then we write:

$$a:b = c:d,$$

and call this statement a proportion. We call the fourth number (d) a **FOURTH PROPORTIONAL** to the other three numbers, and we write:

> *The numbers a, b, c, d are in proportion; d is the fourth proportional to a, b and c.*

In earlier days the proportion would have been written as $a:b::c:d$, but it is simpler to write it using the equality sign.

The following are examples of proportion:

$$2:3 = 4:6, \qquad 3:7 = 9:21, \qquad 5:13 = 35:91.$$

The example from the previous section concerning circles may be stated as follows: *Given two circles with circumferences C, C' and diameters D, D', the numbers C, D, C', D' are in proportion.* (Yet another way of writing this: *C is proportional to D*. We shall meet this kind of sentence again in the chapter on *Variation*.)

The first and fourth terms of a proportion are called its *extremes*, and the second and third terms are called its *means*. The equality $a:b = c:d$ implies that

$$\frac{a}{b} = \frac{c}{d}, \qquad \therefore\ ad = bc,$$

using the cross-multiplication rule. For example, in the relation $2:3 = 4:6$ we have $2\times 6 = 3\times 4$. The property is expressed using words as:

If four numbers are in proportion, the product of the extremes is equal to the product of the means.

Given a, b, c, the fourth proportional d may be found using the formula

$$d = \frac{bc}{a}.$$

A few typical problems concerning ratio and proportion are solved below.

EXAMPLE 1. A school has a teacher-student ratio $(T:S)$ of $1:12$. If there are 600 students in the school, how many more teachers must the school employ for $T:S$ to be $1:10$?

The number of teachers presently employed is $600 \div 12 = 50$. Since the number of students is fixed at 600, for the ratio of teachers to students to be $1:10$, the number of teachers must be $600 \div 10 = 60$. So, the school must employ $60-50$, i.e., 10 more teachers.

EXAMPLE 2. A fourth proportional to the quantities a^2bc, ab^2, ac is

$$\frac{(ab^2)\times(ac)}{a^2bc} = \frac{a^2b^2c}{a^2bc} = b;$$

so a^2bc, ab^2, ac, b are in proportion.

EXAMPLE 3. Given $a:b = 2:3$, to find the ratio $(5a+7b):(4a+9b)$.

We first use the cross-multiplication rule to get $3a = 2b$; this gives us the relation $b = \frac{1}{2}(3a)$. Now substituting for b in the desired ratio, we get:

$$\frac{5a+7b}{4a+9b} = \frac{5a+(7\times 3a)/2}{4a+(9\times 3a)/2} = \frac{10a+21a}{8a+27a} = \frac{31a}{35a} = \frac{31}{35}.$$

So the desired ratio is $31:35$.

EXAMPLE 4. Given $a : b = 3 : 5$, to find the ratio $(a^3 + b^3) : (5a^2b - 2ab^2)$.

We write: $5a = 3b$, therefore $b = \frac{1}{3}(5a)$. Substituting for b in the desired ratio we get:

$$\begin{aligned}
\frac{a^3+b^3}{5a^2b-2ab^2} &= \frac{a^3+\left(125a^3/27\right)}{5a^2\times(5a/3)-2a\times(25a^2/9)} \\
&= \frac{\left(27a^3+125a^3\right)/27}{\left(75a^3-50a^3\right)/9} \\
&= \frac{152a^3}{25a^3}\times\frac{9}{27} = \frac{152}{25}\times\frac{1}{3} = \frac{152}{75}.
\end{aligned}$$

So the desired ratio is $152 : 75$.

Two ratios in one statement. A statement like $a : b : c = 2 : 3 : 5$ is a convenient way of writing *two* ratio statements in one, namely, $a : b = 2 : 3$ and $b : c = 3 : 5$, i.e.,

$$\frac{a}{b} = \frac{2}{3} \quad \text{and} \quad \frac{b}{c} = \frac{3}{5}.$$

Another way of writing the statement $a : b : c = 2 : 3 : 5$ is

$$\frac{a}{2} = \frac{b}{3} = \frac{c}{5}.$$

6.5 Results concerning proportion

Many of the rules concerning proportions may be deduced using simple algebra. We give a few such rules below (along with their older names, in some cases).

INVERTENDO. If $a : b = c : d$, then $b : a = d : c$.

For, if $\frac{a}{b} = \frac{c}{d}$, then $\frac{b}{a} = \frac{d}{c}$.

ALTERNENDO. If $a : b = c : d$, then $a : c = b : d$.

For, if $\frac{a}{b} = \frac{c}{d}$, then $\frac{a}{c} = \frac{b}{d}$.

MULTIPLICATION OF RATIOS If $a : b = c : d$ and $a' : b' = c' : d'$, then

$$aa' : bb' = cc' : dd'.$$

For, if we have $\frac{a}{b} = \frac{c}{d}$ and $\frac{a'}{b'} = \frac{c'}{d'}$, then by multiplication we get

$$\frac{aa'}{bb'} = \frac{cc'}{dd'}.$$

This rule shows that corresponding terms of two proportions may be multiplied to yield another proportion.

EX EQUALI. If $a : b = c : d$, and $b : x = d : y$, then $a : x = c : y$.

For, if $a : b = c : d$, and $b : x = d : y$, then $a : c = b : d$, and so:

$$\frac{a}{c} = \frac{b}{d}, \qquad \frac{b}{d} = \frac{x}{y}, \qquad \therefore \frac{a}{c} = \frac{x}{y},$$

Therefore, $a : x = c : y$.

COMPONENDO. If $a : b = c : d$, then $a+b : b = c+d : d$.

For, if $\frac{a}{b} = \frac{c}{d}$, then by adding 1 to both sides we get

$$\frac{a}{b}+1 = \frac{c}{d}+1, \qquad \therefore \frac{a+b}{b} = \frac{c+d}{d}, \qquad \therefore a+b : b = c+d : d.$$

DIVIDENDO. If $a : b = c : d$, then $a-b : b = c-d : d$.

For, if $\frac{a}{b} = \frac{c}{d}$, then by subtracting 1 from both sides we get

$$\frac{a}{b}-1 = \frac{c}{d}-1, \qquad \therefore \frac{a-b}{b} = \frac{c-d}{d}, \qquad \therefore a-b : b = c-d : d.$$

COMPONENDO–DIVIDENDO. If $a : b = c : d$, then $a+b : a-b = c+d : c-d$.

For, if $\frac{a}{b} = \frac{c}{d}$, then by componendo and dividendo we get:

$$\frac{a+b}{b} = \frac{c+d}{d}, \qquad \frac{a-b}{b} = \frac{c-d}{d}.$$

Therefore, by division, we get

$$\frac{a+b}{a-b} = \frac{c+d}{c-d}, \qquad \therefore a+b : a-b = c+d : c-d.$$

6.6 Continued proportion

The numbers a, b, c, d, ... are said to be in **CONTINUED PROPORTION** if

$$a:b = b:c = c:d = \dots,$$

i.e., if $\dfrac{a}{b} = \dfrac{b}{c} = \dfrac{c}{d} = \cdots$.

- The following numbers are in continued proportion:

$$1, \quad 2, \quad 4, \quad 8, \quad 16, \quad 32, \quad 64, \quad 128, \quad \dots.$$

- The following numbers are in continued proportion:

$$2, \quad 10, \quad 50, \quad 250, \quad 1250, \quad 6250, \quad \dots.$$

- The following numbers are in continued proportion:

$$24, \quad 16, \quad \frac{32}{3}, \quad \frac{64}{9}, \quad \frac{128}{27}, \quad \frac{256}{81}, \quad \dots.$$

If the numbers a, b, c are in continued proportion, then b is called a **MEAN PROPORTIONAL** between a and c, and c is called a **THIRD PROPORTIONAL** to a and b. From $a:b = b:c$ we get $ac = b^2$. The mean proportional and the third proportional may both be found using this relation.

A technique often used to prove results about equal ratios and continued proportions is the use of a new symbol to denote the equal ratio. We show some examples of this, below, contrasting this approach with the other one.

EXAMPLE 5. Given that $\dfrac{a}{b} = \dfrac{c}{d}$, to show that $\dfrac{xa+yc}{xb+yd}$ is equal to each of these equal ratios, for any values of x and y

Write $\dfrac{a}{b} = \dfrac{c}{d} = k$; then $a = kb$ and $c = kd$. Substituting for a, c we get:

$$\frac{xa+yc}{xb+yd} = \frac{xkb+ykd}{xb+yd} = \frac{k(xb+yd)}{xb+yd} = k.$$

In other words, $\dfrac{xa+yc}{xb+yd}$ is equal to $\dfrac{a}{b}$ and to $\dfrac{c}{d}$.

The same method of proof establishes the following proposition:

Proposition. If $\frac{a}{b}=\frac{c}{d}=\frac{e}{f}=\cdots$, then $\frac{xa+yc+ze+\cdots}{xb+yd+zf+\cdots}$ is equal to each of these ratios, for any values of $x, y, z, \ldots$.

EXAMPLE 6. If a, b, c are in continued proportion, to show that $a:c \;=\; a^2:b^2$.

The rule "Product of the extremes is equal to the product of the means" tells us that to prove the required result we must show that $a\cdot b^2=c\cdot a^2$, i.e., $b^2=ac$. But this is true, since a, b, c are in continued proportion. So, the required result follows.

EXAMPLE 7. If a, b, c are in continued proportion, to show that $a+b:b+c=a:b$.

The same rule ("Product of the extremes is equal to the product of the means") tells us that to prove the required result we must show that $b\cdot(a+b)=a\cdot(b+c)$, i.e., $ab+b^2=ab+ac$, that is, $b^2=ac$. But this holds, since a, b, c are in continued proportion. Hence the result.

EXAMPLE 8. If a, b, c, d are in continued proportion, to show that

$$a+c \;:\; a+b+c+d \;=\; b \;:\; b+c.$$

For the required result to be true, the product of the extremes must be equal to the product of the means, i.e., we must have

$$(a+c)\cdot(b+c)-b\cdot(a+b+c+d) \;=\; 0.$$

Simplifying the expression on the left side, we get

$$ab+ac+bc+c^2-ab-b^2-bc-bd \;=\; \left(ac-b^2\right)+\left(c^2-bd\right).$$

But $b^2=ac$, as a, b, c are in continued proportion, and $c^2=bd$ as b, c, d are in continued proportion. It follows that $(a+c)\cdot(b+c)-b\cdot(a+b+c+d)=0$, and the required result is proved.

EXAMPLE 9. Two numbers made of the same two digits are in the ratio $4:7$. Find the two numbers.

Let the digits of the two numbers be a, b; then the two numbers are $10a+b$ and $10b+a$, and the given information tells us that

$$10a+b \ : \ 10b+a \ = \ 4 \ : \ 7.$$

Using the rule "product of the extremes is equal to the product of the means" we get

$$7\cdot(10a+b) = 4\cdot(10b+a), \qquad \therefore\ 70a+7b = 40b+4a, \qquad \therefore\ 66a = 33b,$$

so $2a=b$, i.e., b is twice a. There are different answers possible here; the two numbers may be any of the following pairs:

12 and 21; 24 and 42; 36 and 63; 48 and 84.

EXAMPLE 10. Given that $x:y:z=a:b:c$, to show that

$$(b-c)x+(c-a)y+(a-b)z = 0.$$

To solve this, we write the given statement as

$$\frac{x}{a} = \frac{y}{b} = \frac{z}{c}.$$

Let k denote the common value of the above three ratios. Then we have $x=ka$, $y=kb$ and $z=kc$. Substituting these into the given expression, we get:

$$\begin{aligned}(b-c)x+(c-a)y+(a-b)z &= (b-c)\cdot ka+(c-a)\cdot kb+(a-b)\cdot kc\\ &= k\cdot(ab-ac+bc-ab+ac-bc)\\ &= k\cdot 0 = 0.\end{aligned}$$

The above solution may be altered slightly to yield the following:

If $x:y:z=b-c:c-a:a-b$, then $ax+by+cz=0$.

6.7 Historical note

The study of ratio and proportion was first done by the Greeks more than two millennia ago; much of the work was done by a mathematician called Eudoxus, and it was further developed by Euclid in THE ELEMENTS. The notion of irrational numbers or **INCOMMENSURABLE RATIOS**, i.e., those that cannot be written as the ratio of two integers, emerged as a by-product of their study of ratios. They showed that the ratio of the diagonal of a square to the side is incommensurable; in other words, *it is not possible to find two integers whose squares are in the ratio* $2:1$. They were also able to show that pairs of integers can be found whose ratio differs from the desired ratio ($\sqrt{2}:1$) by less than any positive quantity we may specify. Otherwise put: *Pairs of integers may be found such that the ratio of their squares differs from the ratio* $2:1$ *by as small a quantity as we may specify.*

For instance, the ratio $17:12$ differs from $\sqrt{2}$ by less than 0.0025; the ratio $99:70$ differs from $\sqrt{2}$ by less than 0.000075; and the ratio $1393:985$ differs from $\sqrt{2}$ by less than 0.000000365. These ratios are known as *approximations* to $\sqrt{2}$, and an unlimited number of them can be generated, for example,

$$\frac{3}{2},\quad \frac{7}{5},\quad \frac{17}{12},\quad \frac{41}{29},\quad \frac{99}{70},\quad \frac{239}{169},\quad \frac{577}{408},\quad \frac{1393}{985},\quad \frac{3363}{2378},\quad \frac{8119}{5741},\quad \ldots.$$

A look at the squares of the numerators and denominators of these fractions is most revealing; we find that for each fraction, the square of the numerator is *nearly* twice the square of the denominator, for example,

$$\begin{array}{lll} 17^2 = 289, & 12^2 = 144, & 17^2 - (2 \times 12^2) = 1, \\ 41^2 = 1681, & 29^2 = 841, & 41^2 - (2 \times 29^2) = -1, \\ 99^2 = 9801, & 70^2 = 4900, & 99^2 - (2 \times 70^2) = 1, \\ 239^2 = 57121, & 169^2 = 28561, & 239^2 - (2 \times 169^2) = 1. \end{array}$$

The manner in which the Greeks showed the incommensurability of $\sqrt{2}$ is both ingenious and elegant, and it shows how other such results may be proved: the incommensurability of numbers such as the square roots of 3 and 5; the cube roots of 2 and 3 and so on.

6.8 Approximations to pi

Producing an incommensurable ratio (in some possibly artificial manner) is not too difficult a task; but showing that a *given* ratio is incommensurable can be difficult. The case of π (the ratio of the circumference of a circle to its diameter) is very interesting in this regard.

As noted earlier, a well-known and much used approximation to π is $\frac{22}{7}$; it is accurate to two decimal places. A much better approximation is $\frac{355}{113}$, but it is not so 'popular' and is much less well-known.

A nice way of remembering the first few digits of the decimal expansion of π is by using the following mnemonic:

HOW I WISH I COULD RECOLLECT PI EASILY.

If we count the letters in the successive words of this sentence we get the first eight digits of π; namely, 3.1415926. For those who are curious, here is π to thirty decimal places:

$$\pi = 3.14159\,26535\,89793\,23846\,26433\,83279\,\ldots.$$

Readers may enjoy composing a rhyme to remember these digits. The fact that there is no 0 among the first thirty decimal places is crucial here!

The definition of π, as a ratio of two significant lengths associated with a commonly found geometric figure, shows that it is a 'natural' and 'absolute' constant, not dependent on units of measurement. Trying to find its value using measurements in a laboratory is not too useful, as too many inaccuracies are involved. During Greek times, the great mathematician Archimedes (287–211 BC) managed to show using ingenious geometric arguments that π must lie between $3\frac{10}{71}$ and $3\frac{1}{7}$. The larger of these fractions is the origin of today's much used approximation, $\frac{22}{7}$. In India, Āryabhaṭa, who lived in the fifth century AD, gave the value of π as 3.1416. It was only in the eighteenth century that Johann Lambert, a Swiss-German mathematician-astronomer, showed π to be incommensurable.

The story of the attempts to compute π is a fascinating one, weaving through the tangled history of mathematics spanning two millennia, and featuring the greatest mathematicians of all time. As of today, the most efficient way known of computing π to vast numbers of decimal places is through the use of certain advanced results proved by the great Indian mathematician Srinivasa Ramanujan (1887–1920).

EXERCISES

1. Find a fourth proportional to:

   (a) $x^3, 3x^2y, xy^2$;

   (b) $a^4, 6a^2b^2, 2ab^3$;

   (c) a, bc, a^2.

2. Find a fourth proportional to

$$x^2+4x+3, \quad x^2-9, \quad x^2-1.$$

3. Find a fourth proportional to

$$x^3-1, \quad x^2+x+1, \quad x^2-1.$$

4. Find a mean proportional to:

   (a) $1, z^6$;

   (b) $3ab^3, 12a^3b$;

   (c) $2x^2y^6, 32x^4$.

5. Find a mean proportional to $x-1,\ x^3-3x^2+3x-1$.

6. If x, y, z are in continued proportion, show that:

   (a) $x-y:y-z=y:z$;

   (b) $x+y:x-y-y+z:y-z$.

7. If $a:b=c:d$, show that:

   (a) $(a+c)^2 \ :\ (b+d)^2 \ =\ ac \ :\ bd$;

   (b) $\dfrac{a}{a-b} \ :\ \dfrac{a+b}{b} \ =\ \dfrac{c}{c-d} \ :\ \dfrac{c+d}{d}$;

   (c) $ab\cdot\left(a^2+b^2\right) \ :\ a^3+b^3 \ =\ cd\cdot\left(c^2+d^2\right) \ :\ \left(c^3+d^3\right)$.

8. Show that if $a:b=c:d$, then $(a-b)-(c-d) \ =\ \dfrac{(a-b)(b-d)}{b}$.

9. Two numbers each made of the same two digits are in the ratio $2:9$. Find all possible such pairs of numbers.

10. Show that if a and b are positive, then the ratio $a+1:b+1$ lies between $1:1$ and $a:b$.

6.9 The Chinese tangram puzzle

To conclude this chapter we dwell briefly on a geometrical construct that elegantly brings out the idea of continued proportion—the Chinese puzzle of **TANGRAM**, of uncertain origin. It consists of seven pieces: five triangles, all isosceles right-angled, and in three different sizes, one square and one parallelogram. These can be fitted together to make a square and also to make a rectangle whose sides are in the ratio 1 : 2. A picture of the actual set with the seven 'tans' is shown in Figure 6.3.

Figure 6.3 A tangram set
(*Source*: `http://en.wikipedia.org/wiki/Tangram`)

What makes the puzzle so appealing is that the seven pieces can be fitted together to make *thousands* of different designs, resembling animals, human figures in particular postures (running, dancing, or playing), and many more. Figures 6.4 and 6.5 show such figures. There is evidence to show that Napoleon diverted himself during his years of exile on the island of St Helena using a tangram set! One of the greatest creators of tangram puzzles is the great puzzlist from 19th century-America—Sam Loyd. Lewis Caroll too was very fond of the puzzle.

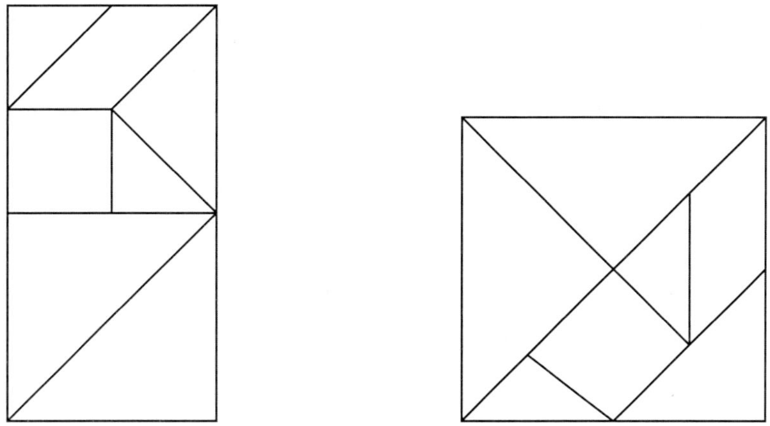

Figure 6.4 A tangram set assembled into a rectangle and then into a square

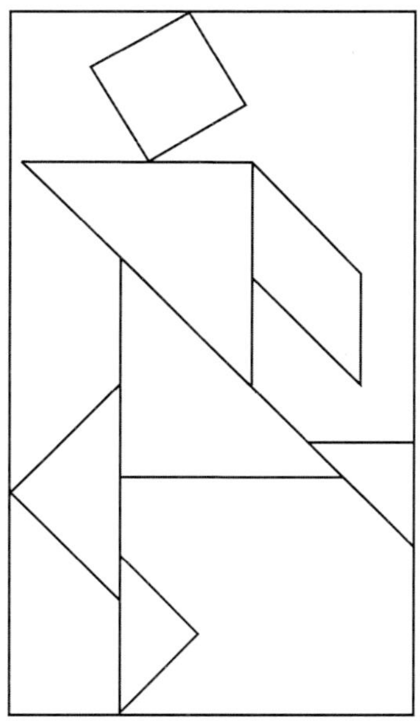

Figure 6.5 A tangram set assembled into a human figure

(*Source*: `http://en.wikipedia.org/wiki/Tangram`)

What connection does all this have to the topic of ratio and proportion? Here is how. Let us look at the *lengths of the sides* of the seven tans. Several lengths are repeated—e.g., the shorter side of the smallest triangle, the side of the square, and the shorter side of the parallelogram all have the same length; the longer side of the parallelogram and the shorter side of the middle-sized triangle have the same length, and so on. How many different lengths are there? If you examine the pictures carefully you will see that there are *five* different lengths. Call them a, b, c, d, e for convenience. We find that these lengths form a continued proportion; indeed, that

$$\frac{b}{a} = \frac{c}{b} = \frac{d}{c} = \frac{e}{d} = \sqrt{2}.$$

Another example of continued proportion in geometry comes from the study of a star-shaped figure called a **PENTAGRAM**; but of that, more later.

Chapter 7

Indices and Exponents

7.1 Introduction

In Chapter 3 we stated the *Fundamental Theorem of Arithmetic*—the statement that every positive integer may be written in just one way as the product of primes or prime powers. For example:

$$800 = 2 \times 2 \times 2 \times 2 \times 2 \times 5 \times 5,$$
$$675 = 3 \times 3 \times 3 \times 5 \times 5,$$
$$882 = 2 \times 3 \times 3 \times 7 \times 7.$$

This theorem allows us to describe the primes as the **BUILDING BLOCKS** of the integers, in the same way as the elements are the building blocks of the world around us. In analogy with the above relations we have formulas in chemistry like H_2SO_4 for sulphuric acid, NH_3 for ammonia, $C_6H_{12}O_6$ for sugar, and so on.

Now it is rather awkward to write the relation $800 = 2 \times 2 \times 2 \times 2 \times 2 \times 5 \times 5$; it is easy to lose count of the numbers! Even worse would be $1728 = 2 \times 2 \times 2 \times 2 \times 2 \times 2 \times 3 \times 3 \times 3$. We need a more convenient notation, and chemistry suggests one for us. Just as we write H_2SO_4 in preference to HHSOOOO, we prefer to write the factorisation of 800 as

$$800 = 2^5 \times 5^2,$$

as this tells you in a glance the number of 2s and 5s in the factorisation of 800. Similarly, we write $675 = 3^3 \times 5^2$, and $882 = 2 \times 3^2 \times 7^2$. This is called the **INDEX NOTATION** or the **EXPONENTIAL NOTATION**.

The number 2^3 means $2 \times 2 \times 2$, and we read it aloud as "2 to the power 3" (or simply "2 to the 3"). The '3' which occurs above the '2' is called the **EXPONENT**. So we have $2^3 = 8$. Similarly we have the following relations:

$$2^4 = 2 \times 2 \times 2 \times 2 = 16,$$

$$2^5 = 2 \times 2 \times 2 \times 2 \times 2 = 32,$$

$$3^6 = 3 \times 3 \times 3 \times 3 \times 3 \times 3 = 729.$$

So in this notation, the powers of 2 may be written as: $2^1, 2^2, 2^3, 2^4, \ldots$.

As noted above, the rationale behind introducing such a notation is that it is a matter of convenience; it saves time as well as space if we write 10^9 instead of 1000000000 or $10 \times 10 \times 10 \times 10 \times 10 \times 10 \times 10 \times 10 \times 10$.

One of the curious things about good notation is that once one grows familiar with it, it starts to assume a life of its own and enables us to do things which we could not have done otherwise; it even helps in finding new results. This is something that has happened time and again in mathematics and science.

EXERCISES

1. List the powers of 2 from 2^1 till 2^{10}.

2. List the powers of 3 from 3^1 till 3^{10}.

3. Compute the quantities 4^5 and 9^4.

4. Compare in each case the two quantities listed below, and describe what you find.

   (a) $10^2 \times 10^3$ and 10^5;

   (b) $2^4 \times 2^5$ and 2^9;

   (c) $3^7 \div 3^4$ and 3^3;

   (d) $10^7 \div 10^3$ and 10^4;

   (e) $7^5 \div 7^2$ and 7^3.

5. Which is greater, 2^8 or 3^5?

6. Which is greater, 2^{20} or 3^{12}?

7. Which is greater, 2^{11} or 3^7?

7.2 The laws of indices

Having introduced a symbol, we must learn how to use it. In this section, we develop the basic laws for working with indices.

RULE FOR MULTIPLICATION Consider the following relations:

$$2^3 \times 2^4 = (2\times 2\times 2)\times(2\times 2\times 2\times 2) = 2^7,$$
$$3^2 \times 3^3 = (3\times 3)\times(3\times 3\times 3) = 3^5.$$

It is not hard to see that when we do multiplication, exponents get *added*. We write the rule thus: *For any quantity a, and any two whole-number exponents m and n,*

$$\boxed{a^m \times a^n = a^{m+n}.} \tag{7.1}$$

Note that this is an identity; we call it the *multiplication rule for exponents*. Written in full, it reads as follows:

$$a^m \times a^n = \underbrace{a\times a\times \cdots \times a}_{m \text{ times}} \times \underbrace{a\times a\times \cdots \times a}_{n \text{ times}} = \underbrace{a\times a\times \cdots \times a}_{m+n \text{ times}} = a^{m+n}.$$

RULE FOR DIVISION Likewise, in division, exponents get *subtracted*. That is, if $m > n$, then we have the identity,

$$\boxed{a^m \div a^n = a^{m-n}.} \tag{7.2}$$

This is the *division rule for exponents*; when written in full it reads as follows:

$$a^m \div a^n = \underbrace{a\times a\times \cdots \times a}_{m \text{ times}} \div \underbrace{a\times a\times \cdots \times a}_{n \text{ times}} = \underbrace{a\times a\times \cdots \times a}_{m-n \text{ times}} = a^{m-n}.$$

For instance, we have:

$$\frac{a^4}{a^2} = \frac{a\times a\times a\times a}{a\times a} = \frac{a\times a}{1} = a^2,$$
$$\frac{a^5}{a^2} = \frac{a\times a\times a\times a\times a}{a\times a} = \frac{a\times a\times a}{1} = a^3,$$

and so on. If n, the index in the denominator, is greater than m, the index in the numerator, then we are left with a term in the *denominator* rather than the numerator, for example:

$$\frac{a^2}{a^4} = \frac{a\times a}{a\times a\times a\times a} = \frac{1}{a\times a} = \frac{1}{a^2} = \text{the reciprocal of } a^2,$$
$$\frac{a^2}{a^5} = \frac{a\times a}{a\times a\times a\times a\times a} = \frac{1}{a\times a\times a} = \frac{1}{a^3} = \text{the reciprocal of } a^3.$$

POWER RULE Next, consider the number $\left(2^4\right)^2$. It is equal to $2^4 \times 2^4 = 2^{4+4} = 2^{2\times 4}$, by applying the multiplication rule. So we have:

$$\left(2^4\right)^2 = 2^{4\times 2}.$$

Similarly, consider the number $\left(3^3\right)^4$. Applying the multiplication rule, we get $3^3 \times 3^3 \times 3^3 \times 3^3 = 3^{3+3+3+3} = 3^{4\times 3}$. So we have:

$$\left(3^3\right)^4 = 3^{4\times 3}.$$

By studying these examples, we arrive at the *power rule for exponents*: *For any quantity a, and any whole-number exponents m and n, the following identity holds:*

$$\boxed{(a^m)^n = a^{mn}.} \tag{7.3}$$

EXERCISES

1. Compute the quantities $\left(2^5\right)^2$ and $\left(2^6\right)^2$.
2. Compute the quantities $\left(3^4\right)^2$ and $\left(3^3\right)^4$.
3. Place the numbers 2^{30}, 8^9 and 16^8 in ascending order.
4. Compare the two quantities $(a^m)^n$ and $(a^n)^m$.

7.3 Big numbers

Playing around with the index notation, one quickly begins to discover very big numbers. If we list the powers of 2, we find that 2^{20} is somewhat more than a million:

$$2^{20} = 1{,}048{,}576,$$

while 2^{30} has crossed the 'billion frontier':

$$2^{30} = 1{,}073{,}741{,}824.$$

Further calculations get tedious, but with a computer to aid us, we make progress and find that

$$2^{100} = 1{,}267{,}650{,}600{,}228{,}229{,}401{,}496{,}703{,}205{,}376,$$

is a thirty one-digit number. Still more impressive is the number 2^{200}; it turns out to have sixty-one digits!

Getting a feel of how large these numbers really are can be difficult, as they lie so completely outside our everyday experience. Here is an example to illustrate what we mean: *If we stack* 10^8 *coins into a single column, how tall is the column?* Taking a coin to be roughly 0.1 cm in width, we see that the column will be $10^8 \times 0.1 = 10^7$ cm high. How high is this? Since 1 m is 100 cm, and 1 km is 1000 m, we see that 1 km is 100000 or 10^5 cm. This means that the column is 10^2 km (or 100 km) in height!

Grains of rice. Here is an example associated with a well-known story. The Shah of Persia was apparently once challenged by a visitor to a game of chess (**SHATRANJ**, as it is also known). The visitor won, and the Shah asked what he desired as a reward. The visitor politely stipulated that he must receive 1 grain of rice for the corner square of the chess board, $2^1 = 2$ grains of rice for the square next to it, $2^2 = 4$ grains for the next square, $2^3 = 8$ grains for the next square, and so on. The Shah was amused at how little the visitor seemed to want, and agreed readily enough.

Let us compute, for fun, how much rice the visitor is actually owed by the Shah. Since the board has 64 squares, he must receive 2^{63} grains of rice for the last square of the board. Let us check how large this number is. Bringing the computer to our aid, we find that

$$2^{63} = 9,223,372,036,854,775,808,$$

a 19-digit number. We see that 2^{63} is 'almost' equal to 10^{19}. (This is written in mathematics as: $2^{63} \approx 10^{19}$.) Just how large a number is 10^{19}? How much rice do these many grains represent? Experimentation suggests that roughly 50 grains of rice will fill a spoon, and that a spoon will hold roughly 5 ml (of water or rice). This means that there are roughly 10 grains of rice per ml. Let the rice be kept in a room measuring (in metres) $10 \times 10 \times 10$. The volume of the hall is 10^3 cubic metres, or $10^3 \times 10^6 = 10^9$ ml (since 1 metre equals 10^2 cm). It follows that the hall will hold $10^9 \times 10 = 10^{10}$ grains of rice. Since the visitor is owed 10^{19} grains, we need $10^{19} \div 10^{10} = 10^9$ such rooms; in other words, a billion large rooms filled with rice. This requires more rice than is available in the entire world!

EXERCISES

1. If I wish to train for long-distance running, would a morning jog of 10^4 strides per day be adequate?

2. A book has roughly 10^5 letters in it. Estimate the thickness of the book.

3. A large sheet of paper 0.01 cm thick is folded ten times in succession. How thick will the resulting wad of paper be? What if it is folded 20 times?

7.4 The four twos

Another 'big numbers' game is the one involving four twos: *Given four twos, which is the largest number that one can make with them?* (We may join them together and form numbers like 2222 and 222^2.) Here are a few such numbers:

$$2222, \qquad 222^2, \qquad 22^{22}, \qquad 2^{222}, \qquad \ldots.$$

Which is the largest of these numbers? Clearly, $222^2 > 2222$. This can be seen without having to do exact computations:

$$222^2 > 100^2 = 10000 > 2222.$$

Next, $22^{22} > 222^2$, for

$$22^{22} > 22^4 = \left(22^2\right)^2 = 484^2 > 222^2.$$

Which is larger, 2^{222} or 22^{22}? As earlier, one can figure this out in a clever way, without having to do exact computations:

$$22^{22} < 32^{22} = \left(2^5\right)^{22} = 2^{110} < 2^{222},$$

so 2^{222} is the larger number. Is this the best we can do? Not quite; we have another candidate, 2^{22^2}. This is the same as 2^{484}, so it is substantially bigger than 2^{222}.

But still better is the number $2^{2^{22}}$. This number is truly gigantic! To see why, observe that $2^{22} = 4194304$, so $2^{2^{22}} = 2^{4194304}$. This is a number with $1,262,612$ digits; writing it out in full would require a book with more than a thousand pages!

Remark

It is important to note that when we write $2^{2^{22}}$, we mean $2^{(2^{22})}$ and *not* $\left(2^2\right)^{22}$. These are not the same. For example,

$$\left(2^3\right)^4 \quad \text{and} \quad 2^{(3^4)}$$

represent two different numbers. In the first number, the bracketing shows that 2^3 is to be computed first. Since $2^3 = 8$, this number equals 8^4 which is the same as 2^{12}. In the second number, 3^4 is to be computed first. Since $3^4 = 81$, the number equals 2^{81}, which is very much larger than 2^{12}.

In general, the quantities

$$\left(a^b\right)^c, \qquad a^{(b^c)}$$

are unequal.

EXERCISES

1. Which number is larger: 4^{3^2} or 2^{3^4}?
2. Which number is larger: 3^{4^5} or 5^{4^3}?
3. Which number is the largest: 444^4, 44^{44} or 4^{444}?
4. Which number is larger, 4^{44^4} or $4^{4^{44}}$?

Estimating the sizes of big numbers

You may wonder how we estimated the size of $2^{2^{22}}$, a number so huge that even the most powerful computer available would think twice before starting to compute it in full! Here is how we went about the task.

Note that $2^{10} = 1024$ has four digits, while $2^{20} = 1048576$ has seven digits. Let us prepare the table shown below, listing the number of digits in 2^n for various values of n.

n	10	15	20	25	30	100	200
# digits in 2^n	4	5	7	8	10	31	61

We notice a pattern soon enough: *The number of digits in 2^n is roughly 1 more than $0.3 \times n$.* For example, 31 is 1 more than 0.3×100, and 61 is 1 more than 0.3×200.

This means that we can expect 2^{1000} to have about 301 digits, and 2^{10000} to have about 3001 digits. And we are close—exact computations show that 2^{1000} has 302 digits, while 2^{10000} has 3011 digits. Continuing, we expect $2^{4194304}$ to have close to $1 + 0.3 \times 4194304$ or roughly $1,258,292$ digits. Using somewhat better estimates, we find that the number of digits is $1,262,612$.

EXERCISES

1. Estimate the number of digits in 2^{222}.

2. Given the following numbers:

$$\begin{aligned} 5^{10} &= 9765625, \\ 5^{20} &= 95367431640625, \\ 5^{40} &= 9094947017729282379150390625, \end{aligned}$$

(so 5^{40} is a 28-digit number), estimate the number of digits in 5^{55}, 5^{555} and $5^{5^{55}}$.

3. Given the following numbers:

$$\begin{aligned} 9^{10} &= 3486784401, \\ 9^{20} &= 12157665459056928801, \\ 9^{40} &= 147808829414345923316083210206383297601, \end{aligned}$$

(so 9^{40} is a 39-digit number), estimate the number of digits in 9^{99}, 9^{999} and $9^{9^{99}}$.

4. *Rumour mongering.* Rumours spread at amazing speed. Suppose that you get hold of a fat juicy rumour and that in the next 5 minutes you go out and tell it to two other persons. Within the next 5 minutes they in turn go out and tell it to two others. And so on ...: each person who hears the story tells it to two others within the next 5 minutes. How many people know the secret within half-an-hour? Within the next 2 hours?

5. Comment on how reasonable the above problem is for describing the actual spread of a rumour.

7.5 Visualising big numbers

It is rather easy, using exponents, to produce numbers so large that visualising them is nearly impossible. So let us start by visualising numbers that are large but not so large that they defy our imagination.

Take a million. Figure 7.1 has 10,000 or 10^4 little squares. If 100 of these are laid out in a 10×10 array, then we will have a million little squares in a square array. If we want to print a book containing one array of 10^4 little squares per page, then the book would have to have 100 pages.

Figure 7.1 Ten thousand little squares!

How much time would it take us to count to a million? If we can speak out the numbers at the rate of one per second, then it will take us $1,000,000$ seconds. This works out to 11 days and $13\frac{7}{9}$ hours: more than $11\frac{1}{2}$ days! And this is with no meal breaks, no sleep, etc.!

If we go back a million minutes into the past, we would find ourselves about two years younger! (A million minutes is a little less than 2 years.)

Jumping to one billion: if we wanted to print a book as earlier, then the book would have to have $100,000$ pages. How thick would it be? Taking a thousand page book to be 5 cm thick, our book works out to be $5 \times 100 = 500$ cm or 5 metres in thickness! And if we had to count to a billion, taking one second per number and no breaks, it would take us 31 years and 259 days!

To conclude, here are some more such tidbits:

- If you go back a billion minutes into the past, you would find yourself in the Roman era.
- If you go back a billion days into the past, you would find yourself in the early period of human evolution. You would not see any humans; this era belongs to the hominids such as the *Australopithecines*.
- If a billion children, each with a shoulder height of 1m, made a 'human tower' by standing on each other's shoulders, the tower would be 1 million kilometres in height. It would go well past the moon! (That would be an easy and inexpensive way of getting to the moon, wouldn't it?)

7.6 Negative exponents

Earlier we had stated that for any quantity a and any two whole number exponents m,n with $m > n$, the following division rule applies:

$$a^m \div a^n = a^{m-n}.$$

But if we apply the rule to the case when $n > m$, we encounter something puzzling. For instance, the rule states that $10^2 \div 10^3 = 10^{-1}$. But what does 10^{-1} mean? How can we possibly multiply a number negative 1 times with itself?

As always in such situations, we must step backwards to resolve the mystery. The question essentially is: *What do we mean by* 10^{-1}? If we succeed in giving it a meaning so that the statement $10^2 \div 10^3 = 10^{-1}$ is both correct and meaningful, then we shall have achieved a victory of sorts. But this is not too hard to do. Since $10^2 \div 10^3$ is the same as $\frac{100}{1000} = \frac{1}{10^1}$, *we agree to give the following meaning to* 10^{-1}:

$$10^{-1} = \frac{1}{10^1}.$$

More generally, we give the following meaning to a^{-m} when m is a whole number exponent, and a is non-zero:

$$\boxed{a^{-m} = \frac{1}{a^m}.}$$

We have one more such 'agreement' to make before proceeding: *we must assign a consistent meaning to* a^0. Let a be non-zero. Applying the rule to the division $a^m \div a^m$, we obtain $a^{m-m} = a^0$. On the other hand, it is obvious that $a^m \div a^m = 1$. So if we wish to apply the multiplication and division rules for exponents uniformly, *with no exceptions*, then we are *forced* to give the following meaning to a^0:

$$\boxed{a^0 = 1} \quad (\text{for } a \neq 0).$$

What have we achieved? The 'victory' we have achieved is this:

The following rules now hold for ***all*** *integer values of m and n, and for any non-zero number a:*

$$a^m \times a^n = a^{m+n}, \qquad a^m \div a^n = a^{m-n}, \qquad (a^m)^n = a^{mn}.$$

For example, we have:

$$a^2 \div a^4 = a^{-2} = \frac{1}{a^2}, \qquad a^3 \div a^3 = 1 = a^0, \qquad a^{-2} \times a^3 = a^1 = a,$$

and so on. So we have brought a certain *consistency* to the rules governing indices. For example, we have $a^3 \times a^0 = a^{3+0} = a^3$ and $a^3 \div a^0 = a^{3-0} = a^3$, showing that a^0 behaves like unity—exactly as it should!

Consistency in notation

The value of the 'victory' mentioned above is not to be underestimated. Consistency in notation is of *great* value in mathematics and science, because notation with consistency and simplicity has a way of acquiring a life of its own, bringing great power into the hands of the user.

A good example is provided by the Hindu-Arabic place value system. To do arithmetic with the Roman system of numeration is most awkward, but with the place value system it becomes easy. More than that, it invites further exploration, whereas bad notation does just the reverse—it inhibits exploration.

Algebra itself provides excellent examples of the efficiency and power of notation, for it enables one to make **GENERALISATIONS** which would otherwise be quite impossible. For example, when we state that for any number $a \neq 0$, and any two whole numbers m and

n, we have $a^m \times a^n = a^{m+n}$, we are stating something in an extremely general form. Into that short statement we have packed *all* possible facts of the kind

$$2^4 \times 2^5 = 2^9, \qquad 3^5 \times 3^7 = 3^{12}, \qquad 4^{11} \times 4^9 = 4^{20}, \qquad 6^{13} \times 6^4 = 6^{17},$$

and so on. This shows the enormous power hidden in good notation. So what we have achieved with regard to the rules governing exponents is of great importance.

Here is another nice example of a generalisation:

THEOREM. *Let n be a positive integer. Then $x+y$ is a factor of x^n+y^n when n is odd, but not when n is even.*

EXAMPLE 1. Let $x=2$ and $y=5$. For $n=3$ we get $x^n+y^n=2^3+5^3=133$, and we can verify that this is divisible by $2+5=7$; indeed, we have $133=7\times 19$. But if $n=4$ we get $x^n+y^n=2^4+5^4=641$, which is not divisible by 7 (in fact, 641 is a prime number).

The use of algebra is indispensable not only in *proving* such a statement, but in *formulating* it in the first place. Here is another example.

FERMAT'S 'LITTLE' THEOREM. *Let p be any prime number and k any whole number; then k^p-k is a multiple of p.*

EXAMPLE 2. Let $p=7$ and $k=3$; then $k^p-k=3^7-3=2184=7\times 312$. Or take $p=11$ and $k=4$; then $k^p-k=4^{11}-4=4194300=11\times 381300$.

The rules for whole-number exponents worked out above ultimately lead the way to a very useful and important topic called **LOGARITHMS**; but more of that later.

EXERCISES

1. Compute the quantities $2^3\times 2^{-5}\times 2^4$ and $\left(10^{-2}\right)^3$.
2. Compute the quantity $\left(2^{-4}\right)^{-5}\div\left(4^{-2}\right)^{-4}$.
3. Compute the quantity $\left(9^{-6}\right)^{-5}\div\left(3^{-10}\right)^{-5}$.

7.7 Fractional exponents

Having worked out the rules for integer exponents, can we do the same for *fractional exponents* too? As earlier, the question of meaning must first be resolved—we must be clear what we *mean* by symbols such as $a^{1/2}$, $a^{1/3}$, $a^{3/5}$, and so on. However, it is not too hard to come up with reasonable meanings. (**Note:** When fractions occur as exponents, we write them as just shown; i.e., we write $a^{1/2}$ and not $a^{\frac{1}{2}}$, which looks very awkward.)

Let a be any ***positive*** number. If we apply the multiplication rule to $a^{1/2} \times a^{1/2}$, we obtain a^1, because $\frac{1}{2} + \frac{1}{2} = 1$. Write b for $a^{1/2}$; then $b \times b = a$, i.e., $b^2 = a$. A positive number b for which $b^2 = a$ is called the **SQUARE ROOT** of a, because when it is squared ('raised to the power 2'), it yields a. We write $b = \sqrt{a}$ to denote this relationship. For example:

- since $2^2 = 4$, we write $\sqrt{4} = 2$;
- since $3^2 = 9$, we write $\sqrt{9} = 3$;
- since $2.5^2 = 6.25$, we write $\sqrt{6.25} = 2.5$; and so on.

Since we want the rules $a^m \times a^n = a^{m+n}$ and $(a^m)^n = a^{mn}$ to hold good for *all* possible values of m and n, and in particular for fractional values, we agree to regard $a^{1/2}$ as the square root of a.

Similarly, $a^{1/3}$ is the **CUBE ROOT** of a, for the rules give:

$$a^{1/3} \times a^{1/3} \times a^{1/3} = \left(a^{1/3}\right)^3 = a^{3\times 1/3} = a^1 = a,$$

and $a^{3/5}$ is the *cube of the fifth root of a*, for

$$\left(a^{1/5}\right)^3 = a^{3\times 1/5} = a^{3/5}.$$

It is also the *fifth root of the cube of a*, for

$$\left(a^{3/5}\right)^5 = a^{5\times 3/5} = a^3.$$

More generally, $a^{1/n}$ is the 'n^{th} root' of a, for we have the relation

$$\left(a^{1/n}\right)^n = a^{n\times 1/n} = a^1 = a$$

and $a^{m/n}$ is the mth power of the nth root of a. Here are some examples:

$$25^{1/2} = 5, \qquad 100^{3/2} = 10^3 = 1000, \qquad 512^{2/3} = 8^2 = 64.$$

We take these rules and definitions to hold for all positive values of a. For fractional values of a, say $a = \frac{b}{c}$ where $c \neq 0$, we apply the rules shown below:

$$\boxed{\left(\frac{b}{c}\right)^m = \frac{b^m}{c^m} \quad \text{and} \quad \left(\frac{b}{c}\right)^{1/m} = \frac{b^{1/m}}{c^{1/m}}}.$$

For example, we have the following:

- $\left(\frac{4}{9}\right)^{1/2} = \frac{2}{3}$; explanation: $4^{1/2} = 2$, and $9^{1/2} = 3$.
- $\left(\frac{8}{27}\right)^{1/3} = \frac{2}{3}$; explanation: $8^{1/3} = 2$, and $27^{1/3} = 3$.
- $\left(\frac{64}{27}\right)^{2/3} = \frac{16}{9}$; explanation:

$$64^{2/3} = \left(64^{1/3}\right)^2 = 4^2 = 16;$$
$$27^{2/3} = \left(27^{1/3}\right)^2 = 3^2 = 9.$$

- $\left(\frac{81}{16}\right)^{-3/4} = \frac{8}{27}$; explanation:

$$81^{-3/4} = \left(81^{1/4}\right)^{-3} = 3^{-3};$$
$$16^{-3/4} = \left(16^{1/4}\right)^{-3} = 2^{-3}.$$

- $(0.008)^{-1/3} = 5$; explanation: $.008 = \frac{8}{1000}$, and:

$$8^{-1/3} = \left(8^{1/3}\right)^{-1} = 2^{-1} = \frac{1}{2};$$
$$1000^{-1/3} = \left(1000^{1/3}\right)^{-1} = 10^{-1} = \frac{1}{10};$$
$$\frac{1}{2} \div \frac{1}{10} = \frac{10}{2} = 5.$$

"The" square root or "a" square root?

Since $2^2 = 4$ and also $(-2)^2 = 4$, you may wonder what we mean when we say '**the** square root of a number'; should we not instead say, "**a** square root"? The resolution of this lies in looking at the number domain within which we work. Generally we work in the set of positive numbers, and we say that 2 is "the" square root of 4, that 5 is "the" square root of 25, and so on. ***By convention, a square root is taken to be positive.***

However, there are different ways in which a question may be framed. If we ask for *all the solutions of the equation* $x^2 = 4$, then the answer is: $x = \pm 2$, where '$\pm$' means 'plus or minus' (so there are *two* solutions). Similarly, the equation $x^2 = 25$ has the solutions $x = \pm 5$. In the case of equations involving cubes, e.g., $x^3 = 8$, we find that there is just one solution ($x = 2$); but this is only because *we confine ourselves to the usual number line*. There are larger domains of numbers within which the equation acquires additional solutions (namely, the so-called *complex numbers*; in this domain the equation $x^3 = 8$ has three solutions!). But this topic will be studied only much later.

Growth properties

The following remarks highlight some important features of the quantity a^x when a is a fixed positive number, and x is allowed to take different values.

- If $a > b > 0$, then $a^x > b^x$ for all positive numbers x, and $a^x < b^x$ for all negative numbers x.
- If $a > 0$ and $a \neq 1$, then from $a^x = a^y$ we can infer that $x = y$.
- If $a > 1$, then a^x *increases* as x increases. Let $a = 3$; then:

$$3^5 = 243, \qquad 3^{10} = 59049, \qquad 3^{20} = 3486784401.$$

- If a lies between 0 and 1, then a^x *decreases* when x increases. Let $a = \frac{1}{2}$; we find that

$$a^5 = \frac{1}{32}, \qquad a^{10} = \frac{1}{1024}, \qquad a^{20} = \frac{1}{1048576}.$$

EXERCISES

1. Simplify the following:

   (a) $\dfrac{3^{25} - 3^{23}}{3^{21}}$;

   (b) $\dfrac{4^{100} + 4^{102} + 4^{104}}{4^{101}}$.

2. Compute the quantities $16^{5/2}$ and $36^{3/2}$.

3. Compute the quantities $27^{2/3}$, $125^{5/3}$ and $32^{6/5}$.

4. Compute the quantities $16^{-3/4}$, $32^{-3/5}$ and $64^{-5/6}$.

5. Compute the quantity $7^{1/4} \times 7^{3/4} \times 7^{5/4} \times 7^{7/4}$.

6. Compute the quantity $9^{1/32} \times 9^{3/32} \times 9^{5/32} \times 9^{7/32}$.

7. Compute the quantity $16^{1/30} \times 16^{2/30} \times 16^{3/30} \times 16^{4/30} \times 16^{5/30}$.

8. Find the square roots of the following numbers: (a) 10^6 (b) 4×10^4 (c) 9×10^6 (d) 1.6×10^5 (e) 19.6×10^3.

9. Compute the values of the following:

   (a) $\left(3^2 + 4^2\right)^{1/2}$;

   (b) $\left(3^3 + 4^3 + 5^3\right)^{1/3}$;

   (c) $\left(4^3 + 4^2 + 4^0\right)^{1/2}$;

   (d) $\left(17^2 + 14^2 + 3^3\right)^{1/9}$;

   (e) $\left(2^9 + 2^7 + 2^6 + 2^4 + 2^3 + 2^0\right)^{1/6}$.

10. Simplify the following:

   (a) $\dfrac{2^{-1}}{3^{-1} + 6^{-1}}$.

   (b) $\dfrac{1}{2^{-1} + 10^{-1}} \times 5^{-1}$.

   (c) $\dfrac{1}{3^{-1} + 11^{-1} + 231^{-1}} \times 7^{-1}$.

11. Simplify to the extent possible: $\dfrac{a^{-1} + b^{-1}}{(ab)^{-1}}$.

12. Simplify to the extent possible: $\dfrac{a^{-1} + b^{-1} + c^{-1}}{(abc)^{-1}}$.

13. Compute the values of the following:

(a) $\sqrt{20\frac{1}{4}}$;

(b) $\sqrt{30\frac{1}{4}}$;

(c) $\sqrt{32\frac{1}{9}}$;

(d) $\sqrt{40\frac{1}{9}}$;

(e) $\left(42\frac{7}{8}\right)^{1/3}$;

(f) $\left(7\frac{19}{32}\right)^{1/5}$.

14. Show that $2^{1/2}$ is equal to $4^{1/4}$.

15. Which is greater: $2^{1/2}$ or $3^{1/3}$?

16. Which is greater: $4^{1/4}$ or $5^{1/5}$?

17. Which is greater: $3^{1/4}$ or $5^{1/6}$?

18. Find a positive integer a such that $\frac{a}{2}$ is a square, and $\frac{a}{3}$ is a cube.

19. Find a positive integer a such that $\frac{a}{5}$ is a square, $\frac{a}{2}$ is a cube, and $\frac{a}{3}$ is a fifth power.

20. Show that if K is a positive number, and a, b, c any three numbers, then

$$K^{a-b} \times K^{b-c} \times K^{c-a} = 1.$$

21. Show that if K is a positive number, and a, b, c any three numbers, then

$$\left(K^a\right)^{b-c} \times \left(K^b\right)^{c-a} \times \left(K^c\right)^{a-b} = 1.$$

22. Show that if K is a positive number, and a, b, c any three numbers, then

$$\left(\frac{K^a}{K^b}\right)^{a+b} \times \left(\frac{K^b}{K^c}\right)^{b+c} \times \left(\frac{K^c}{K^a}\right)^{c+a} = 1.$$

23. Consider the following table, which lists the values of 2^x for $x = 0, 1, 2, \ldots$:

x	0	0.5	1	1.5	2	2.5	3	3.5	4	...
2^x	1	1.414	2		4		8		16	...

Imagine that the table is filled in very finely, with the values of 2^x listed for values of x such as $0.1, 0.2, \ldots$.

(a) Fill in the blanks in the table; that is, find 2^x for $x = 1.5, 2.5, 3.5, \ldots$.

(b) We want to find x such that $2^x = 10$. Clearly $3 < x < 4$, because $2^3 = 8$ and $2^4 = 16$, and $8 < 10 < 16$). Indeed we can expect x to lie closer to 3 than to 4. How would you find the value of x?

(c) Find the approximate value of x if (i) $2^x = 5$ (ii) $2^x = 9$.

24. Given that $\sqrt{3} \approx 1.732$, prepare a table listing the values of 3^x for $x = 0, 0.5, 1, 1.5, 2.5, \ldots$.

25. Find the approximate value of x if (a) $3^x = 10$ (b) $3^x = 20$ (c) $3^x = 50$.

26. If a lies between 0 and 1, and x and y are positive numbers such that $x > y$, will a^x be greater or less than a^y?

27. Prove the identities:

$$2^{n+1} - 1 = 2 \times (2^n - 1) + 1, \qquad 3^{n+1} - 1 = 3 \times (3^n - 1) + 2.$$

28. Prove the identities:

$$4^{n+1} - 1 = 4 \times (4^n - 1) + 3, \qquad 5^{n+1} - 1 = 5 \times (5^n - 1) + 4.$$

7.8 Growth patterns

Consider a square whose side is x cm; here x is any positive number. If we denote the perimeter of the square by P cm, then $P = 4x$. This relationship shows how P may be computed when we know the value of x; it shows how P *changes* with x; it captures what is called the **FUNCTIONAL RELATIONSHIP** between x and P. The relationship may be shown in the form of a table:

x	1	2	3	4	5	6	7	8	$\cdots$
P	4	8	12	16	20	24	28	32	$\cdots$

We see that when x doubles, so does P; when x grows by a factor of 3, so does P. This kind of functional relationship is called **LINEAR**. We say that P *grows linearly with* x.

Now consider the **AREA** of the square. Denote the area by A cm^2; then $A = x^2$. This relation shows the functional relationship between x and A. As earlier we may display the relationship in the form of a table.

x	1	2	3	4	5	6	7	8	...
A	1	4	9	16	25	36	49	64	...

We see that when x doubles, A grows by a factor of 4; when x grows by a factor of 3, A grows by a factor of 9. This kind of functional relationship is called **QUADRATIC**.

If instead we consider the **VOLUME** of a cube whose side is x cm, then we meet yet another kind of relationship. Denoting the volume by V cm^3, we have $V = x^3$. We display the relationship between x and V in the form of a table:

x	1	2	3	4	5	6	7	8	...
V	1	8	27	64	125	216	343	512	...

We see that when x doubles, V grows by a factor of 8; when x grows by a factor of 3, V grows by a factor of 27. This kind of functional relationship is called **CUBIC**.

Another kind of relationship is the **EXPONENTIAL RELATIONSHIP**, associated with population growth. Imagine a single amoeba living in a dish, with a generous supply of food. Amoeba are a very simple form of life, but they can do some nasty things like causing amoebic dysentery to us humans. They grow by dividing into two, through a process called **FISSION**. Every few minutes each new amoeba divides into two, and so it continues; *so the population doubles every few minutes*. Suppose that our amoeba undergoes fission every 10 minutes. We take 10 minutes to be our unit of time, so when we say 'x units of time', we mean $10x$ minutes. If we start with a single amoeba, then how many amoeba will we have after x units of time? Denote the number by N; if we assume that amoeba live forever, then $N = 2^x$. This growth pattern is called *exponential* (as x occurs as an exponent). The table below shows some figures generated by the formula:

x	1	2	3	4	5	6	7	8	...
N	2	4	8	16	32	64	128	256	...

Comparing linear growth, quadratic growth, cubic growth and exponential growth, we may get the impression that cubic growth is the fastest of these; but the smallness of the table has deceived us. If we continue the table from $x = 10$, we find that exponential growth soon overtakes the others.

x	10	11	12	13	14	15	16	17
x^3	1000	1331	1728	2197	2744	3375	4096	4913
2^x	1024	2048	4096	8192	16384	32768	65536	131072

A bit further down, the difference becomes even more dramatic:

$$50^3 = 125000, \qquad 2^{50} = 1125899906842624.$$

The lesson we see here is that *exponential growth is very fast*—much faster than quadratic growth or even cubic growth. Population experts refer to such growth patterns as *explosive*.

It is precisely exponential growth that takes place in a nuclear explosion. The objects that 'grow' in number in such an explosion are not living things but certain subatomic particles called **NEUTRONS**; their numbers increase in an uncontrolled fashion. In a nuclear reactor too they grow in number but the growth is carefully controlled using certain devices called *control rods*. If these did not work then the reactor could blow up or melt down!

We can have less dramatic exponential growth, say 1.1^x; this would mean an increase of 10% for every unit of time. But even this growth is ultimately explosive; e.g., 1.1^{200} is nearly equal to two hundred million, and 1.1^{500} exceeds a hundred billion billion.

7.9 Exponential notation in science

As mentioned several times by now, good notation has a way of coming to life of its own; it helps users think of possibilities which they might not otherwise have considered. The exponential notation has this feature. It is used very widely by scientists and other professionals.

Miscellaneous data

Given in Table 7.1 are various data relating to each planet: r, its distance in km from the sun as given by the length of its *semi-major axis*; T, the time taken in 'earth years' to complete a revolution around the sun (this is its *orbital period*); and D, its *equatorial diameter* in km. Data on the sun are given in Table 7.2.

Observe how easy it is to compare data when given in this form. For example, we see that the distance between Pluto and the Sun is roughly 40 times that between the Earth and

Table 7.1 Miscellaneous data on the solar system

Planet	**Distance,** r (km)	**Orbital period,** T (years)	**diameter,** D (km)
Mercury	5.75×10^6	0.24	3.46×10^3
Venus	10.75×10^6	0.62	4.64×10^3
Earth	14.86×10^7	1.00	1.22×10^4
Mars	22.65×10^7	1.88	6.72×10^3
Jupiter	77.32×10^7	11.86	1.39×10^5
Saturn	141.79×10^7	29.46	1.14×10^5
Uranus	285.28×10^7	84.01	4.70×10^4
Neptune	447.04×10^7	164.79	4.48×10^4
Pluto	587.20×10^7	248.43	2.36×10^3
2003 UB313		560	2.68×10^3

the Sun; for $587.2 \div 14.86$ is roughly $600 \div 15$, i.e., about 40 (this can be done *mentally*). This is expressed by stating that the distance from the Sun to Pluto is 40 Astronomical Units (AU); one astronomical unit being the Earth–Sun distance.

Note: We have included some data on the *tenth planet*, known as '2003 UB313' (it is yet to be christened); it was only recently discovered (July 2005). Measurements suggest that its *aphelion* (furthest point from the Sun) lies at a distance of about 97 AU and its *perihelion* (nearest point) at a distance of about 38 AU.

Table 7.2 lists several physical constants used routinely by scientists. Commonly accepted symbols are also given.

EXERCISES

1. Refer to the 'Solar System Data' table. For each planet, compute its distance (r) from the sun in Astronomical Units. Prepare a table listing r and the orbital period of the planet (T). Make a guess about the relationship between r and T.

2. What is the ratio of volume of Jupiter to that of the Earth? How many Earths would fit into Jupiter? To solve this, you must use the fact that the volume of a sphere is proportional to the *cube* of its radius.

Table 7.2 Miscellaneous physical constants

Constant	Symbol	Value
Speed of light in vacuum	c	3×10^8 metre/second
Charge of an electron	e	1.6022×10^{-19} coulomb
Faraday's constant (electrolysis)	F	96485.309 coulomb/mole
Bohr radius (radius of H atom)		5.2918×10^{-11} metre
Mass of electron	m_e	9.1094×10^{-31} kilogram
Mass of proton	m_p	1.6726×10^{-27} kilogram
Mass of neutron	m_n	1.6749×10^{-27} kilogram
Classical radius of electron	r_e	2.8179×10^{-15} metre
Avogadro constant	A	6.0221×10^{23}
Acceleration due to gravity	g	9.80665 metre/second^2
Newton's constant of gravitation	G	6.67×10^{-14} metre^3/gm $\times$ second^2
Mass of Sun	M_{Sun}	1.99×10^{30} kilogram
Radius of Sun	R_{Sun}	6.96×10^8 metre
Mass of Earth	M_{Earth}	5.98×10^{24} kilogram
Mass of Jupiter		1.899×10^{27} kilogram
Mass of Earth's moon		7.35×10^{22} kilogram
Radius of Earth's moon		1.74×10^6 metre
Mass of Solar System		1.993×10^{30} kilogram

3. What fraction of the mass of the Solar System belongs to the Sun, and what fraction to Jupiter?

4. Compute the acceleration due to gravity on the moon, given that it is about one-sixth of the acceleration due to gravity on Earth.

5. The sun is made almost entirely of hydrogen; it also has some helium, and traces of a few higher elements. Roughly how many hydrogen atoms are there in the Sun? To solve this, you need to know that a hydrogen atom has one proton and one electron.

6. If the Earth were made entirely of hydrogen, roughly how many atoms would be contained in it?

7. If Jupiter were made entirely of hydrogen, roughly how many atoms would be contained in it?

8. How many times the mass of an electron is that of a proton?

9. Roughly how many seconds are there in a year? Express your answer in the form 10^n.

10. What is your age in seconds? (Express your answer in the form 10^n.)

11. Taking the average pulse rate to be 72 beats/minute and the average life span to be 75 years, roughly how many times does the heart beat during an average life span?

12. The *age of the universe* has been estimated as being about 2×10^{10} or 20 billion years. How many seconds old is the universe?

13. A *light year* is the distance travelled by a ray of light in one year. How many kilometres are there in a light-year?

14. How many seconds does light take to travel from the Sun to the Earth, and how many seconds to travel to Pluto? What is the Earth–Sun distance in light minutes?

15. The nearest star, Proxima Centauri, belonging to the Centaurus group of stars, is about 4 light years from the Sun. How many years would it take a spaceship to reach this star if it is travelling at one million kilometres per hour? (At present, we do not have spaceships that can travel at this speed.)

16. Find references to the *Avogadro constant* on the Web or in an encyclopedia. Find what is meant by *molecular weight of a gas* and *gram-mole of a gas*.

    What does Avogadro's law state?

    Using the law, estimate the number of molecules of oxygen that would fill a room measuring 10 m $\times$ 10 m $\times$ 10 m.

7.10 Three diversions

We close this chapter with three 'diversions' involving exponents. The first involves a well-known puzzle in which the powers of 2 make an unexpected appearance; the second is about a celebrated theorem in number theory, recently proved (but after three and half centuries of struggle); and the third is about a closely related *open* problem, also in number theory.

The Tower of Hanoi (The Tower of Brahma)

The puzzle consists of three pegs, labelled A, B and C, and n circular discs $(D_1, D_2, \ldots, D_n)$ where n is a positive integer. Each disc has a hole at its centre. The discs are of different sizes and initially lie on peg A, in the order of increasing size: the largest (D_n) lies at the bottom, and the smallest (D_1) at the top (see Figure 7.1). The object of the puzzle is to move all the discs to peg C, using B as an intermediate junction, with the following constraint: *At no stage must any disc lie upon a smaller disc.* We must transfer the discs one at a time, making as few moves as possible.

Figure 7.1 The Tower of Hanoi
(*Source*: `http://en.wikipedia.org/wiki/Tower-of-Hanoi`)

If $n = 1$, then we need just 1 move to make the transfer. If $n = 2$, then we need three moves: move D_1 to B, then D_2 to C, and then D_1 to C. If $n = 3$, then we find after some trial-and-error that we need seven moves.

At this stage, we introduce a symbol for *the least number of moves we need to make when there are n discs*; we shall call this number h_n. (This may be pronounced as 'h sub n', or 'h subscript n', or simply 'h of n'. The simplest is the first one.) So $h_1 = 1$, $h_2 = 3$ and $h_3 = 7$. It is of great interest to seek a *formula* for h_n. Here is the neat final result:

$$h_n = 2^n - 1. \tag{7.1}$$

Check that the formula fits when $n = 1, 2$, and 3.

It is easy to prove the above formula. We first find a connection between the case when there are $n+1$ discs and the case when there are n discs. We shall show below that

$$h_{n+1} = 2h_n + 1. \tag{7.2}$$

That is, *each successive h-number is* 1 *more than twice the one before it*. So from $h_1 = 1$ we get $h_2 = (2 \times 1) + 1 = 3$, then $h_3 = (2 \times 3) + 1 = 7$, followed by $h_4 = (2 \times 7) + 1 = 15$; and so on. Therefore, the sequence of h-values is the following:

$$1, \quad 3, \quad 7, \quad 15, \quad 31, \quad 63, \quad 127, \quad 255, \quad \ldots.$$

Examining these figures, we discover soon enough that $h_n = 2^n - 1$. So the sequence of h-values is closely related to the powers of 2.

Explanations. Why should the relation $h_{n+1} = 2h_n + 1$ be true? Suppose we start with $n+1$ discs on peg A. Consider the moment when we can first move the largest disc, D_{n+1}. We can move it to peg C only if at that point, *the other n discs are all on peg B*. So the action plan must have three stages to it: (a) Find a way of moving discs $D_1, D_2, \ldots, D_n$ from peg A to peg B; this will naturally take h_n moves. (b) Move D_{n+1} to peg C (this takes 1 move). (c) Finally, move discs $D_1, D_2, \ldots, D_n$ to from peg B to peg C; this will again take h_n moves. The total number of moves is thus $h_n + 1 + h_n = 2h_n + 1$. It is not hard to see that this strategy cannot be bettered, and it shows why $h_{n+1} = 2h_n + 1$.

Using this relation we can now show that $h_n = 2^n - 1$ for every positive integer n. We do not go into the details, but the crucial observation is that

$$2^{n+1} - 1 = 2 \times (2^n - 1) + 1.$$

Fermat's Last Theorem

You will surely have heard about this theorem. The mathematical community has always known of it, ever since it was first conjectured, but since the mid-1990s, it has become known even to the non-mathematical public. There are many popular and well-written books on the Theorem, which is usually abbreviated to FLT.

FLT was first conjectured by a very great amateur mathematician, indeed, the greatest of them all: Pierre de Fermat (1601–65) who worked as a juror for the French government, and 'did' mathematics only in his spare time. He worked in a variety of areas of mathematics: number theory, coordinate geometry, the theory of maxima and minima (this was before the time of Newton), . . . , and in collaboration with Blaise Pascal he even invented a whole new field of mathematics—the *theory of probability*. His famous conjecture probably came about as a result of his practice of reading ancient mathematical texts, in this case the book ARITHMETICA written by the third century AD mathematician Diophantus of Alexandria.

The problem may have occurred to him when he was studying the Pythagorean problem of finding *triples of coprime perfect squares, such that the sum of two of them equals the third one*; e.g., $3^2+4^2=5^2$ $(9+16=25)$; or $5^2+12^2=13^2$ $(25+144=169)$. Infinitely many such triples exist, and nice ways are known of generating all of them. It is a nice exercise to find all such triples in which the difference between the largest two numbers in the triple is some given integer.

It was natural for Fermat to ask, *Can the corresponding problem involving cubes or fourth powers be solved as easily?* One day, while studying Diophantus's text, he scribbled a message in the margin of the book; it translates roughly as follows:

> *It is not possible for a perfect cube to be the sum of two other perfect cubes; or for a perfect fourth power to be the sum of two other perfect fourth powers; or for a perfect fifth power to be the sum of two other perfect fifth powers; and so on. . . . I have found a truly marvellous demonstration of this, but this margin is too small to hold it.*

This may well be the most frustrating marginal comment ever written! After Fermat died and his claim came to be known (thanks to the efforts of his son, Samuel Fermat), it set off a quest for the proof of this statement. The years passed, however, and then the centuries, and no one was able to come up with a proof—though certainly not for want of trying! It would be hard to estimate the amount of amateur and professional manpower that has gone into tackling this problem; it is estimated that there exist *hundreds* of faulty proofs for the FLT, and in many of them the errors in the 'proofs' are very subtle indeed.

Of course, Fermat's conjecture could have been wrong; after all, number theory is a subject where one can easily be fooled by patterns. (This is particularly true with regard to the prime numbers.) But no one was able to find a counter-example to show that the statement is wrong. And to add to the general frustration, no one was able to find any evidence that Fermat had ever found a 'demonstration' (whether marvellous or not) to prove his claim.

The quest for the proof of the FLT lasted no less than three-and-a-half centuries and culminated only in 1994–95, when a proof was given by Andrew Wiles of Princeton University.

The FLT studies the equation $a^n + b^n = c^n$ where a, b, c are required to be positive integers, and n is an integer greater than 2. (For $n = 2$, there are solutions aplenty, as noted above.) Following Fermat, some individual values of n had been treated with success by different mathematicians (Fermat himself had dealt with the case $n = 4$, and Euler had solved the cubic case, $n = 3$), but no one had any idea how the totality of ns could be treated all at once—till Andrew Wiles came along.

The story of Fermat's Last Theorem is a glorious one, one of the great stories in the history of mathematics, not only for the fact that it was ultimately solved, but because the efforts to solve generated such an extraordinary amount of beautiful mathematics (now known as *algebraic number theory*). The student would do well to read about it in a book like Simon Singh's FERMAT'S ENIGMA.

The Beal Conjecture, $a^x + b^y = c^z$

In the Fermat equation, $a^n + b^n = c^n$, the exponents of a, b, c are equal. What happens if we allow them to be different? In other words, what happens if we instead study the equation $a^x + b^y = c^z$, with x, y, $z > 2$? Then, curiously, solutions seem to exist in abundance! For example:

(a) $3^3 + 6^3 = 3^5$;

(b) $3^9 + 54^3 = 3^{11}$;

(c) $3^6 + 18^3 = 3^8$;

(d) $7^6 + 7^7 = 98^3$;

(e) $211^3 + 3165^3 = 422^4$;

(f) $386^3 + 4825^3 = 579^4$;

(g) $307^3 + 614^4 = 5219^3$;

(h) $5400^3 + 90^4 = 630^4$.

Moreover, it is easy to show that infinitely many such examples exist.

On examining these examples, one fact comes to light: *In each instance, the bases share a factor that exceeds* 1. That is, *the* GCD *of the bases exceeds* 1. For example, in examples (a), (b) and (c), all the bases are multiples of 3; in (d) all the bases are multiples of 7; in (e) all the bases are multiples of 211; in (f) all the bases are multiples of 193; and so on. This was first noticed by a Texas millionaire mathematician, Andrew Beal, who formulated it as a conjecture, now called the **BEAL CONJECTURE**.

BEAL CONJECTURE. *If positive integers a, b, c and integers $x > 2$, $y > 2$ and $z > 2$ satisfy the equality $a^x + b^y = c^z$, then* $\text{GCD}(a,b,c) > 1$.

The conjecture remains open, and Andrew Beal himself has announced a reward of \$100,000 for its proof or disproof!

Beal's Conjecture implies the FLT

It is quite easy to show that the Beal Conjecture *implies* Fermat's Last Theorem. So its proof, if found, would provide an alternate proof of FLT.

To see why, suppose that we have $a^n + b^n = c^n$ where a, b, c, n are positive integers with $n > 2$. The Beal conjecture then implies that a, b, c share a common factor $k > 1$. Since all the terms in the equality $a^n + b^n = c^n$ have the same degree (that is, the relation is **HOMOGENEOUS**), this factor can be divided out of the triple, and we get another triple of positive integers satisfying the Fermat relation. That is, if we let $a_1 = \frac{a}{k}$, $b_1 = \frac{b}{k}$, $c_1 = \frac{c}{k}$, then we have

$$a_1^n + b_1^n = c_1^n.$$

But now Beal's claim would apply to this triple as well, i.e., to (a_1, b_1, c_1), and we would be able to divide out a common factor (exceeding 1) from a_1, b_1, c_1. We would thus get *another* triple (a_2, b_2, c_2) satisfying the Fermat relation. And this would go on for ever! Clearly this is an impossibility, as the integers involved are getting smaller and smaller. On the other hand, a positive integer cannot be less than 1, so this process certainly cannot go on forever.

So if Beal's conjecture is true, then the FLT follows from it as a simple corollary.

Remark

The above style of proof is called **INFINITE DESCENT**. The first person to use such a method of proof was Fermat himself. He used it to prove the case $n = 4$ of FLT as well as a remarkable result now called **FERMAT'S TWO SQUARES THEOREM**.

The Catalan Conjecture

A related result is Mihăilescu's Theorem (earlier called *Catalan's Conjecture*); it lay in the 'Unsolved' category for over a century, and was proved only in 2002 by the Romanian mathematician Preda Mihăilescu.

MIHĂILESCU'S THEOREM. *The only pair of consecutive positive integers both of which are perfect powers are* $2^3 = 8$ *and* $3^2 = 9$. *That is, the only solution of the equation* $a^x - b^y = 1$ *in positive integers, with* $x > 1$ *and* $y > 1$, *is* $a = 3, b = 2, x = 2, y = 3$.

In general, statements of this kind are difficult to prove.

EXERCISES

1. Prove the identity:
$$\left(a^2-1\right)^2+(2a)^2 = \left(a^2+1\right)^2,$$
and obtain some Pythagorean triples, i.e., triples of coprime integers such that the sum of the squares of two of them equals the square of the third one. Example: $15^2+8^2 = 17^2$.

2. Prove the identity:
$$\left(a^2-b^2\right)^2 + (2ab)^2 = \left(a^2+b^2\right)^2.$$
Using this identity, list more instances of Pythagorean triples.

3. Find positive integers a, b, c such that $a^2+b^2 = c^3$.

4. Show that infinitely many instances of $a^x+b^y = c^z$ exist in which $a = b = c = 2$ and the exponents are all greater than 2.

5. Prove the identity:
$$[a\,(a^n+b^n)]^n + [b\,(a^n+b^n)]^n = (a^n+b^n)^{n+1}.$$
Using this identity, list more instances of $a^x+b^y = c^z$ where the exponents are all greater than 2. Example: $194^4+291^4 = 97^5$.

Chapter 8

Polynomials

In an earlier chapter we introduced algebra as a 'lazy man's arithmetic' which is surprisingly effective in finding unknown quantities that satisfy given conditions, and in describing and explaining number patterns; it can even be used to find new patterns. In this chapter, we study the notion of *polynomial*. Following this, we shall study *expansions in algebra* and *factorisation* in the following two chapters.

8.1 Polynomials in one variable

Let x represent an unknown quantity. We consider the expressions obtained by multiplying it by itself a number of times:

$$1, \quad x, \quad x \cdot x = x^2, \quad x \cdot x \cdot x = x^3, \quad x \cdot x \cdot x \cdot x = x^4, \quad x \cdot x \cdot x \cdot x \cdot x = x^5, \quad \ldots.$$

Note that they are all of the form $x \cdot x \cdot \cdots \cdot x$. The initial '1' may also be regarded as of this form, except that it is an 'empty product', with no terms at all; i.e., $1 = x^0$. These expressions are called the **PURE POWERS** of x. The exponent used is called the **DEGREE** of the expression; so the degree of $1 = x^0$ is 0, the degree of $x = x^1$ is 1, the degree of x^3 is 3, the degree of x^5 is 5, and so on.

Let any finite number of these powers of x be chosen, let each one be multiplied by any real number, and let the sum of these products be taken. This sum is called a **POLYNOMIAL IN** x, and the different quantities added together are called its **TERMS**. The exponent of the highest power of x which it has is called the **DEGREE** of the polynomial. Examples are given below.

- Pure numbers like 1, $\frac{2}{3}$, $7\frac{1}{5}$ and 10 are polynomials of degree 0.

Such polynomials are also known as **CONSTANTS**.

- Expressions like $x+1$, $2x+5$, $6x-1$, $101x+2007$ and $199x-1999$ are polynomials in x of degree 1.

  Such polynomials are said to be **LINEAR**.

- Expressions like $2x^2-x-7$, $3x^2+6x+3$, $10x^2-1$ and $103x^2+99x-1$ are polynomials in x of degree 2.

  Such polynomials are said to be **QUADRATIC**.

- The expression $x^{101}+x^{37}+\sqrt{113}$ is a polynomial in x of degree 101.

- The expression $\sqrt{7}x^{2007}-x^{1947}+x^{1857}+1$ is a polynomial in x of degree 2007.

So the general polynomial has the form

$$ax^n+bx^{n-1}+cx^{n-2}+\cdots+px+q,$$

where n is a non-negative integer and a is non-zero. The quantities ax^n, bx^{n-1}, cx^{n-2}, …, px and q are the terms of this polynomial, and its degree is n. The term ax^n is called the **HIGHEST DEGREE TERM** or the **LEADING TERM**, and the numbers $a, b, c, \ldots, p, q$ are called the **COEFFICIENTS** of the polynomial.

For example, for the polynomial $5x^7-9x^2+11x-2$, the leading term is $5x^7$, and the degree is 7. We write: $\deg(5x^7-9x^2+11x-2)=7$. Similarly we have: $\deg(x^2+2x)=2$, and $\deg(x^3-x+1)=3$. The word 'deg' stands for *degree*.

Like other things in life, polynomials may be given **NAMES**. For polynomials in x, we use names like $f(x)$, $g(x)$, $h(x)$, $P(x)$, $Q(x)$, $A(x)$, $B(x)$, etc.

Since at the start we consider only non-negative, integral powers of x, the following expressions cannot be obtained through the above prescription:

$$x^{1/2}, \quad x^{1/3}, \quad \frac{1}{x}, \quad \frac{1}{x^2}.$$

Consequently, these are *not* polynomials in x.

Note that we did not list 0 as a polynomial of degree 0; it is the **ZERO POLYNOMIAL**. For reasons which we explain below, the degree of this polynomial is left *undefined*.

Polynomials may arise in mathematics in a natural manner. For example, consider a square with side x. Its perimeter $P(x)$ is given by $P(x)=4x$, which is a linear polynomial in x, and its area $A(x)$ is given by $A(x) = x^2$, which is a quadratic polynomial in x. If we have a cuboid with sides $x+1$, $2x+1$ and $3x-2$, then its volume $V(x)$ is given by

$$V(x) = (x+1)(2x+1)(3x-2) = 6x^3+5x^2-3x-2,$$

which is a polynomial in x, of degree 3.

We have been using the letter x repeatedly, but obviously, other letters can be used just as well. So $f(y) = y^2+1$ is a quadratic polynomial in y; $g(z) = z^5+4z+7$ is a polynomial in z, of degree 5; and $h(w) = w^{11}+3w^2+6$ is a polynomial in w, of degree 11. When a letter (x, y, z, u, v, w, etc.) is used in this manner, it represents an **UNKNOWN QUANTITY**, and any number may be substituted for this letter. It is called the **ARGUMENT** of the polynomial.

8.2 What about the degree of the zero polynomial?

We stated above that the degree of the zero polynomial is left undefined. To see why, consider what happens when we multiply any two polynomials in x of degrees 2 and 3 respectively, say x^2+5 and $2x^3-3x+9$. We get

$$\left(x^2+5\right)\left(2x^3-3x+9\right) = 2x^5+7x^3+9x^2-15x+45.$$

Observe that the degree of the product is 5 which equals $2+3$. *It is always the case that for any two polynomials $f(x)$ and $g(x)$, we have* $\deg(f \cdot g) = \deg(f) + \deg(g)$. You may verify this with the polynomials x^3+1 and x^5-x+3, or with any other pair of polynomials.

What happens if one of the multiplicands is 0? Then the product is always 0, no matter what the other polynomial is; e.g., we have $0 \cdot \left(x^2+1\right) = 0$. If we apply the above rule to this product, we would get: $\deg(0) + \deg(x^2+1) = \deg(0)$, i.e., $\deg(0) + 2 = \deg(0)$. But no matter what value we give to $\deg(0)$, this relation will never be satisfied! This means that the rule stated above gets contradicted. For this reason it is best not to assign any fixed number for the degree of the zero polynomial, and to leave its degree *undefined*.[1]

8.3 Alternate definition of polynomial

Another way to define a polynomial in x is to start with the quantity x and then use it together with the real numbers to build an expression, using the following rules repeatedly, in any order and as many times as we wish.

[1] Some mathematicians prefer to say that degree of the zero polynomial is $-\infty$, that is, negative infinity, because the sum of $-\infty$ and any finite number is $-\infty$; e.g., we may write $-\infty+2 = -\infty$.

- We are allowed to add or subtract any real number, repeatedly.
- We are allowed to multiply by any real number, or divide by any non-zero real number, repeatedly.
- We are allowed to multiply by x, repeatedly.
- We are permitted to use operations like squaring, cubing, raising to the fourth power, or more generally exponentiation to a non-negative power, repeatedly.
- In the case of division, *only division by non-zero real numbers is permitted. We are **not** permitted to divide by x, or by any expression involving x.*

Then the resulting expression is a polynomial in x, and all polynomials in x may be obtained in this manner. For example, if our sequence of operations is

Start with x; add 1; multiply by 3; add 5,

then we first get $x+1$, then $3(x+1)$ which is the same as $3x+3$, and finally we get $3x+3+5$, i.e., $3x+8$. So, $3x+8$ is an example of a polynomial in x.

If the sequence of operations is

Start with x; add 7; square the quantity; add 3; multiply by x; add 1,

then we first get $x+7$; then $(x+7)^2 = x^2+14x+49$; then $x^2+14x+52$; then $x\left(x^2+14x+52\right) = x^3+14x^2+52x$; and finally we get $x^3+14x^2+52x+1$. So $x^3+14x^2+52x+1$ is another example of a polynomial in x. Its degree is 3.

If the sequence of operations is

Start with x; add 1; square the quantity; square the quantity; square the quantity,

then we get, first: $x+1$; then $(x+1)^2$; then $(x+1)^4$; and finally $(x+1)^8$, which simplifies to

$$x^8+8x^7+28x^6+56x^5+70x^4+56x^3+28x^2+8x+1.$$

This is a polynomial of degree 8.

The following are more examples of polynomials:

$$x^3+2x+5, \qquad 2x^4+x-\sqrt{101}, \qquad x^{10}-\sqrt{7}x^4+3x-\sqrt{10}.$$

Since an unlimited number of such operations can be done, the variety of possible polynomials is very large. However some expressions can never occur. Thus, since division by x is not permitted, we can never get expressions like the following:

$$\frac{1}{x}, \qquad \frac{1}{x^2}, \qquad \frac{2x+1}{x^2+1}, \qquad \frac{3x^2+2x+3}{x^4+2x+1},$$

and so on. So such expressions are not polynomials in x.

If we start not with one unknown quantity x, but with *two* such quantities, say x and y, then by using the same rules repeatedly (keeping in mind the restriction that division by x or y is not permitted, nor division by expressions involving x and y), we get a **POLYNOMIAL IN x AND y**. Examples of such polynomials are:

$$x^2+y^3+7, \qquad x^3y+5xy^2+7y^5+2, \qquad x^{10}y^7-4x^3y^{11}+9x^2y^{25}+1001.$$

The degree of the first polynomial is 3; that of the second one is 5 (by virtue of the term $7y^5$); and that of the third is 27 (by virtue of the term $9x^2y^{25}$).

As earlier, it is obvious that the variety of such polynomials is very large. And, as earlier, there are certain expressions which we cannot get using these rules, e.g.,

$$\frac{x}{y}, \qquad \frac{x^2}{y+1}, \qquad 2x^3+3xy^2+\frac{y+1}{x+2}.$$

Such expressions are not polynomials.

For the rest of the chapter we consider only polynomials in a single unknown quantity, which is usually called x. We shall use symbols like P, Q, R, f, g and h as names for the polynomials.

8.4 Multiplication of polynomials

Polynomials can be multiplied in the same way that we multiply integers. The key point to remember is that when we multiply two polynomials P and Q, *every term in P gets multiplied with every term in Q*. This follows from the law of distributivity of multiplication over addition, $a(b+c)=ab+ac$, and its repeated extension to products with more terms, e.g., $(a+b)(c+d)=ac+bc+ad+bd$.

For example, consider the product $(x^2+2x+3)\cdot(x^3+1)$. As there are 3 terms in x^2+2x+3, and two terms in x^3+1, we get $3\times 2=6$ terms when we multiply the two expressions:

$$\begin{aligned}(x^2+2x+3)\cdot(x^3+1) &= x^2\cdot x^3+2x\cdot x^3+3\cdot x^3+x^2\cdot 1+2x\cdot 1+3\cdot 1\\ &= x^5+2x^4+3x^3+x^2+2x+3.\end{aligned}$$

Sometimes we can collect some terms together in the product as they have the same degree. For example, we have:

$$(x-1)\cdot(x^2+x+1)=x^3+x^2+x-x^2-x-1=x^3-1,$$

$$\begin{aligned}(x^2-x+1)\cdot(x^2+x-1) &= x^4+x^3-x^2-x^3-x^2+x+x^2+x-1\\ &= x^4-x^2+2x-1.\end{aligned}$$

Remark

The following general result should be noted:

> *The degree of the product of two non-zero polynomials is equal to the sum of the degrees of the two multiplicands.*

As noted earlier, it is precisely this fact that keeps us from assigning a degree to the zero polynomial.

8.5 Division of polynomials

Division too can be performed, and it is carried out just like long division for numbers. Let us show how the division

$$\frac{x^5+2x^4+3x^3+x^2+2x+3}{x^3+1}$$

is worked out. We know from the computation done above that the answer must be x^2+2x+3, but let us see how this can be found out in a systematic way. We shall exactly mimic the way we do long division with numbers.

The leading term of the dividend is x^5, and that of the divisor is x^3; therefore, the leading term of the quotient must be $x^5 \div x^3 = x^2$. We record this fact, and then subtract x^2 times the divisor from the dividend:

$$(x^5+2x^4+3x^3+x^2+2x+3)-x^2\cdot(x^3+1) \;=\; 2x^4+3x^3+2x+3.$$

The remainder is $2x^4+3x^3+2x+3$.

Now we divide the leading term of the remainder with the leading term of the divisor; we get $2x^4 \div x^3 = 2x$. So the second term of the quotient is $2x$, and we subtract $2x$ times the divisor from the remainder:

$$(2x^4+3x^3+2x+3)-2x\cdot(x^3+1) \;=\; 3x^3+3.$$

The new remainder is $3x^3+3$, and dividing this by the divisor we get 3. The division this time is exact; no remainder is left. So the last term of the quotient is 3, and we see that the desired answer is x^3+2x+3.

Note how the remainder is updated as the division progresses, and how we work only with the leading terms of the updated remainder and of the divisor. This ensures that the division can be done quickly and efficiently.

In actual working, the steps are laid out as shown below. The initial array looks like this:

$$\begin{array}{c||c||c} x^3+1 & x^5+2x^4+3x^3+x^2+2x+3 & \\ \hline \end{array}$$

Since $x^5 \div x^3 = x^2$, the leading term in the quotient is x^2. So we subtract the product of x^3+1 and x^2 from $x^5+2x^4+3x^3+x^2+2x+3$:

$$\begin{array}{c||l||c} x^3+1 & x^5+2x^4+3x^3+x^2+2x+3 & x^2 \\ \hline & x^5 \qquad\qquad\quad + x^2 & \\ \cline{2-2} & \qquad 2x^4+3x^3 \qquad + 2x+3 & \end{array}$$

The remainder after subtraction is $2x^4+3x^3+2x+3$, and its leading term is $2x^4$. Since $2x^4 \div x^3 = 2x$, the next term in the quotient is $2x$. So we subtract the product of x^3+1 and $2x$ from $2x^4+3x^3+2x+3$:

$$\begin{array}{c||l||c} x^3+1 & x^5+2x^4+3x^3+x^2+2x+3 & x^2+2x \\ \hline & x^5 \qquad\qquad\quad + x^2 & \\ \cline{2-2} & \qquad 2x^4+3x^3 \qquad + 2x+3 & \\ & \qquad 2x^4 \qquad\qquad + 2x & \\ \cline{2-2} & \qquad\qquad 3x^3 \qquad\qquad + 3 & \end{array}$$

The remainder now is $3x^3+3$, and the divisor clearly divides into this 3 times. So the next term in the quotient is 3, and there is no remainder left. The final array is shown below.

$$\begin{array}{c||l||c} x^3+1 & x^5+2x^4+3x^3+x^2+2x+3 & x^2+2x+3 \\ \hline & x^5 \qquad\qquad\quad + x^2 & \\ \cline{2-2} & \qquad 2x^4+3x^3 \qquad + 2x+3 & \\ & \qquad 2x^4 \qquad\qquad + 2x & \\ \cline{2-2} & \qquad\qquad 3x^3 \qquad\qquad + 3 & \\ & \qquad\qquad 3x^3 \qquad\qquad + 3 & \\ \cline{2-2} \end{array}$$

We see that the quotient is x^2+2x+3:

$$\frac{x^5+2x^4+3x^3+x^2+2x+3}{x^3+1} = x^2+2x+3.$$

Remark

As with multiplication, we have the following general result:

If P and Q are two non-zero polynomials such that the division $P \div Q$ yields a polynomial S as quotient, with no remainder, then

$$\deg(S) = \deg(P) - \deg(Q).$$

For example, in the division

$$\frac{x^5+2x^2}{x^2} = x^3+2,$$

we have: $\deg(x^5+2x^2)=5$, $\deg(x^2)=2$, and $\deg(x^3+2)=3$; and, of course, $5-2=3$.

An important relation for division of polynomials

In the division $11 \div 4$, we get a quotient of 2 and a remainder of 3. This fact may be written in the following way:

$$11 = (2\times 4)+3,$$

i.e., Dividend = (Quotient × Divisor) + Remainder. Note that the Remainder (which equals 3) is *less* than the Divisor (which is 4). This will always be the case; for if it were not, then we would be able to divide further.

We shall now formulate a similar fact about division for polynomials. Consider the division $(x^3+1) \div (x^2+1)$. Dividing the two leading terms, we get $x^3 \div x^2 = x$. The remainder therefore is

$$\left(x^3+1\right) - x\cdot\left(x^2+1\right) = -x+1.$$

Since the degree of the remainder is 1, which is less than that of the divisor, no further division is possible. So we have the following relation:

$$x^3+1 = x\cdot\left(x^2+1\right)+(-x+1),$$

and this is an *identity*: it is true absolutely, and if we substitute any number for x, we will get a true statement. For example, if we put $x=5$ we get the statement $126=(5\times 26)+(-4)$, which is correct.

Here is another example. Let us divide the polynomial

$$f(x) \;=\; x^6 - 2x^5 + 5x^4 + 8x^3 - 9x^2 - 10x + 11,$$

of degree 6, by the polynomial $g(x) = x^2 - 3x + 2$, whose degree is 2. Going through the division steps, we find that the quotient is $h(x)$ where

$$h(x) \;=\; x^4 + x^3 + 6x^2 + 24x + 51,$$

the remainder being $99x - 91$, whose degree is 1. Observe that the degree of the remainder is strictly less than that of the divisor $(1 < 2)$. Also note that the relation

$$\begin{aligned} &x^6 - 2x^5 + 5x^4 + 8x^3 - 9x^2 - 10x + 11 \\ &\quad = \left(x^4 + x^3 + 6x^2 + 24x + 51\right) \cdot \left(x^2 - 3x + 2\right) \;+\; (99x - 91) \end{aligned}$$

is an identity. For example, if we put $x = 0$ in this relation we get the statement $11 = (51 \times 2) - 91$, which is correct.

The general statement. In general, let P and Q be any two polynomials in x. *Then there is precisely one way of writing the following relation:*

$$\boxed{P \;=\; (S \times Q) + R,} \tag{8.1}$$

with $\deg(R) < \deg(Q)$. The claim that there is 'precisely one way' may worry you, but we shall leave the claim for now.

8.6 GCDs for polynomials

For any given pair of numbers, there is a well-defined greatest common divisor (GCD) which can be computed in a convenient way using **EUCLID'S DIVISION ALGORITHM**. It turns out that the same is true for a given pair of polynomials in one variable. That is, they have a well-defined GCD; for example,

$$\text{GCD}\left(4x \cdot (x+1)^2 \cdot (x+2)^2,\ 6x^3 \cdot (x+1) \cdot (x+2)^4\right)$$

is clearly equal to $2x \cdot (x+1) \cdot (x+2)^2$. Here, the complete factorisations are given for both the polynomials, so it is easy to read off the GCD, in the same way that we can say that $\text{GCD}(2^3\,3^4\,5^2,\ 2^5\,3^2\,5^3) = 2^3\,3^2\,5^2$.

If the factorisations are not given, then the GCD can be found in the same way that it is done for a pair of numbers; i.e., by repeated division. The principle on which this rests is that if A and B are two polynomials in x, then the GCD of A and B is the same as the GCD of A and $A-B$ or the GCD of B and $A-B$, i.e.,

$$\text{GCD}\,(A,B) \;=\; \text{GCD}\,(A,A-B) \;=\; \text{GCD}\,(B,A-B)\,.$$

This means that if we divide A by B and we get a remainder C, then

$$\text{GCD}\,(A,B) \;=\; \text{GCD}\,(B,C)\,.$$

If there is no remainder, i.e., $C=0$, then B itself is the GCD of A and B.

This can now be repeated for the pair of polynomials B, C; we 'forget' the original pair of polynomials (A, B) and work instead with the new pair (B, C). That is, we divide B by C, and obtain, say, a remainder D; then

$$\text{GCD}\,(B,C) \;=\; \text{GCD}\,(C,D)\,.$$

We continue this way till we get a remainder of 0; and once this happens (which it must), the latest divisor is the GCD we want.

You may wonder what happens if at the start we decided to divide B by A rather than A by B. We find that at the end we get the very same answer. In an actual application, we choose to divide the polynomial having larger degree with the one having smaller degree.

EXAMPLE 1. Let us compute the $\text{GCD}(A,B)$ where $A = x\cdot(x+1)^2\cdot(x+2)^2$ and $B = x^3\cdot(x+1)\cdot(x+2)^4$. Here, $\deg(A) = 5$ and $\deg(B) = 8$; so we choose to divide B by A. We find that the quotient is x^3+3x^2+x-1, and the remainder is

$$C \;=\; x\cdot\left(x^3+5x^2+8x+4\right).$$

Observe that $\deg(C) = 4$, which is less than that of A. Dividing A by C, we find that the division is exact, with quotient $x+1$. So the desired GCD is C; i.e.,

$$\text{GCD}(A,B) \;=\; C \;=\; x\cdot\left(x^3+5x^2+8x+4\right) \;=\; x\cdot(x+1)\cdot(x+2)^2.$$

8.7 Roots of a polynomial

Till now, we have looked at polynomials only as expressions produced by certain rules. Now we shall give a more active role to polynomials—we shall permit them to *act*, and to *do* things. So we shall be giving them a more dynamic role.

Take any polynomial in x, say x^2+3x+2. We shall name it $P(x)$:

$$P(x) = x^2+3x+2.$$

Now suppose we give the value 1 to x; then the expression x^2+3x+2 takes the value $1+3+2=6$. We write this fact as follows:

$$P(1) = 6.$$

The symbol $P(1)$ tells us that we have substituted 1 for x. Similarly, $P(0)$ refers to the number obtained when we substitute 0 for x; so we have

$$P(0) = 2.$$

We can similarly list the values of $P(x)$ for different numbers x. The action of producing the number $P(x)$ from the number x may be regarded as being 'done' by the polynomial P. We may also regard P as a **MACHINE** that takes the number x and produces from it the number $P(x)$. We depict this action as follows:

$$x \longrightarrow \boxed{P\text{-Machine}} \longrightarrow P(x).$$

We call x the **INPUT VALUE** into the machine, and $P(x)$ the **OUTPUT VALUE**. It is particularly useful to think of P as a computer program that takes in an input, x, processes it, and prints an output, i.e., the value of $P(x)$.

What choice of input value will yield 0 as the output value? In other words, for which value(s) of x will it be true that $x^2+3x+2=0$? Such a value is called a **ZERO** or a **ROOT** of P. Note that a root of P is a **SOLUTION** of the equation $P(x)=0$. In this case we can find the roots by trial-and-error. Thus, $x=-1$ is a root, because

$$P(-1) = 1-3+2 = 0.$$

Another root is -2, because

$$P(-2) = 4-6+2 = 0.$$

Will there be any other roots? You are invited to make a check and to think about this question.

The important result that provides a connection between the roots of a polynomial $P(x)$ and its factors follows.

Theorem 8.1 (Factor Theorem) *If $P(x)$ is a polynomial in x, and a is a root of P, then $x-a$ is a factor of $P(x)$.*

This is a very useful result, as it provides a practical way to attack the problem of factorisation. It is also a neat result! The proof uses the idea of division and remainders. Let $P(x)$ be divided by $x-a$. We will get as a result some quotient Q, and possibly some remainder R. Since $\deg(x-a)=1$, and $\deg(R)<\deg(x-a)$, it must be that $\deg(R)=0$ (for, 0 is the only non-negative integer less than 1). This means that the remainder R is a constant! Now we study the identity

$$P(x)=(x-a)\cdot Q+R.$$

The fact that it is an identity means that we are free to substitute for x any value we please. In particular, we may substitute a for x. Doing so, we get

$$P(a) \;=\; 0\cdot Q+R \;=\; R.$$

But as a is a root of $P(x)$, we have $P(a)=0$. This means that $R=0$, i.e., that the remainder is zero. Hence, there is no remainder left in the division of $P(x)$ by $x-a$. This means that $x-a$ is a factor of $P(x)$.

Note that the reverse statement too is true, but in a much more obvious way: *If $x-a$ is a factor of $P(x)$, then a is a root of $P(x)$*. For, if $x-a$ is a factor, then $P(x)=(x-a)\cdot Q(x)$ where Q is some other polynomial. Now, substituting a for x, we get $P(a)=0\cdot Q(a)=0$, and this means that a is a root of P.

We consider some examples below.

EXAMPLE 2. Consider the polynomial $f(x)=x^2-3x+2$. Since $1-3+2=0$, we have $f(1)=0$. The factor theorem now assures us that $x-1$ must be a factor of $f(x)$. And indeed we find that

$$x^2-3x+2 \;=\; (x-1)\cdot(x-2).$$

If we consider the polynomial $g(x)=x^3-3x+2$, the same logic applies (for $1-3+2=0$, so $g(1)=0$), and $x-1$ is a factor of this polynomial too. Here is a check:

$$x^3-3x+2 \;=\; (x-1)\cdot\left(x^2+x-2\right).$$

But this logic would apply to the fourth degree polynomial $h(x)=x^4-3x+2$ just as well; and we have:

$$x^4-3x+2 \;=\; (x-1)\cdot\left(x^3+x^2+x-2\right).$$

Similarly we have:

$$\begin{aligned} x^5-3x+2 &= (x-1)\cdot\left(x^4+x^3+x^2+x-2\right), \\ x^6-3x+2 &= (x-1)\cdot\left(x^5+x^4+x^3+x^2+x-2\right), \end{aligned}$$

and so on; x^n-3x+2 is divisible by $x-1$ for every positive integer n.

This example shows that if the sum of the coefficients of a polynomial is 0 (with the signs of the coefficients taken into account, naturally), then the polynomial is divisible by $x-1$. So, without actual division, we can assert that the polynomial

$$x^8-8x^7+7x^6+5x^5-14x^4+21x^3-23x^2+24x-13$$

is divisible by $x-1$; for its sum of coefficients is $1-8+7+5-14+21-23+24-13=0$.

Some corollaries of the factor theorem

1. *x^n-1 is divisible by $x-1$ for any positive integer n.*

   For, when we substitute 1 for x in x^n-1, we get $1^n-1=1-1=0$.

   If we divide x^n-1 by $x-1$ for different values of n, we find a nice pattern:

   $$\begin{aligned} x^2-1 &= (x-1)\cdot(x+1), \\ x^3-1 &= (x-1)\cdot\left(x^2+x+1\right), \\ x^4-1 &= (x-1)\cdot\left(x^3+x^2+x+1\right), \\ x^5-1 &= (x-1)\cdot\left(x^4+x^3+x^2+x+1\right), \\ x^6-1 &= (x-1)\cdot\left(x^5+x^4+x^3+x^2+x+1\right), \end{aligned}$$

   and it is easy to guess that the quotient is always a polynomial all of whose coefficients are 1:

   $$x^n-1 = (x-1)\cdot\left(x^{n-1}+x^{n-2}+\cdots+x^2+x+1\right).$$

2. *x^n+1 is divisible by $x+1$ for any odd positive integer n, but not for an even positive integer.*

   For, if we substitute $x=-1$ in x^n+1, we get $(-1)^n+1$. When n is odd this equals $-1+1=0$; but when n is even it equals $1+1=2\neq 0$.

If we divide $x^n - 1$ by $x - 1$ for different values of n, we find a nice pattern once again:

$$x^3 + 1 = (x+1)\cdot(x^2 - x + 1),$$
$$x^5 + 1 = (x+1)\cdot(x^4 - x^3 + x^2 - x + 1),$$
$$x^7 + 1 = (x+1)\cdot(x^6 - x^5 + x^4 - x^3 + x^2 - x + 1),$$
$$x^9 + 1 = (x+1)\cdot(x^8 - x^7 + x^6 - x^5 + x^4 - x^3 + x^2 - x + 1).$$

We see that for an odd value of n, if we divide $x^n + 1$ by $x + 1$, the quotient is a polynomial whose coefficients are alternately 1 and -1:

$$x^n + 1 = (x+1)\cdot(x^{n-1} - x^{n-2} + x^{n-3} - \cdots + x^2 - x + 1).$$

The first and last coefficients have a positive sign in each case.

8.8 The remainder theorem

The factor theorem can be extended to the following:

Theorem 8.2 (Remainder Theorem) *Let $P(x)$ be a polynomial in x, and let a be any number. Then the remainder left in the division $P(x) \div (x - a)$ is $P(a)$.*

Here is an example showing how the remainder theorem may be used.

EXAMPLE 3. Let a and b be unknown numbers. Suppose that the polynomial $x^4 + ax^3 + bx^2 - 3x + 4$ leaves remainder 5 when divided by $x - 1$, and remainder -3 when divided by $x + 1$. What are the values of a and b?

The remainder theorem tells us that the remainder when the given polynomial is divided by $x - 1$ is

$$1 + a + b - 3 + 4 = a + b + 2,$$

and the remainder when it is divided by $x + 1$ is

$$1 - a + b + 3 + 4 = -a + b + 8.$$

So the given information tells us that

$$\begin{cases} a + b + 2 = 5, \\ -a + b + 8 = -3. \end{cases}$$

Consequently we have $a+b=3$ and $-a+b=-11$. Adding these two relations we get $2b=-8$, which yields $b=-4$. From this we get $a=7$. We have obtained the desired values.

The factor theorem sometimes allows us to factorise polynomials in an elegant and impressive way. We show some examples of this in Chapter 10 (*Factorisation of Polynomials*).

8.9 Symmetric polynomials

Later (perhaps in college, if you study mathematics further) you will learn about the notion of a symmetric polynomial. A **SYMMETRIC POLYNOMIAL** in a and b is one which remains unchanged if we swap a and b. Here are some examples of such polynomials:

$$a^2+b^2, \quad a^3+b^3, \quad ab+a+b, \quad a^3b^3+a^2+b^2+1, \quad a^2b+ab^2.$$

But $ab+a$ and or $a+b^2$ are not symmetric; the former changes to $ab+b$ if we swap a and b, while the latter changes to a^2+b.

It turns out that any such polynomial may be expressed in terms of the two quantities $S=a+b$ and $P=ab$ (both of which are symmetric polynomials in a and b), together possibly with some constants. Here are some examples:

- $a^2+b^2=(a+b)^2-2ab=S^2-2P$;
- $a^3+b^3=(a+b)^3-3ab(a+b)=S^3-3SP$;
- $a^4+b^4=S^4-6P^2-4P(S^2-2P)$.

Symmetric polynomials in three variables

For the case of *three* quantities a, b, c, a symmetric polynomial is one which remains unchanged no matter how we swap these three variables. Here are some examples of such polynomials:

$$\begin{aligned}
F &= a^2b+a^2c+b^2a+b^2c+c^2a+c^2b,\\
G &= a^2bc+b^2ca+c^2ab,\\
H &= a^3b+a^3c+b^3a+b^3c+c^3a+c^3b,\\
K &= a^3b^2c+b^3c^2a+c^3a^2b+a^3c^2b+c^3b^2a+b^3a^2c.
\end{aligned}$$

Clearly, if we add or subtract polynomials which are symmetric in a, b, c, then the resulting polynomial too will be symmetric in a, b, c. The same can be said for the product of two symmetric polynomials in a, b, c.

It turns out that any such polynomial may be expressed in terms of the three quantities P, Q, R, where

$$P = a+b+c, \qquad Q = ab+bc+ca, \qquad R = abc.$$

The reader will find it a nice challenge to express the polynomials F, H and K (above) in terms of P, Q, R. We give the answer only for K; it is:

$$K = P \cdot Q \cdot R - 3R^2.$$

These notions may be easily extended to the case of four or more variables, but we do not do so here.

EXERCISES

1. Compute the product: $\left(x^4+3x^3+5x^2+7x+9\right)\cdot\left(x^2-2x+4\right)$.

2. Find the coefficients of x^5 and x^7 in the product

$$\left(3x^4-5x^3+8x^2-9x+1\right)\cdot\left(2x^5-3x^3+6x^2-8x+2\right)$$

without having to fully multiply the two polynomials.

3. Compute the following using long division:

$$\left(x^6-2x^5-7x^4+93x^3-187x^2+280x-255\right) \div \left(x^2-5x+15\right).$$

4. Compute the quotient in the division

$$(a+b+c)^5-\left(a^5+b^5+c^5\right) \div (a+b)\cdot(b+c)\cdot(c+a).$$

5. Find the remainder when $x^4+x^3+x^2+x+1$ is divided by $x-2$.

6. Find the remainder when x^8+1 is divided by x^2-2x+1.

7. Find the remainder when x^7-1 is divided by x^3-1.

8. Find the number a if the polynomial $x^4-5x^3+ax^2-39x+34$ is divisible by $x-2$.

9. Find the numbers a and b if the polynomial

$$x^5 + 2x^4 + ax^3 + bx^2 - 67x + 66$$

is divisible by $x^2 - 5x + 6$.

10. Check which of the following polynomials is divisible by $x + 1$:

(a) $x^5 - 2x^4 + 3x^3 - 4x^2 + 5x - 6$;

(b) $x^9 - 3x^8 + 5x^7 - 7x^6 + 9x^5 - 11x^4 + 13x^3 - 15x^2 + 17x + 81$.

11. ✪ Find a and b, given that $x^9 + ax^5 + bx^2 - 10$ is divisible by $x^2 - 1$.

12. For $n = 1, 2, 3, \ldots$, divide $x^n - 1$ by $(x - 1)^2$ and tabulate the results as shown below (the first line has already been filled for you):

n	$x^n - 1$	Quotient	Remainder
1	$x - 1$	0	$x - 1$
2	$x^2 - 1$		
3	$x^3 - 1$		

Continue the computation till $n = 8$, and then make a guess about the patterns you see in the 'Quotient' and 'Remainder' columns.

13. For $n = 1, 2, 3, \ldots$, divide $x^n + 1$ by $(x + 1)^2$ and tabulate the results as shown below (the first line has already been filled for you):

n	$x^n - 1$	Quotient	Remainder
1	$x + 1$	0	$x + 1$
2	$x^2 + 1$		
3	$x^3 + 1$		

Continue the computation till $n = 8$, and then make a guess about the patterns you see in the 'Quotient' and 'Remainder' columns. (The pattern is a little more intricate than the one in the previous problem.)

14. ✪ We had claimed that if we are given two polynomials A and B, then there is just one pair Q, R of polynomials such that

$$A = Q \cdot B + R, \qquad \deg(R) < \deg(B).$$

Try to explain we cannot find more than one such pair of polynomials.

Hint. Suppose there happened to be *two* such pairs, say $\{Q,R\}$ and $\{Q',R'\}$, with $Q \neq Q'$ and $R \neq R'$. Then we would have $A = Q \cdot B + R$ and $A = Q' \cdot B + R'$. By subtraction we would now get the relation $(Q' - Q) \cdot B = R - R'$. But is this relation possible? (Compare the degrees of the two sides and check.)

Chapter 9

Expansions in Algebra

In this chapter we continue our study of algebraic manipulation; now we focus on *expansions* of various kinds. Along the way we shall make a brief study of the well-known **PASCAL TRIANGLE.**

To *expand* an algebraic expression is to open up all its brackets fully and to perform all its implied multiplications. For example, by actual multiplication we get:

$$(a+2b+3c)(4a-3b+5c) = 4a^2-6b^2+15c^2+5ab+17ac+bc,$$
$$\left(x^2+x+1\right)^3 = x^6+3x^5+6x^4+7x^3+6x^2+3x+1.$$

Sometimes shortcuts may be available for performing the multiplication; this is typically the case when the multiplicands possess some visible patterns and are related to one another in a convenient way. But if this is not the case, then we simply have to multiply out the terms the long way.

Remarks

Several remarks are needed here.

1. When the expression contains different powers of a single quantity x (or y, z, t, ...), the terms are generally arranged in descending order of their exponents—that is, highest degree first, and lowest degree last.

2. When the expression contains terms in different quantities (a, b, c, d, ...), they are arranged (to the extent possible) in 'dictionary order' (also known as *lexicographic order*). Thus, in the expansion of $(a+2b+3c)(4a-3b+5c)$, above, we listed the terms involving a^2, b^2 and c^2 first, and then the other terms.

3. Consider the expression $ab+ac+bc$; its terms are arranged in lexicographic order. However, some mathematicians prefer to write it as $ab+bc+ca$, because this shows its cyclic symmetry. We may imagine the three quantities arranged on a circle, so that when we go around the circle we meet them in the order $a \to b \to c \to a$. The cross-products are therefore read in the same order. For this same reason, we write ca rather than ac. This is, of course, not essential; it is only done to preserve the symmetry in the expression.

4. Note that the above guidelines are merely conventions which are generally agreed upon.

9.1 Homogeneous expressions

In the expansion of $(a+2b+3c)(4a-3b+5c)$, the two bracketed factors, namely, $a+2b+3c$ and $4a-3b+5c$, contain only terms with degree equal to 1; so, in the product, all the terms have degree equal to $1+1$, i.e., 2 (so all the terms are **QUADRATIC**). Such an expression, in which all the terms have equal degree, is said to be **HOMOGENEOUS**.

The expansion of $(a+2b+3c)(4a-3b+5c)(9a+7b-4c)$ is likewise homogeneous; all the terms have degree equal to $1+1+1=3$ (so here all the terms are **CUBIC**). If we actually multiply out the terms, we get:

$$36a^3-42b^3-60c^3+73a^2b-19ab^2+137a^2c+67ac^2+31b^2c+101bc^2+108abc.$$

Note carefully how each of the different terms in the expansion has total degree 3.

9.2 Expansions without complete multiplication

If we wish to find the coefficient of just one particular term, then we may be able do so without having to do a complete multiplication. For example, consider the product $(a+2b+3c)(4a-3b+5c)$. Suppose we want only the coefficient of bc. The term bc can be produced in only two ways from the given product: $(2b)\times(5c)$, and $(3c)\times(-3b)$. These yield $10bc$ and $-9bc$, respectively, and together they yield bc. So the coefficient of bc in the product is 1. Similarly, the coefficient of ca is $(1\times 5)+(3\times 4)=17$.

Or consider the product $(a+2b+3c)(4a-3b+5c)(9a+7b-4c)$. Take any typical term that must occur in the expansion, say a^2b. It can be produced in *three* different ways:

$$(a)\times(4a)\times(7b), \qquad (a)\times(-3b)\times(9a), \qquad (2b)\times(4a)\times(9a),$$

so the desired coefficient is $28-27+72=73$. Similarly, the coefficient of b^2c is the sum of

$$2\times(-3)\times(-4), \qquad 2\times5\times7, \qquad 3\times(-3)\times7$$

and so is equal to $24+70-63=31$. In the case of abc, there are *six* different ways in which this term can be produced; do you see why?

9.3 Binomial expansions I

Of particular importance in mathematics are the expansions of $(a+b)^2$, $(a+b)^3$, $(a+b)^4$, $(a+b)^5$, ...; i.e., $(a+b)^n$ where n represents any arbitrary positive integer. These are known as *binomial expansions* because $a+b$ is a **BINOMIAL** (a sum of two quantities); in contrast, a sum of three quantities is called a **TRINOMIAL**. Binomial expansions crop up repeatedly in diverse areas of mathematics (e.g., in statistics; combinatorics; the theory of probability), and are of great importance. They also have a large number of very pleasing patterns associated with them, as we shall now see.

Let us begin by listing the expansions of $(a+1)^2$, $(a+1)^3$, $(a+1)^4$, $(a+1)^5$, ..., and see what we find. By direct multiplication we get:

$$(a+1)^2 = a^2+2a+1.$$

Now let us obtain the expansion of the cubic $(a+1)^3$. We could write it as a triple product, $(a+1)\times(a+1)\times(a+1)$, but it makes more sense to make use of the expansion above. We choose to write $(a+1)^3 = (a+1)\times(a+1)^2$, i.e.,

$$(a+1)^3 = (a+1)\times\left(a^2+2a+1\right).$$

The highest degree term in the product is a^3, which arises from $a\times a^2$; its coefficient is 1. The term with the next lower degree (a^2) is obtained from $1\times a^2$ and $a\times 2a$, i.e., in two different ways, so its coefficient is $1+2=3$. The a-term is also obtained in two different ways, $1\times 2a$ and $a\times 1$, so its degree is $2+1=3$. Finally, the constant term (with zero degree) is $1\times1=1$. So the desired expansion is

$$(a+1)^3 = a^3+3a^2+3a+1.$$

But it is more revealing and more instructive to write the expansion as

$$a^3+(1+2)a^2+(2+1)a+1,$$

as this shows how we get it from the product $(a+1)\times(a^2+2a+1)$.

Next, we find the expansion of $(a+1)^4$. This has degree equal to 4, and it is called a **QUARTIC** or a **BIQUADRATIC** expression. We shall obtain the expansion by writing it as

$$(a+1)\times(a^3+3a^2+3a+1).$$

The highest degree term is $a\times a^3 = a^4$. The a^3-term is obtained from the products $1\times a^3$ and $a\times 3a^2$, so its coefficient is $1+3=4$. The a^2-term is obtained from the products $1\times 3a^2$ and $a\times 3a$, so its coefficient is $3+3=6$. The coefficient of the a-term is, similarly, $3+1=4$, and the constant term is 1. So the desired expansion is

$$(a+1)^4 = a^4+4a^3+6a^2+4a+1,$$

and, as earlier, it is more instructive to write the expansion as

$$a^4+(1+3)a^3+(3+3)a^2+(3+1)a+1,$$

to show how we get it from the product $(a+1)\times(a^3+3a^2+3a+1)$.

We can similarly find the expansion of $(a+1)^5$. It has degree equal to 5, so it is called a **QUINTIC**. By writing $(a+1)^5$ as

$$(a+1)\times(a^4+4a^3+6a^2+4a+1),$$

we quickly find that the required expansion is

$$a^5+(1+4)a^4+(4+6)a^3+(6+4)a^2+(4+1)a+1.$$

The pattern should be quite visible now—i.e., the sequential way in which we get the coefficients of the successive powers of $(a+1)$. Let us write only the *coefficients* in these expansions, starting with $(a+1)^0=1$, in which the only coefficient is equal to 1, and $(a+1)^1=a+1$, in which the coefficients are $1,1$. We get this array:

$(a+1)^0$	1					
$(a+1)^1$	1	1				
$(a+1)^2$	1	2	1			
$(a+1)^3$	1	3	3	1		
$(a+1)^4$	1	4	6	4	1	
$(a+1)^5$	1	5	10	10	5	1

We can see now how the successive rows are computed; *each number equals the sum of the number immediately above it and the one to the left of that number*. If we write the array in a triangular form, then this property becomes more visible:

$$
\begin{array}{ccccccccccccccccc}
&&&&&&&&1&&&&&&&&\\
&&&&&&&1&&1&&&&&&&\\
&&&&&&1&&2&&1&&&&&&\\
&&&&&1&&3&&3&&1&&&&&\\
&&&&1&&4&&6&&4&&1&&&&\\
&&&1&&5&&10&&10&&5&&1&&&\\
&&1&&6&&15&&20&&15&&6&&1&&\\
&1&&7&&21&&35&&35&&21&&7&&1&\\
1&&8&&28&&56&&70&&56&&28&&8&&1
\end{array}
$$

Here, *each number equals the sum of the two numbers immediately above it*. From the last row, we deduce that the expansion of $(a+1)^8$ is

$$a^8+8a^7+28a^6+56a^5+70a^4+56a^3+28a^2+8a+1.$$

This array has been known since early times (e.g., in ancient China, and in India from the time of Bhāskarāchāryā II, but it is known as **PASCAL'S TRIANGLE**, in honour of Blaise Pascal (1623–62), a French Jesuit-mathematician and philosopher who in correspondence with Pierre de Fermat (1601–65) invented the field of **PROBABILITY THEORY** and **COUNTING** (a topic also known as **COMBINATORICS** to mathematicians).

The Pascal triangle is blessed by an unusually large number of patterns—it possesses so many properties that several volumes would be needed to catalog them. And new properties are being discovered! We list a few of them below, labelling each one as '*Easy*', '*Medium*', '*Challenging*' or '*Hard*'. Try proving them for yourself, and do not give up too quickly! We use the following notation: the numbers in the nth row of the Pascal array will be denoted respectively by

$$C(n,0),\quad C(n,1),\quad C(n,2),\quad \ldots,\quad C(n,n-2),\quad C(n,n-1),\quad C(n,n).$$

So $C(n,0)$ denotes the 1st entry in the nth row, $C(n,1)$ denotes the 2nd entry, etc. *This means that $C(n,k)$ is the coefficient of x^{n-k} in the expansion of $(x+1)^n$.* Thus, $C(4,1)=4$,

$C(4,2) = 6$, $C(5,2) = 10$, etc. By definition these coefficients obey the following rule:

$$\boxed{C(n,k) \;=\; C(n-1,k-1)+C(n-1,k).} \tag{9.1}$$

For example, $C(7,3) = 35 = 15+20 = C(6,2)+C(6,3)$.

Note that *the identity is true precisely because of the way in which the coefficients of* $(x+1)^n$ *are related to the coefficients of* $(x+1)^{n-1}$.

Pascal-1 *Each row in the Pascal array is palindromic*—it reads the same left-to-right and right-to-left. This may be written in symbols as:

$$C(n,k) \;=\; C(n,n-k), \quad \text{for all possible } n \text{ and } k.$$

Example: $C(6,2) = 15 = C(6,4)$.

Pascal-2 $C(n,1) = n$ *for each positive integer* n.

Pascal-3 *The sum of the numbers in the* n^{th} *row is* 2^n. In symbols:

$$C(n,0)+C(n,1)+C(n,2)+\cdots+C(n,n-1)+C(n,n) \;=\; 2^n.$$

Example: $C(3,0)+C(3,1)+C(3,2)+C(3,3) = 1+3+3+1 = 8 = 2^3$.

Pascal-4 *If we 'join up' the entries of the* n^{th} *row, treating each entry as a digit, we get the base-ten form of the number* 11^n. For example, we have:

$$11^1 \;=\; 11, \qquad 11^2 \;=\; 121, \qquad 11^3 \;=\; 1331, \qquad 11^4 \;=\; 14641.$$

For the next row, we have 10 as an entry. As 10 has two digits, we must allow a 'carry' into the place to its left. So we get:

$$11^5 \;=\; \overline{1,5,10,10,5,1} \;=\; 161051,$$

and similarly,

$$\begin{aligned}
11^6 &= \overline{1,6,15,20,15,6,1} &&= 1771561,\\
11^7 &= \overline{1,7,21,35,35,21,7,1} &&= 19487171,\\
11^8 &= \overline{1,8,28,56,70,56,28,8,1} &&= 214358881.
\end{aligned}$$

Pascal-5 *In each row of the Pascal array, the sum of the first, third, fifth, seventh, ... entries equals the sum of the second, fourth, sixth, ... entries. That is, the sum of the entries in the odd numbered places equals the sum of the entries in the even numbered places.* In symbols:

$$C(n,0)+C(n,2)+C(n,4)+\cdots = C(n,1)+C(n,3)+C(n,5)+\cdots.$$

Example: $C(4,0)+C(4,2)+C(4,4)=1+6+1=8$ and $C(4,1)+C(4,3)=4+4=8$.

Pascal-6 $C(n,2)$ *equals the sum of the numbers* 1, 2, 3, ..., $n-2$, $n-1$. That is,

$$C(n,2) = 1+2+3+\cdots+(n-2)+(n-1).$$

Example: $C(7,2)=21=1+2+3+4+5+6$.

Pascal-7 *Given any set S containing n elements, the number of subsets of S that contain exactly k elements is* $C(n,k)$.

Example: Take the 4-element set $S=\{a,b,c,d\}$. The subsets of S that have exactly 2 elements are $\{a,b\}$, $\{a,c\}$, $\{a,d\}$, $\{b,c\}$, $\{b,d\}$ and $\{c,d\}$. These are 6 in number. Note that $C(4,2)=6$.

Or take the 5-element set $S=\{a,b,c,d,e\}$. The subsets of S that have exactly 3 elements are $\{a,b,c\}$, $\{a,b,d\}$, $\{a,b,e\}$, $\{a,c,d\}$, $\{a,c,e\}$, $\{a,d,e\}$, $\{b,c,d\}$, $\{b,c,e\}$, $\{b,d,e\}$ and $\{c,d,e\}$, and these are 10 in number. Note that $C(5,3)=10$.

Pascal-8 *The sum of the squares of the entries in the* n^{th} *row equals the middle entry of the* $2n^{\text{th}}$ *row.* That is,

$$C(n,0)^2+C(n,1)^2+C(n,2)^2+\cdots+C(n,n-1)^2+C(n,n)^2 = C(2n,n).$$

Example: $C(4,0)^2+C(4,0)^2+C(4,0)^2+C(4,0)^2+C(4,0)^2$ is equal to $1^2+4^2+6^2+4^2+1^2=70$. This is also the value of $C(8,4)$.

Pascal-9 *We have the following identities:*

$$\frac{C(n,k)}{C(n,k-1)} = \frac{n-k+1}{k}, \qquad \frac{C(n,k)}{C(n-1,k)} = \frac{n}{n-k}.$$

Example:

- $\dfrac{C(7,3)}{C(7,2)} = \dfrac{35}{21} = \dfrac{5}{3} = \dfrac{7-3+1}{3}$
- $\dfrac{C(7,3)}{C(6,3)} = \dfrac{35}{20} = \dfrac{7}{4} = \dfrac{7}{7-3}$

Pascal-10 *$C(n,k)$ may be written as the product of k fractions, as follows:*

$$C(n,k) = \frac{n}{1} \times \frac{n-1}{2} \times \frac{n-2}{3} \times \cdots \times \frac{n-k+2}{k-1} \times \frac{n-k+1}{k}.$$

Example: $C(6,3) = 20$, and we have:

$$20 = \frac{6}{1} \times \frac{5}{2} \times \frac{4}{3}.$$

Pascal-11 *If p is a prime number, then all the numbers*

$$C(p,1), \quad C(p,2), \quad \ldots, \quad C(p,p-2), \quad C(p,p-1)$$

are multiples of p.

Example: The numbers $C(7,1), C(7,2), C(7,3), C(7,4), C(7,5), C(7,6)$ are 7, 21, 35, 35, 21, 7; all these numbers are multiples of 7 (a prime number).

Pascal-12 *If n is composite, then at least one of the following numbers*

$$C(n,1), \quad C(n,2), \quad \ldots, \quad C(n,n-2), \quad C(n,n-1),$$

is ***not*** *a multiple of n.*

Example: The numbers $C(8,1)$, $C(8,2)$, $C(8,3)$, $C(8,4)$, $C(8,5)$, $C(8,6)$, $C(8,7)$ are 8, 28, 56, 70, 56, 28, 8; they include at least one non-multiple of 8 (note that 28 and 70 are non-multiples of 8).

Of these, we judge the following to be *Easy* (we have written **P** for **Pascal**, as a short form): **P-1**, **P-2**, **P-3**, **P-4**, **P-5**; the following is *Medium*: **P-6**; the following are *Challenging*: **P-7**, **P-8**, **P-9**, **P-10**, **P-11**; and the following is *Hard*: **P-12**.

A consequence of these properties is that in each row of the Pascal array, the largest number is the one in the middle (or, in the case of odd-numbered rows, the two middle numbers). Those who like computing large numbers will find that the Pascal coefficients grow in size rapidly; e.g., we have

$$C(40,20) = 137846528820, \qquad C(60,30) = 118264581564861424.$$

9.4 Using the Pascal triangle

Having explored at length how to get the expansion of $(a+1)^n$ for different positive integral values of n, we now show how to put our findings to use.

We first state our basic finding in a slightly different form. We have seen, above, that

$$(a+1)^n = C(n,0)a^n + C(n,1)a^{n-1} + C(n,2)a^{n-2} + \cdots + C(n,n-1)a + C(n,n).$$

Since $(a+1)^n$ is just the same as $(1+a)^n$, and each row in the Pascal array is palindromic, we can rewrite the above as:

$$\boxed{(1+a)^n = C(n,0) + C(n,1)a + C(n,2)a^2 + \cdots + C(n,n-1)a^{n-1} + C(n,n)a^n.} \quad (9.2)$$

The important point about this relation is that it is an *identity*; so it is true no matter what we substitute in place of a. If we put $a = 0$, then we get $1 = C(n,0)$, i.e., the first number in each row is 1. If we put $a = 1$, then on the LHS we get $(1+1)^n$, i.e., 2^n. On the RHS we get

$$C(n,0) + C(n,1) + C(n,2) + \cdots + C(n,n-1) + C(n,n),$$

i.e., the sum of all the numbers in the nth row. *This explains why the sum of all the numbers in the nth row is 2^n* (observation **P-3**).[1] And if we put $a = -1$, then on the LHS we get $(1-1)^n$ or 0^n, which is 0 for any positive integral value of n. On the RHS we get:

$$C(n,0) - C(n,1) + C(n,2) - + - \cdots \pm C(n,n-1) \mp C(n,n)$$

Here the signs are alternately plus and minus, which is why we have written $\pm$ for the sign of $C(n,n-1)$, meaning that it could be plus or minus, and $\mp$ for the sign of $C(n,n)$. Now this expression is the difference between the sum of the entries in the odd numbered places and the sum of the entries in the even numbered places. *This explains why the sum of the entries in the odd numbered places equals the sum of the entries in the even numbered places* (observation **P-5**).

So by giving appropriate values to a we are able to account for many of the observed properties! The reader should check what happens if $a = 10$. Which property are we now able to explain?

[1] This is not the only way of proving this property. Try to find your own way.

9.5 Binomial expansions II

We emphasise once more that equation 9.2, above, represents an *identity*, so we are free to substitute any value or expression for a that we may please. Now we choose to replace a by a fraction, $\frac{y}{x}$. We get:

$$\left(1+\frac{y}{x}\right)^n = C(n,0)+C(n,1)\frac{y}{x}+C(n,2)\frac{y^2}{x^2}+\cdots+C(n,n)\frac{y^n}{x^n}. \qquad (9.3)$$

Now, in place of the successive powers of a in the RHS of equation 9.2, we have the successive powers of $\frac{y}{x}$. The expression on the LHS is

$$\left(1+\frac{y}{x}\right)^n = \frac{(x+y)^n}{x^n}.$$

Multiplying both sides of equation 9.3 by x^n we get:

$$\boxed{(x+y)^n = C(n,0)\,x^n+C(n,1)\,x^{n-1}y+C(n,2)\,x^{n-2}y^2+\cdots+C(n,n)\,y^n.} \qquad (9.4)$$

This equation is very important; it represents the general form of the **BINOMIAL THEOREM**. You will study this theorem in detail in grades 11–12. Note the structure of the terms on the RHS; hiding the coefficients, the terms are:

$$x^n, \quad x^{n-1}y, \quad x^{n-2}y^2, \quad \ldots, \quad x^2y^{n-2}, \quad xy^{n-1}, \quad y^n.$$

Observe that the exponents of x in the successive terms form a descending sequence, coming down from n to 0 in steps of 1, whereas the exponents of y form an increasing sequence, going up from 0 to n in steps of 1. In consequence, each term has a total degree of n (i.e., the exponents of x and y add up to n); so the expression on the RHS is homogeneous, of degree n.

Having got the general form of the binomial theorem, we can now put it to use. Say we want the expansion of

$$(2a-3b)^5.$$

In equation 9.4 we substitute $2a$ for x; $-3b$ for y; and 5 for n. We get the following on the RHS:

$$C(5,0)\,(2a)^5+C(5,1)\,(2a)^4\,(-3b)^1+\,C(5,2)\,(2a)^3(-3b)^2+C(5,3)\,(2a)^2\,(-3b)^3$$
$$+\,C(5,4)\,(2a)^1\,(-3b)^4+C(5,5)\,(-3b)^5.$$

From the Pascal array we know that the numbers in the fifth row are 1, 5, 10, 10, 5, 1. Substituting these numbers in the above expression we get:

$$(2a-3b)^5 = 32a^5 - 240a^4b + 720a^3b^2 - 1080a^2b^3 + 810ab^4 - 243b^5.$$

This is the required expansion. Or say we want the expansion of

$$(3a-5c)^6.$$

In the binomial theorem we substitute $3a$ for x; $-5c$ for y; and 6 for n. We get the expansion

$$\begin{aligned}&C(6,0)\,(3a)^6 + C(6,1)\,(3a)^5\,(-5c)^1\\&\quad + C(6,2)\,(3a)^4\,(-5c)^2 + C(6,3)\,(3a)^3\,(-5c)^3\\&\qquad + C(6,4)\,(3a)^2\,(-5c)^4 + C(6,5)\,(3a)^1\,(-5c)^5\\&\qquad\quad + C(6,6)\,(-5c)^6.\end{aligned}$$

Since the numbers in the sixth row of the Pascal array are 1, 6, 15, 20, 15, 6, 1, we deduce that the expansion of $(3a-5c)^6$ is

$$729a^6 - 7290a^5c + 30375a^4c^2 - 67500a^3c^3 + 84375a^2c^4 - 56250ac^5 + 15625c^6.$$

9.6 Squares of multinomial expressions

Recall that a binomial expression is the sum of two quantities or terms. In contrast, a **MULTINOMIAL EXPRESSION** is a sum of several terms. We now consider how to get the square of such an expression.

Consider the expansion of $(a+b+c)^2$. Treating $a+b$ as a single term, we get:

$$\begin{aligned}(a+b+c)^2 &= (a+b)^2 + 2(a+b)c + c^2\\&= a^2+b^2+c^2+2\,(ab+ac+bc)\,.\end{aligned}$$

Next, we consider the expansion of $(a+b+c+d)^2$. Treating $a+b+c$ as a single term and using the above equation, we get:

$$\begin{aligned}(a+b+c+d)^2 &= (a+b+c)^2 + 2(a+b+c)d + d^2\\&= a^2+b^2+c^2+d^2+2\,(ab+ac+ad+bc+bd+cd)\,.\end{aligned}$$

The pattern is now easy to spot. There are two types of terms in the expansions: (i) *squares of all the individual terms, each with a coefficient of* 1; (ii) *products of two individual terms, in all possible combinations, each with a coefficient of* 2. So we see that the square of a sum of several terms is

$$\begin{aligned} & \text{sum of the squares of all the individual terms} \\ + \ & 2\,(\text{sum of all pair-wise products of the individual terms})\,. \end{aligned}$$

It is easy to explain this rule. Write the square of the given multinomial expression, say $(a+b+c+d+e+\cdots)^2$, as a product:

$$(a+b+c+d+e+\cdots) \times (a+b+c+d+e+\cdots).$$

Since each bracketed expression is homogeneous with degree 1, each term in the product will have degree $1+1=2$. Therefore, two types of terms will occur in the expansion: *squares of individual terms*, like a^2; and *products of pairs of terms*, like ab. The only way to get a^2 is by multiplying the a from the first bracketed expression with the a from the second expression; so all such terms must have a coefficient of 1. But for terms like ab, there are *two* ways of getting them: multiply a from the first expression with b from the second one, or multiply b from the first expression with a from the second one; hence, all such terms must have a coefficient of 2. Hence the rule stated.

In actually using it, it is easy to miss some cross-product terms. A simple way of avoiding this is: *multiply each term with all the terms that follow it.*

For example, the expansion of $(3a+2b-5c+4d)^2$ will be

$$9a^2+4b^2+25c^2+16d^2+2\,(6ab-15ac+12ad-10bc+8bd-20cd)\,,$$

and the expansion of $\left(a+\dfrac{1}{a}+b+\dfrac{1}{b}\right)^2$ will be

$$a^2+\frac{1}{a^2}+b^2+\frac{1}{b^2}+2ab+\frac{2}{ab}+\frac{2a}{b}+\frac{2b}{a}+4.$$

The verbal explanation given above helps in finding expansions even in cases where the exponent exceeds 2. Let us tackle a more complicated example.

Expansion of $(a+b+c)^3$. The product here is

$$(a+b+c)\times(a+b+c)\times(a+b+c).$$

Each bracketed expression is homogeneous with degree 1, so the product will also be homogeneous with degree $1+1+1=3$; each term in the product will have degree 3. The expressions with degree 3 that can be made using the symbols a, b and c are the following:

- terms with just one symbol: a^3, b^3, and c^3;
- terms with two different symbols: a^2b, a^2c, b^2a, b^2c, c^2a, and c^2b;
- terms with three different symbols: abc.

Now let us work out the coefficients of these different terms. Since a^3 can only be obtained by multiplying the as in each of the three bracketed expressions, its coefficient is 1. To get a^2b we must choose 'b' from any one bracketed expression and 'a' from each of the other two expressions. There are three ways of doing this, as there are three different bracketed expressions from which to choose 'b', and once this has been done no more choice is available. So the coefficient of a^2b is 3, and this is so for all the terms of this type. For the term abc, we must select 'a' from one bracketed expression, 'b' from another, and 'c' from the remaining one. There are $3\times 2\times 1=6$ ways of doing this (three choices for a, two choices for b, and just one choice for c). Accordingly, the coefficient of abc is 6. It follows that the expansion of $(a+b+c)^3$ is

$$a^3+b^3+c^3+3\left(a^2b+a^2c+b^2a+b^2c+c^2a+c^2b\right)+6abc.$$

Sum-of-coefficients check. If we assign the value 1 to each of a, b, c, then $(a+b+c)^3 = 3^3=27$. The above expansion yields, with the same substitutions, $3+(3\times 6)+6=27$. The two figures are equal, as they should be. *If they were not equal, then we would know that we have made an arithmetical error.*

Expansion of $(a+b+c)^4$. This expansion may be obtained in the same way, but the reasoning is more involved. We have terms of the following types:

- a^4 (three such terms, namely: a^4, b^4 and c^4);
- a^3b (six such terms, namely: a^3b, a^3c, b^3a, b^3c, c^3a and c^3b);
- a^2b^2 (three such terms, namely: a^2b^2, a^2c^2, and b^2c^2);
- a^2bc (three such terms, namely: a^2bc, b^2ca and c^2ab).

The coefficient of a^4 is 1; that of a^3b is 4; that of a^2b^2 is 6; and that of a^2bc is 12. So the expansion is

$$\begin{aligned} & a^4+b^4+c^4 \\ & \quad + 4\left(a^3b+a^3c+b^3a+b^3c+c^3a+c^3b\right) \\ & \quad\quad + 6\left(a^2b^2+a^2c^2+b^2c^2\right) \\ & \quad\quad\quad + 12\left(a^2bc+b^2ac+c^2ab\right). \end{aligned}$$

Sum-of-coefficients check: $(1+1+1)^4 = 81$, and $3+(4\times 6)+(6\times 3)+(12\times 3) = 81$.

The expansion of *(a+b+c+d)*^{4}. We can get this expansion in just the same way. The expansion is homogeneous with degree 4, so there are terms like a^4 (four such terms); a^3b (twelve such terms); a^2b^2 (six such terms); a^2bc (twelve such terms); and $abcd$ (only one such term). We leave it to the reader to explain how the following expansion is obtained:

$$\begin{aligned} & a^4+b^4+c^4+d^4 \\ & \quad + 4\left(a^3b+a^3c+a^3d+b^3a+b^3c+b^3d+c^3a+c^3b+c^3d+d^3a+d^3b+d^3c\right) \\ & \quad\quad + 6\left(a^2b^2+a^2c^2+a^2d^2+b^2c^2+b^2d^2+c^2d^2\right) \\ & \quad\quad\quad + 12\left(a^2bc+a^2bd+a^2cd+b^2ac+b^2ad+b^2cd\right) \\ & \quad\quad\quad\quad + 12\left(c^2ab+c^2ad+c^2bd+d^2ab+d^2ac+d^2bc\right) \\ & \quad\quad\quad\quad\quad + 24\,abcd. \end{aligned}$$

Sum-of-coefficients check: $(1+1+1+1)^4 = 256$, and

$$4+(4\times 12)+(6\times 6)+(12\times 12)+24 = 256.$$

Remark

The idea of a sum-of-coefficients check is applicable to any such expansion. For example, consider the expansion of $(5a-2b)^5$; it is:

$$3125\,a^5 - 6250\,a^4b + 5000\,a^3b^2 - 2000\,a^2b^3 + 400\,ab^4 - 32b^5.$$

If we put $a=b=1$ then $(5a-2b)^5 = 3^5 = 243$. The sum of the coefficients is $3125-6250+5000-2000+400-32 = 243$.

9.7 Sum and product formulas

For two given numbers a and b, let S denote their sum and P their product:

$$S = a+b, \qquad P = ab.$$

Let $X_n = a^n + b^n$ denote the sum of the nth powers of a and b. Then X_n is a polynomial which is symmetric in a, b, and so we should be able to express it in terms of S and P. (Recall that we discussed symmetric polynomials in Chapter 8.) Let us find these expressions. Of course, $X_0 = 2$ and $X_1 = S$. For X_2, note that

$$(a+b)^2 = a^2+b^2+2ab, \qquad \therefore\ a^2+b^2 = (a+b)^2-2ab,$$

giving

$$\boxed{X_2 = S^2-2P.} \tag{9.5}$$

For X_3 we use the following form of the expansion of $(a+b)^3$:

$$(a+b)^3 = a^3+b^3+3ab(a+b).$$

Substituting, we get $S^3 = a^3+b^3+3PS$, which yields

$$\boxed{X_3 = S^3-3PS.} \tag{9.6}$$

For X_4 we use the expansion of $(a+b)^4$; we write it in the form

$$(a+b)^4 = a^4+b^4+\left(4a^3b+4ab^3\right)+6a^2b^2,$$

i.e.,

$$a^4+b^4 = (a+b)^4-4ab\left(a^2+b^2\right)-6a^2b^2.$$

This yields $X_4 = S^4-4PX_2-6P^2$. Since $X_2 = S^2-2P$ (just obtained, above), we get, by substitution, $X_4 = S^4-4P\left(S^2-2P\right)-6P^2$, i.e.,

$$\boxed{X_4 = S^4-4PS^2+2P^2.} \tag{9.7}$$

For X_5 we have:

$$(a+b)^5 = a^5+b^5+5ab\left(a^3+b^3\right)+10a^2b^2(a+b),$$

giving $X_5 = S^5-5PX_3-10P^2S$. Since we already know that $X_3 = S^3-3PS$ we get $X_5 = S^5-5P\left(S^3-3PS\right)-10P^2S$, and so:

$$\boxed{X_5 = S^5-5PS^3+5P^2S.} \tag{9.8}$$

We can go on in this manner and find expressions for any X_n in terms of S and P.

9.8 The difference of two squares

Of great importance is the expansion

$$(a-b)(a+b) = a^2-b^2, \tag{9.9}$$

called the **DIFFERENCE OF TWO SQUARES** formula. We express it verbally as: *The difference of two squares equals the product of their sum and their difference.* It comes of use in diverse expansions as well as factorisations (as we shall see in Chapter 10). Here are some examples:

$$\begin{aligned} a^4-b^4 &= \left(a^2+b^2\right)\cdot\left(a^2-b^2\right) \\ &= \left(a^2+b^2\right)\cdot(a+b)\cdot(a-b), \end{aligned}$$

$$\begin{aligned} a^8-1 &= \left(a^4-1\right)\cdot\left(a^4+1\right) \\ &= \left(a^2-1\right)\cdot\left(a^2+1\right)\cdot\left(a^4+1\right) \\ &= (a-1)\cdot(a+1)\cdot\left(a^2+1\right)\cdot\left(a^4+1\right). \end{aligned}$$

It can play a role in factorisation of integers too:

$$899 = 30^2-1 = 29\times 31,$$

$$1599 = 40^2-1 = 39\times 41 = 3\times 13\times 41.$$

9.9 Visual representations of some expansions

We describe here how the expansions for $(a+b)^2$, $(a+b)(a-b)$, $(a+b+c+d)^2$ and $(a+b)^3$ can be represented *visually*. We draw on the following geometric facts:

- The area of a rectangle with sides a and b is ab. In particular, the area of a square with side a is a^2.
- The volume of a cuboid with sides a, b and c is abc. In particular, the volume of a cube with side a is a^3.

We shall simply present the figures, and trust that the relevant expansion can be 'seen' in the figure.

Expansion of $(a+b)^2$

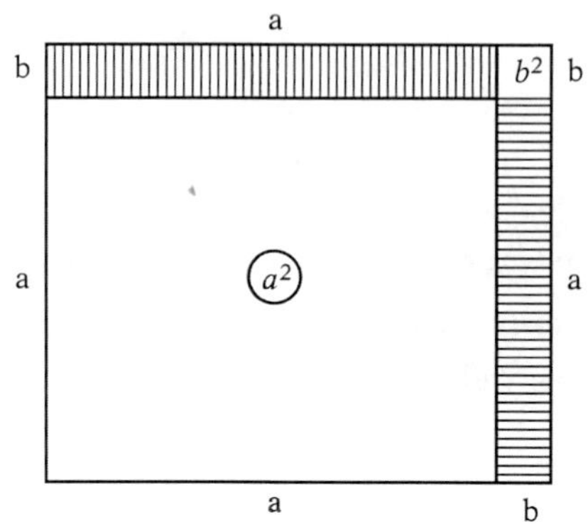

Figure 9.1

Here we see a square with side $(a+b)$ dissected into: a square with side a; a square with side b; and two $a \times b$ rectangles. Consideration of the areas of the different parts yields: $(a+b)^2 = a^2 + b^2 + 2ab$.

Expansion of $(a+b)(a-b)$

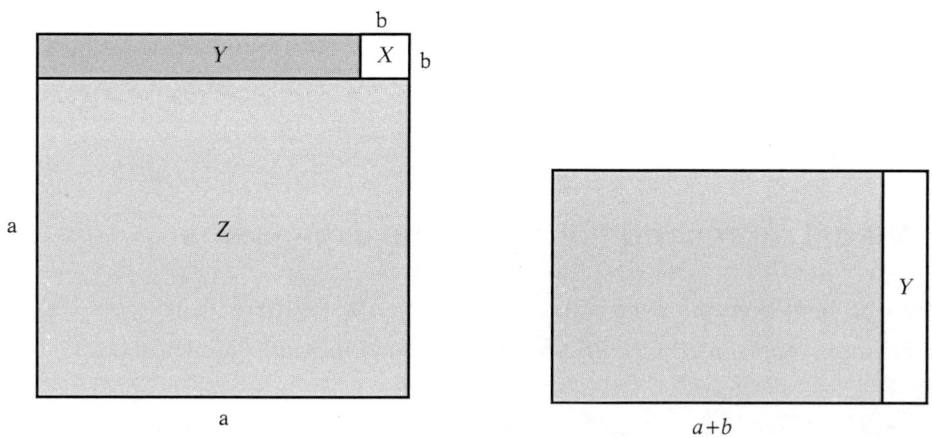

Figure 9.2

Here we assume that $a > b$. From one corner of a square of side a we remove a square of side b (marked 'X'), and a $a \times b$ rectangle from one side of the remaining piece (marked 'Y'). The left over rectangle (marked 'Z') and the rectangle Y can then be assembled into a $(a+b) \times (a-b)$ rectangle.

Expansion of $(a+b+c)^2$

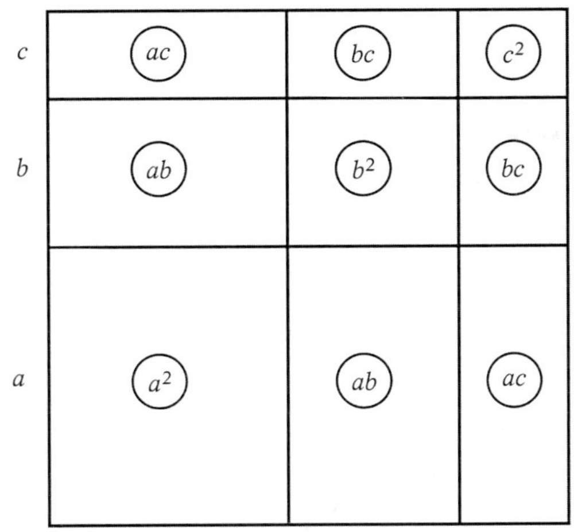

Figure 9.3 Showing that $(a+b+c)^2 = a^2+b^2+c^2+2(ab+ac+bc)$

Expansion of $(a+b)^3$

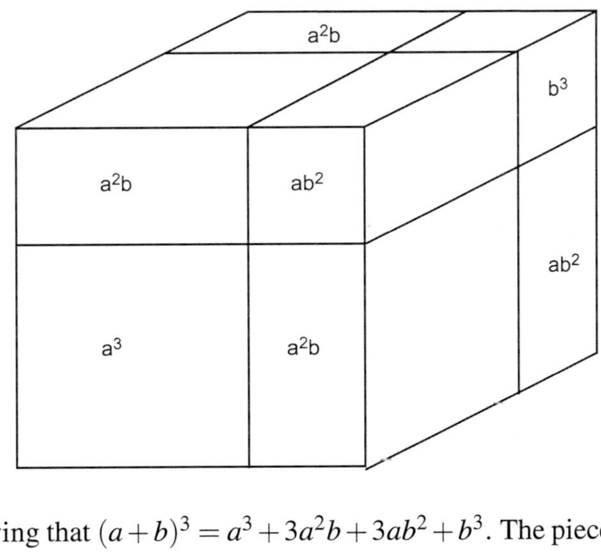

Figure 9.4 Showing that $(a+b)^3 = a^3+3a^2b+3ab^2+b^3$. The pieces include: one cube of volume a^3, one cube of volume b^3, three cuboid slabs each with dimensions $a \times a \times b$ and volume a^2b, and three cuboid slabs each with dimensions $a \times b \times b$ and volume ab^2.

9.10 Miscellaneous expansions

In this section we list some frequently used expansions that are particular cases of the various formulas presented above.

- We have the formulas:

$$(a+b)^2+(a-b)^2=2\left(a^2+b^2\right),$$
$$(a+b)^2-(a-b)^2=4ab.$$

- In the expansions for $(a+b)^2$ and $(a-b)^2$, put $b=\dfrac{1}{a}$; we get:

$$\left(a+\frac{1}{a}\right)^2=a^2+\frac{1}{a^2}+2,$$
$$\left(a-\frac{1}{a}\right)^2=a^2+\frac{1}{a^2}-2.$$

So we also have:

$$\left(a+\frac{1}{a}\right)^2+\left(a-\frac{1}{a}\right)^2=2\left(a^2+\frac{1}{a^2}\right),$$
$$\left(a+\frac{1}{a}\right)^2-\left(a-\frac{1}{a}\right)^2=4.$$

- Again, in the cubic expansions,

$$(a+b)^3=a^3+b^3+3ab(a+b),$$
$$(a-b)^3=a^3-b^3-3ab(a-b),$$

if we put $b=\dfrac{1}{a}$ we get:

$$\left(a+\frac{1}{a}\right)^3=a^3+\frac{1}{a^3}+3\left(a+\frac{1}{a}\right),$$
$$\left(a-\frac{1}{a}\right)^3=a^3+\frac{1}{a^3}-3\left(a-\frac{1}{a}\right).$$

9.11 A claim from a notebook of Ramanujan

We shall close this chapter with a discussion of an item from the famous NOTEBOOK of Srinivasa Ramanujan. The entry is made in the style now identified with Ramanujan—it is a bare statement of fact, with no build up and no explanation. It occurs on page 23 (entry number 11).

$$\textit{If } x = y+\left(\frac{z}{y}-y^3\right)^{1/3}, \quad \textit{then } 3y = x+\left(\frac{9z}{x}-x^3\right)^{1/3}.$$

We shall justify this claim and show at the same time that the '3' and '9' in the relation cannot be replaced by any other pair of numbers.[2]

We first write the claim in rationalised form by clearing the roots:

$$\textit{If } (x-y)^3 = \frac{z}{y}-y^3, \quad \textit{then } (3y-x)^3 = \frac{9z}{x}-x^3. \tag{9.10}$$

The 'IF' condition in (9.10) is equivalent to $x^3-3x^2y+3xy^2 = \frac{z}{y}$, and therefore to

$$x^2-3xy+3y^2 = \frac{z}{xy}.$$

The 'THEN' condition in (9.10) is equivalent to $27y^3-27y^2x+9yx^2 = \frac{9z}{x}$. Dividing through by $9y$, we see that it is equivalent to

$$x^2-3xy+3y^2 = \frac{z}{xy}.$$

The two conditions in (9.10) therefore assert exactly the same thing. So Ramanujan's claim is justified.

Now suppose that we replace the coefficients '3' and '9' in 9.10 by literals a and b; we get:

$$\textit{If } (x-y)^3 = \frac{z}{y}-y^3, \quad \textit{then } (ay-x)^3 = \frac{bz}{x}-x^3. \tag{9.11}$$

The 'IF' condition in (9.11) is equivalent to $x^3-3x^2y+3xy^2 = \frac{z}{y}$, and therefore to

$$x^2-3xy+3y^2 = \frac{z}{xy}.$$

[2]The author has based this part on a communication received from Mr TSKV Iyer of Pune.

The 'THEN' in (9.11) is equivalent to $a^3y^3 - 3a^2y^2x + 3ayx^2 = \dfrac{bz}{x}$, and therefore to

$$3ax^2 - 3a^2xy + a^3y^2 = \frac{bz}{xy}.$$

The two conditions in (9.11) are therefore equivalent if and only if

$$\frac{1}{3a} = \frac{3}{3a^2} = \frac{3}{a^3} = \frac{1}{b}.$$

These lead to $a = 3$ and $b = 9$, as claimed. ❑

We can deduce an analogous result for quadratics, by arguing in the same way. The result is:

$$\textit{If } (x+y)^2 = \frac{z}{y} + y^2, \quad \textit{then } (4y+x)^2 = \frac{8z}{x} + x^2.$$

This may be stated using radicals as:

$$\textit{If } x = -y + \left(\frac{z}{y} + y^2\right)^{1/2}, \quad \textit{then } 4y = -x + \left(\frac{8z}{x} + x^2\right)^{1/2}.$$

We leave the proof to the reader.

EXERCISES

1. Expand the following (without doing 'long multiplication'):

   (a) $(2a - 3b + 4c - 5d)^2$;

   (b) $(1 - x + x^2 - x^3)^2$;

   (c) $(1 - 2x + 3x^2 - 4x^3)^2$;

   (d) $(1 + 3x + 5x^2 + 7x^3)^2$;

   (e) $(1 - 2x + 3x^2)^3$.

2. Using the Pascal triangle, find the expansions of the following:

   (a) $(3x - 4y)^6$;

   (b) $\left(\dfrac{a}{2} - \dfrac{b}{3}\right)^5$;

(c) $\left(2x^2 - \dfrac{5}{x}\right)^7$.

3. Using the Pascal triangle, find:

   (a) the coefficient of x^4 in $(5-2x)^7$;

   (b) the coefficient of x^6 in $\left(3x^2-4\right)^6$.

4. In the expansion of $\left(5x^2 - \dfrac{2}{x}\right)^7$:

   (a) show that there is no x^3 term and no x^4 term;

   (b) find the coefficients of x^2 and x^5.

5. In the expansion of $\left(2x^3 - \dfrac{5}{\sqrt{x}}\right)^6$, find the coefficients of x^4 and x^{11}.

6. Simplify: $\left(a+\dfrac{1}{a}\right)^3 - \left(a-\dfrac{1}{a}\right)^3$.

7. Simplify: $\left(a+\dfrac{1}{a}\right)^4 - \left(a-\dfrac{1}{a}\right)^4$.

8. Show how from the Pascal triangle we can deduce that the value of

$$C(n,0)-2C(n,1)+4C(n,2)-8C(n,3)+16C(n,4)+-+\cdots\pm 2^n\,C(n,n)$$

   will always be 1 or -1.

   For example, try $n=5$. The required sum is then

$$\begin{aligned} &C(5,0)-2C(5,1)+4C(5,2)-8C(5,3)+16C(5,4)-32C(5,5) \\ &= 1-10+40-80+80-32 \;=\; -1. \end{aligned}$$

   In what way is the sign ($+$ or $-$) related to the value of n?

9. Given that $a+\dfrac{1}{a}=3$, find the values of $a^2+\dfrac{1}{a^2}$ and $a^3+\dfrac{1}{a^3}$.

10. Given that $a+\dfrac{1}{a}=4$, find the values of $a^4+\dfrac{1}{a^4}$ and $a^5+\dfrac{1}{a^5}$.

11. Given that $a+\dfrac{1}{a}=5$, find the values of $a^6+\dfrac{1}{a^6}$ and $a^7+\dfrac{1}{a^7}$.

12. Given that $a+b=6$ and $ab=4$, find the value of a^3+b^3.

13. Given that $a+b=5$ and $ab=3$, find the value of a^4+b^4.

14. Given that $a-b=3$ and $ab=4$, how would you find the value of $a+b$? Can it be given a definite value? (You will find that it is one of two possible values; but there is no way of saying which one.)

15. Given that $a-b=4$ and $ab=1$, how would you find the value of a^3-b^3? Can it be given a definite value?

16. Compute the expansions of the following:

    (a) $(1-x)\left(1+x+x^2\right)$;
    (b) $(1-x)\left(1+x+x^2+x^3\right)$;
    (c) $(1-x)\left(1+x+x^2+x^3+x^4\right)$;
    (d) $(1-x)\left(1+x+x^2+x^3+x^4+x^5\right)$;
    (e) $(1-x)\left(1+x+x^2+x^3+x^4+x^5+x^6\right)$.

    Based on your answers, deduce the expansion of

    $$(1-x)\left(1+x+x^2+x^3+x^4+\cdots+x^n\right)$$

    for general positive integers n.

17. Compute the expansions of the following:

    (a) $(1+x)\left(1-x+x^2\right)$;
    (b) $(1+x)\left(1-x+x^2-x^3\right)$;
    (c) $(1+x)\left(1-x+x^2-x^3+x^4\right)$;
    (d) $(1+x)\left(1-x+x^2-x^3+x^4-x^5\right)$;
    (e) $(1+x)\left(1-x+x^2-x^3+x^4-x^5+x^6\right)$.

    Based on your answers, deduce the expansion of

    $$(1+x)\left(1-x+x^2-x^3+x^4-+-\cdots\pm x^n\right)$$

    for general positive integers n. The sign of x^n inside the bracketed expression is plus if n is even, and minus if n is odd; it can be written compactly as $(-1)^n$.

18. ✪ For given quantities a and b, let $S = a+b$ and $P = ab$. Let X_N denote the sum of the nth powers of a and b. Find expressions for X_6 and X_7 in terms of S and P. Also, show that

$$X_{n+2} = (a+b)X_{n+1} - abX_n.$$

19. ✪ Compute the expansions of the following:

(a) $(1+x+x^2)^2$;

(b) $(1+x+x^2+x^3)^2$;

(c) $(1+x+x^2+x^3+x^4)^2$;

(d) $(1+x+x^2+x^3+x^4+x^5)^2$;

(e) $(1+x+x^2+x^3+x^4+x^5+x^6)^2$.

Based on your answers, make a guess about the expansion of

$$(1+x+x^2+x^3+x^4+\cdots+x^n)^2$$

for general positive integers n, and also make a guess about the value of the largest coefficient in the expansion.

20. *An investigation involving the square root of* 2.

We consider the expanded and simplified form of the quantity $\left(1+\sqrt{2}\right)^n$. Thus we have: $\left(1+\sqrt{2}\right)^2 = 3 + 2\sqrt{2}$, and:

$$\left(1+\sqrt{2}\right)^3 = 7 + 5\sqrt{2}, \qquad \left(1+\sqrt{2}\right)^4 = 17 + 12\sqrt{2}.$$

(a) Find the expanded and simplified forms of $(1+\sqrt{2})^5$ and $(1+\sqrt{2})^6$.

(b) Let $(1+\sqrt{2})^n$ be written in the form $a_n + b_n\sqrt{2}$ where a_n, b_n are numbers that depend on n. Given only a_n and b_n, how will you find a_{n+1} and b_{n+1} without having to expand $(1+\sqrt{2})^{n+1}$ in full?

(c) ✪ Why is it true that for large values of n, the fraction $\dfrac{a_n}{b_n}$ is very nearly equal to $\sqrt{2}$? For example, we have:

$$\left(1+\sqrt{2}\right)^{10} = 3363+2378\sqrt{2}, \qquad \left(1+\sqrt{2}\right)^{12} = 19601+13860\sqrt{2}.$$

Now we find that:

$$\frac{3363}{2378} \approx 1.414213624, \qquad \frac{19601}{13860} \approx 1.4142135642,$$

and $\sqrt{2} = 1.41421356237309\ldots$.

Chapter 10

Factorisation of Polynomials

In Chapter 9, we studied expansions of various kinds. Now we study the reverse problem—that of *factorisation*. When we form a product $P \times Q$, the multiplicands P and Q are called **FACTORS** of $P \times Q$, in the same way that, say, 3 and 7 are factors of $3 \times 7 = 21$. For example:

- x and $x+1$ are factors of $x \cdot (x+1) = x^2 + x$;
- $x+1$ and $x-2$ are factors of $(x+1) \cdot (x-2) = x^2 - x - 2$;
- x^2+1 and x^3-x-1 are factors of

$$\left(x^2+1\right) \cdot \left(x^3-x-1\right) \; = \; x^5 - x^2 - x - 1.$$

Multiplication is easy to do, but the reverse problem—that of *factorising a given polynomial*—can be a very challenging problem, and this is so even if you have a powerful computer to help you! There is no single method that is suitable for all problems of factorisation. In this chapter, we look at some approaches that can help.

Remark

The problem of factorising integers is challenging enough, so it is not surprising that the problem of factorising polynomials is considered difficult! If you doubt this claim, we invite you to find the factors of the number 13338001. Or, if that seems too easy, try the number 51706883699. (Use a computer if you wish!) Each of these numbers is the product of just two prime numbers, but this information may not be of much help!

10.1 Using the 'difference of two squares' identity

An often used idea in factorisation is to exploit the identity

$$\boxed{(a-b)(a+b) \;=\; a^2-b^2}, \tag{10.1}$$

and to use it 'in reverse'. For example, take the expression $16x^4-9$. Since $16x^4$ and 9 are both squares, we have:

$$16x^4-9 \;=\; \left(4x^2\right)^2-3^2 \;=\; \left(4x^2-3\right)\cdot\left(4x^2+3\right).$$

EXAMPLE 1. Similarly, we have, for the expression $81a^4-16b^4$:

$$\begin{aligned} 81a^4-16b^4 &= \left(9a^2\right)^2-\left(4b^2\right)^2 \\ &= \left(9a^2-4b^2\right)\cdot\left(9a^2+4b^2\right) \\ &= (3a-2b)\cdot(3a+2b)\cdot\left(9a^2+4b^2\right). \end{aligned}$$

EXAMPLE 2. Here is another example: we shall factorise the trinomial $x^2-8x+15$. Here we first use the identity $(a-b)^2=a^2-2ab+b^2$ to 'complete the square' and only then invoke the difference of two squares formula. We have:

$$\begin{aligned} x^2-8x+15 &= \left(x^2-8x+16\right)-1 \\ &= (x-4)^2-1^2 \\ &= (x-4-1)\cdot(x-4+1) \\ &= (x-5)\cdot(x-3). \end{aligned}$$

EXAMPLE 3. Here is how we factorise $1-x^2-y^2+2xy$:

$$\begin{aligned} 1-x^2-y^2+2xy &= 1-\left(x^2-2xy+y^2\right) \\ &= 1^2-(x-y)^2 \\ &= (1-x+y)\cdot(1+x-y). \end{aligned}$$

EXAMPLE 4. To factorise $a^2+b^2-c^2-d^2-2ab+2cd$, we write:

$$a^2+b^2-c^2-d^2-2ab+2cd \;=\; \left(a^2-2ab+b^2\right) \;-\; \left(c^2-2cd+d^2\right)$$

$$\begin{aligned} &= (a-b)^2-(c-d)^2 \\ &= (a-b-c+d)\cdot(a-b+c-d). \end{aligned}$$

EXAMPLE 5. Another nice application is the factorisation of x^4+4. Is this expression a square? Not quite; x^4 is the square of x^2, and 4 is the square of 2; but the square of x^2+2 is x^4+4x^2+4, and not x^4+4. So an extra term has got introduced into the expression as a result of squaring. But this extra term is itself a square!—indeed, $4x^2=(2x)^2$. Putting back all these pieces together, we are able to find the desired factorisation:

$$\begin{aligned} x^4+4 &= (x^4+4x^2+4)-(4x^2) \\ &= (x^2+2)^2-(2x)^2 \\ &= (x^2+2-2x)\cdot(x^2+2+2x). \end{aligned}$$

So the desired factorisation is

$$x^4+4 = (x^2-2x+2)\cdot(x^2+2x+2). \tag{10.2}$$

EXAMPLE 6. The same idea works for x^4+1, but this time an irrational quantity enters the factorisation:

$$\begin{aligned} x^4+1 &= (x^4+2x^2+1)-(2x^2) \\ &= (x^2+1)^2-\left(\sqrt{2}x\right)^2 \\ &= \left(x^2+1-\sqrt{2}x\right)\cdot\left(x^2+1+\sqrt{2}x\right). \end{aligned}$$

So the desired factorisation is,

$$x^4+1=\left(x^2-\sqrt{2}x+1\right)\cdot\left(x^2+\sqrt{2}x+1\right). \tag{10.3}$$

EXAMPLE 7. We shall find the factors of $x^4+x^2y^2+y^4$:

$$\begin{aligned} x^4+x^2y^2+y^4 &= (x^2+2x^2y^2+y^4) - x^2y^2 \\ &= (x^2+y^2)^2 - (xy)^2 \\ &= (x^2-xy+y^2)\cdot(x^2+xy+y^2). \end{aligned}$$

10.2 Application to integer factorisation

The difference of two squares formula can be applied just as well to yield the factorisation of a given number, provided we are able to express the number as a difference of two squares. Here are some examples:

$$\begin{aligned}
91 &= 100-9 &&= 10^2-3^2 &&= (10-3)\times(10+3) &&= 7\times 13;\\
391 &= 400-9 &&= 20^2-3^2 &&= (20-3)\times(20+3) &&= 17\times 23;\\
899 &= 900-1 &&= 30^2-1^2 &&= (30-1)\times(30+1) &&= 29\times 31;\\
1591 &= 1600-9 &&= 40^2-3^2 &&= (40-3)\times(40+3) &&= 37\times 43;\\
3599 &= 3600-1 &&= 60^2-1^2 &&= (60-1)\times(60+1) &&= 59\times 61.
\end{aligned}$$

As these examples will suggest, this idea is particularly useful if the number to be factorised is close to and a bit less than a perfect square. An early approach towards solving the problem of factorisation of numbers is based on just this idea; it is due to Fermat.

Similarly, the factorisation of x^4+4 which we got above allows us to factorise any integer which is 4 more than a fourth power. For example, if we substitute 5 for x, we get the factors of $5^4+4=629$:

$$5^4+4 = \left(5^2+2-2\times 5\right)\cdot\left(5^2+2+2\times 5\right),$$

i.e., $629=17\times 37$. If we substitute 15 for x, we get the factors of $15^4+4=50629$:

$$15^4+4 = \left(15^2+2-2\times 15\right)\cdot\left(15^2+2+2\times 15\right),$$

i.e., $50629=197\times 257$. And the substitution $x=25$ yields the factorisation of 390629 as 577×677.

This idea does not help, however, in the factorisation of an integer that is 1 more than a fourth power, because in the factorisation obtained above we got an irrational quantity. For example, if we put $x=10$, we get the number $10^4+1=10001$ in the LHS of (10.3). In its RHS we get

$$10^4+1 = \left(101-10\sqrt{2}\right)\times\left(101+10\sqrt{2}\right).$$

This is not of much use! (In fact the desired factorisation is $10^4+1=73\times 137$, but this has to be found by other means.)

Remark

As a corollary to the above we can show the following:

The only prime number of the form n^4+4 *is* 5 *which equals* 1^4+4.

However, no such statement can be made for prime numbers that are 1 more than some fourth power, i.e., of the form n^4+1. Indeed, there are many such prime numbers, e.g.,

$$2=1^4+1, \qquad 17=2^4+1, \qquad 1297=6^4+1,$$

$$65537=16^4+1, \qquad 160001=20^4+1, \qquad 331777=24^4+1,$$

and so on. There are probably infinitely many such prime numbers; but this is not known for certain. (Mathematicians would call this an 'open problem' because it is yet to be settled one way or another.)

10.3 Factorisation by breaking up an expression

Another idea used in factorisation is to write the given expression as a sum of two expressions which share some common factor in an obvious way; then this same factor divides the given expression too. That is, if in the sum $P+Q$ we observe that both P and Q are divisible by some factor S, then S will be a divisor of $P+Q$ too. If we replace the word 'sum' by 'difference' then the same conclusion holds good.

For example, consider the expression $x^2-8x+15$ which we factorised (above) using the 'difference of two squares' formula. We shall accomplish the factorisation in a different way here. Observe that

$$\begin{aligned} x^2-8x+15 &= x^2-5x-3x+15 \\ &= \left(x^2-5x\right)-(3x-15). \end{aligned}$$

Now observe that $x^2-5x=x\cdot(x-5)$ and $3x-15=3\cdot(x-5)$. So both the bracketed expressions have $x-5$ as a factor, and we get:

$$\begin{aligned} x^2-8x+15 &= x\cdot(x-5)-3\cdot(x-5) \\ &= (x-3)\cdot(x-5). \end{aligned}$$

The difference of two squares formula itself can be derived using this approach:

$$\begin{aligned} a^2-b^2 &= a^2-ab+ab-b^2 \\ &= a\cdot(a-b)+b\cdot(a-b) \\ &= (a+b)\cdot(a-b). \end{aligned}$$

We shall examine this idea again, when we consider the problem of factorising quadratic polynomials in general.

Factorisation of a sum of two cubes

An impressive application of the idea described above is the factorisation of the expression a^3+b^3. To factorise this, we insert additional 'bridge' terms in between a^3 and b^3, thus:

$$a^3+b^3 = a^3+a^2b-a^2b+b^3 = \left(a^3+a^2b\right)-\left(a^2b-b^3\right).$$

Now observe that $a^3+a^2b=a^2\cdot(a+b)$ and

$$a^2b-b^3 = b\cdot\left(a^2-b^2\right) = b\cdot(a-b)\cdot(a+b).$$

So both a^3+a^2b and a^2b-b^3 have $a+b$ as a factor, and we get:

$$\begin{aligned} a^3+b^3 &= a^2\cdot(a+b)-b\cdot(a-b)\cdot(a+b) \\ &= (a+b)\cdot\left[a^2-b(a-b)\right]. \end{aligned}$$

Hence:

$$\boxed{a^3+b^3 = (a+b)\cdot\left(a^2-ab+b^2\right).} \qquad (10.4)$$

In the same way we get the factorisation of a^3-b^3. Or, more simply, we use the fact that $(-b)^3=-b^3$. So by writing $-b$ in place of b in the factorisation of a^3+b^3 we get:

$$\boxed{a^3-b^3 = (a-b)\cdot\left(a^2+ab+b^2\right).} \qquad (10.5)$$

These two factorisations are worth remembering, for they frequently come of use. Likewise for the particular case obtained when $b=1$ and we write x for a:

$$\boxed{x^3+1 = (x+1)\cdot\left(x^2-x+1\right),} \qquad (10.6)$$

and

$$\boxed{x^3-1 = (x-1)\cdot\left(x^2+x+1\right).} \qquad (10.7)$$

Factorisation of a sum of two fifth powers

We may similarly factorise the expression a^5+b^5, by inserting bridge terms:

$$\begin{aligned} a^5+b^5 &= a^5+a^4b-a^4b+b^5 \\ &= a^4\cdot(a+b)-b\cdot\left(a^4-b^4\right). \end{aligned}$$

Since $a^4 - b^4$ has $a^2 - b^2$ as a factor, and $a^2 - b^2$ has $a+b$ as a factor, we get:

$$a^5 + b^5 = a^4 \cdot (a+b) - b \cdot (a-b) \cdot (a+b) \cdot (a^2+b^2).$$

We see that $a+b$ is a factor of $a^5 + b^5$, and that

$$a^5 + b^5 = (a+b) \cdot \left[a^4 - b \cdot (a-b) \cdot (a^2+b^2)\right].$$

This is better written as follows:

$$\boxed{a^5 + b^5 = (a+b) \cdot \left(a^4 - a^3 b + a^2 b^2 - ab^3 + b^4\right).} \tag{10.8}$$

By writing $-b$ in place of b, we get the factorisation of $a^5 - b^5$:

$$\boxed{a^5 - b^5 = (a-b) \cdot \left(a^4 + a^3 b + a^2 b^2 + ab^3 + b^4\right).} \tag{10.9}$$

The particular cases obtained by putting $b = 1$ and writing x in place of a are useful to remember:

$$\boxed{x^5 + 1 = (x+1) \cdot \left(x^4 - x^3 + x^2 - x + 1\right),} \tag{10.10}$$

$$\boxed{x^5 - 1 = (x-1) \cdot \left(x^4 + x^3 + x^2 + x + 1\right).} \tag{10.11}$$

Of course, these can be obtained directly, using the idea of bridge terms. Thus, for $x^5 - 1$ we have:

$$\begin{aligned} x^5 - 1 &= x^5 - x^4 + x^4 - x^3 + x^3 - x^2 + x^2 - x + x - 1 \\ &= x^4 \cdot (x-1) + x^3 \cdot (x-1) + x^2 \cdot (x-1) + x \cdot (x-1) + 1 \cdot (x-1) \\ &= (x-1) \cdot \left(x^4 + x^3 + x^2 + x + 1\right). \end{aligned}$$

The sum of two 7th powers, two 9th powers, two 11th powers, and in general the sum of two n^{th} powers where n is an odd positive integer, may be factorised in the same way, as can the difference $a^n - b^n$ of any two n^{th} powers.

10.4 Factorisation of quadratic trinomials

Earlier in the chapter we performed the factorisation of $x^2 - 8x + 15$ in two different ways (by writing it as a difference of two squares; and by writing it as a sum of two expressions having a common factor). We now consider how to factorise quadratic trinomial expressions in general, i.e., expressions of the kind

$$ax^2+bx+c,$$

where a, b, c are given numbers (with, of course, $a \neq 0$). It is convenient to consider the cases $a=1$ and $a \neq 1$ separately.

The case when a is equal to 1. Consider first the case when $a=1$, i.e., when the expression is **MONIC**. (Polynomials for which the leading term has a coefficient of 1 are called 'monic'.) Then the expression is x^2+bx+c. Suppose that it factorises as $(x+r)\cdot(x+s)$, where r, s are some numbers. Expanding this product, we get:

$$x^2+bx+c = x^2+(r+s)x+rs.$$

For this relation to be an identity, we must have

$$b = r+s, \qquad c = rs.$$

Of course, we do not as yet know r and s; we only know b and c, and we must find r and s from b and c. The above relations tell us that we need to find two numbers with sum b and product c. In many cases, the desired pair of numbers can be found by trying out the different possibilities.

EXAMPLE 8. To factorise $x^2+8x+15$, we look for two numbers with sum 8 and product 15. Such a pair of numbers may be found by trial-and-error: $\{3,5\}$. Hence, the desired factorisation is $(x+3)\cdot(x+5)$.

General points to be kept in mind

- If $b>0$ and $c>0$, then the sum and product of r and s are both positive, so *both of them must be positive.*
- If $b<0$ and $c>0$, then the sum of r and s is negative whereas their product is positive, so *both of them must be negative.*
- If $c<0$ then the product of r and s is negative, so *they have opposite sign*; one of them must be negative, and the other one must be positive.

EXAMPLES

1. To factorise $x^2 - 8x + 15$, we look for two numbers with sum -8 and product 15. Here we have $b < 0$ and $c > 0$, so the two numbers must both be negative.

   Pairs of negative numbers whose product is 15 are $\{-1, -15\}$ and $\{-3, -5\}$. The second pair fits our requirement. So the two numbers are -3, -5, and the desired factorisation is $(x-3) \cdot (x-5)$.

2. To factorise $x^2 + 2x - 35$, we look for two numbers with sum 2 and product -35. Here we have $c < 0$, so the two numbers must be of opposite sign.

   Pairs of numbers with product -35 are $\{-1, 35\}$, $\{-35, 1\}$, $\{-5, 7\}$ and $\{-7, 5\}$. The third pair fits our requirement, as their sum is 2. So the two numbers are -5, 7, and the desired factorisation is $(x-5) \cdot (x+7)$.

3. To factorise $x^2 - 3x - 28$, we look for two numbers with sum -3 and product -28. Here we have $c < 0$, so the two numbers must be of opposite sign.

   Pairs of numbers with product -28 are $\{-1, 28\}$, $\{-28, 1\}$, $\{-4, 7\}$ and $\{-7, 4\}$. The last pair fits our requirement, as their sum is -3. So the two numbers are 4, -7, and the desired factorisation is $(x+4) \cdot (x-7)$.

The case when a is not equal to 1. Now we consider the case when the given expression is not monic, i.e., the coefficient $a \neq 1$. As often happens, the lead on how we should proceed is found by studying a problem in reverse. Consider a product like $(3x-5) \cdot (4x+3)$. Expanding it, we get

$$\begin{aligned}(3x-5) \cdot (4x+3) &= 12x^2 - 20x + 9x - 15 \\ &= 12x^2 - 11x - 15.\end{aligned}$$

Observe that in the expression in the middle (namely, $12x^2 - 20x + 9x - 15$), the coefficients of the x-terms are -20 and 9, whose sum is -11 (which is the coefficient of x in the final product), and whose product is -180 (which is equal to the product of the coefficient of the x^2-term and the constant term in the final product). Now, given the expression $12x^2 - 11x - 15$, if we were given the hint that we should write the middle term, $-11x$, as $-20x + 9x$, then we would be able to find the desired factorisation:

$$\begin{aligned}12x^2 - 11x - 15 &= 12x^2 - 20x + 9x - 15 \\ &= 4x \cdot (3x-5) + 3 \cdot (3x-5)\end{aligned}$$

$$= \quad (4x+3)\cdot(3x-5).$$

In general, given the expression ax^2+bx+c, we must find two numbers with sum b and product ac, keeping the signs of these two numbers in mind. Then, by breaking up the term bx suitably, we find the desired factorisation. To see why, let the factorisation of ax^2+bx+c be $(px+q)\cdot(rx+s)$, where p, q, r, s are numbers to be found. Expanding this product, we get:

$$ax^2+bx+c \;=\; (pr)x^2+(ps+qr)x+qs,$$

implying that,

$$a = pr, \qquad b = ps+qr, \qquad c = qs.$$

Observe that b is the sum of two quantities (ps and qr) whose product ($pqrs$) equals ac.

EXAMPLES

1. To factorise $10x^2-11x+3$, we look for two numbers with sum -11 and product $10\times 3=30$. The two numbers must be negative; we find that the pair $\{-5,-6\}$ satisfies the requirements, and so:

$$\begin{aligned} 10x^2-11x+3 &= 10x^2-5x-6x+3 \\ &= 5x\cdot(2x-1)-3\cdot(2x-1) \\ &= (5x-3)\cdot(2x-1). \end{aligned}$$

2. To factorise $28x^2-27x-10$, we look for a pair of numbers with sum -27 and product $28\times(-10)=-280$. The desired numbers must naturally be of opposite sign. Here are some pairs of numbers whose product is -280:

$$\{-280,1\},\ \{-140,2\},\ \{-70,4\},\ \{-40,7\},\ \{-35,8\},\ \{-20,14\}\ \ldots.$$

The fifth pair $\{-35,8\}$ satisfies our requirements. So:

$$\begin{aligned} 28x^2-27x-10 &= 28x^2-35x+8x-10 \\ &= 7x\cdot(4x-5)+2\cdot(4x-5) \\ &= (4x-5)\cdot(7x+2). \end{aligned}$$

3. To factorise $8x^2-30x-77$, we look for two numbers with sum -30 and product $8\times(-77)=-616$. The desired numbers must naturally be of opposite sign. Here are some pairs of numbers with product -616:

$$\{-616,1\},\quad \{-308,2\},\quad \{-154,4\},\quad \{-77,8\},\quad \{-88,7\},$$

$$\{-56,11\},\quad \{-28,22\},\quad \{-14,44\},\quad \{-44,14\},\quad \ldots.$$

The last pair listed above satisfies our requirements. So:

$$\begin{aligned} 8x^2-30x-77 &= 8x^2-44x+14x-77 \\ &= 4x\cdot(2x-11)+7\cdot(2x-11) \\ &= (4x+7)\cdot(2x-11) \end{aligned}$$

10.5 A more complex example of factorisation

Here is a more complex example (which you may skip at the first reading—but then please come back to it later!); we shall factorise the following polynomial P which is symmetric in a, b, c, and has degree 4:

$$P = \left(a^4+b^4+c^4\right) - 2\left(a^2\cdot b^2+b^2\cdot c^2+c^2\cdot a^2\right).$$

Our approach uses a blend of different approaches—the ideas developed above for factorising quadratic trinomials, and the 'difference of two squares' idea.

We choose to give more prominence to a than to b or c, and we express P in a non-symmetric way:

$$P = a^4-a^2\left(2b^2+2c^2\right)+\left(b^4-2b^2c^2+c^4\right).$$

Note that P may be regarded as a quadratic expression in a^2. Note also that the last bracketed expression is a perfect square:

$$b^4-2b^2c^2+c^4 = \left(b^2-c^2\right)^2 = [(b-c)\cdot(b+c)]^2 = (b-c)^2\cdot(b+c)^2.$$

We now make use of the following relation:

$$(b-c)^2+(b+c)^2 = 2b^2+2c^2.$$

For convenience, we write r for $b-c$ and s for $b+c$. Then we find that

$$P = a^4 - \left(r^2+s^2\right)\cdot a^2 + r^2\cdot s^2.$$

Observe that the coefficient of a^2 is $(-r^2)+(-s^2)$, and the constant term is $r^2\cdot s^2$ which may also be written as $(-r^2)\cdot(-s^2)$. So the 'shape' of the expression is just right (the coefficient of a^2 is the sum of $-r^2$ and $-s^2$, and the constant term is the product of $-r^2$ and $-s^2$), and we deduce that

$$P = \left(a^2 - r^2\right) \cdot \left(a^2 - s^2\right).$$

The two bracketed expressions factorise further, and we get:

$$P = (a-r) \cdot (a+r) \cdot (a-s) \cdot (a+s).$$

Substituting back $b-c$ for r and $b+c$ for s, we get the desired factorisation: $P = (a-b-c) \cdot (a-b+c) \cdot (a+b-c) \cdot (a+b+c)$. We rewrite this as follows to show its symmetry a little more clearly:

$$P = (a+b+c) \cdot (a-b-c) \cdot (b-c-a) \cdot (c-a-b).$$

10.6 Factorisation using the factor theorem

We now show how the factor theorem, which we had studied in Chapter 8 on *Polynomials*, can help in finding the factors of a polynomial. We first state the theorem again.

Theorem 10.1 (Factor Theorem) *If $P(x)$ is a polynomial in x, and a is a zero of P, then $x-a$ is a factor of $P(x)$.*

EXAMPLE 9. We consider the factorisation of the polynomial P given below, of degree 3:

$$P(x) = 3x^3 - 10x^2 - 11x + 42.$$

Here is a list of values taken by $P(x)$ for $x=-5$, $x=-4$, $x=-3$, ..., $x=4$, $x=5$; the list may be produced by hand calculation, or by using a computer.

x	-5	-4	-3	-2	-1	0	1	2	3	4	5
$P(x)$	-528	-266	-96	0	40	42	24	4	0	30	112

We observe that $P(-2) = 0$ and $P(3) = 0$. The factor theorem now assures us that both $x-(-2)$ and $x-3$ are factors of $P(x)$. So we have already obtained two factors of the given expression, $x+2$ and $x-3$, and as the expression is a cubic, there is just one more factor.

As the leading term of $P(x)$ is $3x^3$, and the product of the leading terms of the two factors just found is x^2, the leading term of the third factor must be $3x^3 \div x^2 = 3x$. And as the constant term of $P(x)$ is 42, and the product of the constant terms of the two factors found above is $2 \times (-3) = -6$, the constant term of the third factor must be $42 \div (-6) = -7$. So, the third factor must be $3x-7$, and we have the complete factorisation:

$$3x^3 - 10x^2 - 11x + 42 = (x+2) \cdot (x-3) \cdot (3x-7).$$

Note that since $3x-7$ takes the value 0 when we substitute $x = \frac{7}{3}$, we can anticipate that the same will happen for $P(x)$. And, indeed:

$$P\left(\frac{7}{3}\right) = 3 \cdot \left(\frac{7}{3}\right)^3 - 10 \cdot \left(\frac{7}{3}\right)^2 - 11 \cdot \left(\frac{7}{3}\right) + 42 = \frac{343 - 490 - 231 + 378}{9} = 0.$$

EXAMPLE 10. We consider the factorisation of the polynomial Q given below, of degree 4:

$$Q(x) = 6x^4 - 13x^3 - 63x^2 + 82x - 24.$$

Here is a list of values taken by $Q(x)$ for $x = -5, x = -4, x = -3, \ldots, x = 4, x = 5$; the list may be produced by hand calculation, or by using a computer.

x	-5	-4	-3	-2	-1	0	1	2	3	4	5
$Q(x)$	3366	1008	0	-240	-150	-24	-12	-120	-210	0	936

We observe that $Q(-3) = 0$ and $Q(4) = 0$. The factor theorem now assures us that both $x - (-3)$ and $x - 4$ are factors of $Q(x)$. So we have already obtained two factors of the given expression, $x+3$ and $x-4$, and as the expression has degree 4, the remaining factor must be of degree 2. As the product of the two factors found is $(x+3) \cdot (x-4) = x^2 - x - 12$, we get the quadratic factor by straightforward division:

$$\frac{6x^4 - 13x^3 - 63x^2 + 82x - 24}{x^2 - x - 12} = 6x^2 - 7x + 2.$$

The factor, $6x^2 - 7x + 2$, being a quadratic trinomial, may be factorised using the ideas of the previous section. We need two numbers with sum -7 and product $6 \times 2 = 12$; the obvious pair is $\{-3, -4\}$. So,

$$6x^2 - 7x + 2 = 6x^2 - 3x - 4x + 2 = 3x \cdot (2x-1) - 2 \cdot (2x-1) = (3x-2) \cdot (2x-1).$$

We now have the complete factorisation:

$$6x^4 - 13x^3 - 63x^2 + 82x - 24 = (x+3) \cdot (x-4) \cdot (2x-1) \cdot (3x-2).$$

Following the remark made in the previous example, we can anticipate that both $Q\left(\frac{1}{2}\right) = 0$ and $Q\left(\frac{2}{3}\right) = 0$.

EXAMPLE 11. We consider the factorisation of the polynomial $P = a^2 - b^2$. In this, we think of b as fixed and a as a variable. (This is an idea that we shall use again, below.) Writing x for a, we have:

$$P(x) = x^2 - b^2.$$

We see immediately that if we substitute b for x, we get 0; i.e., $P(b) = 0$. The same is the case if we substitute $-b$ for x, because $(-b)^2 = b^2$. The factor theorem now assures us that both $x - b$ and $x - (-b) = x + b$ are factors of $P(x)$. And indeed we have:

$$P(x) = (x-b) \cdot (x+b).$$

Substituting back a for x, we get

$$a^2 - b^2 = (a-b) \cdot (a+b).$$

Note that we have obtained the difference of two squares formula. Using the same logic, we may get the factors of $a^3 - b^3$, $a^3 + b^3$, etc.

MORE EXAMPLES

The following examples feature some impressive applications of the factor theorem.

EXAMPLE 12. We shall show that the following polynomial F which is symmetric in a, b, c,

$$F = a^3 + b^3 + c^3 - 3abc,$$

is divisible by $a + b + c$.

There are *three* unknowns here (a, b and c), but we shall think of just one of them as a variable, treating the other two as constants or plain numbers. Let a be the one treated as a variable. Calling it x to make things look more familiar, we have:

$$F(x) = x^3 + b^3 + c^3 - 3bcx.$$

Invoking the factor theorem, we realise that if $x + b + c$, which is the same as $x - (-b - c)$, is to be a factor of F, then we must have $F(-b-c) = 0$. So, we substitute $-b - c$ in place of x; we get:

$$\begin{aligned} F(-b-c) &= (-b-c)^3 + b^3 + c^3 + 3bc(b+c), \\ &= 0, \end{aligned}$$

after an easy expansion. So $x+b+c$ is indeed a factor of $F(x)$. This means that $a+b+c$ is a factor of $a^3+b^3+c^3-3abc$, as claimed. If we perform the division of $a^3+b^3+c^3-3abc$ by $a+b+c$, we get the following:

$$a^2+b^2+c^2-ab-bc-ca.$$

It should not come as a surprise that the quotient is symmetric in a, b, c, and has degree 2.

EXAMPLE 13. We shall find in the same way the factors of the polynomial G, where

$$G = (a+b+c)^3 - \left(a^3+b^3+c^3\right).$$

Writing x for a as earlier, we have:

$$G(x) = (x+b+c)^3 - \left(x^3+b^3+c^3\right).$$

If we substitute $-b$ for x we get

$$G(-b) = c^3-c^3 = 0,$$

and this tells us that $x-(-b)$ is a factor of $G(x)$, i.e., that $x+b$ is a factor of $G(x)$. In the same way we find that

$$G(-c) = b^3-b^3 = 0,$$

so that $x+c$ is a factor of $G(x)$. Reverting to the original symbols, we see that both $a+b$ and $a+c$ are factors of $G=(a+b+c)^3-\left(a^3+b^3+c^3\right)$.

Drawing on the fact that G is symmetric in a, b, c, we realise that $b+c$ too must be a factor of G; and this means that the polynomial $H=(a+b)\cdot(b+c)\cdot(c+a)$ must be a factor of G. Performing the division $G\div H$ we get a quotient of 3 (a constant, i.e., a polynomial of degree 0; but this should not come as a surprise, for both G and H have degree 3). It follows that

$$(a+b+c)^3-\left(a^3+b^3+c^3\right) = 3(a+b)\cdot(b+c)\cdot(c+a).$$

EXAMPLE 14. We now 'stretch' the factor theorem a bit.

Consider the quadratic polynomial x^2-2. It can be factorised using the factor theorem (via the substitution $x=\sqrt{2}$) as:

$$x^2-2 = \left(x-\sqrt{2}\right)\cdot\left(x+\sqrt{2}\right).$$

In this factorisation we see an irrational quantity ($\sqrt{2}$) as a coefficient. If we were not permitted to use irrational quantities, then we would not be able to factorise x^2-2. Such polynomials are called **IRREDUCIBLE**. *Their coefficients are integers, but to factorise them we are forced to use irrational quantities as coefficients.*

Let $f(x)$ be any polynomial with integer coefficients. Then the following is true:

$$\text{If } f\left(\sqrt{2}\right) = 0, \text{ then } x^2-2 \text{ is a factor of } f(x). \tag{10.12}$$

For example, take the polynomial $f(x) = 3x^5 - x^4 + x^3 + x^2 - 14x + 2$; note that its coefficients are integers. The substitution $x = \sqrt{2}$ yields:

$$\begin{aligned} f\left(\sqrt{2}\right) &= 3\left(\sqrt{2}\right)^5 - \left(\sqrt{2}\right)^4 + \left(\sqrt{2}\right)^3 + \left(\sqrt{2}\right)^2 - 14\left(\sqrt{2}\right) + 2 \\ &= 12\sqrt{2} - 4 + 2\sqrt{2} + 2 - 14\sqrt{2} + 2 = 0. \end{aligned}$$

And indeed we find the following factorisation:

$$3x^5 - x^4 + x^3 + x^2 - 14x + 2 = \left(x^2-2\right)\cdot\left(3x^3 - x^2 + 7x - 1\right).$$

There is nothing peculiar to $\sqrt{2}$ in this example; a similar statement may be made using the quantity $\sqrt{n}$ where n is any integer which is not a perfect square. The statement corresponding to (10.12) would be:

> *Suppose that n is not a perfect square. If $f(x)$ is a polynomial with integer coefficients such that $f(\sqrt{n}) = 0$, then x^2-n is a factor of $f(x)$.*

For example, the polynomial x^2-3 is irreducible, as its factorisation uses the irrational quantity $\sqrt{3}$. Using this fact we may show that the polynomial

$$x^6 - 10x^4 + 2x^3 + 10x^2 - 6x + 33$$

is a multiple of x^2-3. For, substituting $\sqrt{3}$ into the polynomial we get

$$3^3 - 10\cdot 3^2 + 2\cdot 3\sqrt{3} + 10\cdot 3 - 6\sqrt{3} + 33 = 0,$$

and we may verify that

$$x^6 - 10x^4 + 2x^3 + 10x^2 - 6x + 33 = (x^2-3)\cdot(x^4 - 7x^2 + 2x - 11).$$

THE CASE $n = -1$. We can stretch this idea further, by introducing the notion of **COMPLEX NUMBERS**; they correspond to the case $n = -1$ in the above discussion. Take the polynomial $x^2 + 1$. It is clearly irreducible. To factorise it we would have to 'invent' the number $\sqrt{-1}$ which is not a real number at all; it cannot be placed anywhere on the number line, because the square of a real number cannot be negative. We get the number by 'solving' the equation $x^2 + 1 = 0$; we get $x^2 = -1$, $\therefore x = \pm\sqrt{-1}$. The numbers $\sqrt{-1}$ and $-\sqrt{-1}$ are called **IMAGINARY UNITS**, and they are denoted by the symbols $i, -i$, respectively. Each one is an example of a complex number. The rules by which such numbers are handled are the following:

$$i^2 = -1, \quad i^3 = -i, \quad i^4 = 1, \quad i^5 = i, \quad \ldots,$$

and $(1+2i)+(3-4i) = 4-2i$ and so on. Using this rather ghostly number we are able to factorise $x^2 + 1$; for we have:

$$x^2 + 1 = (x-i)\cdot(x+i).$$

This may be verified using the difference of two squares identity:

$$(x-i)\cdot(x+i) = x^2 - i^2 = x^2 - (-1) = x^2 + 1.$$

The statement analogous to (10.12) is the following. Let $f(x)$ be a polynomial with integer coefficients, and let us substitute $x = i$ in $f(x)$. We now have:

$$\textit{If } f(i) = 0, \textit{ then } x^2+1 \textit{ is a factor of } f(x). \tag{10.13}$$

Example: Take the polynomial $4x^5 - 5x^4 + 11x^3 - 14x^2 + 7x - 9$; call it $f(x)$. Substituting $x = i$ in $f(x)$ we get:

$$\begin{aligned} f(i) &= 4i^5 - 5i^4 + 11i^3 - 14i^2 + 7i - 9 \\ &= 4i - 5 - 11i + 14 + 7i - 9 = 0. \end{aligned}$$

And indeed we have:

$$4x^5 - 5x^4 + 11x^3 - 14x^2 + 7x - 9 = \left(x^2+1\right)\cdot\left(4x^3 - 5x^2 + 7x - 9\right).$$

EXAMPLE 15. The idea of 'inventing' numbers may seem farfetched and outrageous, but it is certainly very useful! We consider one more such example and along the way find a nice application to a problem in integer factorisation.

We know that x^3-1 may be factorised as $(x-1)\cdot\left(x^2+x+1\right)$. Can the polynomial x^2+x+1 be factorised further? (Note that it has integer coefficients.) We can check that it cannot; it is irreducible. (It can be factorised using complex numbers as coefficients, but we do not permit this for now.) Let us now 'invent' a number w which is a root of x^2+x+1. We can do algebra with w using the usual rules; e.g., we have

$$w^3-1 = (w-1)\cdot\left(w^2+w+1\right) = (w-1)\cdot 0 = 0.$$

So $w^3=1$, which also means that $w^4=w$, $w^5=w^2$, $w^6=1$, $w^7=w$, $w^8=w^2$, etc. So as we raise w to higher and higher powers, the same numbers keep coming back in a cycle: 1, w, w^2, 1, w, w^2, 1, w, w^2, ...

The statement analogous to (10.12) and (10.13) is as follows: Let $f(x)$ be a polynomial with integer coefficients. We now substitute $x=w$ in $f(x)$ and find the following:

$$\textit{If } f(w) = 0, \textit{ then } x^2+x+1 \textit{ is a factor of } f(x). \tag{10.14}$$

EXAMPLE 16. Let $f(x)=x^5-10x^4+3x^3-5x^2+6x-7$; we have:

$$\begin{aligned} f(w) &= w^5-10w^4+3w^3-5w^2+6w-7 \\ &= w^2-10w+3-5w^2+6w-7 \\ &= -4w^2-4w-4 = -4\cdot\left(w^2+w+1\right) = 0. \end{aligned}$$

And indeed we have:

$$x^5-10x^4+3x^3-5x^2+6x-7 = \left(x^2+x+1\right)\cdot\left(x^3-11x^2+13x-7\right).$$

An easy application of this idea shows that x^2+x+1 is a factor of each of the following polynomials:

$$x^5+x+1, \qquad x^5+x^4+1, \qquad x^8+x+1, \qquad x^8+x^4+1, \qquad \ldots.$$

If we substitute integer values for x we get some nice factorisations; e.g., using $x=200$, we deduce that 40201 is a divisor of 320000000201; and using $x=300$, that 90301 is a divisor of 2438100000001.

There is a rich theory that lies behind such mathematics, called **ALGEBRAIC NUMBER THEORY**, much of which was born through efforts to solve Fermat's Last Theorem.

10.7 A square investigation

An often discovered property of the sequence of integers is the following:

The product of four consecutive positive integers is 1 *less than a square.*

For example, we have:

$$\begin{aligned} 1\times2\times3\times4 &= 24 = 5^2-1, \\ 2\times3\times4\times5 &= 120 = 11^2-1, \\ 3\times4\times5\times6 &= 360 = 19^2-1, \\ 4\times5\times6\times7 &= 840 = 29^2-1, \end{aligned}$$

and so on. Why is this so? How do we explain this property?

Consider any four consecutive positive integers, say n, $n+1$, $n+2$, $n+3$. We must show that their product is 1 less than some square, for any value of n. Here is how we may do so. We first note that *in any list of four consecutive integers, the product of the middle two exceeds the product of the outer two by* 2. For example, considering the list 4, 5, 6, 7, we have: $5\times6=30$, $4\times7=28$, and $30-28=2$. It is easy to account for this property; in the list n, $n+1$, $n+2$, $n+3$, the product of the middle two integers is

$$(n+1)\cdot(n+2) = n^2+3n+2,$$

and the product of the outer two integers is

$$n\cdot(n+3) = n^2+3n;$$

and we have $\left(n^2+3n+2\right)-\left(n^2+3n\right) = 2$.

We next note that the product of any two positive integers that differ by 2 is 1 less than a square; e.g., we have $1\times3=3=2^2-1$; $2\times4=8=3^2-1$; $3\times5=15=4^2-1$, and so on. This is easy to explain: if the two integers are n and $n+2$, then we have:

$$n\cdot(n+2) = n^2+2n = \left(n^2+2n+1\right)-1 = (n+1)^2-1.$$

Even simpler is to write the two integers as $n-1$ and $n+1$; then their product is n^2-1, and this is 1 less than a square.

The pieces of the puzzle have now fallen into place, and the solution is at hand: given four consecutive integers n, $n+1$, $n+2$, $n+3$, we write

$$A=(n+1)(n+2)=n^2+3n+2, \qquad B=n(n+3)=n^2+3n.$$

Then $A=B+2$, so,

$$A\cdot B \;=\; (B+2)\cdot B \;=\; B^2+2B \;=\; (B+1)^2-1.$$

In other words, we have:

$$n\cdot(n+1)\cdot(n+2\cdot(n+3) \;=\; \left(n^2+3n+1\right)^2-1,$$

and this explains what we had observed at the start.

Remark

The 'four' in this property is very special—there is no other integer k for which it is true that the product of any k consecutive positive integers is always a certain amount less than a square, or cube, etc.

EXERCISES

1. Factorise each of the following quadratic trinomials.

   (a) x^2+4x+3

   (b) x^2+5x+6

   (c) $x^2+7x+12$

   (d) $x^2+11x+30$

   (e) $x^2+9x+14$

   (f) $x^2-5x-14$

   (g) $x^2-6x-27$

   (h) $x^2+7x-30$

   (i) $x^2-7x-44$

   (j) $x^2-8x-65$

2. Factorise each of the following trinomials.

   (a) $2x^2-11x+5$

   (b) $5x^2-13x+6$

   (c) $-5x^2+18x+8$

   (d) $-8x^2+23x+3$

   (e) $-10x^2+17x-7$

   (f) $-18x^2+51x-35$

3. Factorise each of the following expressions.

(a) $a^2 - 9b^2$

(b) $49 - b^4$

(c) $16 - 81c^4$

(d) $4a^2b^2 - c^4$

(e) $x^{10} - 9y^6$

(f) $x^8 - 16y^4$

4. Factorise each of the following expressions.

(a) $a^2 + b^2 - c^2 - 2ab$

(b) $9a^2 + 4b^2 - 16c^2 + 12ab$

(c) $9a^2 + 16b^2 - c^2 - 24ab + 2c - 1$

(d) $a^2 + b^2 - c^2 - 2ab - 2a + 2b + 1$

(e) $a^2 + b^2 - c^2 - 2ab - 4a + 4b + 6c - 5$

5. Factorise each of the following expressions.

(a) $a^3 + 8b^3$

(b) $27a^3 - 64b^6$

(c) $8a^3b^6 - c^3$

(d) $125x^3 + 729y^6$

(e) $p^3q^3r^3 - 64$

6. Factorise each of the following expressions.

(a) $x^4 + x^2 + 1$

(b) $x^6 + 3x^4 - x^3 + 3x^2 + 1$

(c) $x^4 + 4x^2 + 16$

(d) $x^8 + x^4 + 1$

(e) $x^4 - 18x^2 + 1$

7. Factorise the following integers using the ideas of polynomial factorisation. Look up a table of squares to assist you in your computations.

(a) 221

(b) 399

(c) 1599

(d) 1763

(e) 2303

(f) 5183

(g) 6083

(h) 8099

(i) 10403

(j) 11663

(k) 14351

(l) 14399

(m) 32399

(n) 57599

8. Factorise the following integers using the ideas of polynomial factorisation. Look up a table of cubes to assist you in your computations.

(a) 1727
(b) 1729
(c) 4097
(d) 7999
(e) 8001
(f) 13823
(g) 21951
(h) 21953
(i) 32767
(j) 32769

9. Factorise each of the following expressions using the factor theorem.

(a) $3x^3 - 2x^2 - 11x + 10$
(b) $2x^3 + 11x^2 - 31x - 180$
(c) $4x^3 - 11x^2 - 6x + 9$
(d) $6x^4 + 5x^3 - 82x^2 - 31x + 210$
(e) $10x^4 + 9x^3 - 54x^2 - 23x + 30$

10. Show that $H = (a+b)\cdot(b+c)\cdot(c+a)$ is a factor of P, where

$$P = (a+b+c)^5 - \left(a^5 + b^5 + c^5\right),$$

and find the quotient in the division $P \div H$.

11. Show that $H = (a+b)\cdot(b+c)\cdot(c+a)$ is a factor of Q, where

$$Q = (a+b+c)^7 - \left(a^7 + b^7 + c^7\right).$$

12. Is it true that $H = (a+b)\cdot(b+c)\cdot(c+a)$ is a factor of the following expression:

$$(a+b+c)^n - (a^n + b^n + c^n),$$

wherever n is an odd positive integer?

13. ✪ Factorise the following polynomial which is symmetric in a, b, c:

$$\left(a^3 + b^3 + c^3\right) + 2abc - \left(a^2b + a^2c + b^2a + b^2c + c^2a + c^2b\right).$$

14. ✪✪ Factorise the following polynomial which is symmetric in a, b, c:

$$2\left(a^3 + b^3 + c^3\right) - 3\left(a^2b + a^2c + b^2a + b^2c + c^2a + c^2b\right) + 12abc.$$

15. ✪ Show without actual division that $x^{2012} + x^{2011} + 1$ is divisible by $x^2 + x + 1$.

    (The author would not ever want to inflict the actual division on anyone—even as a punishment!)

16. ✪ Show without actual division that 10240000000401 is divisible by 421.

    (Hint: Observe that the number 10240000000000 is a power of 20.)

17. ✪ Show without actual division that 10100000001 is divisible by 10101.

    (Hint: Observe that the number 10000000000 is a power of 100.)

18. ✪ Show without actual division that 318750001 is divisible by 2551.

19. ✪ Find a divisor of the number $\frac{6252501}{3} = 2084167$ and thus show that it is not prime.

20. ✪ ✪ Using the ideas developed in Examples 14 and 15 (section 10.6), show without complete division that $x^4 + x^3 + x^2 + x + 1$ is a divisor of each of the following polynomials:

    (a) $7x^6 - 5x^5 + 18x^4 + 18x^3 + 18x^2 + 11x + 23$;

    (b) $x^8 + 8x^7 + 10x^6 - x^5 + 12x^4 + 11x^3 + 4x^2 + 2x + 13$;

    (c) $x^{14} + x^{13} + x^7 + x + 1$.

Chapter 11

Linear Equations

11.1 Introduction to equations

Consider the statement $3x+5=20$. It states that two given expressions ($3x+5$ and 20) are equal to each other, but says nothing further about x. Are there some values of x that make the statement true? Let us try: $x=0$ yields $5=20$ (false); $x=1$ yields $8=20$ (false); $x=2$, 3 and 4 yield the false statements $11=20$, $14=20$ and $17=20$ (respectively); but $x=5$ finally yields a true statement ($20=20$).

A statement like $3x+5=20$ is called an **EQUATION**. In general, by an equation we mean a statement that two given expressions are equal to each other, with one or both of the expressions involving some unknown quantity; the act of finding that quantity (generally denoted by x, but it could also be some other letter, e.g., y) is called **SOLVING THE EQUATION**. The task is to find all the values of x which make the equation valid. Some examples of equations are shown below.

1. $2x+1=11$; this is an example of a **LINEAR EQUATION**. It involves just one unknown quantity which occurs in the simplest possible form—not raised to any power. It is also known as a **SIMPLE EQUATION**.

2. $\frac{2x-1}{3}=\frac{5x+3}{7}$; this too is a simple equation, involving fractions.

3. $x^2+7x+6=0$; this is an example of a **QUADRATIC EQUATION**; the unknown quantity x occurs as a *square*, i.e., to the second power.

4. $x^3+x=10$; this is an example of a **CUBIC EQUATION**; the unknown quantity x occurs as a *cube*, i.e., to the third power.

5. $x^4+x^3+x=111$; this is an example of a **QUARTIC EQUATION**; here the unknown quantity x occurs as a *fourth power*.

6. $x^5=x^4+x+14$; this is an example of a **QUINTIC EQUATION**; here the unknown quantity x occurs as a *fifth power*.

7. $2^x=3x+4$; this is an example of an **EXPONENTIAL EQUATION**; the unknown quantity x now occurs as an *exponent*.

8. $3^x+2^x=10$; this is another example of an exponential equation.

9. $x^x+x^2+x=100$; this is also an exponential equation—of a particularly nasty type!

In all these examples there is a *single unknown*, x, and a *single equation*. But we can also have equations where there are *several equations* in *several unknowns*; we then talk of a **SYSTEM OF EQUATIONS**. Examples of situations where the number of equations or the number of unknowns exceeds one are given below.

10. $2x+3y=19$

    This is an example of a *single equation* in *two unknowns*, x and y. The equation is linear.

11. $$\left\{\begin{array}{rcl} 2x+y &=& 11 \\ 3x-y &=& 14 \end{array}\right\}$$

    This is an example of a system with *two equations* in *two unknowns*, x and y. The equations are linear.

12. $x^2+y^2=25$

    This is an example of a *single equation* in *two unknowns*, x and y. The equation is **NON-LINEAR**.

13. $$\left\{\begin{array}{rcl} x^2+y^2+z^3 &=& 14 \\ x^3+y^3+z^3 &=& 36 \\ x^4+y^4+z^4 &=& 98 \end{array}\right\}$$

    This is an example of a system with *three equations* in *three unknowns*, x, y and z. The equations are non-linear.

In all these examples, no further conditions have been placed on the unknowns, apart from the stated equation(s). But additional restrictions may be placed on them; for example, they may be required to be integers, or be required to be rational numbers. Three famous instances of this are the following:

14. *The equation* $x^2+y^2=z^2$ *in which x, y and z are required to be positive integers.*

    A triple (x,y,z) of positive integers satisfying the above equation is called a **PYTHAGOREAN TRIPLE**. (We have met such triples in Chapter 3, *Families of Numbers*, and Chapter 5, *Fractions: Special Topics*.) If the integers are coprime, then the triple is known as a **PRIMITIVE PYTHAGOREAN TRIPLE**, or **PPT** for short. Examples: $(x,y,z)=(3,4,5)$, $(5,12,13)$, and $(7,24,25)$.

15. *The equation* $x^n+y^n=z^n$ *in which x, y, z and n are required to be positive integers and n must be greater than* 2. (Note the similarity of this with the Pythagorean equation; the only change is the exponent.)

    This is known as the **FERMAT EQUATION**, after the amateur mathematician Pierre de Fermat (1601–65)—the greatest amateur mathematician ever—who had conjectured, in a famously written marginal note, that it has no solutions.

16. *The equation* $3^m-2^n=\pm 1$ *in which both m and n are required to be positive integers exceeding* 1.

    This is a particular case of the **CATALAN EQUATION**, named after the Belgian mathematician Eugène Charles Catalan (1814–94). In words it asks: *Find all instances where a power of* 3 *and a power of* 2 *are consecutive integers.*

    It is not too difficult to solve this problem, but the general version, *Find all instances where the powers of two integers differ by* 1, is extremely difficult. It was solved only in 2003, after remaining unsolved for over a century.

11.2 Genesis of equations

Equations arise when there is a number (or numbers) to be determined, with some features or properties specified. We consider a few examples:

1. We want a number with the property that *when we subtract the number from its square, we get* 12.

Here a property has been specified, and we must identify the number (or numbers) with that property. To find a suitable equation we denote the desired number by x; then the equation is, clearly:

$$x^2 - x = 12.$$

2. We want a number such that *the sum of the number and its reciprocal is* 3. Denoting the number by x, we get the equation

$$x + \frac{1}{x} = 3.$$

3. Here is an example where the property involves a *pair* of numbers: *Find two numbers such that the square of the first number exceeds the second one by* 21, *and the square of the second number exceeds the first one by* 11. Now we need two symbols for the two unknowns. Call them x and y, respectively; then the equations become

$$\left\{ \begin{array}{rcl} x^2 - y &=& 21, \\ y^2 - x &=& 11. \end{array} \right\}$$

4. Here is an example concerning the digits of a two-digit number:

   Find a two-digit number such that the sum of its digits is 8, *and if its tens and units digits are interchanged, the new number exceeds the old one by* 36.

   Here we denote the tens digit of the number by x, and the units digit by y; then the number is $10x+y$, the number obtained by interchanging the digits is $10y+x$, and the difference between the new number and the old one is $(10y+x)-(10x+y)=9y-9x$. The sum of the digits is 8. So the equation system is:

$$\left\{ \begin{array}{rcl} 9y - 9x &=& 36, \\ x + y &=& 8. \end{array} \right\}$$

   For the answer to 'make sense' we must further require that both x and y are single-digit numbers. (Why?) But it so happens that even if we do not impose this extra requirement we get exactly the same answer.

5. *Find three consecutive integers with the property that the sum of the squares of the first and third exceeds the square of the middle one by* 486.

   If we denote the *middle integer* by x, then the other two integers are $x-1$ and $x+1$. The equation is, therefore:

$$(x-1)^2 + (x+1)^2 - x^2 = 486.$$

For the answer to make sense it must be that x is an integer. But even if we do not impose this requirement we get exactly the same answer.

6. *Find all instances when a triangular number is a perfect square.*

   The triangular numbers $1, 3, 6, 10, 15, 21, 28, 36, 45, 55, \ldots$ are given by the formula $\frac{1}{2}m(m+1)$, and the perfect squares are given by the formula n^2. So we seek all pairs (m, n) of positive integers such that

   $$\tfrac{1}{2}m(m+1) \;=\; n^2.$$

   Here, unlike the earlier problems, the requirement that m and n are positive integers cannot be dropped. Otherwise we could list 'solutions' such as $m = 2$, $n = \sqrt{3}$, which clearly has no meaning with regard to the original problem.

11.3 Solution sets

A number that makes an equation true is called a **SOLUTION** of the equation; the set of solutions is called the **SOLUTION SET** of the equation. Different possibilities can arise with regard to the solutions of an equation in one unknown quantity:

I. The equation may be true for *just one value of* x, in which case it is said to have a **UNIQUE SOLUTION**.

   An example of such an equation is $2x + 1 = 11$; it has just one solution, namely: $x = 5$. Its solution set is $\{5\}$.

II. The equation may be true for *two or more values of* x, in which case it is said to have **MULTIPLE SOLUTIONS**.

   An example of such an equation is $x^2 = 9$ (it is true for $x = 3$, and also for $x = -3$). Its solution set is $\{-3, 3\}$.

   Another example: the equation $x^3 - 4x = 0$; it is true for the following three values: $x = -2$; $x = 0$; $x = 2$, so its solution set is $\{-2, 0, 2\}$.

III. The equation may be true for *all possible values of* x; it is then known as an **IDENTITY**. Its solution set is the entire set $\mathbf{R}$ of real numbers.

   An example of such an equation is $x^2 - 1 = (x - 1)(x + 1)$. More such examples are easy to come by.

IV. The equation may be true for *no value of* x, in which case its solution set is the empty set Φ.

An example of such an equation is $x+1=x$. An equation of this kind in some way contradicts the basic laws of algebra, and hence can never be true.

The very same statements can be made for equation systems having more than one unknown quantity. We give some examples below.

1. The equation system

$$\left\{\begin{array}{rcl} 2x-y &=& 5 \\ 3x+y &=& 10 \end{array}\right\}$$

has a unique solution, namely, $(x,y)=(3,1)$. So its solution set is $\{(3,1)\}$.

2. The equation system

$$\left\{\begin{array}{rcl} x^2+y^2 &=& 25 \\ x-y &=& 1 \end{array}\right\}$$

has two solutions, namely, $(x,y)=(4,3)$ and $(x,y)=(-3,-4)$. So its solution set is $\{(4,3),\ (-3,-4)\}$.

3. The single equation $x+y=10$ in two unknowns $(x,\ y)$ has *infinitely many solutions*, some of which are listed here:

$$(x,y) \;=\; (0,10),\ (1,9),\ (2,8),\ (3,7),\ \ldots,\ (10,0),\ (11,-1),\ \ldots.$$

Its solution set has infinitely many elements.

4. The equation system

$$\left\{\begin{array}{rcl} x^2+y^2 &=& 25 \\ x+y &=& 15 \end{array}\right\}$$

is not made true by *any* pair of values of x and y; its solution set is Φ. (It may not be clear to you why this is so, but we leave this matter for now.)

Remark

Here we are assuming that x and y are *real numbers*. If we enlarge the set of numbers to include the *complex numbers*, then the system does indeed have solutions. But this is not a topic we shall be studying now.

11.4 Basic principles used in solving an equation

Centuries back, in his great book THE ELEMENTS (Book I), Euclid made certain assertions which he called **COMMON NOTIONS** (or 'CMN' for short). We shall modify Euclid's list and present the common notions as follows:

COMMON NOTION 1. *Quantities which are equal to the same quantity are equal to one another.*

COMMON NOTION 2. *If equals are added to equals, or subtracted from equals, then the resulting quantities are equal.*

COMMON NOTION 3. *If equals are multiplied by equals, or divided by equals which are not zero, then the resulting quantities are equal.*

These statements were originally made in a *geometric* context (Euclid's book is mostly about geometry), but they serve just as well in the context of algebra. The algebraic way of stating CMN-2 and CMN-3 is: if $a = b$, and $c = d$, then

$$a+c = b+d, \qquad a-c = b-d, \qquad ac = bd,$$

and if $c, d \neq 0$, then

$$\frac{a}{c} = \frac{b}{d}.$$

A useful rule that comes from the CMNs is the **CROSS-MULTIPLICATION RULE**:

$$\boxed{\text{If } \frac{a}{b} = \frac{c}{d}, \text{ then } ad = bc.}$$

This is obtained by multiplying both sides of the relation $\frac{a}{b} = \frac{c}{d}$ by bd, which is the LCM of b and d. It works because multiplication is associative.

Using the common notions to solve linear equations. In each case, the strategy will be to *isolate* the unknown quantity on one side, say the left side. Take a simple equation in some unknown quantity x, say:

$$3x+7 = 49.$$

To solve this, we add the additive inverse of 7 (namely, -7) to both sides of the equation, making use of CMN-2, and get:

$$(3x+7)+(-7) = 42, \quad \therefore\ 3x+\Big(7+(-7)\Big) = 42, \quad \therefore\ 3x = 42.$$

Note how we have 'isolated' x on the left side.

Now we multiply both sides of the last equation by the multiplicative inverse of 3, namely, $\frac{1}{3}$, making use of CMN-3, and get:

$$\frac{1}{3}\times(3x) = \frac{1}{3}\times 42, \quad \therefore\ \left(\frac{1}{3}\times 3\right)\times x = \frac{1}{3}\times 42, \quad \therefore\ x = 14.$$

Note how we have used the fact that *addition and multiplication are associative.*

Verifying the solution. Having got this far, one final step remains; *we must verify that the solution we have found fits the given equation.* So we substitute $x = 14$ in the expression $3x+7$, and get: $(3\times 14)+7 = 42+7 = 49$, as given. So the solution does 'fit'. *This is a necessary final step.*

The general case. All such equations are solved in much the same way. The general situation is described below, with the symbols a, b, c used to represent given numbers. (They are called the **CONSTANTS** of the equation.)

- If $x+b=c$, then $x=c-b$ (obtained by adding the additive inverse of b, i.e., $-b$, to both sides).
- If $ax = c$, where $a \neq 0$, then $x = \frac{c}{a}$ (obtained by multiplying both sides by the multiplicative inverse of a, namely, $\frac{1}{a}$).

  What happens if $a = 0$? Then there are two possible outcomes.

  - ☐ Either c too is 0, in which case the equation reads $0x = 0$; this equation is made true by *every possible number* (because 0 times any number is 0), so it has infinitely many solutions. Its solution set is **R**.
  - ☐ Or $c \neq 0$, in which case the equation does not have any solution at all. This is because the product of x and 0 cannot be non-zero for any value of x.

So if $a = 0$, then the equation $ax = c$ either has infinitely many solutions or no solutions; what a curious situation!

- If the equation is $ax + b = c$, where a is assumed to be non-zero (note that this equation includes both the earlier ones as special cases), then we first add the additive inverse of b to both sides:

$$ax + b = c, \quad \therefore\ ax + b + (-b) = c + (-b), \quad \therefore\ ax = c - b.$$

Now we multiply both sides by the multiplicative inverse of a (recall that it is not zero):

$$ax = c - b, \quad \therefore\ \frac{1}{a} \times ax = \frac{1}{a} \times (c - b), \quad \therefore\ x = \frac{c - b}{a}.$$

So the solution of $ax + b = c$ is $x = \frac{c-b}{a}$, provided that $a \neq 0$.

If it happens that $a = 0$, then the equation either has no solution or infinitely many solutions.

Remark

Observe how associativity plays its part in the solution:

- ☐ it ensures that $(ax + b) + (-b)$ is the same as $ax + \big(b + (-b)\big)$, which simplifies to ax because $b + (-b) = 0$, and $ax + 0 = ax$;
- ☐ it ensures that $\frac{1}{a} \times (ax)$ is the same as $\left(\frac{1}{a} \times a\right) x$, which simplifies to x because $\frac{1}{a} \times a = 1$ and $1x = x$.

So associativity is of crucial importance in our solution procedure.

EXAMPLES

EXAMPLE 1. Solve the equation $\dfrac{2x+3}{5} - \dfrac{x+4}{7} = 8$.

We first 'clear the fractions' by multiplying both sides by the LCM of the denominators, i.e., by $\text{LCM}(5, 7) = 35$. On the left side we get:

$$35\left(\frac{2x+3}{5} - \frac{x+4}{7}\right) = 7(2x+3) - 5(x+4) = 14x + 21 - 5x - 20 = 9x + 1,$$

and on the right side we get: $8 \times 35 = 280$. The equation now reads

$$9x+1 = 280,$$

so the solution is

$$x = \frac{280-1}{9} = \frac{279}{9} = 31.$$

Now we check whether this fits. On the left side we get:

$$\frac{(2\times 31)+3}{5} - \frac{31+4}{7} = \frac{62+3}{5} - \frac{35}{7} = \frac{65}{5} - \frac{35}{7} = 13-5 = 8,$$

as given, and the verification is complete.

EXAMPLE 2. Solve the equation $\dfrac{10}{x+3} = \dfrac{21}{3x-1}$.

Observe that this does not 'look' linear. But appearances can be deceptive. By applying the cross-multiplication rule we get:

$$10(3x-1) = 21(x+3), \quad \therefore\ 30x-10 = 21x+63, \quad \therefore\ 30x-21x = 63+10,$$

and we finally get:

$$9x = 73, \quad \therefore\ x = \frac{73}{9}.$$

Now we must check our solution (a not very inviting task this time, but let us toil on). Substitute $x = \frac{73}{9}$ on both sides of the given equation. On the left side we get:

$$\frac{10}{\frac{73}{9}+3} = \frac{10}{\frac{73+27}{9}} = \frac{10}{\frac{100}{9}} = \frac{90}{100} = \frac{9}{10}.$$

On the right side we get:

$$\frac{21}{\left(3\times\frac{73}{9}\right)-1} = \frac{21}{\frac{73}{3}-1} = \frac{21}{\frac{73-3}{3}} = \frac{21}{\frac{70}{3}} = \frac{63}{70} = \frac{9}{10}.$$

The two sides are equal, so the verification is complete.

EXAMPLE 3. *A* is twice as old as *B*, and in five years *A* will be two years older than *B*. How old are they?

Here the problem has some 'red herrings' which mislead us; the 'in five years' is irrelevant, as the difference between *A*'s age and *B*'s age is not going to change from one year to the next!

Let B's age in years be denoted by x; then A's age in years is $2x$ ('twice as old'); it is also $x+2$ ('two years older'). So $2x = x+2$. This leads to $2x - x = 2$, and we get $x = 2$. So B is 2 years old, and A is 4 years old. The answer fits the stated conditions (the 'data'), so the check works out.

EXAMPLE 4. The rule for changing from the Fahrenheit scale (°F) to the Celsius scale (°C) for measurement of temperature is the following:

$$\mathrm{C} = \frac{5}{9}(\mathrm{F}-32).$$

Given that $\mathrm{C} = 10$, find F.

We must solve the equation

$$\frac{5}{9}(\mathrm{F}-32) = 10$$

in the unknown F. By cross-multiplication followed by addition of 32 to both sides, we get:

$$\mathrm{F}-32 = \frac{9}{5}\times 10 = 18, \qquad \therefore\ \mathrm{F} = 32+18 = 50.$$

So the answer is: 10°C corresponds to 50°F.

Check: $\frac{5}{9}\times(50-32) = \frac{5}{9}\times 18 = 5\times 2 = 10$, as required.

EXAMPLE 5. Solve the equation $(x+1)^3 + (x-1)^3 - 2x^3 = 72$.

The equation *looks* like a cubic equation; but here too we shall see that appearances are deceptive. First we open out the cubed expressions. Since

$$(x+1)^2 = (x+1)\times(x+1) = (x^2+x)+(x+1) = x^2+2x+1$$

we get:

$$\begin{aligned}(x+1)^3 &= (x+1)\times(x^2+2x+1)\\ &= (x^3+2x^2+x)+(x^2+2x+1)\\ &= x^3+3x^2+3x+1,\\ (x-1)^3 &= x^3-3x^2+3x-1 \qquad \text{(similarly)}.\end{aligned}$$

Therefore, we get:

$$\begin{aligned}(x+1)^3+(x-1)^3-2x^3 &= (x^3+3x^2+3x+1)+(x^3-3x^2+3x-1)-2x^3\\ &= 6x,\end{aligned}$$

a surprising simplification! So the given equation takes a very simple form indeed:

$$6x = 72,$$

and the solution is: $x = \frac{72}{6} = 12$.

Now for the check. Substituting $x = 12$ into the given equation, we get:

$$13^3 + 11^3 - (2 \times 12^3) = 2197 + 1331 - (2 \times 1728) = 3528 - 3456 = 72,$$

as required.

EXAMPLE 6. Solve the equation $ax + b = cx + d$.

Here we need to be clear what we are solving. It is assumed that x is the unknown, and that a, b, c and d are constants (i.e., given numbers).

- If $a \neq c$ then we get:

$$\begin{aligned} ax + b &= cx + d, \\ \therefore\ ax + b + (-b) &= cx + d + (-b), \\ \therefore\ ax &= cx + d - b, \\ \therefore\ ax - cx &= d - b, \\ \therefore\ (a - c)x &= d - b, \\ \therefore\ x &= \frac{d - b}{a - c}. \end{aligned}$$

Check: Substituting $x = \dfrac{d - b}{a - c}$ into $ax + b$ we get:

$$a \times \left(\frac{d - b}{a - c}\right) + b = \frac{ad - ab + ab - bc}{a - c} = \frac{ad - bc}{a - c}.$$

Substituting $x = \dfrac{d - b}{c - a}$ into $cx + d$ we get:

$$c \times \left(\frac{d - b}{a - c}\right) + d = \frac{cd - bc + ad - cd}{a - c} = \frac{ad - bc}{a - c}.$$

Both sides are equal to $\dfrac{ad - bc}{a - c}$, so the solution has been verified.

- If $a = c$, then the above solution is not valid, for it involves division by 0.

  As earlier, we must distinguish between two possibilities: $b = d$, and $b \neq d$.

  If $b = d$, then every number is a solution of the equation (for the equation reduces to $0x = 0$).

  If $b \neq d$, then the equation has no solutions.

EXAMPLE 7. Solve the equation $\dfrac{x+1}{2x+3} = \dfrac{x+4}{2x+7}$.

Invoking the cross-multiplication rule we get:

$$\begin{aligned} \frac{x+1}{2x+3} &= \frac{x+4}{2x+7}, \\ \therefore\ (x+1)(2x+7) &= (x+4)(2x+3), \\ \therefore\ \left(2x^2+7x\right)+(2x+7) &= \left(2x^2+8x\right)+(3x+12), \\ \therefore\ 2x^2+9x+7 &= 2x^2+11x+12, \\ \therefore\ 2x^2+9x-2x^2-11x &= 12-7, \\ \therefore\ -2x &= 5, \\ \therefore\ x &= -\frac{5}{2}. \end{aligned}$$

Check: On the left side of the given equation we get

$$\frac{-\frac{5}{2}+1}{\left(2\times-\frac{5}{2}\right)+3} = \frac{\frac{-5+2}{2}}{-5+3} = \frac{-\frac{3}{2}}{-2} = \frac{3}{4}.$$

On the right side we get:

$$\frac{-\frac{5}{2}+4}{\left(2\times-\frac{5}{2}\right)+7} = \frac{\frac{-5+8}{2}}{-5+7} = \frac{\frac{3}{2}}{2} = \frac{3}{4}.$$

The two sides are equal, and the verification is complete.

EXAMPLE 8. Find four consecutive integers such that the product of the second and fourth integers exceeds the product of the first and third integers by 47.

Let the smallest of the four integers be x; then the other three are $x+1$, $x+2$, $x+3$. The stated condition translates into the following:

$$(x+1)(x+3)-x(x+2) = 47.$$

Expanding the products on the left side, we get:

$$\left(x^2+x+3x+3\right)-\left(x^2+2x\right) \;=\; 47.$$

This yields $4x+3-2x=47$, and:

$$2x+3 \;=\; 47, \qquad \therefore\; 2x \;=\; 44, \qquad \therefore\; x \;=\; \frac{44}{2} \;=\; 22.$$

So the four integers are 22, 23, 24 and 25. Check: $23\times 25=575$; $22\times 24=528$; $575-528=47$, as required.

EXAMPLE 9. Break 80 into two parts so that the larger part is $\frac{3}{2}$ of the smaller part.

Let x be the larger part; then the smaller part is $80-x$. The stated condition tells us that

$$x \;=\; \frac{3}{2}(80-x), \qquad \therefore\; 2x \;=\; 240-3x, \qquad \therefore\; 5x \;=\; 240, \qquad \therefore\; x \;=\; \frac{240}{5} \;=\; 48.$$

So the two numbers are 48, and $80-48=32$.

Remark

Note that the words 'larger' and 'smaller' played no part in the solution. If we had said, "let x be the smaller part", then the stated condition would translate to

$$80-x \;=\; \frac{3}{2}\cdot x,$$

giving $2(80-x)=3x$, $\therefore 160-2x=3x$, $\therefore 5x=160$, $\therefore x=\frac{160}{5}=32$. This gives $80-x=80-32=48$. We get the same two numbers we got earlier: 32 and 48.

11.5 Linear equations in two unknowns

We proceed now to study equation systems that have *two equations in two unknowns* (generally denoted by x,y, or occasionally by u,v). Such systems are commonly known as **SIMULTANEOUS EQUATIONS**. We shall only study cases where the equations are linear (i.e., where x and y occur to the first power only).

Earlier we saw an example of a single equation in two unknowns which has infinitely many solutions: the equation $x+y=10$, in Section 11.3. It is in general true (with some exceptions) that a single equation in two unknowns has infinitely many solutions. For example, take the equation

$$2x+3y = 20.$$

We treat y as an unknown by itself, and solve for it; we get:

$$3y = 20-2x, \qquad \therefore y = \frac{20-2x}{3}.$$

We have 'expressed y in terms of x'. Now we can freely give values to x (*any value that we wish*), and *assign to y the value dictated by the above relation*. In this manner, we may list an unlimited number of solution pairs to the given equation.

For example, if we put $x=0$, then we get $y=\frac{20}{3}$; if we put $x=1$, then we get $y=\frac{18}{3}=6$; if we put $x=2$, then we get $y=\frac{16}{3}$; if we put $x=3$, then we get $y=\frac{14}{3}$; and so on. So the solution set is

$$\left\{\left(0,\frac{20}{3}\right),\ (1,6),\ \left(2,\frac{16}{3}\right),\ \left(3,\frac{14}{3}\right),\ \ldots\right\},$$

an infinite set.

Remark

Though we will not study examples which are not linear, the same can be said for non-linear equations too. For example, take the equation

$$x^2+y^2 = 100.$$

This is a single non-linear equation in two unknowns. As earlier we can solve for y:

$$y^2 = 100-x^2, \qquad \therefore y = \sqrt{100-x^2} \quad \text{or} \quad y = -\sqrt{100-x^2}.$$

Now we may freely assign values to x, get the corresponding values of y, and so get an unlimited number of solutions to $x^2+y^2=100$. For example, $x=0$ yields $y=\pm 10$; $x=1$ yields $y=\pm\sqrt{99}$; $x=6$ yields $y=\pm 8$; and so on.

So a single equation in two unknowns generally gives rise to an infinite solution set. But if we have *two* equations in two unknowns, then typically the infinity can come crashing down to just one, and we get a unique solution! In some instances, the equations may even contradict each other, and then we get no solution at all.

Two methods of solution present themselves here; we illustrate both by studying the system

$$\left\{\begin{array}{rcl} 2x+y &=& 11, \\ 3x-y &=& 14. \end{array}\right\}$$

Method 1. We first solve for y using each of the given equations. From the equation $2x+y=11$ we get:

$$y = 11-2x.$$

From the equation $3x-y=14$ we get:

$$y = 3x-14.$$

We now have two expressions for the same quantity, y. We equate them:

$$3x-14 = 11-2x,$$

and *solve this equation for* x, using the usual strategy:

$$3x+2x = 11+14, \qquad \therefore\ 5x = 25, \qquad \therefore\ x = \frac{25}{5} = 5.$$

Having found x, we find y from either of the expressions we got earlier for y; since $y=11-2x$, we have:

$$y = 11-(2\times 5) = 11-10 = 1.$$

So the answer is $(x,y)=(5,1)$. The solution is unique.

As always, we must check the answer. Substituting $x=5$, $y=1$ into $2x+y$ we get $(2\times 5)+1=11$, as given; and substituting the same values into $3x-y$ we get $(3\times 5)-1=14$, as given. So the checks work out.

Method 2. The other method, which is generally more convenient to use, is called the **METHOD OF ELIMINATION**. We have,

$$\begin{aligned} 2x+y &= 11, \\ 3x-y &= 14. \end{aligned}$$

Using Common Notion-2, we add the left sides of these two equations, and also the two right sides; on the left side we get: $(2x+y)+(3x-y)=5x$ (the y cancels out), and on the right side we get $11+14=25$; therefore:

$$5x = 25, \qquad \therefore\ x = \frac{25}{5} = 5.$$

Having found x we now find y in the same way as earlier.

In this method we 'eliminated' y by adding the two equations. We could do so quite easily as the first equation has a $+y$ and the second equation has a $-y$. But elimination is possible in any such situation.

For example, suppose we choose to eliminate x and not y. Note that the coefficient of x in the first equation is 2; in the second equation it is 3. If we multiply each equation by the coefficient of x in the *other* equation, then the coefficients of $x$in the two resulting equations will clearly be the same. Here is what we get when we multiply the first equation by 3 and the second equation by 2:

$$\begin{aligned} 6x+3y &= 33, \\ 6x-2y &= 28. \end{aligned}$$

Note that each equation features a $6x$. If we subtract the left side of the second equation from the left side of the first one, and do the same on the right side, the resulting expressions will still be equal (Common Notion-2), and the $6x$ will conveniently get eliminated; so we get:

$$3y-(-2y) = 33-28, \qquad \therefore\ 5y = 5, \qquad \therefore\ y = \frac{5}{5} = 1.$$

Having found y, we find x by substituting for y in either of the given equations. Thus, from $2x+y=11$, substituting $y=1$ we get

$$2x+1 = 11, \qquad \therefore\ 2x = 11-1 = 10, \qquad \therefore\ x = \frac{10}{2} = 5,$$

and we have found the same solution as earlier.

Remark

Though we have listed these as two different methods, they are clearly related; in both cases we eliminate one unknown, and thus obtain a single equation in the *other* unknown. We now solve this equation, substitute in the given equation(s), and thus find the value of the eliminated quantity.

The idea of elimination works even in cases where the equations are not linear, though the algebra may get messy. For example, consider this pair of non-linear equations:

$$\left\{ \begin{aligned} x^2-y &= 21, \\ y^2-x &= 11. \end{aligned} \right\}$$

We solve for y from each equation; the first one yields

$$y = x^2 - 21, \qquad \therefore\ y^2 = \left(x^2 - 21\right)^2,$$

and the second one:

$$y^2 = x + 11.$$

By equating the two expressions in y^2, we get a single equation in x:

$$\left(x^2 - 21\right)^2 = x + 11, \qquad \therefore\ x^4 - 42x^2 + 441 = x + 11,$$

and finally:

$$x^4 - 42x^2 - x + 430 = 0.$$

This is an example of a quartic equation, because x occurs to the fourth power (but for the moment, we shall not attempt to solve it).

EXAMPLES

EXAMPLE 10. Solve the following equations for x and y:

$$\begin{aligned} 7x - 5y &= 50, \\ 3x + 2y &= 9. \end{aligned}$$

We choose to eliminate y. Multiplying the first equation by 2 and the second one by 5, we get:

$$\begin{aligned} 14x - 10y &= 100, \\ 15x + 10y &= 45. \end{aligned}$$

Addition of the two equation now yields:

$$29x = 145, \qquad \therefore\ x = \frac{145}{29} = 5.$$

Substituting this into the equation $3x + 2y = 9$ we get:

$$(3 \times 5) + 2y = 9, \qquad \therefore\ 2y = 9 - 15 = -6, \qquad \therefore\ y = -\frac{6}{2} = -3.$$

So the solution is: $(x, y) = (5, -3)$. The solution is unique.

Check: $(7 \times 5) - [5 \times (-3)] = 35 - (-15) = 50$, and $(3 \times 5) + [2 \times (-3)] = 15 - 6 = 9$.

EXAMPLE 11. Solve the following pair of equations for x and y:

$$\left\{ \begin{aligned} \frac{x}{2} - \frac{y}{3} &= \frac{1}{4}, \\ \frac{x}{5} + \frac{y}{4} &= \frac{1}{3}. \end{aligned} \right\}$$

We opt to clear the fractions first: we multiply the first equation by $\text{LCM}(2,3,4) = 12$, and the second equation by $\text{LCM}(5,4,3) = 60$; we get:

$$\left\{ \begin{aligned} 6x - 4y &= 3, \\ 12x + 15y &= 20. \end{aligned} \right\}$$

We solve this by eliminating x. Subtracting twice the first equation from the second one, we get:

$$\left\{ \begin{aligned} 12x - 8y &= 6, \\ 12x + 15y &= 20, \end{aligned} \right\} \qquad \therefore\ 15y - (-8y) = 20 - 6, \qquad \therefore\ 23y = 14,$$

giving $y = \frac{14}{23}$.

Now we substitute this value of y into the equation $6x - 4y = 3$:

$$6x - 4 \times \frac{14}{23} = 3, \qquad \therefore\ 6x = 3 + \frac{56}{23} = \frac{69+56}{23} = \frac{125}{23},$$

giving

$$x = \frac{1}{6} \times \frac{125}{23} = \frac{125}{138}.$$

So the solution is

$$(x,y) = \left(\frac{125}{138}, \frac{14}{23}\right) = \left(\frac{125}{138}, \frac{84}{138}\right).$$

Now for the check:

$$\frac{x}{2} - \frac{y}{3} = \frac{125}{276} - \frac{28}{138} = \frac{125-56}{276} = \frac{69}{276} = \frac{1}{4},$$

and

$$\frac{x}{5} + \frac{y}{4} = \frac{25}{138} + \frac{21}{138} = \frac{46}{138} = \frac{1}{3}.$$

The verification has worked out correctly.

EXAMPLE 12. Solve the following equations for x and y:

$$\left\{\begin{array}{rcl} ax+by &=& e, \\ cx+dy &=& f. \end{array}\right\}$$

Here a, b, c, d, e, and f are constants. So the task is to express x and y in terms of these six quantities.

We choose to eliminate y first. Multiplying the first equation by d and the second one by b, we get:

$$\left\{\begin{array}{rcl} adx+bdy &=& de, \\ bcx+bdy &=& bf. \end{array}\right\}$$

Subtracting the second equation from the first one, we get:

$$(ad-bc)x = de-bf, \qquad \therefore\ x = \frac{de-bf}{ad-bc},$$

provided $ad-bc \neq 0$. Next, we eliminate x from the original pair of equations. Multiplying the first equation by c and the second one by a, we get:

$$\left\{\begin{array}{rcl} acx+bcy &=& ce, \\ acx+ady &=& af. \end{array}\right\}$$

Subtracting the first equation from the second one, we get:

$$(ad-bc)y = af-ce, \qquad \therefore\ y = \frac{af-ce}{ad-bc},$$

provided $ad-bc \neq 0$. It follows that the solution is

$$\boxed{(x,y) = \left(\frac{de-bf}{ad-bc}, \frac{af-ce}{ad-bc}\right), \quad \text{provided that } ad-bc \neq 0.} \qquad (11.1)$$

Observe that x and y have the same denominator: $ad-bc$.

When we check the solution we find that it works out correctly:

$$\frac{a(de-bf)}{ad-bc} + \frac{b(af-ce)}{ad-bc} = \frac{ade-abf+abf-bce}{ad-bc} = \frac{e(ad-bc)}{ad-bc} = e,$$

and

$$\frac{c(de-bf)}{ad-bc} + \frac{d(af-ce)}{ad-bc} = \frac{cde-bcf+adf-cde}{ad-bc} = \frac{f(ad-bc)}{ad-bc} = f.$$

Can we get into any difficulties in this solution? Yes: if the denominator in these fractions is zero! The above solution involves division by $ad - bc$ and is valid only if $ad - bc \neq 0$. So if $ad - bc \neq 0$, then the given equation system has a unique solution as given above.

What happens if $ad - bc = 0$ may not be obvious to you at this point in time; we shall not take up the matter here. It turns out that two possible situations may occur, one in which there are infinitely many solutions, and one in which there are no solutions.

EXAMPLE 13. A two-digit number is 7 times the sum of its digits. If 27 be subtracted from the number, the digits get interchanged. Find the number.

Let the units digit of the number be x, and let the tens digit be y; then the number is $10y + x$, its sum of digits is $x + y$, and the number obtained by interchanging the digits is $10x + y$. The stated conditions ('the data') then translate into the equations $10y + x = 7(x + y)$, and $10y + x - 27 = 10x + y$. These may be rearranged to yield the following pair of equations:

$$\left\{\begin{array}{rcr} 6x - 3y &=& 0, \\ 9x - 9y &=& -27. \end{array}\right\}$$

From the first equation we get $3y = 6x$, $\therefore \quad y = 2x$. From the second equation we get $9y = 9x + 27$, $\therefore y = x + 3$. So we get, combining these two;

$$2x = x + 3, \qquad \therefore x = 3, \qquad \therefore y = 3 + 3 = 6.$$

So the desired number is 63. Check: $63 = 7 \times (6 + 3)$, and $63 - 27 = 36$.

EXAMPLE 14. Two numbers are in the ratio $4 : 5$. If 10 be added to each number, then the ratio becomes $6 : 7$. Find the two numbers.

Let the two numbers be x and y; then the stated conditions tell us that

$$\frac{x}{y} = \frac{4}{5}, \qquad \frac{x + 10}{y + 10} = \frac{6}{7}.$$

Using the cross-multiplication rule, we get

$$5x = 4y, \qquad 7(x + 10) = 6(y + 10).$$

Therefore:

$$\left\{\begin{array}{rcr} 5x - 4y &=& 0, \\ 7x - 6y &=& -10. \end{array}\right\}$$

We choose this time to directly use formula (11.1). Since

$$a = 5, \quad b = -4, \quad c = 7, \quad d = -6, \quad e = 0, \quad f = -10,$$

we get:

$$x = \frac{0-(40)}{-30+28} = \frac{-40}{-2} = 20, \qquad y = \frac{-50-0}{-30+28} = \frac{-50}{-2} = 25.$$

So the two numbers are 20 and 25. (Check: $20:25 = 4:5$ and $30:35 = 6:7$, as required.)

There are of course other ways to proceed. Since the numbers are given to be in the ratio $4:5$, we may take the numbers as $4k, 5k$, respectively, where k is to be found. The second piece of information yields:

$$4k+10 : 5k+10 = 6:7, \qquad \therefore\ 7(4k+10) = 6(5k+10), \qquad \therefore\ 28k+70 = 30k+60,$$

giving $2k = 10$, and hence $k = 5$. So the numbers are 20 and 25.

EXAMPLE 15. Choose any three-digit number. Form a new three-digit number by *reversing its digits*. Show that the difference between this integer and the earlier one is a multiple of 99.

This is not a typical 'find the number' problem, but may be conveniently solved using algebra.

Let the units digit of the number be x, let the the tens digit be y, and let the hundreds digit be z. Then the number chosen is

$$100z + 10y + x,$$

and the number obtained by reversing the digits is

$$100x + 10y + z.$$

The difference between the two integers is

$$(100z+10y+x) - (100x+10y+z) = 99z - 99x = 99(z-x).$$

The difference is 99 times some integer, and hence is a multiple of 99.

11.6 Application I: Clock problems

In today's world, watches with moving hands and a dial are not seen too often, having been edged out by digital watches. This, sadly, denies us the pleasure of some interesting problems based on the movements of the hour-hand and minute-hand. We pose and solve a few such problems here. (We shall ignore the position of the second-hand in our problems.)

EXAMPLE 16. It is visually clear that the positions of the hour- and minute-hands coincide exactly at 12 noon. In the minutes that follow, the minute-hand is always ahead of the hour-hand, but sometime after 1 PM the minute-hand 'catches up' with the hour-hand. We ask, *When does this happen?* That is, *at what time after* 1 PM *do positions of the hour- and minute-hands exactly coincide?* By examining a watch we see that the desired event takes place between 1.05 PM and 1.06 PM. To find the exact time, we set up an equation. Let the positions of the two hands coincide at x minutes after 1 PM.

The crucial observations that we use to solve this problem (and all others of its kind) are the following:

- *In each hour, the minute-hand makes a complete movement around the dial, so it turns at a speed of* 360° *every* 60 *minutes; that is,* 6° *every minute, or* 30° *every* 5 *minutes.*
- *The hour-hand makes a complete movement around the dial every* 12 *hours, so it turns at the rate of* 360° *every* 12 *hours, that is,* 30° *every hour, or* $\frac{1}{2}^\circ$ *every minute. This means, in particular, that the minute-hand moves* 12 *times as fast as the hour-hand.*

Now consider the interval from 1 PM till x minutes past 1 PM. During this interval, the minute-hand moves through an angle of $6x^\circ$, while the hour-hand moves through an angle of $\frac{1}{2}x^\circ$. At the start of this interval the two hands are separated by an angle of 30°, and at the end of the interval the two hands coincide. It follows that

$$6x = 30 + \frac{x}{2}.$$

This is the equation we have set up in x. Solving it is easy; we get,

$$6x - \frac{x}{2} = 30, \qquad \therefore \frac{11x}{2} = 30, \qquad \therefore x = \frac{2 \times 30}{11} = \frac{60}{11} = 5\tfrac{5}{11}.$$

It follows that the two hands are coincident at $5\frac{5}{11}$ minutes past 1 PM.

EXAMPLE 17. At 3 PM the angle between the hour-hand and minute-hand is 90°. At what time, exactly, does this happen next?

By examining a watch we see that the desired event takes place between 3.30 PM and 3.35 PM. To find the exact time, we set up an equation as earlier. Let the event happen at x minutes after 3 PM.

Consider the interval from 3 PM till x minutes past 3 PM. During this interval, the minute-hand moves through an angle of $6x^\circ$, while the hour-hand moves through an angle of $\frac{1}{2}x^\circ$. At the start of this interval the hour-hand is ahead of the minute hand by 90°, and at the end of the interval the minute-hand is ahead of the hour-hand by 90°; so the minute-hand has gained 180° on the hour-hand. It follows that

$$6x = 180 + \frac{x}{2}.$$

This is the equation we have set up in x. Solving it is easy; we get,

$$6x - \frac{x}{2} = 180, \qquad \therefore\ \frac{11x}{2} = 180, \qquad \therefore\ x = \frac{2 \times 180}{11} = \frac{360}{11} = 32\tfrac{8}{11}.$$

It follows that the desired event takes place at $32\frac{6}{11}$ minutes past 3 PM.

11.7 Application II: Pythagorean triples

We show a nice application of the topic of this chapter to the problem of generating *Pythagorean triples*—that is, triples of positive integers such that the square of the largest of them equals the sum of the squares of the two smaller ones. If the integers share no common factors, then the triple is said to be *primitive*; the triple is then called a *primitive Pythagorean triple*, or **PPT** for short. Examples of such triples are $(3,4,5)$, $(5,12,13)$ and $(20,21,29)$. These triples have lots of very interesting properties. For example, we may show that among the three integers in a PPT, there is always a multiple of 3, a multiple of 4 and a multiple of 5. [These could be the same integer; for example, in the PPTs $(60,221,229)$ and $(60,899,901)$.]

We now show how such triples can be generated in a systematic way. Let (a,b,c) be a PPT, with c as the largest of the three integers; then $c^2 = a^2 + b^2$. This equation may be written, after division by a^2, as:

$$\frac{c^2}{a^2} = 1 + \frac{b^2}{a^2}, \qquad \text{i.e.,} \qquad \left(\frac{c}{a}\right)^2 = 1 + \left(\frac{b}{a}\right)^2.$$

For convenience we write

$$x = \frac{c}{a}, \qquad y = \frac{b}{a}.$$

Then x and y are fractions with the same denominator, and $x^2 = 1 + y^2$. We write this relation as $x^2 - y^2 = 1$, and then as:

$$(x+y)(x-y) = 1.$$

So the product of $x+y$ and $x-y$ is 1; in other words, *the fractions $x+y$ and $x-y$ are reciprocals of each other*. We now write $r = x+y$; then we must have

$$x - y = \frac{1}{r}.$$

So we have obtained a pair of equations: $x+y = r, \quad x - y = \dfrac{1}{r}$.

Now we shall solve the above pair of equations for the unknowns x and y in terms of r (it too is an unknown, but at present we shall not treat it as such). Adding the two equations, we get:

$$(x+y)+(x-y) = r + \frac{1}{r}, \qquad \therefore\ 2x = r + \frac{1}{r}, \qquad \therefore\ x = \frac{1}{2}\left(r + \frac{1}{r}\right).$$

Similarly we get, by subtraction:

$$(x+y)-(x-y) = r - \frac{1}{r}, \qquad \therefore\ 2y = r - \frac{1}{r}, \qquad \therefore\ y = \frac{1}{2}\left(r - \frac{1}{r}\right).$$

In this way we have expressed both x and y in terms of a third quantity r. It may seem that we have only succeeded in replacing one pair of unknowns by another unknown, but in fact we have accomplished a whole lot more; for we may now give *any value* to r that we wish, and obtain from the above a suitable PPT. For example:

- Choose $r = 2$; then we get

  $$x = \frac{1}{2}\left(2 + \frac{1}{2}\right) = \frac{5}{4}, \qquad y = \frac{1}{2}\left(2 - \frac{1}{2}\right) = \frac{3}{4}.$$

  We get the relation $\left(\frac{5}{4}\right)^2 - \left(\frac{3}{4}\right)^2 = 1$, and from it the PPT $(4, 3, 5)$.

- Choose $r = 4$; then we get

  $$x = \frac{1}{2}\left(4 + \frac{1}{4}\right) = \frac{17}{8}, \qquad y = \frac{1}{2}\left(4 - \frac{1}{4}\right) = \frac{15}{8}.$$

  We get the relation $\left(\frac{17}{8}\right)^2 - \left(\frac{15}{8}\right)^2 = 1$, and from it the PPT $(8, 15, 17)$.

- Choose $r = 6$; then we get

$$x = \frac{1}{2}\left(6+\frac{1}{6}\right) = \frac{37}{12}, \qquad y = \frac{1}{2}\left(6-\frac{1}{6}\right) = \frac{35}{12}.$$

We get the relation $\left(\frac{37}{12}\right)^2 - \left(\frac{35}{12}\right)^2 = 1$, and from it the PPT $(12, 35, 37)$.

- Choose $r = \dfrac{8}{3}$; then we get

$$x = \frac{1}{2}\left(\frac{8}{3}+\frac{3}{8}\right) = \frac{73}{48}, \qquad y = \frac{1}{2}\left(\frac{8}{3}-\frac{3}{8}\right) = \frac{55}{48}.$$

We get the relation $\left(\frac{73}{48}\right)^2 - \left(\frac{55}{48}\right)^2 = 1$, and from it the PPT $(48, 55, 73)$.

We can go on in this way and generate an unlimited number of PPTs. If you like the feel of very large numbers, then try something like $r = \frac{1000000}{101}$; this yields the relation

$$\left(\frac{1000000010201}{202000000}\right)^2 - \left(\frac{999999989799}{202000000}\right)^2 = 1,$$

and the following PPT:

$$(202000000,\ 999999989799,\ 1000000010201).$$

11.8 Application III: Squares in arithmetic progression

Anyone playing with a table of squares is likely to stumble upon the fact that the three squares 1^2, 5^2, 7^2 lie in **ARITHMETIC PROGRESSION** or AP for short; that is, 5^2 lies exactly halfway between 1^2 and 7^2 (for we have $25 - 1 = 49 - 25$). This fact prompts us to ask whether we can find more such triples, in some systematic way. We shall find such a way by following exactly the same method as the one used above.

Let the three squares be a^2, b^2 and c^2. Then we have

$$b^2 - a^2 = c^2 - b^2,$$

$$\therefore\ 1 - \left(\frac{a}{b}\right)^2 = \left(\frac{c}{b}\right)^2 - 1.$$

For convenience we write:

$$x = \frac{a}{b}, \qquad y = \frac{c}{b}.$$

The two fractions have the same denominator, and we have:

$$1 - x^2 = y^2 - 1.$$

Factorising both sides we get $(1-x)(1+x) = (y-1)(y+1)$, and hence:

$$\frac{1+x}{y+1} = \frac{y-1}{1-x}.$$

Let t be the common value of each of the above two fractions. Then we get, using cross-multiplication:

$$1 + x = t(y+1),$$
$$y - 1 = t(1-x).$$

In other words:

$$x - ty = t - 1,$$
$$tx + y = t + 1.$$

We shall treat these as a pair of equations in x and y and solve for the two unknowns in terms of t. Multiplying the second one by t and adding it to the first one, we get:

$$\left(t^2+1\right)x = t - 1 + t^2 + t, \qquad \therefore\ x = \frac{t^2+2t-1}{t^2+1}.$$

Similarly, multiplying the first equation by t and subtracting from the second one, we get:

$$\left(t^2+1\right)y = t + 1 - t^2 + t, \qquad \therefore\ y = \frac{-t^2+2t+1}{t^2+1}.$$

We can now give any value we wish to t, and each resulting pair of values of x and y will yield a triple of squares in AP

- Let $t = \frac{1}{2}$; then we get:

$$x = \frac{\frac{1}{4}+1-1}{\frac{1}{4}+1} = \frac{1}{5}, \qquad y = \frac{-\frac{1}{4}+2+1}{\frac{1}{4}+1} = \frac{7}{5}.$$

  This tells us that the quantities $\left(\frac{1}{5}\right)^2$, 1^2 and $\left(\frac{7}{5}\right)^2$ are in AP and hence that $1^2, 5^2, 7^2$ are three squares in arithmetic progression.

- Let $t = \frac{2}{3}$; then we get:

$$x = \frac{\frac{4}{9} + \frac{4}{3} - 1}{\frac{4}{9} + 1} = \frac{7}{13}, \qquad y = \frac{-\frac{4}{9} + \frac{4}{3} + 1}{\frac{4}{9} + 1} = \frac{17}{13}.$$

This tells us that the quantities $\left(\frac{7}{13}\right)^2$, 1^2 and $\left(\frac{17}{13}\right)^2$ are in AP and hence that 7^2, 13^2, 17^2 are three squares in arithmetic progression.

- Let $t = \frac{3}{4}$; then we get:

$$x = \frac{\frac{9}{16} + \frac{3}{2} - 1}{\frac{9}{16} + 1} = \frac{17}{25}, \qquad y = \frac{-\frac{9}{16} + \frac{3}{2} + 1}{\frac{9}{16} + 1} = \frac{31}{25}.$$

This tells us that the quantities $\left(\frac{17}{25}\right)^2$, 1^2 and $\left(\frac{31}{25}\right)^2$ are in AP and hence that 17^2, 25^2, 31^2 are three squares in arithmetic progression.

In some cases you will find that the triple contains negative numbers; but this should not worry you. Try generating more triples of squares in AP using these formulas.

Remark

Using the above method we can generate an unlimited number of instances of three unequal squares in AP. It is astonishing, however, that there does not exist even a single instance of *four* unequal perfect squares in AP! But to prove this statement is a great challenge. (Fermat was the first mathematician to assert that one cannot find four unequal squares in AP; but, as usual, he provided no proof ....)

11.9 Application IV: Unit fractions

We now consider one more such problem, concerning unit fractions (those with unit numerator). Playing around with unit fractions, we soon come across the relation

$$\frac{1}{2} = \frac{1}{3} + \frac{1}{6},$$

in which *one unit fraction has been written as the sum of two others*. Can we find more such instances?

The equation we need to solve is

$$\frac{1}{a} = \frac{1}{b} + \frac{1}{c}, \tag{11.2}$$

where a, b and c are positive integers. From the equation we get:

$$\begin{aligned} \frac{1}{a} &= \frac{b+c}{bc}, \\ \therefore\ bc &= a(b+c), \\ \therefore\ bc - a(b+c) &= 0. \end{aligned}$$

We now employ a device which comes of use in many such equations: of adding some quantity to both sides of the equation in such a way that one side becomes factorisable in a visible way. In this case, we choose to add a^2 to both sides, because we have the nice and easy factorisation:

$$bc - a(b+c) + a^2 = (b-a)(c-a).$$

So we get $(b-a)(c-a) = a^2$. Now remember that a, b, c are *integers*. So this equation tells us that $b-a$, $c-a$ are divisors of a^2, indeed, that they are a pair of **COMPLEMENTARY DIVISORS** of a^2. (Given an integer N and two of its divisors, say r, s, we say that r and s are a pair of complementary divisors of N if their product is N. For example, 4 and 5 are a pair of complementary divisors of 20, and 3 and 12 are a pair of complementary divisors of 36.)

So we choose a pair of complementary divisors of a^2, say r and s, and write

$$b - a = r, \qquad c - a = s.$$

From this we get $b = a + r$ and $c = a + s$. This gives us the following prescription for finding triples (a, b, c) of positive integers such that $\frac{1}{a} = \frac{1}{b} + \frac{1}{c}$.

ALGORITHM

Step 1 Select any positive integer a.

Step 2 Factorise a^2, and select any pair (r, s) of complementary divisors of a^2, i.e., express a^2 as a product $r \times s$.

Step 3 Let $b = a + r$ and $c = a + s$.

Step 4 Then the triple (a,b,c) has the required property.

For example, choose $a = 6$; then $a^2 = 36$. We can write 36 as a product of two positive integers in many ways:

$$36 = 1\times 36 = 2\times 18 = 3\times 12 = 4\times 9.$$

The factorisation $36 = 1\times 36$ yields $r = 1$, $s = 36$, $b = 6+1 = 7$, $c = 6+36 = 42$, and we get:

$$\frac{1}{6} = \frac{1}{7}+\frac{1}{42}.$$

The factorisation $36 = 2\times 18$ yields $r = 2$, $s = 18$, $b = 6+2 = 8$, $c = 6+18 = 24$, and we get:

$$\frac{1}{6} = \frac{1}{8}+\frac{1}{24}.$$

Note the presence here of a common factor that divides all three numbers appearing in the relation (2 divides each of 6, 8 and 24). So this solution is not 'primitive' (in the sense used for Pythagorean triples). The factorisation $36 = 3\times 12$ yields another solution,

$$\frac{1}{6} = \frac{1}{9}+\frac{1}{18},$$

which too is not primitive.

The factorisation $36 = 4\times 9$ yields $r = 4$, $s = 9$, $b = 6+4 = 10$, $c = 6+9 = 15$, and we get another primitive solution:

$$\frac{1}{6} = \frac{1}{10}+\frac{1}{15}.$$

So we have obtained two primitive solutions:

$$(a,\, b,\, c) = (6,\, 7,\, 42), \qquad (a,\, b,\, c) = (6,\, 10,\, 15).$$

We can in this way produce solutions at will. Observe that the second solution $(6,10,15)$ has the curious feature that $\text{GCD}(a,b) > 1$, $\text{GCD}(b,c) > 1$, $\text{GCD}(c,a) > 1$, yet $\text{GCD}(a,b,c) = 1$.

Remark

The alert reader may notice that in all the primitive solutions obtained, namely, $(2,3,6)$, $(6,7,42)$ and $(6,10,15)$, the *sum of the two larger numbers is a perfect square*:

$$3+6 = 9 = 3^2, \qquad 7+42 = 49 = 7^2, \qquad 10+15 = 25 = 5^2.$$

But the non-primitive solutions do not show such a property. Is there some deeper result at play here? There is, but we shall leave you with the task of finding it.

EXERCISES

1. Solve the following equations for x.

   (a) $7x-15 = 9-5x.$

   (b) $7x-3 = 22+2x.$

   (c) $\dfrac{x-3}{4}-\dfrac{x+1}{10}=2.$

   (d) $x^2+(x+1)^2+(x+2)^2+225 = (x+3)^2+(x+4)^2+(x+5)^2.$

   (e) $\dfrac{x+1}{2x-3} = \dfrac{x+8}{2x+6}.$

2. Two numbers differ by 12, and one is five times the other one; find them.

3. Find two numbers who sum is 32 and whose difference is 6.

4. Find the number whose double exceeds its half by 15.

5. Divide 63 into two parts so that one part is two-seventh of the other one.

6. Find two consecutive odd numbers whose product exceeds the square of the smaller one by 38.

7. Find two numbers differing by 6 whose product exceeds the square of the smaller one by 42.

8. The squares of two consecutive numbers differ by 99; find them.

9. The sum of the squares of three consecutive numbers exceeds 3 times the square of the least number by 101. Find the three numbers.

10. The sum of the squares of four consecutive numbers exceeds 4 times the square of the second number by 70. Find the four numbers.

11. A is four times as old as B. In 16 years, he will be twice as old as B. Find their present ages.

12. Ten years ago my age was three-eighths of what it will be 15 years from now. How old am I?

13. I am twice as old as my brother, but five years ago, I was three times as old as my brother. How old are we at present?

14. Solve the following pairs of equations for x and y:

(a) $\left\{\begin{array}{rcl} 7x+3y &=& 27 \\ 2x+5y &=& 16 \end{array}\right\}$

(b) $\left\{\begin{array}{rcl} x+5y &=& 18 \\ 3x+2y &=& 41 \end{array}\right\}$

(c) $\left\{\begin{array}{rcl} 4x+3y &=& 17 \\ 7x+5y &=& 23 \end{array}\right\}$

(d) $\left\{\begin{array}{rcl} 5x+6y &=& 1 \\ 4x+5y &=& 2 \end{array}\right\}$

(e) $\left\{\begin{array}{rcl} ax+by &=& c \\ bx+ay &=& d \end{array}\right\}$ (here a, b, c, d are constants)

(f) $\left\{\begin{array}{rcl} x/2 - y/3 &=& 1/4 \\ x/3 - y/4 &=& 1/6 \end{array}\right\}$

(g) $\left\{\begin{array}{rcl} x + y &=& -3 \\ x/2 + y/4 &=& 0 \end{array}\right\}$

15. Find x and y given that $\left\{\begin{array}{rcl} 8x + 9/y &=& 7 \\ 6x - 1/y &=& 8/3 \end{array}\right\}$.

16. Find x and y given that $\left\{\begin{array}{rcl} 12/x - 15/y &=& 1 \\ 3/x + 10/y &=& 3 \end{array}\right\}$.

17. Find x, y and z given that $\left\{\begin{array}{rcl} (x+5)/2 &=& y \\ (y+5)/4 &=& z \\ (z+3)/5 &=& x \end{array}\right\}$.

18. Find x, y and z given that $\left\{\begin{array}{rcl} x+y &=& 34 \\ y+z &=& 49 \\ z+x &=& 63 \end{array}\right\}$.

19. Find x, y and z given that $\left\{\begin{array}{lcl} x+y+z &=& 10 \\ 2x-y+3z &=& 21 \\ 3x+4y-z &=& 4 \end{array}\right\}$.

20. Check what happens when you try to solve the equations $\left\{\begin{array}{lcl} x-y &=& 43 \\ y-z &=& 39 \\ z-x &=& -82 \end{array}\right\}$. How many solutions does the system have?

21. Show that the system of equations $\left\{\begin{array}{lcl} x-y &=& 41 \\ y-z &=& 56 \\ z-x &=& -95 \end{array}\right\}$ has no solution.

22. A certain two-digit number is four times the sum of its digits. If 27 is added to the number, its digits get reversed. Find the number.

23. A certain two-digit number is five times the sum of its digits. If its digits are reversed, we get a number which exceeds it by 9. Find the number.

24. In a certain three-digit number, the first and third digits are equal, and the sum of the digits is 9. If 52 is added to the number, the second and third digits of the answer are equal. Find the number. (Hint: Can there be any 'carry' when we add 52 to the number?)

25. In a certain four-digit number, the second and third digits are equal, and the first digit exceeds the fourth digit by 4. If the digits are reversed, and the resulting number subtracted from the original one, what is the answer?

26. At 4 PM, the angle between the hour-hand and the minute-hand of a clock is $120°$. At what time, exactly, does this happen next?

27. At 6 PM, the hour-hand and the minute-hand are in a straight line (pointing in opposite directions). At what time, exactly, does this happen next?

28. Show that the hour-hand and minute-hand coincide in position (one hand over the other) at $10\frac{10}{11}$ minutes past 2 PM.

29. ✪ We bring in the second-hand too into this problem.

    At 12 noon and again at 12 midnight, the hour-hand, minute-hand and second-hand all coincide in position. *Is there any other time when this happens?*

30. ✪ I start out for a walk one evening at some time between 5 PM and 6 PM, and when I return home I find that the hour-hand and the minute-hand have exchanged positions. For how many minutes did I walk?

Chapter 12

Problem Corner

This chapter features miscellaneous problems that do not fall exactly into any category. The one feature they do share is that they are a lot of fun to tackle! So we do not give any preamble or build-up to the problems.

12.1 Appetisers

The problems in this section are minor adaptations of problems from junior-level mathematics olympiads across the world. They are only meant to serve as appetisers; there is more weighty fare to come, shortly!

1. The sum of two numbers is 12 and their product is $29\frac{3}{4}$. What is the larger of these two numbers?

2. How many positive three-digit integers are there whose units digit is 5?

3. Find a positive number with the property that one-ninth of it multiplied by one-seventh of it equals the number itself.

4. The average of a set of 10 numbers is 72. If two of the numbers, 39 and 65, are discarded, what will be the average of the remaining set of numbers?

5. When I write $\langle a,b\rangle$, I mean the quantity $a+b-3$. What is $\langle\langle 2,3\rangle,\langle 4,5\rangle\rangle$ equal to?

6. There are three snakes in the snake house at the zoo. The two smallest snakes total 13 feet in length, and the two largest snakes total 22 feet in length. The average length of all the snakes is 9 feet. How many feet long is the middle snake?

7. The sum of two integers is 37. If the larger is divided by the smaller, the quotient is 3, and the remainder is 5. What is the larger number?

8. The number 81 has five distinct positive integer divisors. What is the product of all these divisors?

9. (a) The number 19321 is a perfect square. What is the next perfect square?

   (b) The number 103041 is a perfect square. What is the next perfect square?

10. If $\langle a,b\rangle$ means the quantity $2a+b-2$, what is $\langle\langle 2,3\rangle,\langle 4,5\rangle\rangle$ equal to?

11. How many whole numbers between 100 and 999 have three different digits in increasing order?

12. How many distinct seven letter sequences can be made using all of the letters in the word COMPUTE?

13. If 6 paleontologists can unearth 4 dinosaurs in 10 days, how many days will it take 9 paleontologists to unearth 12 dinosaurs?

14. A total of 15 handshakes were exchanged at the conclusion of a party. If each person shook hands exactly once with every other person, how many people were at the party?

15. In a certain book, the only numbers that appear are the page numbers. If the pages are numbered from 1 to 333, how many times does the digit '3' appear in the book?

16. What positive number gets tripled when its square is added to it?

17. Solve the following cryptarithm (this means that digits have to be assigned to the letters so that two different letters do not represent the same digit, and in such a way that the indicated arithmetical sum works out right:

    SEND + MORE + GOLD = MONEY.

18. Imagine meeting a man who lived in the 19th century. He says that he was exactly X years old in the year X^2. In which year was he born?

19. Find the digit in the *hundreds place* of the following sum:

$$7+77+777+7777+77777+\cdots+7777777777777777777.$$

20. If you continue the following triangle of numbers in the indicated pattern,

1						
2	3	4				
5	6	7	8	9		
10	11	12	13	14	15	16
17	18	19	$\ldots$,			

what number would be directly below 196? What number would be directly below 2007?

21. What is the 150th letter in the pattern $ABBCCCDDDDE, \ldots$?

22. I pick a three-digit number. Then I reverse the digits, so that the units digit and the hundreds digit are interchanged. I find that the reversed number is larger than the original one, and the product of the original number and the reversed one is 65125. What is the number I picked at the start?

23. How many whole numbers less than 1000 contain at least one '2' but no '3' in their base-ten representations?

24. The ten digits from 0 till 9 are coded using the letters A, B, C, D, E, F, G, X, Y, Z, in some order. If the following two 'sums' are correct:

$$\texttt{XYZ} + \texttt{AB} = \texttt{CDEF}, \quad \text{and} \quad \texttt{XYZ} - \texttt{AB} = \texttt{BGA},$$

find the digit represented by each letter.

25. If $A = 1, B = 2, C = 3, \ldots, Z = 26$, find a mathematical word the sum of whose letters is 75.

26. Use three 9s and each of the operations $+, -, \times, \div$ once and only once to write an expression equal to 1.

27. If A, B, and C are digits, such that ABC + ABC + ABC = BBB, find the digit represented by each letter.

28. Two friends, Alpha and Beta, are playing a game of Heads or Tails. Alpha wagers half of the money in his pocket each time the coin is flipped. If it is Head, Alpha wins the wagered amount from Beta. If it is Tails, then Beta wins the wagered amount from Alpha. After the two friends play the game for one hour, exactly the same number of Heads and Tails have occurred, and the two stop playing. Did Alpha win money, lose money, or break even? Explain your reasoning.

29. Each letter in the following sum:

$$\text{FOUR} + \text{ONE} + \text{THREE} + \text{THREE} = \text{ELEVEN},$$

represents a distinct digit. Find the value of each letter that will correctly solve this puzzle.

30. Five teams (Alpha, Beta, Gamma, Delta and Epsilon) participated in a football tournament. Each team played once against each of the other teams. The winner of each match received two points, the losing team received 0 points; in case of a tie, each team received 1 point. We are told that Alpha got 6 Points, Beta got 5 Points, Gamma got 3 Points and Delta got 1 Point. How many points did Epsilon get?

31. Using the ten digits once each, I form two whole numbers and subtract the smaller from the larger. For example, I may get $986420 - 1357 = 985063$. Or I may get $45678 - 12390 = 33288$. What is the *least possible answer* I can get by doing this?

32. A **PALINDROMIC NUMBER** is a number that reads the same backwards as forwards, such as 1881. How many palindromic years will occur in the next 2000 years?

33. An enclosure at the zoo contains ostriches and giraffes. If the zookeeper counts 32 eyes and 44 feet in this pen, how many giraffes must there be?

34. The sum of two numbers is 10. Their product is 20. What must be the sum of their reciprocals?

35. A **TRUNCATED OCTAHEDRON** is a solid figure with 8 hexagonal faces and 6 square faces. Since each edge belongs to two faces, the number of edges is 36. How many vertices does it have?

36. If $\langle a,b \rangle$ is a short form for $(a+2b) \div 3$, what does $\langle \langle 1,2 \rangle , \langle 3,4 \rangle \rangle$ equal?

37. (a) In a **MAGIC TRIANGLE**, a distinct number is associated with each vertex and each side, in such a way that the sum of the three numbers corresponding to each side is the same. The common sum is called the *magic sum* of the triangle. Form a magic triangle with a magic sum of 21, using the numbers 4, 5, 6, 7, 8, and 9.

(b) Form a magic triangle with the largest possible magic sum using the six numbers 23, 34, 45, 56, 67 and 78.

12.2 For the junior mathlete

The problems in this section are from the TOURNAMENT OF THE TOWNS (Junior Level), a famous and remarkable mathematics contest played between towns of Russia (formerly USSR). These problems are of the 'long-answer' type, requiring proofs or detailed solutions. Some of them are quite challenging, and we hope that you enjoy pitting your wits against them!

1. The positive integer n is obtained from the positive integer m by permuting its digits. Show that the sum of the digits is the same for the following pairs of numbers:

   (a) $2n$ and $2m$

   (b) $5n$ and $5m$

   (c) $\frac{1}{2}n$ and $\frac{1}{2}m$ (assuming m and n are both even)

2. A game of billiards is played on a triangular table with angles 30°, 60° and 90°. There are pockets at each corner. A ball is hit from just outside the 30° pocket towards the middle of the opposite side. Show that if it goes far enough it will end up in the 60° pocket after hitting the edge 8 times.

3. $ABCDE$ is a convex pentagon such that

$$AD = AE, \qquad AB = AC, \qquad \measuredangle CAD = \measuredangle ABE + \measuredangle AEB$$

Show that the length of CD is twice the length of the median from A in $\triangle ABE$.

4. Let $p(n)$ denote the product of the digits of n, and $s(n)$ the sum of the digits. Find the number of n that satisfy the relation

$$p(p(n))+p(s(n))+s(p(n))+s(s(n)) = 1984.$$

5. We are given 68 coins all with different weights. Show how to find the lightest and the heaviest amongst them with at most 100 weighings on a balance.

6. Let $s(n)$ denote the sum of the digits of n. A sequence of numbers $a(n)$ is defined by the relations

$$a(1) = 1, \qquad a(n+1) = a(n)+s(a(n)).$$

Does the number 123456 occur in the sequence?

7. The proportion of blue-eyed people with fair hair exceeds the proportion of all people who have fair hair. Which is greater: *the proportion of fair-haired people with blue eyes*, or *the proportion of all people with blue eyes*?

8. Show that in any set of 7 positive integers there must be three whose sum is divisible by 3.

9. ABC is a triangle with AM a median. Can the inradius of ABM be twice the inradius of ACM?

10. The number `8...8D9...9` has fifty 8s, followed by the digit `D`, followed by fifty 9s. What is `D` if the number is divisible by 7?

11. A cube of side 3 has each face divided into 9 squares of side 1. Is it possible to draw a closed path on the surface of the cube which crosses each small square just once and does not pass through the vertex of any square?

12. A, B and C ran a race. Immediately after the start, A was first, B second, and C third. During the race C exchanged positions with A or B six times, and A exchanged position with B or C five times. B finished ahead of A and there were no ties. What was the finishing order?

13. Find all positive integer triples (a,b,c) such that

$$a+\cfrac{1}{b+\cfrac{1}{c}} = \frac{10}{7}.$$

14. Can 9 red, 9 blue and 9 white unit cubes be arranged to form a $3\times3\times3$ cube in which every row parallel to an edge of the cube has just two different colours?

15. Find 10 different positive integers such that each divides the sum of the integers.

16. One square of a 100×100 board is removed. Is it possible to tile the remaining squares with triangular tiles sides 2, $\sqrt{2}$, $\sqrt{2}$, so that the side length 2 of each tile lies along the sides of two adjacent squares?

17. We are given n integers such that the difference between any number and the product of the others is divisible by n. Show that the sum of the squares of the numbers is divisible by n.

18. A player plays a game against a computer. The game starts with the number 123. The player may permute the digits of the number, then the computer adds 102 to the new number. The player loses if this process produces a 4-digit number (and wins if it produces a 5-digit number). Can the player win?

19. A flying rook can move to any square in the same row or column which is not adjacent. Can a flying rook tour a 4×4 board and return to its starting square in 16 moves?

20. For any positive integer n, show that there is a multiple of n whose sum of digits is odd.

21. Some cats and dogs live in two flats in house A and two flats in house B. The ratio cats/dogs is higher for $A1$ than $B1$ and for $A2$ than $B2$. Is it necessarily higher for A than B?

22. If a and b are fractions as shown below,

$$a=\cfrac{1}{2+\cfrac{1}{3+\cfrac{1}{4+\cfrac{1}{5+\cfrac{1}{\cdots+\cfrac{1}{1991}}}}}},\qquad b=\cfrac{1}{1+\cfrac{1}{1+\cfrac{1}{3+\cfrac{1}{4+\cfrac{1}{5+\cfrac{1}{6\cdots+\cfrac{1}{1991}}}}}}},$$

show that $a+b=1$.

23. If the positive integers a, b, c have no common divisor greater than 1, and

$$c = \frac{ab}{a-b},$$

show that $a-b$ must be a square.

24. A number is written on each side of a hexagon and then the sum of the two adjoining sides is written on each vertex. All the side numbers and one vertex number are then deleted. Is it possible to deduce the missing vertex number from the remaining numbers?

25. Given a positive integer n, an allowed move is to replace it with the integer $n+d$, where $1 < d < n$ is a divisor of n. Show that starting with 4, one can reach any composite number by a sequence of moves.

26. A, B, and C each play the other the same number of times. They score 1 for a win, and $1/2$ for a draw. Is it possible that A scored more than B, who scored more than C, but that C had more wins than B, who had more wins than A?

27. Find five positive integers such that the greatest common divisor of each pair is the difference between them.

28. 20 pupils find that every two have a common grandfather. Show that at least 14 have a common grandfather.

29. Sonia has 30 stamps, each worth 10 cents, 15 cents or 20 cents, with a total value of 500 cents. Show that she must have more 20-cent stamps than 10-cent stamps.

30. Three grasshoppers are placed on a line. Every second one of the grasshoppers jumps over one of the others to land an equal distance the other side. After several jumps they have returned to the three points they occupied initially (but they may have changed places). Show that the middle grasshopper must have been in the middle at the start.

31. Do 100 positive integers exist such that their sum is equal to their least common multiple?

32. A rectangle $ABCD$ with area 1 is folded so that the vertex C coincides with the vertex A. The resulting figure has a pentagonal shape. Show that its area is less than $3/4$.

33. Does there exist an integer n such that $n-96$, n and $n+96$ are all positive primes? What about $n-1996$, n and $n+1996$?

34. Two players play a game on a 10×10 board. Each player alternately places a counter on an unoccupied square. The first player uses red counters and the second player uses blue counters. When all 100 squares are occupied, the first player scores 1 for 5 adjacent red counters in a row, column or diagonal; 2 for 6 adjacent red counters; 3 for 7 adjacent red counters and so on. The second player scores similarly for adjacent blue counters. The player with the higher total wins. Which player has a winning strategy?

35. Do 19 consecutive positive integers exist such that the sum of the squares of the first ten among them equals the sum of the squares of the last nine among them?

36. For how many integers from 1 to 1997 is the sum of digits a multiple of 5?

37. A person can move down an escalator (moving or stationary) at a speed d relative to the escalator, and up the elevator at a speed $u < d$ relative to the escalator. The escalator moves at speed $e < u$ up or down. Which is quicker: to descend and then ascend an upward moving escalator, or to descend and then ascend a downward moving escalator?

38. A, B, C listed words that met some conditions. A listed the most and C the least. A word listed by only one contestant scored 2 points, a word listed by two contestants scored 1 point, and a word listed by all three scored 0. Is it possible that C got the highest score and A the lowest?

39. A king tours every square of an 8×8 chess board, visiting each square exactly once and returning to his starting position. Show that he made an even number of diagonal moves. [A king can move one square in any direction, horizontally, vertically or diagonally.]

40. A $20 \times 20 \times 20$ cube is divided into 8000 cells. A real number is assigned to each cell, so that the sum of the numbers in any row of 20 cells parallel to an edge of the cube is 1. One of the cells has the number 10. Let S be the set of 58 cells which includes this cell and the others in the same row (parallel to some edge). Find the sum of all the numbers not in S.

41. A square has 09 as its last two digits. Show that the previous digit (in the hundreds place) is even.

42. Twelve candidates were on a TV talk show. One candidate said "one lie has been told". Another said "Now two lies have been told". A third said "Now three lies have

been told". This continued until the twelfth candidate said "Now twelve lies have been told.". It turned out that just one of the candidates correctly stated the number of lies told before his claim. How many lies were told by the candidates?

43. Some pieces move on a chessboard. A piece is said to be an (m,n) piece if it can move m squares parallel to one of the edges of the board and then n squares in the perpendicular direction. For example, a knight is a $(1,2)$ piece. Show that the squares can be coloured with two colours (each square with just one colour), so that an (m,n) piece always moves from one colour to the other.

44. A father and son skate at constant speeds around a circular rink. The father periodically overtakes his son. The son then changes direction and they meet five times more often. How much faster does the father skate than his son?

45. A square is cut into 100 rectangles by 9 lines parallel to one side and 9 lines perpendicular to them. If just 9 of the rectangles are squares, show that two of the squares must be the same size.

46. a, b, c are integers such that $a+b+c=0$. Can $a^{1999}+b^{1999}+c^{1999}$ be a prime?

47. Can we find positive integers m,n such that

$$m(m+1) = 2n(2n+2)?$$

48. Can we place a positive integer at each vertex of a cube so that numbers m and n are joined by an edge if and only if m divides n or n divides m?

49. A number is written in each square of a 4×4 board so that for each square the sum of the numbers in the squares that share a side with it is 1. Find the sum of all the 16 numbers.

50. A *move* consists of replacing a given integer n by ab, where a and b are positive integers with sum n. Can 2001 be obtained from 22 by a sequence of such moves?

51. Fifteen rooks are placed on a board each in a different row and column. Each rook then makes a knight's move (to the opposite corner of a 3×2 rectangle). Show that after the moves, there will be two rooks in the same row or column.

52. All coins are *genuine* or *fake*. All genuine coins have the same weight, and all fake coins have the same weight, but are heavier than genuine coins. You have 4 coins and

suspect that 2 may be fake. Can you decide whether this is true or not by using a balance twice?

53. There is a set of at least 4 points in the plane. If any one of the points is removed, then the others have an axis of symmetry. Must the set of all the points have an axis of symmetry?

54. Can any triangle be divided into a triangle, a convex quadrilateral, a convex pentagon and a convex hexagon?

55. (a) There are 128 coins of two different weights, 64 of each. Show that one can always find a coin of each weight by not more than 7 uses of a balance.

    (b) There are 8 coins of two different weights, 4 of each. Show that one can always find a coin of each weight with not more than 2 uses of a balance.

Chapter 13

Investigations

In this chapter, which is the last one in this volume, we shall pose open problems for you; 'open' means that your task is not to derive or prove a given result, but to search for interesting results. The result may refer to a pattern in some sequence of numbers, or some unexpected equality, or some striking inequality; in fact, it could refer to anything that seems significant and worth examining. We shall merely describe the situations, and then leave the rest to you.

13.1 Mischievous cancellations

Observe the identity

$$\frac{16}{64} = \frac{1\not{6}}{\not{6}4} = \frac{1}{4}.$$

The 6 has been illegally cancelled ('struck away'), yet the answer is correct! Find other identities of this kind. *Harder.* Find all such identities.

13.2 Mischievous square roots

Observe the identity

$$\sqrt{\mathbf{2}\frac{2}{3}} = \mathbf{2}\sqrt{\frac{2}{3}},$$

in which the '**2**' (shown in bold font) has illegally jumped outside the square root sign. But the value of the expression remains unchanged! Find other identities of this kind. *Harder.* Find all such identities.

13.3 Prime numbers

1. Find all prime numbers which are (a) one less than a square (b) one less than a cube.

2. Find all positive integers n such that the numbers $2^n - 1$ and $2^n + 1$ are both prime.

13.4 Digital sums

Consider the number 40. The sum of its digits is 4, and 40 is 10×4. So, the number 40 is equal to 10 times the sum of its digits. We shall call 40 a 10-*good number*.

Or consider the number 24. Its sum-of-digits is 6, and 24 is 4×6. So, the number 24 is equal to 4 times the sum of its digits. We shall call 24 a 4-*good number*.

More generally, for any given number k, if a positive integer n has the property that it is k times the sum of its digits, we call it a *k-good number*.

1. Find all positive integers which are 2-good.

2. Find all positive integers which are 3-good.

3. Find all positive integers which are 4-good.

4. Find all positive integers which are 5-good.

5. Find all positive integers which are 6-good.

6. Find all positive integers which are 7-good.

7. Find all positive integers which are 8-good.

8. Find all positive integers which are 9-good.

9. Find all positive integers which are 10-good.

10. Find all positive integers which are 11-good.

11. Find all positive integers which are 12-good.

13.5 Digital reversals

Given any positive integer n, let us denote by $\text{Rev}(n)$ the integer obtained when we reverse the digits of n. For example,

$$\text{Rev}(123) = 321, \qquad \text{Rev}(20060) = 6002, \qquad \text{Rev}(120300) = 3021.$$

Observe that zeroes occurring at the 'units end' of the number do not make any contribution to the reversed number; therefore,

$$\text{Rev}(n) = \text{Rev}(10n) = \text{Rev}(100n) = \text{Rev}(1000n) = \cdots.$$

In this section we shall focus on the question of when (if at all), $\text{Rev}(n)$ is an *integer multiple* of n.

1. Show that there are no two-digit or three-digit positive integers n such that $\text{Rev}(n) = 4n$.

2. Show that there is just one four-digit positive integer n such that $\text{Rev}(n) = 4n$, and find this number.

3. Show that there is just one five-digit positive integer n such that $\text{Rev}(n) = 4n$, and find this number.

4. Are there any positive integers n such that $\text{Rev}(n) = 2n$? Investigate the question as fully as possible.

5. Are there any positive integers n such that $\text{Rev}(n) = 3n$? Investigate the question as fully as possible.

6. Are there any positive integers n such that $\text{Rev}(n) = 5n$?

7. Are there any positive integers n such that $\text{Rev}(n) = 6n$?

8. Are there any positive integers n such that $\text{Rev}(n) = 7n$?

9. Are there any positive integers n such that $\text{Rev}(n) = 8n$?

10. Show that there is just one four-digit positive integer n such that $\text{Rev}(n) = 9n$, and find this number.

11. Show that there is just one five-digit positive integer n such that $\text{Rev}(n) = 9n$, and find this number.

13.6 Squares and 2006 ...

This book was written during the years 2006–2011; this may explain the choice of the numbers occurring in the problem.

1. Are there any integers n for which $n^2 + 20n + 6$ is a perfect square? Find all of them, or show that there are no such integers.

2. Are there any integers n for which $n^2 + 20n + 7$ is a perfect square? Find all of them, or show that there are no such integers.

3. Are there any integers n for which $n^2 + 20n + 8$ is a perfect square? Find all of them, or show that there are no such integers.

4. Find all integers n for which $n^2 + 20n + 9$ is a perfect square.

5. Show that there are no integers n for which $n^2 + 20n + 10$ is a perfect square.

6. Find all integers n for which $n^2 + 20n + 11$ is a perfect square.

13.7 Squares and cubes

The number 121 has the property that it is a perfect square with more than two digits, and when its units and tens digits are deleted, then the number left over (namely, 1) is also a perfect square. Trivially, any perfect square which is a multiple of 10 has this property (e.g., 12100 or 2500), so such instances are not of much interest.

1. Find all perfect squares $N > 100$, such that (a) N is not a multiple of 10 and (b) if the last two digits of N are deleted, then the resulting number too is a perfect square.

   Remark. There are only finitely many such perfect squares!

2. Find all perfect squares $N > 10000$, such that (a) N is not a multiple of 10 and (b) if the last four digits of N are deleted, then the resulting number too is a perfect square.

   Remark. There are only finitely many such perfect squares!

3. Find all perfect cubes $N > 1000$, such that (a) N is not a multiple of 10 and (b) if the last three digits of N are deleted, then the resulting number too a perfect cube.

   Remark. There are only finitely many such perfect cubes!

13.8 Still more squares

The perfect square 2025 has the property that if we 'slice' it through its middle into two parts, getting the numbers 20 and 25, add these two parts, and then square the sum, we get back the original number:

$$2025 \longrightarrow \{20,\ 25\}, \qquad 20+25 = 45, \qquad 45^2 = 2025.$$

1. Find all four-digit perfect squares with this property.

2. Find all six-digit perfect squares with this property. (Here, we slice the six-digit number into two parts each with three digits, add the two parts, and then square the sum.)

13.9 And yet more squares ...

The number 1233 has the property that if we 'slice' it through its middle into two parts, getting the numbers 12 and 33, then *square these two parts* and *add the squares*, we get back the original number:

$$1233 \longrightarrow \{12,\ 33\}, \qquad 12^2+33^2 = 144+1089 = 1233.$$

1. Find all four-digit integers with this property.

2. Find all six-digit integers with this property. (Here, we slice the six-digit number into two parts each with three digits, square the two parts, and then add the squares.)

13.10 Accommodating numbers

Take the number 25. If we insert a '7' between its tens and units digits, we get a number (275) which is 11 times the original number ($275 = 11 \times 25$).

Or take the number 15. If we insert a '0' between its tens and units digits, we get a number (105) which is 7 times the original number ($105 = 7 \times 15$).

We shall refer to this phenomenon using the word **ACCOMMODATION**. More precisely, for given integers N, x, k, we shall say that N *accommodates* x*, to a multiplicity of* k, if the integer obtained by inserting x between the tens and units digits of N is equal to $k \times N$. So:

- 25 accommodates 7 to a multiplicity of 11;
- 25 accommodates 2 to a multiplicity of 9 (for $225 = 9 \times 25$);
- 15 accommodates 0 to a multiplicity of 7;
- 15 accommodates 6 to a multiplicity of 11 (for $165 = 11 \times 15$);
- 16 accommodates 7 to a multiplicity of 11 (for $176 = 11 \times 16$);

and so on. Observe that a multiplicity of 11 occurs repeatedly.

Find all integer pairs N, x such that N accommodates x to a multiplicity of 13.

Answers to Exercises

Chapter 1

Page 1: [1] 1024; [2] 59049; [3] 2^{11} is smaller; [4] 1 m; [5] 3 km; [6] 5 km; *Note.* Answers could vary for the last two.

Page 3: [1] 999999; [2] 875400; [3] 10^3 and 10^4; 10^4 and 10^5; 10^5 and 10^6; [4] $24318 = 24 \times 1000 + 3 \times 100 + 18 = 243 \times 100 + 18$;

Page 8: [1] XLI, LXXIII, fCIII, CIII, MCXXIII, MMMMMLXXXI; [2] 18, 97, 1123, 84; [3] $18 + 97 + 1110 = 1225$, or MCCXXV; [4] $18 \times 97 = 1746$, or MDCCXLVI;

Page 12: [1] $-4, -3, -2, -1, 0, 1, 2, 3, 4$; [2] $-10, -9, \ldots, 9, 10$; [3] 101; [4] 201; 1001; [5] $6, 7, \ldots, 15, 16$; [6] $-12, -11, \ldots, 25, 26$; [7] 63; [8] 37 or 63; [9] 3 or 47; [10] 21, 39, 61 or 79;

Page 18: [1] $a = b$; [3] 174, 392, 826; [4] $210 - 2 = 208$; [5] 541; [6] 5734; [7] 3765; [8] $c = 0$;

Page 28: [1] 3, 2; [2] $5, 1, 6, 2, 7, 3, 8, 4, 0, 5, 1, 6, 2, \ldots$; [3] Ditto; [5] 1; [6] 5; [8] No; [9] A single digit number; [10] n is a multiple of 9; [11] n is a multiple of 9;

Page 31: [1] $1 + 7 = 8$; [2] $1 \times 7 = 7$; [3] lhs: 4, rhs: 3; error; [4] lhs: 6, rhs: 7; error;

Page 33: [1] 15; [2] 4127; [3] 7;

Page 35: [1] Multiply by 1000, then divide by 8; [3] $\overline{ab} \times 11 = \overline{acb}$ where $c = a + b$. If c is 10 or more, there is a 'carry' of 1 to the hundreds place; [5] $\overline{ab} \times 101 = \overline{abab}$;

Page 39: [3] The units digit repeats after 4 steps; [4] Ditto;

Page 41: (Misc problems I) [2] 15050; [3] 1500500; [4] 22500; [5] 27; [6] 47; [7] 67; [8] 19; [9] 21; [10] 149 and 1499; [11] 124 and 1249; [12] 110 and 1032; [13] 200 and 2000; [14] 198 and 1998; [15] 249 and 2499; [16] 400; [17] 432; only two, 432 and 3456;

Page 43: (Misc problems II) [1] True; [2] True; [3] False; [4] True; [5] True; [6] True; [7] True; [8] 2178; [9] 1089; [10] 6534; [11] 21978; [12] 1001 is divisible by 13; [13] $1001 = 7 \times 11 \times 13$; [14] 10101 is divisible by 37; [15] 1010101 is divisible by 137; [16] 101010101 is divisible by 41;

Chapter 2

Page 60: [9] $(x+1)(x+3)$, $(x+1)(x+9)$, $(x-5)(x-7)$, $(x-2)(x^2+2x+4)$, $(x+3)(x^2-3x+9)$, $(x-2)(x+2)(x^2+4)$; [10] Divisible by $2+3=5$; [11] Divisible by $4^2+7^2=65$; [12] 29×31; [13] 7×139; [14] (a) 39 (b) 117, since $5^3-2^3=117=3^2\times13$; [15] $8^3-5^3=387$; [16] $7^3-4^3=279$; [17] $7+4=11$, $7^3+4^3=407=11\times37$; [18] $8+5=13$, $8^3+5^3=637=7^2\times13$; [20] $(a^2+ab+b^2)(a^2-ab+b^2)$; [21] $(x^2+2x+2)(x^2-2x+2)$; [22] $n=3$; [23] $n=3$; [24] $117+78$; [25] 74; [26] $x^2-x=42$; [27] $7x-(x/2)^2=3x$, $x=16$ or $x=0$; [28] 21, 22, 23, 24; [29] 11, 12, 13, 14, 15, 16; [30] $-1, 0, 1, 2$; [37] Yes;

Chapter 3

Page 68: [6] Odd; [7] Even; nothing can be said;

Page 72: [1] **2**, **6**; [2] **5**, **0**; [3] No; [4] No; [5] Yes, $\mathbf{2}\times\mathbf{4}=\mathbf{0}$; [6] Yes, $\mathbf{2}\times\mathbf{5}=\mathbf{0}$;

Page 77: [2] 199, 257, 277; [3] 101 and 103; [4] 227 and 229; [5] $861=3\times7\times41$, $957=3\times11\times29$, $1001=7\times11\times13$, $1295=5\times7\times37$; [6] $1309=7\times11\times17$, $1547=7\times13\times17$, $1729=7\times13\times19$, $3731=7\times13\times41$; [7] 30; [8] 10; [9] 12345; [10] $30^2=900$;

Page 84: [1] 36; [6] 1; [7] d^2; [8] No; 2; [9] 1 or 2; [10] 1 or 3; [11] 1, 2 or 4; [12] 1; [13] 1; [14] 1; [15] $\{10,120\}$ or $\{30,40\}$; [16] $\{6,210\}$ or $\{30,42\}$; [17] $\{6,240\}$ or $\{30,48\}$; [18] d and d^2; [19] Try $a=2, b=3, c=4$;

Page 91: [3] 117; [4] 366;

Page 100: [4] $a=0$ or 4; [5] 144; [8] $689=13\times53$, $1003=17\times59$; [9] $893=19\times47$, $1363=29\times47$; [10] 29×47; [11] When the number is the product of two primes very close to each other; [13] 68; [14] 25; [20] One example: $3^3+4^3+5^3=6^3$; $1^3+12^3=9^3+10^3$; [22] 370, 371, 407;

Page 108: [1] $\frac{2n}{n+1}$; [8] Length of cycle is 20; [12] $1, 36, 1225, 41616, 1413721, \ldots$; [13] $\{3,6\}$, $105,210\}$, $3570,7140\}$, $\ldots$; [14] $\{1,3\}$, $\{15,45\}$, $\{210,630\}$, $\{2926,8778\},\ldots$; [15] $\{3,15\}$, $\{21,105\}$, $\{990,4950\},\ldots$;

Page 113: [1] $50=2^5+2^4+2^1$, $101=2^6+2^5+2^2+2^0$, $1003=2^9+2^8+2^7+2^6+2^5+2^3+2^1+2^0$, $2005=2^{10}+2^9+2^8+2^7+2^6+2^4+2^2+2^0$;

Page 114: [1] 100; [2] 320; [3] 9; [4] 3; [5] 1; [6] 648; [7] 432; [8] 60, 72, 84, 90 and 96 all have 12 divisors, the maximum; [9] 180 has 20 divisors, the maximum; [10] 11; [11] 101; [12] 201; [13] 10201; [14] 25 divisors; [15] 121 divisors; [16] 256 divisors; [19] 12 and 18; [20] 60 and 72; [21] 144 and 324; [22] Primes; [23] Squares of primes; [24] Cubes of primes, and products of two unequal primes; [25] Fourth powers of primes;

Chapter 4

Page 127: [1] (a) $\frac{2}{5}$ (b) $\frac{3}{8}$ (c) $\frac{5}{14}$ (d) $\frac{5}{11}$ (e) $\frac{9}{19}$ (f) $\frac{11}{31}$; [2] $\frac{94}{315}$; [3] $\frac{103}{168}$; [4] $\frac{5}{6}$; [6] $n=7$; [7] (a) $\frac{1}{2}$ (b) 20 (c) 5 (d) 35 (e) $1/12$ (f) $126=70+56$ (g) $120=84+36$ (h) $56=35+21$; [9] When n is odd; [10] When n is not a multiple of 3; [11] Many solutions; e.g., 20679 and 41358; [12] Many solutions;e.g., 23058 and 69174;

Page 135: [1] 200%; [2] 80%; [3] $\frac{25000}{x}\%$; [4] $9\frac{1}{11}\% \approx 9.09\%$; [5] 25%; [6] Single discount of 20%; [7] Single discount of 30%; [8] 28%; [9] $D=\frac{10000}{B}-100$; [10] $\frac{xy}{100}$;

Page 141: [1] 0.97%; [2] 180; [3] 7 km; [4] 20%; [5] $\frac{1}{11}$; $\frac{10}{11}$; equal!; [6] 800 ml; [7] 8 cups; [8] 56%; [9] 25%; [10] $\frac{1000}{47}\% \approx 21.3\%$; $\frac{10100}{121}\% \approx 83.5\%$;

Chapter 5

Page 148: [5] $\frac{2}{15}$, $\frac{1}{5}$, $\frac{19}{90}$, $\frac{11}{30}$; [6] $\frac{13}{99}$, $\frac{25}{99}$, $\frac{19}{99}$, $\frac{53}{99}$; [7] 8, 20, 25, 40, 64; [8] Pure recurring: $\frac{2}{3}$, $\frac{5}{11}$, $\frac{20}{23}$, $\frac{5}{27}$, $\frac{12}{19}$. Others are mixed recurring; [10] $n=3$ or 9; [11] $n=11, 33$ or 99; [12] $n=111, 333, 999$; [13] $\frac{242}{303}=0.\overline{7986}$; [14] $\frac{189}{271}=0.\overline{69741}$;

Page 164: [2] $\frac{1}{39}=0.\overline{025641}$, $\frac{1}{41}=0.\overline{02439}$; [3] True; [4] The repetend is very large — it has 7866 digits!; [9] $\frac{1}{12}=\frac{1}{3}-\frac{1}{4}$, $\frac{1}{20}=\frac{1}{4}-\frac{1}{5}$, $\frac{1}{30}=\frac{1}{5}-\frac{1}{6}$; [10] $\frac{1}{1}-\frac{1}{10}=\frac{9}{10}$; [11] $\frac{1}{2}\left(\frac{1}{1}-\frac{1}{11}\right)+\frac{1}{2}\left(\frac{1}{2}-\frac{1}{10}\right)=\frac{36}{55}$;

Chapter 6

Page 182: [1] $3y^3$, $\frac{12b^5}{a}$, abc; [2] $(x-1)(x-3)=x^2-4x+3$; [3] $x+1$; [4] z^3, $6a^2b^2$, $8xy^3$; [5] $(x-1)^2$; [9] 18 and 81;

Chapter 7

Page 187: [5] $2^8>3^5$; [6] $2^{20}>3^{12}$; [7] $3^7>2^{11}$;

Page 189: [1] 2^{10}, 2^{12}; [2] 3^8, 3^{12}; [3] $16^8>2^{30}>8^9$; [4] Equal;

Page 190: [1] Over 10 km; more than adequate!; [2] Roughly 50 pages (but answers can vary); [3] 10.2 cm; slightly over 100 m;

Page 192: [1] $2^{3^4}>4^{3^2}$; [2] $3^{4^5}>5^{4^3}$; [3] $4^{444}>44^{44}$; [4] $4^{4^{44}}>4^{44^4}$; [5] 67 digits; [6] 39 digits, 388 digits, more than 1.9×10^{38} digits; [7] 95 digits, 954 digits, more than 2.8×10^{94} digits;

Page 197: [1] 2^2, 10^{-6}; [2] 2^4; [3] 3^{10};

Page 200: [1] 72, $68\frac{1}{4}$; [2] 1024, 216; [3] 9, 3125, 64; [4] $\frac{1}{8}$, $\frac{1}{8}$, $\frac{1}{32}$; [5] $7^4=2401$; [6] 3; [7] 4; [8] 10^3, 200, 3000, 400, 140; [9] 5, 6, 9, 2, 3; [10] 1, $\frac{1}{3}$, $\frac{1}{3}$; [11] $a+b$; [12] $ab+bc+ca$; [13] (a) $\frac{9}{2}$ (b) $\frac{11}{2}$ $\frac{17}{3}$ $\frac{19}{3}$ $\frac{7}{2}$ $\frac{3}{2}$; [15] $3^{1/3}>2^{1/2}$; [16] $4^{1/4}>5^{1/5}$; [17] $3^{1/4}>5^{1/6}$; [18] $2^33^4=648$; [19] $2^{10}3^65^{15}$; [23] (b) $x\approx3.3$ (c) (i) $x\approx2.3$ (c) (ii) $x\approx3.2$; [25] (a) $x\approx2.1$ (b) $x\approx2.7$ (c) $x\approx3.6$; [26] $a^x<a^y$;

Page 205: [2] 1479; [3] Sun: 99.85%, Jupiter: 0.095%; [4] 1.634 metre/second^2; [5] 1.2×10^{57}; [6] 3.6×10^{51}; [7] 1.1×10^{54}; [8] 1836 times; [9] 3×10^7 seconds in a year; [10] 5×10^8 seconds; [11] 2.8×10^9, about 3 billion; [12] 6×10^{17} seconds; [13] 9.46×10^{12} km; [14] Sun to Earth: 495 seconds, Sun to Pluto: 19573 seconds, Earth-Sun: $8\frac{1}{3}$ light minutes; [15] 3.7 million years;

Page 213: [3] Example: $26^2+39^2=13^3$; [4] Example: $2^3+2^3=2^4$;

Chapter 8

Page 230: [1] $x^6+x^5+3x^4+9x^3+15x^2+10x+36$; [2] 76 and 7; [3] $x^4+3x^3-7x^2+13x-17$; [4] $5(a^2+b^2+c^2+ab+bc+ca)$; [5] 31; [6] $8x-6$; [7] $x-1$; [8] $a=17$; [9] $a=-31,\ b=63$; [10] (a) Not divisible (b) Divisible; [11] $a=-1,\ b=10$; [12] The remainder in the division $(x^n-1)\div(x-1)^2$ is $nx-n$; [13] The remainder in the division $(x^n+1)\div(x+1)^2$ is $nx+n$ if n is odd, and $-nx-n+2$ if n is even;

Chapter 9

Page 253: [1] (a) $4a^2+9b^2+16c^2+25d^2-12ab+16ac-20ad-24bc+30bd-40cd$, (b) $x^6-2x^5+3x^4-4x^3+3x^2-2x+1$, (c) $16x^6-24x^5+25x^4-20x^3+10x^2-4x+1$, (d) $49x^6+70x^5+67x^4+44x^3+19x^2+6x+1$, (e) $27x^6-54x^5+63x^4-44x^3+21x^2-6x+1$; [2] (a) $729x^6-5832x^5y+19440x^4y^2-34560x^3y^3+34560x^2y^4-18432xy^5+4096y^6$, (b) $\frac{a^6}{64}-\frac{a^5b}{16}+\frac{5a^4b^2}{48}-\frac{5a^3b^3}{54}+\frac{5a^2b^4}{108}-\frac{ab^5}{81}+\frac{b^6}{729}$, (c) $64x^{12}-960x^9+6000x^6-20000x^3+37500-\frac{37500}{x^3}+\frac{15625}{x^6}$; [3] (a) 70000, (b) 34560; [4] (b) 70000 and 175000; [5] 37500 and 6000; [6] $6a+\frac{2}{a^3}$; [7] $8a^2+\frac{8}{a^2}$; [8] $+$ for even n, and $-$ for odd n; [9] 7 and 18; [10] 194 and 724; [11] 12098 and 57965; [12] 144; [13] 343; [14] $\pm\sqrt{17}$; [15] Yes, 76; [16] $1-x^3,\ 1-x^4,\ 1-x^5,\ 1-x^6,\ 1-x^7$; in general: $1-x^{n+1}$; [17] $1+x^3,\ 1-x^4,\ 1+x^5,\ 1-x^6,\ 1+x^7$; in general, $1\pm x^{n+1}$, with $+$ sign for odd n, and $-$ sign for even n; [18] $X_6=S^6-6PS^4+9P^2S^2-2P^3$, $X_7=S^7-7PS^5+14P^2S^3-7P^3S$; [19] The expansion of $(1+x+x^2+\cdots+x^n)^2$ has the form $1+2x+3x^2+4x^3+\cdots+nx^{n-1}+(n+1)x^n+nx^{n+1}+\cdots+3x^{2n-2}+2x^{2n-1}+x^{2n}$;

Chapter 10

Page 277: [1] (a) $(x+1)(x+3)$ (b) $(x+1)(x+5)$ (c) $(x+3)(x+4)$ (d) $(x+5)(x+6)$ (e) $(x+2)(x+7)$ (f) $(x-7)(x+2)$ (g) $(x-9)(x+3)$ (h) $(x+10)(x-3)$ (i) $(x-11)(x+4)$ (j) $(x-13)(x+5)$; [2] (a) $(x-5)(2x-1)$ (b) $(x-2)(5x-3)$ (c) $(4-x)(5x+2)$ (d) $(3-x)(8x+1)$ (e) $(1-x)(10x-7)$ (f) $(5-3x)(6x-7)$; [3] (a) $(a-3b)(a+3b)$ (b) $(7-b^2)(7+b^2)$ (c) $(2-3c)(2+3c)(4+9c^2)$ (d) $(2ab-c^2)(2ab+c^2)$ (e) $(x^5-3y^3)(x^5+3y^3)$ (f) $(x^2-2y)(x^2+2y)(x^2-2xy+2y^2)(x^2+2xy+2y^2)$; [4] (a) $(a-b+c)(a-b-c)$ (b) $(3a+2b+4c)(3a+2b-4c)$ (c) $(3a-4b-c+1)(3a-4b+c-1)$ (d) $(a-b+c-1)(a-b-c-1)$ (e) $(a-b-c+1)(a-b+c-5)$; [5] (a) $(a+2b)(a^2-2ab+4b^2)$, (b) $(3a-4b)(9a^2+12ab+16b^2)$, (c) $(2ab^2-c)(4a^2b^4+2ab^2c+c^2)$ (d)

$(5x+9y^2)(25x^2-45xy^2+81y^4)$ (e) $(pqr-4)(p^2q^2r^2+4pqr+16)$; [6] (a) $(x^2+x+1)(x^2-x+1)$ (b) $(x^2-x+1)(x^4+x^3+3x^2+x+1)$ (c) $(x^2+4x-1)(x^2-4x-1)$ (d) $(x^2+x+1)(x^2-x+1)(x^4-x^2+1)$; [7] 13×17, $3\times 7\times 19$, $3\times 13\times 41$, 41×43, $7^2\times 47$, 71×73, $7\times 11\times 79$, $7\times 13\times 89$, 101×103, 107×109, 113×127, $7\times 11^2\times 17$, 179×181, 239×241; [8] 11×157, $7\times 13\times 19$, 17×241, 19×421, $3^2\times 7\times 127$, 23×601, $3^4\times 271$, 29×757, $7\times 31\times 151$, $3^2\times 11\times 331$; [9] $(x-1)(x+2)(3x-5)$, $(x-4)(x+5)(2x+9)$, $(x+1)(x-3)(4x-3)$, $(x+2)(x-3)(2x+7)(3x-5)$, $(x+1)(x-2)(2x+5)(5x-3)$; [10] $5(a^2+b^2+c^2+ab+bc+ca)$; [12] True; [13] $(a-b+c)(-a+b+c)(-a-b+c)$; [14] $(a-2b+c)(-a-b+2c)(-2a+b+c)$; [19] $19\times 43\times 2551$;

Chapter 11

Page 310: [1] (a) $x=2$ (b) $x=5$ (c) $x=19$ (d) $x=10$ (e) $x=6$; [2] 3 and 15; [3] 13 and 19; [4] 10; [5] 14 and 49; [6] 19 and 21; [7] 7 and 13; [8] 49 and 50; [9] 16, 17 and 18; [10] 15, 16, 17 and 18; [11] $A=32$, $B=8$; [12] 25 years; [13] 20 years and 10 years; [14] (a) $(x,y)=(3,2)$ (b) $(x,y)=(13,1)$ (c) $(x,y)=(-16,27)$ (d) $(x,y)=(-7,6)$ (e) $x=\frac{ac-bd}{a^2-b^2}$, $y=\frac{ad-bc}{a^2-b^2}$ (f) $(x,y)=(\frac{1}{2},0)$ (g) $(x,y)=(3,-6)$; [15] $(x,y)=(\frac{1}{2},3)$; [16] $(x,y)=(3,5)$; [17] $(x,y,z)=(1,3,2)$; [18] $(x,y,z)=(24,10,39)$; [19] $(x,y,z)=(1,2,7)$; [20] Infinitely many solutions; [22] 36; [23] 45; [24] 414; [25] 3996; [26] $43\frac{7}{11}$ minutes past 4 PM; [27] $5\frac{5}{11}$ minutes after 7 PM; [29] No; [30] Start at $32\frac{4}{13}$ minutes after 5 PM, and walk for $55\frac{5}{13}$ minutes;

Chapter 12

Page 314: [1] $8\frac{1}{2}$; [2] 179; [3] $63^2=3969$; [4] 77; [5] 5; [6] 8 feet; [7] 29; [8] 59049; [9] 19600, 103684; [10] 19; [11] 648; [12] 5040; [14] 6; [15] 102; [16] 2; [17] Many solutions; e.g., $9478+1634+5628=16740$; [18] 1806 (he is 43 years old in 1849); [19] 0; [20] 223 and 2096; [21] Q; [22] 125; [23] 217; [24] $945+78=1023$, $945-78=867$; [27] $A=1$, $B=4$, $C=8$; [28] A loses money; [29] Two solutions: $8769+721+45911+45911=101312$ and $9824+871+60411+60411=131517$; [30] 5 points; [31] $90123-87654=2469$; [32] 20; [33] 10 ostriches, 6 giraffes; [34] $\frac{1}{2}$; [35] 24; [36] 3; [37] (a) (7, 6, 8, 4, 9, 5); max sum: 168, with (56, 45, 67, 23, 78, 34);

Page 318: We give answers to only some of the questions. [4] 0; [7] Fair-haired people with blue eyes; [6] No; [10] 5; [11] Yes; [13] $(a,b,c)=(1,2,3)$; [15] One possibility: 1, 2, 3, 6, 12, 24, 48, 96, 192, 384; [19] No; [21] No; [24] No; [31] Yes, e.g., 4, 102 with ninety eight 1s; sum and lcm are 204; [33] Yes, e.g., $n=101$; No; [35] Yes, starting with 171; [36] 399; [46] No; [47] No;

Chapter 13

Page 325: [13.1] Example: $\frac{19}{95}$; [13.2] Example: $\sqrt{3\frac{3}{8}} = 3\sqrt{\frac{3}{8}}$;

Page 326: [13.3] (1a) 3 (1b) 7 (2) $n = 2$; [13.4] 2-good: 18; 3-good: 27; 4-good: 12, 24, 36, 48; 5-good: 45; 6-good: 54; 7-good: 21, 42, 63, 84; 8-good: 72; 9-good: 81; 10-good: 10, 20, 30, 40, 50, 60, 70, 80, 90; 11-good: 198; 12-good: 108;

Page 327: [13.5] (2) 2178 (3) 21978 (4)–(9): No (10) 1089 (11) 10989;

Page 328: [13.6] (1) None (2) $n = 7, 37$ (3) $n = 14$ (4) $n = 36$ (5) None (6) $n = 35$; [13.7] (1) 121, 144, 169, 196, 441, 484, 961 and 1681 (2) There are many of these; e.g., 10201, 10404, ...; the largest such number is 24019801 (3) 1331 and 1728;

Page 329: [13.8] (1) 2025, 3025 and 9801 (2) 494209 and 998001; [13.9] (1) 1233 and 8833 (2) Only 990100; [13.10] $(5,6)$, $(10,3)$, $(15,8)$, $(20,6)$ and $(30,9)$;